# Making and remaking saints in nineteenth-century Britain

Manchester University Press

# Making and remaking saints in nineteenth-century Britain

Edited by Gareth Atkins

Manchester University Press

Copyright © Manchester University Press 2016

While copyright in the volume as a whole is vested in Manchester University Press, copyright in individual chapters belongs to their respective authors, and no chapter may be reproduced wholly or in part without the express permission in writing of both author and publisher.

Published by Manchester University Press
Altrincham Street, Manchester M1 7JA
www.manchesteruniversitypress.co.uk

*British Library Cataloguing-in-Publication Data is available*

ISBN 978 0 7190 9686 0 hardback
ISBN 978 1 5261 5633 4 paperback

First published by Manchester University Press in hardback 2016

This edition first published 2021

The publisher has no responsibility for the persistence or accuracy of URLs for any external or third-party internet websites referred to in this book, and does not guarantee that any content on such websites is, or will remain, accurate or appropriate.

Typeset by Servis Filmsetting Ltd, Stockport, Cheshire

# Contents

| | | |
|---|---|---|
| List of figures | | *page* vii |
| List of contributors | | viii |
| Preface | | xi |
| Introduction: thinking with saints<br>*Gareth Atkins* | | 1 |
| 1 | Paul<br>*Michael Ledger-Lomas* | 29 |
| 2 | The Virgin Mary<br>*Carol Engelhardt Herringer* | 44 |
| 3 | Claudia Rufina<br>*Martha Vandrei* | 60 |
| 4 | Patrick<br>*Andrew R. Holmes* | 77 |
| 5 | Thomas Becket<br>*Nicholas Vincent* | 92 |
| 6 | Thomas More<br>*William Sheils* | 112 |
| 7 | Ignatius Loyola<br>*Gareth Atkins* | 127 |
| 8 | English Catholic martyrs<br>*Lucy Underwood* | 144 |
| 9 | Richard Baxter<br>*Simon Burton* | 161 |
| 10 | The Scottish Covenanters<br>*James Coleman* | 177 |

| 11 | John and Mary Fletcher<br>*David R. Wilson* | 193 |
| 12 | William Wilberforce and 'the Saints'<br>*Roshan Allpress* | 209 |
| 13 | Elizabeth Fry and Sarah Martin<br>*Helen Rogers* | 226 |
| 14 | John Henry Newman's *Lives of the English Saints*<br>*Elizabeth Macfarlane* | 245 |
| 15 | Thérèse of Lisieux<br>*Alana Harris* | 262 |

Index     279

# Figures

1   *In the Painting Studio*, reproduced from Wilfrid Wilberforce, *The House of Burns and Oates* (London: Burns and Oates, 1908), p. 20. Courtesy of the State Library of Victoria.   2
2   Dante, Hus, Francis, detail of stained-glass window, c. 1907–10, Mansfield College, Oxford, by Powell and Sons, Whitefriars. Photograph © Rex Harris.   3
3   Robert Sayer, *John Wesley: That Excellent Minister of the Gospel, Carried by Angels into Abraham's Bosom,* coloured engraving, 1791. Courtesy of the Methodist Archive, John Rylands Library, Manchester. © University of Manchester.   11
4   *Our Lady of Victories*, statue, mid nineteenth century. Photograph © Brompton Oratory.   45
5   *The marriage of Pudens and Claudia; Paul explaining the Gospel to Caractacus and Bran the Blessed; Sts Prasside and Pudenziana*, three-light window, 1897, Church of St Llonio, Llandinam, Powys. Photograph © Martin Crampin.   61
6   *Mrs Fry Visiting Newgate, 1818*, exhibited 1876; engraving by T. D. Atkins. Photograph © Joseph Crisalli.   231
7   Jerry Barrett, *Mrs Fry Reading to the Prisoners in Newgate, 1816*, engraving. Courtesy of the British Museum. © Trustees of the British Museum.   233
8   W. Dickes, *The Jail Missionary*, reproduced from *Women of Worth: A Book for Girls* (1859: New York, 1863), p. 85.   237
9   [Joseph] Swain, *Sarah Martin Conducting Service in Yarmouth Gaol*, wood engraving. Reproduced from Edwin Hodder, *Heroes of Britain in War and Peace* (London, [1879–80]), p. 186. © The British Library Board, 10804. ee.5.   238
10   Unknown photographer, *Postcard of the Shrine of the Little Flower, Ribbleton*, c. 1928. Courtesy of the Talbot Library, Preston.   271

# Contributors

**Roshan Allpress** is a Senior Teaching Fellow at the Venn Foundation and a consultant in the non-profit and charitable sector in New Zealand and Australia. His research focuses on social and cultural change in the eighteenth and nineteenth centuries, and particularly on the intersections of religious, commercial and reform networks. He is currently working on developing his recently completed Oxford D.Phil. thesis, 'Making Philanthropists: Entrepreneurs, Evangelicals and the Growth of Philanthropy in the British World, 1756–1840', into a book.

**Gareth Atkins** is a Fellow and Director of Studies in History at Magdalene College, and a member of the Bible and Antiquity Research Project at CRASSH, both in Cambridge. He has published on Anglican identity, religious politics and networks, and the use of religious heroes and heroines in eighteenth- and nineteenth-century religious and popular culture. He is preparing a monograph, provisionally entitled *The Politics of Patronage: Anglican Evangelicals and British Public Life, 1770–1850*.

**Simon Burton** is an Assistant Professor in the Faculty of Artes Liberales, University of Warsaw. His research focuses on late medieval and early modern theology, especially the movement of Reformed Scholasticism. His monograph *The Hallowing of Logic: The Trinitarian Method of Richard Baxter's Methodus Theologiae* (2012) explores the theology of the celebrated English Puritan theologian Richard Baxter. He has published further research on Baxter in *Ecclesiology* and the *Calvin Theological Journal* and a number of other articles and book-chapters relating to sixteenth- and seventeenth-century Reformed theology in international journals and edited collections.

**James Coleman** is a freelance historian specialising in the cultural history of Scotland since the Reformation. His recent book, *Remembering the Past in Nineteenth-Century Scotland* (2014), examines the role of collective memory in reflecting and generating a sense of Scottish national consciousness. He currently works in fundraising.

**Alana Harris** teaches Modern British History at King's College London. Her research interests span the transnational history of Catholicism, gender and sexuality, pilgrimage and material culture. She has published extensively on Catholic saints and devotional cultures, and recent books include *Faith in the Family: A Lived Religious*

*History of English Catholicism* (2014), *Love and Romance in Britain 1918-1970* (2014, co-edited with Timothy Willem Jones) and *Rescripting Religion in the City: Migration and Religious Identity in the Modern Metropolis* (2014, co-edited with Jane Garnett).

**Carol Engelhardt Herringer** is a Professor of History at Wright State University. Her work focuses on religious and cultural history. She is the author of *Victorians and the Virgin Mary: Religion and Gender in England, 1830-85* (2008) and the co-editor of *Edward Bouverie Pusey and the Oxford Movement* (2012). Her current project examines the religious and cultural significance of eucharistic debates in the Victorian Church of England.

**Andrew R. Holmes** is a Lecturer in Modern Irish History at Queen's University Belfast. He has published widely on religion, politics, and intellectual life in Ireland and Britain from the early eighteenth century to the twentieth century. He is author of *The Shaping of Ulster Presbyterian Belief and Practice 1770-1840* (2006) and co-editor of four edited collections.

**Michael Ledger-Lomas** is a Lecturer in the Theology and Religious Studies Department, King's College London and a Director of the Bible and Antiquity research project at CRASSH, Cambridge. His previous publications include the edited volumes *Cities of God: the Bible and Archaeology in Nineteenth-Century Britain* (2013) and *Dissent and the Bible in Britain, c. 1650–1950* (2013). He is currently writing a religious biography of Queen Victoria.

**Elizabeth Macfarlane** is Chaplain and Fellow of St John's College, Oxford. Her research focuses on nineteenth-century attitudes to the British saints, commemorative cultures, and book history.

**Helen Rogers** is a Reader in Nineteenth-Century Studies at Liverpool John Moores University. She edited the *Journal of Victorian Culture* (2008-15) and her publications include *Women and the People: Authority, Authorship and the Radical Tradition in Nineteenth-Century England* (2000) and *Gender and Fatherhood in the Nineteenth Century* (2007, co-edited with Trev Lynn Broughton). She has written widely on crime and punishment and blogs about her book-in-progress, *Conviction: Stories from a Nineteenth-Century Prison* at www.convictionblog.com.

**William Sheils** is Professor Emeritus and Leverhulme Fellow in the History Department at the University of York. His research has been largely focused on the history of post-Reformation England, sharing his time between papists, puritans and conformists. He was President of the Ecclesiastical History Society 2008-09, and is currently writing a study of the 'posthumous life' of Thomas More, of which his chapter forms a part.

**Lucy Underwood** is a Leverhulme Early Career Fellow in History at the University of Warwick, having previously held fellowships at the Folger Shakespeare Library and the British School at Rome. Her first book, *Childhood, Youth and Religious Dissent in*

*Post-Reformation England* was published by Palgrave Macmillan in 2014. Her current research is on national identity and early modern English Catholicism.

**Martha Vandrei** received her PhD from King's College London in 2013 and is now Lecturer in Modern and Public History at the University of Exeter. She is currently completing her first monograph under the title *An Image of Truth: Queen Boudica and the Growth of Historical Culture in Britain since 1600*.

**Nicholas Vincent** is Professor of Medieval History at the University of East Anglia and a Fellow of the British Academy.

**David R. Wilson** teaches theology, ethics, and church history at George Fox Evangelical Seminary and Warner Pacific College in Portland, Oregon. His research has been primarily focused on ecclesiology, theology and gender in the long eighteenth century, although he has published articles and book chapters on hermeneutics and contemporary theology. David is currently working on editing an annotated collection of the sermons of Mary Bosanquet Fletcher. He is co-editor of the series *Explorations in Social Holiness* (Emeth Press) and Co-Executive Director of Gemeinde, a non-profit organization in Portland, Oregon focused on social justice in the margins of society. His book, *Church and Chapel in Industrializing Society*, is forthcoming this year (2016).

# Preface

THE SEEDS OF THIS book were sown at a colloquium in July 2012 at Magdalene College, Cambridge, funded by the British Academy. In addition to the attenders, and to contributors who have joined the project more recently, many others have played a part in its development, especially Shinjini Das, Simon Ditchfield, Michael Hetherington, James Kirby, Tim Larsen, Brian Murray, Rowan Williams, John Wolffe, and members of the IHR Modern Religious History Seminar. I am also grateful to my colleagues at Magdalene, and in the Bible and Antiquity Project at CRASSH, who have provided stimulating and supportive environments in which to complete it.[1] In particular I should like to thank Michael Ledger-Lomas, whose intellectual contribution to this book goes far beyond providing a chapter for it. I should also like to acknowledge the parts played by the two anonymous readers who provided such helpful feedback, and by Emma Brennan and the staff at Manchester University Press, who have made the process of editing this volume such an agreeable one. My final debt is to Sarah, who became a mother just as this book was coalescing, but who nevertheless continues to show the patience and grace of a saint. Anna is not yet old enough to know what a saint is, but her infectious delight in everything around her is a constant challenge to see the mundane and ordinary afresh.

### Note

1 The author acknowledges support from the European Research Council under the European Union's Seventh Framework Programme (FP7/2007–2013)/ERC Grant Agreement n.295463

# Introduction: thinking with saints

## Gareth Atkins

'WHAT'S A SAINT?' GIBBER the demons in John Henry Newman's 1865 poem *The Dream of Gerontius*. 'One whose breath doth the air taint before his death; a bundle of bones, which fools adore, ha! ha!'[1] Newman's knowing swipe against sceptical Protestants assumed that the correct answer to the question was the Roman one: that saints were to be venerated, and that miracles and relics were at the centre of what they stood for. For Victorian and Edwardian visitors to Burns and Oates, 'the headquarters of Catholic publishing', near Marble Arch, Newman's point would have been underlined wherever they looked. For children, the bookselling department poured forth one-shilling copies of the illustrated *Alphabet of Saints* (1905). Below street level saints were made in a series of workshops devoted to plaster moulding, statue-painting, gilding, woodcarving and mural-making (figure 1).[2] Photographs in the 1908 conspectus showed studios littered with crucifixes, angels and cowled saints: scenes that might have evoked a shudder from any Protestant observer who strayed that far. Burns and Oates also used saints to underpin a Catholic reading of the national past. The firm was located only a few hundred yards along Oxford Street from Tyburn, 'where the gallows, that lifted the English Martyrs to Paradise, once stood'. Its celebration of this bespoke a growing confidence among Catholics following the beatifications of sixteenth-century English martyrs by Leo XIII in 1886 and 1895, as well as a canny commercial desire to market the works of Francis Thompson (1859–1907), 'the poet of Tyburn tree'.[3] At the same time, the business was also a highly modern operation: dismayingly so, perhaps, for those accustomed to dismissing Catholicism as backward and barbarous. Its publicity trumpeted the possibilities of cheap print in much the same way as Protestant flagships like the Bible Society. Customers could order by telephone (2706 Mayfair), or even by telegram from across the world. There were discounts for cash purchasers and those buying in bulk.

It is hard to imagine an institution further removed from this than Mansfield College, Oxford. Established in 1889 to train Congregational ministers, it set forth staunch Free Church principles: reformed religion, civil liberty, religious freedom. Yet here too, amid the triumphal gothic of Basil Champneys (1842–1935), the inmates were surrounded by saints. Their significance was highlighted in a sermon by R. W. Dale (1829–95) preached at the College's opening.[4] Taking as his text Jude 3 ('Contend for

1 *In the Painting Studio*, reproduced from Wilfrid Wilberforce, *The House of Burns and Oates* (London: Burns and Oates, 1908), p. 20.

the faith which was once for all delivered unto the saints'), Dale reminded his hearers that the religion Mansfield proclaimed was no innovation: it was descended from the apostles 'through sixty generations of saints'. No one denomination or confession could claim a monopoly. 'We who have erected this college have broken with the politics of the Great Churches of Christendom, and are unable to accept their confessions, creeds, articles and canons of doctrine. But we listen with reverence to the saints of all Churches, when they speak concerning those great things which may be actually verified in the saintly life.'⁵ When Free Churchmen like Dale invoked the saints they referred not to some special category of believer set apart by ecclesiastical officialdom, but to the entirety of the elect. Yet this did not stop them from singling some out for especial notice. The entrance to the chapel was flanked by doctors of the early Church: Origen, Athanasius, Augustine. Oliver Cromwell's portrait stood over the Senior Combination Room, the expelled ministers of 1662 in the Library, Milton's statue above the main entrance and Bunyan's outside the chapel door. Inside, the chapel was crowded with reformed 'saints': sculptures of Wycliffe, Calvin, Cartwright, Baxter, Howe and Whitefield in one aisle and Wesley, Watts, Owen, Hooker, Knox and Luther in the other.⁶ Still more expansive was the stained-glass scheme masterminded by the first Principal, A. M. Fairbairn (1838–1912), and installed in the first decade of the twentieth century.⁷ The seventy men and women that comprised it broadcast an exuberantly ecumenical vision, pairing the prophet Amos with Plato and ranging from the New Testament, Latin and Greek Churches through the medieval and Reformation periods (both continental and British) to contemporary Nonconformity, which latter category encompassed Elizabeth Fry, Thomas Chalmers, David Livingstone, Friedrich Schleiermacher and the recently deceased Dale. For the German modernist theologian Friedrich Heiler (1892–1967) Mansfield was 'the most Catholic place in Oxford' (figure 2).⁸

These two contrasting examples introduce the central contention of this book: that 'saints' – holy men and women – were pivotal in religious discourse throughout the nineteenth century, and remained so well beyond it. For despite their qualms about

2 Dante, Hus, Francis, detail of stained-glass window, c. 1907–10, Mansfield College, Oxford, by Powell and Sons, Whitefriars.

popery, Protestants were as fascinated by such figures as Catholics were. Long after the mechanisms of canonisation had disappeared, their need for spiritual patterns was just as pressing. They not only still engaged with the saints of the past but continued to make their own saints in all but name, investing them with the trappings of sanctity – hagiographies, iconography, relics, shrines. Each of the sixteen chapters in this volume focuses on the reception of a particular individual or group. They seek to explore the enduring appeal of sanctity in our period. Together they define sainthood in broad terms, as encompassing both those who were recognised by Catholics as such and those who functioned in similar ways for Protestants. Yet none of this is to imply that it was a stable category that commanded universal agreement. While the appeal of figures like the Apostle Paul and the Virgin Mary spanned confessional and indeed religious divides, one of our recurring themes is how different groups sought to stake exclusive claims to them. We show how saints acted as sparkpoints for some of the most controverted debates between Catholics and Protestants: the nature of miracles, the validity of intercession, the reliability of traditions and texts. Yet we also emphasise that there was never complete consensus within confessions or denominations as to what saints stood for. They were used at once to articulate religious identities and to contest those identities and blur their boundaries.

As will become clear, much of the heat of such debates was generated by enduring narratives of confessional rivalry. As Kirstie Blair and Timothy Larsen have demonstrated, the Book of Common Prayer and the King James Bible were among several inherited texts whose authority was questioned, but which continued to govern religious life in the nineteenth century and beyond.[9] The Reformation was unfinished business: recent work has explored in rich detail the intensification of confessional conflict across the British Isles from the 1820s onwards.[10] While our essays pick up on this, they also collectively warn against the assumption that 'Protestant' and 'Catholic' were labels for self-evident, coherent, diametrically opposed categories. From the late eighteenth century the explosion of evangelical Dissent span off new sects that competed for converts and influence. Catholicism, too, was far from monolithic. All the churches operated in a vibrant religious and commercial marketplace in which existing authority structures were eroded by the exploitation of new media to appeal to religious customers. Consumers and producers as much as religious hierarchies made saints, influencing their representation and their commodification, too. Such figures helped to sell a vast range of media, from multi-volume Lives and Letters to Sunday-school books, historical novels, cheap engravings, mass-produced ceramic figurines, lantern slides, and much else besides: hence our insistence that sainthood was not just bestowed from above but was also forged in everyday existence, with all the messiness that this entailed.

If saints were not the preserve of one group, it follows that they did not belong to orthodox believers alone. To an extent that has often been remarked upon but seldom examined, freethinkers and atheists appropriated the language of hagiography in order to advance their own ideas about what constituted 'holiness'. The 1849

*Calendrier Positiviste* of Auguste Comte (1798–1857) retained Gregory the Great and Francis of Assisi alongside mythical heroes, philosophers, literary greats, scientists and statesmen in a radically re-imagined version of the Catholic calendar.[11] Or take George Eliot (1819–80), whose dismay on encountering a 'very amiable atheist' in Edward Bulwer-Lytton's 1829 potboiler *Devereux* prompted the revelation, unsettling for a serious-minded young evangelical, 'that religion was not a prerequisite to moral influence'.[12] The mature Eliot had read not only Comte but Carlyle, Coleridge and Ludwig Feuerbach (1804–72), which encouraged her to see sympathy and love not as deriving from God but as innate human qualities.[13] When she began and ended *Middlemarch* (1871–72) with evocations of Teresa of Avila it was to conjure up the numerous anonymous women who did not share her piety but brought about 'the growing good of the world' nevertheless.[14] A major theme running through this book is that one did not have to be an unbeliever to conceive sanctity in similarly inclusive terms. Fresh from Thomas Arnold's Rugby, the future Dean of Westminster and Broad Churchman A. P. Stanley (1815–81) voiced his conviction that the communion of saints encompassed 'all good men, including, therefore, chiefly Christians, but also the Jewish saints, who lived before Christ, and all those, such as Socrates &c. whom we value among the pagans, or those whom we might have to value among the Unitarians and Deists'.[15] Inclusivity, however, had consequences. Stanley's comment serves to underline the heuristic value of the term but also its instability, a point that we return to time and again. Once shorn of their ecclesiastical significance, it was easier to write off saints' antics as psychological or historical case-studies. Imperial expansion, moreover, continued to confront Europeans with reminders that Christianity was only part – and not necessarily a privileged part – of a much bigger story. Buddha, Mohammed and Confucius could all be 'canonised' provided that the net was cast wide enough.[16]

This book uses saints, then, to show that devotional practices and language survived into an age of confessional strife, doubt and secularisation. It demonstrates that they provided ways for Christians and their opponents to reflect on what those profound changes meant for religion. And it emphasises that saints were also invoked in broader discussions about gender, morality and national identity that were not necessarily linked to religious issues at all. Why was this? One aspect of the answer, we suggest, lies in the interaction between two Victorian obsessions: the cultivation of character and the 'cult of history'. If the nineteenth century was, as Clyde Binfield claims, 'hagiology's high noon', this was because men and women of faith provided subject matter for everything from stained glass, statuary and paintings to tracts, poems and children's books.[17] At the same time, however, the fact that our subject does not fit straightforwardly into categories like celebrity or heroism goes some way towards explaining why sainthood has received such minimal scholarly attention. This book makes a broader and much more fundamental claim about the centrality of saints to how commentators in Britain (and, by extension, further afield) conceptualised religion, both in historical and in experiential terms.[18] To browse nineteenth-century periodicals and publications is – to adapt Stuart Clark's phrase – to encounter numerous writers 'thinking with saints'.[19] However one defined them, 'saints' clearly mattered. Fundamentally this was because they have always been crucial to how Christianity is lived. From the earliest days, such figures were important because their lives were patterned on Scripture and, more specifically, on the life of Christ. This identification became particularly apt whenever it involved the shedding of blood: martyrs ('witnesses') gradually became figures to whom believers prayed, whose deaths they commemorated annually, often among their tombs.[20] All believers were saints, but some were more saintly than others. Beliefs about them varied according to time and place: for some Christians – many Protestants among them – veneration could lead to idolatry, which happened the life of the saint became of parallel or greater importance than the scriptural narrative, or when relics were ascribed power in and of themselves. But as the chapters that follow show, this should not be allowed to obscure their enduring importance, or indeed the ways in which practices, gestures and postures, along with attitudes to time, place and touch, sayings and superstitions, defied the doctrinal frameworks intended to limit or exclude them. Of course, medieval and early modern scholars may not be much surprised by the idea that saints and sanctity are central to accounts of belief. All the same, by examining the reception of saints in a self-consciously modern age, this book underlines how not just they but the questions they raise have always been intrinsic to Christian existence.[21]

The remainder of this introduction sketches the contexts against which individual chapters should be read. In doing so it seeks to elucidate the questions that unite them, and to offer suggestions for new approaches to the issues they raise. The first section examines the ambivalent legacies of the Reformation for nineteenth-century ideas about sainthood. It makes the case for methodological as well as thematic continuity, recognising that scholars of medieval and early modern religion have been more alive than their modern counterparts to notions of sanctity revolving around temporality, materiality and place. By employing their tools we uncover ideas that Protestants repudiated officially but in practice never entirely eschewed. The next section turns from continuities to discontinuities. It identifies the 1840s as a key moment in which claims by different groups to have 'rediscovered' Britain's religious heritage sparked intense debate. These contentions drove and were driven by deepening confessional divisions: while Roman and Anglo-Catholics embraced figures from the deeper Christian past, for Protestants they made that past appear distant and strange. One result, as many of our chapters suggest, was selective appropriation. Another was the generation of models of 'modern' sanctity: overseas missionaries, Christian soldiers, feminist campaigners. Here we intersect closely with a growing corpus of work on 'lived religion' in the nineteenth and twentieth centuries that stresses the importance of consumer behaviour, everyday practices and materiality in constituting belief.[22] The final section explores the enduring importance of sainthood for agnostics and unbelievers. It examines how secularists remoulded sanctity to fit new notions of morality. And it also shows the extent to which practitioners of secular-minded academic disciplines like history, anthropology and psychology remained fascinated by saints and the societies that created them. Far from being dismissed, by the early twentieth century, as we shall show, the 'holy' and the numinous were still live categories that science promised to develop rather than to debunk.

## Survival

It might seem perverse to start from the premise that saints mattered in nineteenth-century Britain because they had never really gone away. Relics, shrines, images and festivals stood condemned by Protestant reformers, and their insistence on the sainthood of all believers cut sharply against the idea that the Church could single individuals out for special treatment. 'Whatever else the Reformation was,' writes Eamon Duffy, 'it represented a great hiatus in the lived experience of religion. It dug a ditch, deep and dividing, between people and their religious past, and in its rejection of purgatory and of the cult of the saints, of prayer to and from the holy dead, it reduced Christianity to the mere company of the living.'[23] Yet to see the Reformation as an unbridgeable chasm is to ignore the continuities of behaviour and belief that spanned it. The saints of the past did not vanish overnight. British churchgoers still worshipped in buildings dedicated to them. Biblical figures in particular were held up as paragons for imitation: Peter the Apostle, for example, was reclaimed from Rome by Elizabethan reformers as a proto-Protestant who would have cast off the trappings in which Catholics had disguised him.[24] And the physical and mental gaps where saints had once stood continued to matter. Memories of medieval cults were central to the reforming project, which used 'superstitious' images and tall tales to throw the Protestant present into brighter contrast.[25] Saint Thomas of Canterbury was effaced from liturgies and prayers, but was by no means forgotten, being repainted as Becket the papal catspaw. As Nicholas Vincent shows in chapter 5, those who revered and those who reviled him in the nineteenth century drew on very long polemical traditions.[26] More subtly, we suggest, time, stuff and space continued to be infused with half-articulated notions about the role of individuals in embodying or even mediating divine power, notions that problematise the assumption among scholars of modernity that Protestants did not make saints.[27]

While the Apostle Paul's injunction against observing 'days, and months, and times, and years' fuelled a wariness among the hotter sort of Protestants about treating any time as holier than any other, save the Sabbath, in England the liturgical calendar was attenuated rather than abolished.[28] Cranmer's 1552 Prayer Book retained most of the principal traditional feasts among its twenty-four red-letter days, keeping all the Apostles and Evangelists, Stephen, the Holy Innocents, All Saints, Michaelmas, John the Baptist, the Purification of the Blessed Virgin and the Annunciation.[29] These remained fixtures, but the lesser black-letter days proliferated as time went on. The initial four – Saints George, Lawrence and Clement, plus Lammas Day – were joined by Mary Magdalene and fifty-six others in 1561, the otherwise obscure Saint 'Enurchus' (a misreading of Evurtius) on 7 September 1604, to mark the late Queen

Elizabeth's birthday, and Alban and the Venerable Bede in 1661. How such days were to be celebrated, if at all, was a matter of debate: all were labelled as 'saints', but what this meant theologically was unclear. The eclectic nature of those included added to the ambiguity. Figures from pre-Reformation England – Alban, Chad and Etheldreda, Archbishops Augustine, Alphege and Dunstan of Canterbury – rubbed shoulders with early Christians – Augustine of Hippo, Cyprian of Carthage, Jerome, Nicholas, Lucy – and, more bizarrely, several popes – Clement, Silvester, Gregory the Great. To exacerbate the confusion, in 1662 three more red-letter days were added: liturgies for the monarchist cult of King Charles on 30 January, 'Charles II: Nativity and Return' for 29 May and 'Papists Conspiracy' for 5 November, all of which remained in the Prayer Book until 1859.[30] 'Sainthood' was clearly a grey area. By the second half of the nineteenth century, scholars and satirists[31] had laid bare the haphazard processes by which the Prayer Book saints had been selected; but despite widespread calls for change,[32] the 1662 calendar continued to dictate Anglican times and seasons until the early twentieth century.[33]

Such dates were not, of course, the same as Catholic festivals. In a superb survey of Reformation Britain, Alec Ryrie maintains that calendars of heroes, martyrs and biblical anniversaries were 'essentially almanacs or even curiosities'. Protestants sought not to *make* saints but to *be* saints and, having swept away old ways of marking time, required new ways of punctuating 'the long monologue of the Protestant life'.[34] The best-known English calendar was that attached to John Foxe's *Actes and Monuments*, which was probably a marketing device intended to make the book look more liturgical.[35] Yet if martyrologies were not devotional as such, we should not overlook their hagiographical potential in other respects. Catholic saints represented a spiritual bloodline, and in tracing their descent from the apostles, Protestants necessarily looked to exemplary figures in the intervening centuries in order to prove that their own beliefs were no innovation.[36] Four major European martyrologies were issued in the 1550s alone, all of which had very long afterlives.[37] The nineteenth century alone witnessed a new scholarly edition of Foxe (1837–41), expurgated versions for children, fresh illustrations and its reproduction in a variety of media.[38] This volume investigates two less familiar inherited lineages. Lucy Underwood shows how the campaign to beatify the English Martyrs became a focal point for Catholic conceptions of 'Englishness', prompting an explosion in confessional historiography and setting sixteenth-century figures forth in architecture, literature and devotion. James Coleman advances a similar argument for the Covenanters of the late seventeenth century, highlighting their centrality to Scottish and Presbyterian identity, but demonstrating that their doctrines and words – not to mention commemorative rituals in a stoutly anti-papal society – were deeply contested matters.

Constructing doctrinal pedigrees was an unexceptionably Protestant practice. But historians of early modern religion have also been intrigued at the extent to which Protestants continued to behave in ways that looked conservative.[39] The material remains of martyrs are a case in point. In the 1550s Catholic observers sneered at the 'heretics' who scooped up bones and bits from among the ashy sludge of Marian burnings to wear next to their hearts or even to consume. Others fought to touch the hands and garments of the condemned.[40] In Germany, too, Protestant 'saints' seemed to retain powers once ascribed to their Catholic predecessors.[41] Ulinka Rublack has written about 'grapho-relics': Luther's or Melanchthon's autographs, inscribed under a line of Scripture: salvation and personal charisma mediated in the same scrap of paper.[42] While Alexandra Walsham rightly doubts whether such practices indicate 'survivalism and syncretism' among a stubbornly semi-reformed laity, their spiritual, emotional and sometimes thaumaturgical uses demonstrate the enduring significance of individual sanctity, even at a time when 'superstition' was under attack.[43] Similar ambiguities can be glimpsed beneath nineteenth-century commemorations of martyrs. Militant Protestants broadcast their doctrines, but they also marked the places where they had lived and suffered, and preserved artefacts connected with them.[44] The language they employed reveals layers of ambivalence. One visitor in Valladolid reflected on how the Spanish Inquisition had thrown Protestant ashes into the Esqueva that flowed through it. Rather than effacing the gospel, he mused, such actions had metaphorically carried it far and wide.[45] Scottish Presbyterians were fond of quoting John Knox (c. 1514–72) on Patrick Hamilton (1504–28), whose dying smoke 'infected all on whom it did blow'.[46] No doubt this was intended to be figurative. But while Protestants were undoubtedly 'word people', they continued to engage with the stuff of sanctity in ways that defy easy categorisation. Witness the man who wished to be buried under the sacred turf of Baxter's Kidderminster, or the pilgrimages of Wesleyan relic-seekers to the house of the Fletchers at Madeley, as discussed in chapters 9 and 11 by Simon Burton and David Wilson.[47]

Nor did saints die out during the Enlightenment. Far from being dispelled by the advent of Newtonian science, the idea that 'wonders' and portents were signs of divine action in a law-governed universe often drew fresh justification from it.[48] Debate about sanctity came to revolve around evidence and epistemology. Jane Shaw places David Hume's influential essay 'Of Miracles' (1748) within a broader discussion about how to distinguish between 'true' and 'false' miracles, a discussion in which Anglican moderates sought to steer a middle way between extravagant sectarian (and Catholic) claims, on one hand, and corrosive scepticism on the other.[49] To be sure, many rejected post-apostolic miracles as papist moonshine. But they remained a perplexing subject for nineteenth-century Protestants who wanted to believe the stories recounted in the Gospels but who dismissed later prodigies as monkish fables.[50] Catholic Europe, for its part, poured immense resources into the cult of the saints, wrapping them in an assertive baroque aesthetic that portrayed miraculous healings, levitations and ecstatic visions in marble and gilded splendour.[51] Yet here also there was evidence of new priorities. Undergirding Catholic confidence was the 'science of sanctity': the painstaking collation of eyewitness testimony and even autopsies as part of a rigorous canonisation process designed to ward off critical attacks.[52] Its apogee was the massive Bollandist *Acta Sanctorum* (sixty-eight volumes, 1643–1940). As Clare Haynes has shown, English art collectors were by no means allergic to Counter-Reformation glitz, but Protestants also read much of the Catholic hagiological literature produced in this period, some of them avidly.[53] Alban Butler's *Lives of the Fathers, Martyrs, and Other Principal Saints* (four volumes, 1756–59) was the most significant such work, distilling the *Acta* into moderate, didactic biographies that fitted perfectly the practical piety of Hanoverian Britain.[54] Like Thomas à Kempis's *Imitation of Christ*, Butler was deemed safe and, in some circles, profitable for Protestant consumption.[55]

Saints were also taken up by new religious movements. In few places was cross-confessional borrowing more evident than in the restless search of John Wesley (1703–91) for modern saints worthy of the name. His fascination with Catholic holy men such as the aristocratic philanthropist Gaston de Renty (1611–49) and the eccentric hermit Gregory Lopez (1542–96) was not to everyone's taste.[56] Bishop Lavington's polemic on *The Enthusiasm of Methodists and Papists Compar'd* (1749–51) suggested that the new movement shaded into semi-popery, repeatedly likening Wesley's stern asceticism to that of 'Romish' saints.[57] Although, as David Wilson shows in chapter 11, the ecstatic but impeccably Protestant spirituality of John Fletcher (1729–85) and his wife Mary Bosanquet (1739–1815) came later to be regarded as the pinnacle of Methodist perfection, elsewhere John Walsh has brilliantly explored how contemporaries described Wesley himself as a holy man, albeit one of a more inimitable kind.[58] The aged preacher with his long, silver hair certainly looked the part. 'I have read or heard of saints, surely this is one', marvelled one observer.[59] George Eliot later put similar words into the mouth of Dinah Morris in the evocative open-air sermon in *Adam Bede*.[60] (As the cover image of this volume shows, Morris herself was one of several figures in Victorian fiction whose presentation evoked their saintly status.) Wesley's posthumous presentation is also instructive. Robert Sayer's extraordinary print of the recently deceased great man being wafted up to heaven by angels, for instance, smacked of Counter-Reformation iconography (figure 3). Even less conventionally Protestant were the biscuits distributed to mourners at his funeral in 1791, on which was a likeness of Wesley in his canonicals, with a halo and a crown.[61] Trees under which he had preached, chairs and beds on which he reposed, teapots that refreshed him, locks of his hair, pens and items of clothing were all cherished. The fact many of these ended up in the Museum of Methodist Antiquities suggests that they were treated more as curios than as sacred objects, but the dividing line was seldom clear.[62]

By the early nineteenth century there was also growing interest in the saints of the more distant past. Clerical antiquaries had long been sympathetic to aspects of the pre-Reformation Church, but it now enjoyed a new vogue, boosted by romantic nostalgia for hermits, holy wells and ruined abbeys, and mediated through the novels of Walter Scott.[63] In the hands of the Poet Laureate Robert Southey (1774–1843), this temper could be put to conservative purposes, as Bill Sheils shows in chapter 6 in his discussion of the former's 'colloquies' with the ghost of Thomas More, published in 1829 to defend the embattled established Church.[64] Better known is how the Tractarians deployed it to more radical effect as they sought to reawaken the Church of England

3 Robert Sayer, *John Wesley: That Excellent Minister of the Gospel, Carried by Angels into Abraham's Bosom*, coloured engraving, 1791.

to its Catholic ancestry in the 1830s and 40s. A fuller awareness of England's saints, Newman proclaimed in 1843, would 'serve to make us love our country better, and on truer grounds than heretofore; to teach us to invest her territory, her cities and villages, her hills and springs with sacred associations'.[65] It was a seductive vision, but it is worth pointing out that it drew on sympathies that already existed, and that manifested themselves in different ways in different parts of Britain. Newman's comments were certainly influential for the Scottish Tractarian bishop Alexander Forbes of Brechin (1817–75), whose *Kalendars of Scottish Saints* (1872) excavated the Catholic strata that underlay the Presbyterian present.[66] Forbes's saints were undoubtedly Catholics, but in his reading they were also entrepreneurial philanthropists in the mould of Chalmers or Carnegie who were integral to a whiggish national story as pioneers of agriculture, weaving and women's rights.[67] Forbes was also an outspoken advocate of saints as a solution to the problems of the modern city, founding a sisterhood dedicated to Mary and Modwenna in Dundee in 1871.[68] In Wales, too, saints were figureheads for churchmen keen to reinforce continuity narratives. In chapter 3 Martha Vandrei shows how both middle-of-the-road Anglicans and advanced High Churchmen used classical literature, medieval mythology and early modern scholarship to connect Christian antiquity with the British Church, via the elusive ancient princess Claudia Rufina: 'Saint Gwladys'. In Ireland, meanwhile, as Andrew Holmes demonstrates in chapter 4, Ulster Presbyterians decried Anglican and Catholic claims to Patrick, presenting him instead as a Scottish-Irish Unionist figure who, like them, had abhorred episcopacy and championed pure biblical Christianity.

England cared less about its patron saint: it has been argued that Saint George received so little attention because 'Englishness' had become so thoroughly subsumed within imperial 'Britishness'.[69] More marked was an appreciation of saints as regional or even local figures. For the scholarly amateur Frances Arnold-Forster (1857–1921) 'England's patron saints' were its Church dedicatees, and her magisterial work on the subject pioneered it as a subject of serious study for folklorists and historians.[70] Such figures were claimed most vociferously by Anglicans, who came in our period to regard themselves as spiritual descendants of the great pre-Conquest 'native' founder-saints: Etheldreda at Ely, Chad at Lichfield, Frideswide at Oxford, Cuthbert at Durham, as well as a host of more obscure local figures.[71] Church restoration was one catalyst for this. Another was crisis. Anglicans were becoming aware that the established Church could no longer command the allegiance of all or even most people. The pageants, banners, processions and rituals created for the newly revived patronal festivals were part of its retooling as a 'national Church', one that saw itself less as a denomination than as guardian of England's cultural patrimony, not least as custodian of her finest ancient monuments. If ancient dioceses could at least claim continuities, new ones had to be more strenuously creative. By far the most ambitious was Truro (1876), whose stunning stained glass, conceived by the first bishop, Edward White Benson (1829–96), was installed between 1887 and 1913. The resulting scheme included 108 luminaries, beginning with the commission to Peter and weaving in the fifth- and sixth-century Cornish saints Piran, German and Petroc, the preaching of John Wesley to tin miners, and the locally born missionary to India, Henry Martyn (1781–1812), who appeared alongside John Keble (1792–1866) and F. D. Maurice (1805–72) in a triptych representing evangelical, High and Broad churchmanship, the sequence culminating with a window showing Benson laying the foundation stone for the new cathedral. Recent scholarship reveals how overseas expansion transplanted familiar saints into still more exotic settings. Alex Bremner has brilliantly documented their export by High Churchmen who sought to extend the symbolic and visual languages of Anglicanism into imperial settings, while Joseph Hardwick notes the clerical and lay freemasonry of St George's societies that conjoined Anglicans amid the often hostile voluntarism of the rapidly expanding Anglo-world.[72]

## Revival

Saints, as we have seen, had not gone away. But this did not prevent some from claiming to have rediscovered them, and others from contesting that claim. The flamboyantly Italianate piety adopted by the convert-priest Frederick William Faber (1814–63) was not to most English tastes. Yet even he was taken aback by the storm that erupted after the publication of the first volumes in a projected series of *Lives of the Saints* in 1848.[73] Protestant distaste was a given; but the *Lives* were also savaged by Catholics. In September the usually moderate *Dolman's Magazine* published a blistering review of the volume on Saint Rose of Lima, warning that its subject's extreme asceticism seemed calculated to repel modern readers. 'Alban Butler had doubtless read all this, and perhaps more. He wisely and prudently omitted it. Why resuscitate such more than charnel horrors?' 'A good biography of a saint of God', the reviewer stated, 'is an invaluable work', but the main aim should be 'edification': improbable stories were unhelpful.[74] After a short period of suspension the scheme was resumed under the auspices of Newman's Birmingham Oratory, eventually being completed in forty-two volumes (1847–56). The furore evinced a wide spectrum of beliefs about saints and what they were for.[75] 'Old' or 'English' Catholics brought up on Butler found the excesses of Faber's Counter-Reformation subjects hard to stomach: what he sniffily dismissed as 'mezzo-Protestante freddezza' was what they called common sense.[76] In the 1860s the future Lord Acton (1834–1902) would annoy his fellow believers by exposing factual errors in the legends of the saints, later lambasting Pius V and Saint Charles Borromeo for celebrating the murders of Protestants.[77] By the end of the century, however, unapologetic supernaturalism was becoming the order of the day. As Alana Harris shows in chapter 15, the remarkable but hitherto unexplored popularity among British Catholics of the miraculous healing cult of the 'Little Flower', Saint Thérèse of Lisieux, showed the prevalence of this temper in grassroots religiosity, while in chapter 2 Carol Engelhardt Herringer describes how devotion to the Virgin Mary became an identifying badge for Catholics of all stripes.

Such figures were not, however, the property of Catholics alone. Faber's extravagances were part of a much wider debate about saints and sanctity which blew up with particular vigour in the 1840s. While the rising interconfessional temperature undoubtedly played a part, this section, like our book as a whole, examines how such contentions overflowed into broader intellectual discussion and cultural production. There was no single sparkpoint, but, as Elizabeth Macfarlane shows in chapter 14, John Henry Newman's abortive *Lives of the English Saints* undoubtedly fuelled the flames, all the more so because the series issued from a figure who was still – for now – a member of the established Church. Newman's circle had long considered the Church of England ripe for the revival of more full-bloodedly Catholic forms of worship. To achieve this they sought initially to capitalise on existing reverence among High Churchmen for the 'Caroline divines' of the seventeenth century, as mediated, for instance, through Izaak Walton's gently hagiographical *Lives* of John Donne (1572–1631), George Herbert (1593–1633), Richard Hooker (1554–1600) and others.[78] *Tract 75* (1836) even contained a proposed liturgy venerating that most saintly of Restoration churchmen, the non-juring bishop Thomas Ken (1637–1711).[79] By 1842, however, Newman was living in self-imposed exile among a small band of followers at Littlemore, and from there he projected a multi-authored series featuring figures derived not from Anglican history but from pre-Reformation hagiologies, eventually published in 1844–45. It was not a success. The uncritical inclusion of miracles, apparitions and ecstatic visions, alongside favourable references to papal authority, monasticism and celibacy, elicited outraged reviews.[80] In autumn 1845 Newman, Faber and several other contributors departed for Rome, but this served only to inflame matters further. Commentators railed against the vogue for preferring shadowy and distant figures above more tangible ones. 'What have Dunstan, and George of Cappadocia, and Swithin the bishop, and Margaret the virgin, and Crispin the martyr, done for us' asked one commentator, that they should 'elbow out' Charles Simeon of Cambridge?[81] The series also fell foul of family values. 'Fanatical panegyrics of virginity' were decried as unbiblical and unhealthy, not least in *The Saint's Tragedy* (1848), the first of many attacks by Charles Kingsley (1819–75) on 'Newmanism', which used the sufferings of Saint Elizabeth of Hungary to hammer home the point.

To some degree such reactions represented old prejudices writ large. Many on both sides of the confessional divide felt that obscure popish legends belonged amid the credulous peasantry of southern Europe, not the inhabitants of modern Britain. Yet the controversies of the 1840s served also to crystallise more current questions about how Christianity related to its past. Saints forced religious commentators to wrestle with questions about authority, lineage, miracles, testimony. Existing work often assumes that the answers tended to run along confessional lines.[82] It also tends to swallow Anglo- and Roman Catholic claims to medievalising 'innovation' in the teeth of hysterical Protestant abuse. Behind the polemical white noise, however, there often existed considerable consensus, as several of our chapters demonstrate. Francis of Assisi: for instance, was universally revered, even if Protestants concentrated more on his poverty and preaching than his supernatural feats, stigmata and papal obedience, while the social reformer Josephine Butler (1828–1906) lauded Catherine of Siena for her proto-feminist activism and diligent life of prayer.[83] Such figures appealed to Protestants and Catholics alike, often being construed simply as exemplars who demonstrated how to live better lives; how to follow Christ. Yet this was also why Faber's and Newman's efforts were so controversial. For if saints were to be imitated as well as applauded, it was necessary to render accounts of them believable, burrowing through 'superstitious' detritus to get to the original truths beneath. Textual archaeology, of course, generated problems of its own. One of the most serious accusations against Newman's series was that it opened the back door to unbelief, collapsing the distinction between the genuine miracles of Scripture and the 'sophistry, lying legends, forged writings' of later ages in much the same way that had scandalised readers of Edward Gibbon (1737–94) in the 1770s and 80s.[84] Yet at a time when radical biblical critics were beginning to 'demythologise' the Gospels, historians eager to deconstruct medieval accounts, likewise, risked opening similar Pandora's boxes. The faith of earlier ages could be incorporated or dismissed, but it could not safely be ignored.

These skirmishes were intensified by the articulation of more expansive definitions of sanctity. Few were more expansive than those of Thomas Carlyle (1795–1881), whose subjects in *On Heroes, Hero-Worship, and the Heroic in History* (1841) were presented as incursions of the divine into human history. It is not always easy to tell whether Carlyle's God was anything more than a metaphor, and his juxtaposition of Jesus with Cromwell, Mohammed, Luther and Odin was hardly calculated to reassure the orthodox. Nevertheless, his rejection of 'cant' and dead creeds in favour of example and action appealed to Protestants allergic to cloistered mummery. 'All religions, and all ages, have their saints; their men of unearthly mould; self-conquerors, sublime even in their errors; not altogether hateful in their crimes', declaimed the second-generation Claphamite Sir James Stephen (1789–1859) in *Essays in Ecclesiastical Biography* (1849). 'If a man will understand the dormant powers of his own nature, let him read the *Acta Sanctorum*.'[85] Stephen's vision of a Protestant hagiology owed as much to his watered-down inherited evangelicalism as it did to Carlyle.[86] But his *Essays* also chimed with a growing sense among liberal Christians of the need to define the Church more inclusively. Broad Church Anglicans like A. P. Stanley and F. W. Farrar (1831–1903) and Presbyterians like John Tulloch (1823–86) made frequent and often playful use of wildly contrasting figures from across the Judaeo-Christian epoch in order to expose the narrowness of ecclesiastical combatants in the present day. They venerated F. D. Maurice as gentle, 'saint-like', even 'CHRIST-like': Kingsley thought him 'the most beautiful human soul' he had ever met, the embodiment of John, 'the Apostle of Love'.[87] And they prized open-mindedness in figures from the past. Not for nothing did progressives from Samuel Taylor Coleridge (1772–1834) to James Martineau (1805–1900) claim the Puritan Richard Baxter as their patron saint, as Simon Burton explains in chapter 9. Baxter's mildness, his eirenicism, his prescription of 'mere Christianity' and his dying words ('I would as willingly be a martyr for charity as for faith') led them to hail him as a man ahead of his time.[88]

To mid-Victorians steeped in the certainties of Samuel Smiles's *Self Help* and that other shrine to the cultivation of character, the National Portrait Gallery (both 1859), the gospel of the life well lived made sense. The catalogues of the Religious Tract and Catholic Truth Societies were packed with exemplary biographies tailored for readers in particular walks of life.[89] This-worldly 'usefulness' trumped other-worldly mysticism as a criterion for inclusion. Helen Rogers shows in chapter 13 how readily commentators deployed the language of sanctity to praise philanthropic heroines like the prison visitors Elizabeth Fry and Sarah Martin. Protestants sometimes chafed at the lack of official mechanisms for recognising virtuous achievement. 'Could I canonise Sarah Martin,' declared one bishop, 'I would do so.'[90] Roshan Allpress advances a similar argument regarding Wilberforce and the Clapham 'saints' in chapter 12. What began as a derogatory nickname was by the 1820s a genuine accolade. In an age of moral renovation at home and abroad, Allpress argues, 'practical saints' spearheaded institutional and individual reform, at once expiating national and imperial sins – above all, the slave trade – and being constructed as exemplary models of Christian life. The flipside of this practical emphasis was a revulsion against the futility of the self-punishment held to characterise Catholic accounts. Readers of the Nonconformist *Eclectic Review*, for instance, might have been startled to read that there were indeed Protestant ascetic 'saints', but were reassured that theirs were more Jesus-centred and less showy than the Catholic variety. In setting the Italian mystic Saint Paul of the Cross (1695–1775) against the recently deceased urban missionary Travers Madge (1823–66), the *Eclectic* contrasted the former's 'thaumaturgic marvels', misogyny and narrow-spiritedness with the latter's simplicity, self-sacrifice and non-dogmatic devotion, related in a 'small and exceedingly modest volume' that far outshone the exhibitionism of any Desert Father or phoney medieval miracle worker.[91]

For those seeking modern martyrs and heroes fit to rank alongside those of the past, a rich source was overseas missions. Brian Stanley outlines an 'apostolic succession' whose sufferings and deaths elevated them to martyr status: John Williams (Vanuatu, 1839), Allen Gardiner (Tierra del Fuego, 1851), John Coleridge Patteson (Santa Cruz Islands, 1871), David Livingstone (Chitambo's village, 1873), James Hannington (Busoga, 1885), James Chalmers (Papua New Guinea, 1901).[92] The prototype was Henry Martyn, whose preaching, biblical translation, travels and death in Persia in 1812 made him a totemic figure (Charlotte Brontë's stern and self-denying St John Rivers in *Jane Eyre* (1847) was almost certainly modelled on him).[93] Pious commentators seldom tired of repeating the inscription placed on his tomb at Tokat, which emphasised the power of his cross-cultural appeal: 'he will long be remembered in the East, where he was known as a man of God'.[94] Interestingly, Martyn modelled attributes that Protestants did not always prize – asceticism, fasting, celibacy. It is significant that early modern Jesuits provided some of the most compelling models of missionary sanctity: Martyn himself was 'exceedingly roused' at the 'astonishing example of that great saint' Francis Xavier.[95] Popular collections of missionary lives were often ambitiously ecumenical, conjoining Hudson Taylor's China Inland Mission with Augustine of Canterbury, the Irish preacher Columba, the Anglo-Saxon Boniface, the Lutheran Schwartz and the American David Brainerd, and constructing similar edifices of 'missionary women'.[96] 'Soldier-saints', likewise, could be assembled into eclectic spiritual bloodlines, running from the biblical warriors Joshua, Gideon and David through the Catholic saints George, Alban and Martin of Tours to contemporary paragons like the Baptist Henry Havelock and Captain Hedley Vicars.[97]

While Victorians relished reading about such figures, they also developed new ways of representing them. Although there is little room to expand upon this here, it is worth emphasising that as well as being discussed in print, saints became much more visible in our period. Between the 1830s and the 1860s there was an explosion in the demand for stained glass, which within a generation dramatically transformed churches and chapels.[98] What little scholarship exists on this has focused on the revivalism of A. W. N. Pugin (1812–52) and his High Church counterparts in the Ecclesiological Society. Here tradition was all-important. The influential *Ecclesiologist*, for instance, recommended that the spaces created by gothic tracery be filled with biblical characters and haloed saints.[99] New firms like Hardman and Co. (1838), Clayton and Bell (1855) and Charles Eamer Kempe (1866) catered to this vogue, fulfilling major commissions as well as supplying catalogues of standard figures that could be purchased cheaply 'off the peg'. Stained glass also, though, encouraged less conventional treatment. It became a feature of schools, colleges and museums, whose windows were now peopled with founders, ancestors and alumni. Such figures were sanctified by the medium in which they appeared. From 1897 ordinands at chapel in Ridley Hall, Cambridge, for example, were scrutinised from above by a sequence of teachers of the faith, running from Irenaeus in the second century to Joseph Barber Lightfoot in the nineteenth, via Anselm, Tyndale, Luther, Cranmer, Ridley and George Herbert, the whole designed to assert that evangelical Anglicanism was no recent innovation.[100] Frescoes and ceramics, too, attracted saint-makers. Saint Jude's Church, Hampstead Garden Suburb embodied the go-ahead Christian Socialism of its founder, Henrietta Barnett (1851–1936). Its Lady Chapel was, and is, a shrine to female ministry, placing Saints Helena, Cecilia and Genevieve in an imagined empyrean that also includes Joan of Arc, Madame Guyon, Harriet Beecher Stowe, Florence Nightingale, Grace Darling, Elizabeth Barrett Browning, Edith Cavell and Queen Victoria.[101]

## Doubting saints

Francis William Newman (1805–97) is often remembered as the black sheep of his family. Whereas his brother's *Apologia Pro Vita Sua* (1864) became a classic of spiritual autobiography, Frank's notorious *Phases of Faith* (1850) mapped a journey in the opposite direction, from evangelicalism via 'honest doubt' to freethought and vegetarianism. Among his friends, however, the *enfant terrible* was regarded very differently. For W. M. Thackeray (1811–63) he was 'a very pious loving humble soul … with an ascetical continence … and a beautiful love and reverence', while George Eliot called him 'our blessed St Francis' 'whose soul is a blessed yea'.[102] 'He is so holy!' sighed Elizabeth Gaskell (1810–65). 'The face and the voice at first sight told "He had been with Christ".'[103] His funeral address, by the Anglican clergyman John Temperley Grey (c. 1837–1903), was explicit: 'Without depreciating in the least his illustrious brother, it may truly be said that while one was a saint in the cloister, the other was a saint in the very thick of life's battle.' Grey praised his sympathy for the downtrodden, support for women's suffrage, anti-vivisectionism, philanthropy and hospitality. It mattered little that he rejected almost all dogmatic statements beyond the Lord's Prayer and was morally outraged by aspects of conventional Christianity: 'our friend was a truth seeker'. 'Francis Newman stood by himself in his greatness, his goodness, his simplicity', Temperley concluded. 'We shall not find his like again.'[104] Such comments were characteristic of late Victorian freethought, where action trumped contemplation and good intentions were everything. They also underline the extent to which sanctity and its *topoi* could be decoupled from orthodox belief.[105] Starstruck devotees burst into tears or enthused breathlessly about their quasi-religious experiences at the feet of Charles Darwin (1809–82).[106] Positivist Temples of Humanity showed that one did not need to believe in the Christian God or indeed any God at all to assemble collections of *de facto* saints.[107]

We have seen already how Protestants laid claim to Catholic saints by paring away the superstitions that disfigured them. This final section examines how liberal thinkers took a step further, resolving the difficulties inherent in regarding past figures as spiritually or behaviourally normative by studying them as products of their times and cultures. Just as source critics sought not to destroy the Gospels but to discover the Jesus of history, the aim was not to debunk saints but to discern what they were really like. Granted, historicism raised as many questions as it answered, suggesting that if 'God' existed at all he worked inscrutably through time rather than intervening directly in it. But while theological conservatives regarded such treatment as corrosive, to liberals it was creative. If it could be proven that religion was embedded in the human psyche, or in the needs of society, it altered its significance, to be sure, but made it more true, not less. This trajectory is implicit in several of the essays that follow, but it emerges with particular clarity in chapter 7, on Ignatius Loyola. British Protestants had always dismissed his miraculous visions, retched at his unhealthy self-mortification and shivered at the sight of Jesuits. But increasingly they were also intrigued by his iron will and manly endurance, comparing him with other charismatic figures in analyses of religious leadership and speculating about how his beliefs were shaped by his nationality, rather than dismissing them out of hand.[108]

To historicise saints also meant exchanging old models for new ones. This idea reappears throughout *Robert Elsmere* (1888), the provocative bestselling novel by Mrs Humphry Ward (1851–1920), wherein the eponymous clergyman-hero's crisis of faith is brought on by the study of early French saints' lives. Unable to reconcile credulous legends with either reason or religion, Elsmere loses his faith, becoming a self-sacrificial prophet of the religion of humanity in the slums of London's East End, proclaiming Jesus not as saviour but as the noblest of all men. Elsmere dies exhausted but ecstatic, a 'real-life' saint.[109] The French scholar and controversialist Ernest Renan (1823–92) mischievously argued that the Dutch philosopher and reputed atheist Baruch Spinoza (1623–77) ought to be regarded in similar terms. Far from 'traversing his life like a demon incarnate, and ending it in despair', as believing critics expected him to, he beatifically refused the patronage that might have constrained his freedom to think, eschewing polemic and revering reason above all.[110] 'The cause of the supernatural is compromised, the cause of the ideal is unscathed; and so it will ever be', Renan crowed.[111]

Historicism encouraged the deconstruction of saints' cults as well as their characters. This, too, was constructive as well as sceptical. In the introduction to her *Sacred and Legendary Art* (1848), the critic and liberal Protestant Anna Jameson (1794–1860), for instance, denounced the 'puritanical jealousy' that held Catholic art in contempt, reminding readers that myths and miracles were the natural subject matter of an ignorant age whose piety was, nonetheless, beyond question.[112] The essayist and historian James Anthony Froude (1818–94) pushed the point further. As a young don he had participated in Newman's disastrous series, but he later broke with the Tractarians and with orthodox belief, resigning his fellowship and scandalising Oxford with a sensational semi-autobiographical novel, *The Nemesis of Belief* (1849), eventually coming under the spell of Carlyle. His 1850 essay on 'The lives of the saints' marked an important step in his intellectual journey, combining something like Newman's awe at the 'faith of fourteen hundred years' with Carlyle's sense that great men were projections of deep human needs, 'the heroic patterns of a form of human life which every Christian within his own limits was endeavouring to realise'.[113] Legends had been a characteristic of Christianity ever since it emerged from Galilee, when 'the devout imagination, possessed with what was often no more than the rumour of a name, bodied it out into life, and form, and reality'. Were they true? Froude sneered at the question: 'Doubtless the "Lives of the Saints" are full of lies. Are then none in the Iliad?' he asked, 'in the legends of Æneas? Were the stories sung in the liturgy of Eleusis all so true? so true as fact? Are the songs of the Cid or of Siegfried?'[114] Saints were real enough for those who made pilgrimages to them on bleeding knees. The young J. R. Seeley (1834–95) hoped that this affective power might be harnessed to the uses of current society and politics. Having already presented a provocatively human Jesus in *Ecce Homo* (1865), he published an 1868 essay on 'The Church as a teacher of morality' that blamed the Church's problems on its espousal of obsolete exemplars. Drawing on Carlyle ('every nation's true Bible is its history') and sounding like Comte ('we should form, as it were, a national calendar, consecrate our ancestors – keep their images near us, and so reap the inestimable advantage'), Seeley argued that the inculcation of civic duty and social morality required up-to-date saints, drawn not from the ancient East but from British history. His quasi-Coleridgean blueprint re-envisaged the Anglican clergy as curator-priests of a patriotic pantheon designed to cater to current needs.[115]

For the 'father of anthropology' Edward Burnett Tylor (1832–1917), by contrast, saints had no place whatsoever in modern culture. They were a 'survival' from the 'animism' that characterised primitive belief systems, and their continued existence defied the evolutionary progress of human culture. As Timothy Larsen has shown in a sparkling recent study, Tylor's Quaker upbringing informed a savage anti-Catholicism that lost none of its ferocity when he lost his faith.[116] The Catholic cult of the saints, Tylor stated, was merely a modified form of pre-Christian ancestor worship: having taken over Roman basilicas, it preserved Roman polytheism, parcelling out responsibility for professions and illnesses. In worshipping their dead, Tylor observed waspishly, contemporary Catholics (and, by implication, Christians more generally) were as bad as the primitive peoples of Zululand, Madagascar, Ceylon and elsewhere.[117] Tylor's protégé J. G. Frazer (1854–1941) was similarly dismissive. Frazer's *The Golden Bough* (1890, and various revisions) is most famous for its claim that Christian resurrection stories grew from the universal pagan myth of the dying and revived god, but it also situated saints in nature rites. Amid the greenery of Manx and Highland spring celebrations, Frazer remarked, 'it is obvious that St. Bride, or St. Bridget, is an old heathen goddess of fertility, disguised in a threadbare Christian cloak'.[118] Brought up in the Free Church of Scotland, Frazer, like Tylor, was the product of a deeply anti-Catholic milieu, and he peppered his work with similarly acerbic commentary, chuckling at Sicilian peasants who, 'within our own lifetime', had held their saints responsible for a drought, turning them 'like naughty children' to the wall and shaking fists at them because they 'either could not or would not help'.[119] It is worth pointing out, however, that this was the high-water mark for such condescension. The notion of 'survivals' was already unfashionable by the time of Tylor's death, while his refusal to accept that notions of a spiritual realm pointed to any reality beyond the material was criticised by the Jesuit Alfred Weld (1823–90), the evolutionist Alfred Russel Wallace (1823–1913) and the folklorist Andrew Lang (1844–1912).[120]

By the end of the century modernist theologians and idealist philosophers of a liberal Protestant bent were coming to argue that new forms of enquiry offered richer understandings of human personality that would in turn throw new light on belief. As Michael Ledger-Lomas points out in chapter 1, spiritualism, occultism and psychical research provided inviting material for the latest among many attempts to explain the experiences of the Apostle Paul on the road to Damascus. Inviting, but problematic, in that any attempt to vindicate the biblical account in physiological or psychological terms raised the disquieting possibility that Paul's vision and therefore his teaching were self-generated. The attempt to resolve such tensions was central to the work of the Harvard psychologist and philosopher William James (1842–1910), whose 1901–02 Gifford Lectures became *Varieties of Religious Experience*. James's beliefs are notoriously hard to pin down: although sympathetic to what subjects said about their encounters with the divine, he havered at the edges of theistic commitment, preferring to advance a pragmatist understanding of humanity's search for God that held all such experiences to be meaningful, if not necessarily true in the traditional sense.[121] In endeavouring 'to test saintliness by common sense, [and] to use human standards to help us decide how far the religious life commends itself as an ideal kind of human activity', he was well aware that such standards were themselves historically specific.[122] But as in comparative ethnology, 'there is a certain composite photograph of universal saintliness, the same in all religions, of which the features can easily be traced'.[123] Thus Pascal jostles with Frank Bullen's *With Christ at Sea* (1900), Augustine with the Buddha and the Bhagavad-Gita, and the holy poverty of Jesuits and Franciscans with that of 'Hindu fakirs, Buddhist monks, and Mohammedan dervishes'.[124] Uniting them was the possession of one powerful emotional faculty and a lack of balancing inhibitions. If saints were single-minded it was because they had resolved their internal tensions: and while their enthusiasm (for fasting, say) could tip over into pathology, it was, at base, a fundamentally healthy mental state.[125]

It has been argued that James's ecumenism should not be allowed to obscure the essentially Protestant nature of his taxonomy.[126] His sharpest criticisms of saintly excess were reserved for Catholic self-punishment and over-scrupulousness. 'It is better that a life should contract many a dirt-mark, than forfeit usefulness in its efforts to remain unspotted', he sniffed of the Jesuit Louis Gonzaga (1568–91), whose intellect (and idea of God) James crushingly thought 'no larger than a pin's head'.[127] Whether or not saints bespoke the action of a deity – James was deliberately vague about this – their value could nevertheless be judged through the effect they had on others. Holiness was therefore a matter of moral influence and action. James influenced a range of younger thinkers, notably the Lutheran scholar of comparative religion Rudolf Otto (1869–1937) and the Presbyterian systematic theologian John Wood Oman (1860–1939), both of whom developed the idea that religious consciousness – a sense of the sacred – was something intrinsic to humanity that nevertheless pointed beyond the merely material or mental. Our story does not end in the first decade of the twentieth century. Nevertheless, *Varieties* forms an appropriate endpoint for this introduction, in that James, like most nineteenth-century commentators, was concerned as much with what saints were for as with what they were. He concluded that they mattered because they offered men and women an ideal to emulate, one that was 'holy' because it was so different from that of the strutting strong man imagined by Nietzsche and others like him. Saints were a mirror that gave humanity glimpses of its better self and – perhaps – of something beyond.

## What's a saint?

This introduction has shown that the question posed by Newman's sceptical demons was so resonant because there was no single answer to it. And yet it has also shown that saints – however defined – were central to belief, unbelief and everything in between. British people worshipped alongside saints, but they also thought with them, using them to articulate or challenge identities, and returning repeatedly to the historical, ethical and theological issues they raised. *Making and Remaking Saints in Nineteenth-Century Britain* can only scratch the surface of this vast and extraordinarily rich subject.

But if the essays that follow succeed in provoking further research, this book will have achieved its purpose.

## Notes

1. John Henry Newman, *Verses on Various Occasions* (1867; London: Burns and Oates, 1880), p. 341.
2. Wilfrid Wilberforce, *The House of Burns and Oates* (London: Burns and Oates, 1908), pp. 15–21.
3. *Ibid.*, pp. 6–7.
4. *Mansfield College, Oxford: Its Origin and Opening* (London: James Clarke, 1890), p. 54.
5. *Ibid.*, pp. 68–9.
6. *Ibid.*, pp. 47–8. See also Elaine Kaye, *Mansfield College, Oxford: Its Origin, History and Significance* (Oxford: Oxford University Press, 1996), pp. 77–81; Clyde Binfield, '"We claim our part in the great inheritance": the message of four Congregational buildings', in Keith Robbins (ed.), *Protestant Evangelicalism: Britain, Ireland, Germany and America, c. 1750–c. 1950* (Oxford: Blackwell, 1990), pp. 201–24.
7. William B. Selbie, *The Life of Andrew Martin Fairbairn* (London: Hodder and Stoughton, 1914), pp. 426–30.
8. Andrew L. Drummond, *The Church Architecture of Protestantism* (Edinburgh: T. & T. Clark, 1934), p. 293.
9. Kirstie Blair, *Form and Faith in Victorian Poetry and Religion* (Oxford: Oxford University Press, 2012); Timothy Larsen, *A People of One Book: The Bible and the Victorians* (Oxford: Oxford University Press, 2011).
10. Irene Whelan, *The Bible War in Ireland* (Madison: University of Wisconsin Press, 2005); Michael Wheeler, *The Old Enemies* (Cambridge: Cambridge University Press, 2006), Dominic Janes, *Victorian Reformation: The Fight over Idolatry in the Church of England, 1840–1860* (Oxford and New York: Oxford University Press, 2009); Peter Nockles and Vivienne Westbrook (eds), *Reinventing the Reformation in the Nineteenth Century*, Special Issue of the Bulletin of the John Rylands Library, 90 (2014).
11. Auguste Comte, *Calendrier Positiviste, ou, Système Général de Commémoration Publique* (Paris: L. Mathias, 1849).
12. Gordon S. Haight (ed.), *The George Eliot Letters*, 9 vols (New Haven: Yale University Press, 1954–78), I: pp. 45, 63.
13. David Hempton, *Evangelical Disenchantment: Nine Portraits of Faith and Doubt* (New Haven: Yale University Press, 2008), pp. 19–40.
14. George Eliot, *Middlemarch: A Study of Provincial Life*, 4 vols (Edinburgh and London: William Blackwood and Sons, 1871–72), I: pp. v–vii; IV: p. 371.
15. Rowland E. Prothero, *The Life and Correspondence of Arthur Penrhyn Stanley*, 2 vols (London: John Murray, 1893), I: p. 116.
16. Philip C. Almond, *The British Discovery of Buddhism* (Cambridge: Cambridge University Press, 1988); Almond, *Heretic and Hero: Muhammad and the Victorians* (Wiesbaden: O. Harrassowitz, 1989); Clinton Bennett, *Victorian Images of Islam* (London: Grey Seal, 1992); Norman J. Girardot, *The Victorian Translation of China: James Legge's Oriental Pilgrimage* (Berkeley and Los Angeles: California University Press, 2002).

17 Clyde Binfield (ed.), *Sainthood Revisioned: Studies in Hagiography and Biography* (Sheffield: Sheffield Academic Press, 1995), p. 13.
18 For discussion of similar issues in Europe and in North America, see Marina Warner, *Joan of Arc: The Image of Female Heroism* (1981; new edn, Oxford: Oxford University Press, 2013), pp. 184–257; Jonathan Dewald, *Lost Worlds: The Emergence of French Social History, 1815–1970* (Philadelphia: Penn State University Press, 2006), pp. 7–96; Patricia Appelbaum, 'St Francis in the nineteenth century', *Church History*, 78 (2009), 792–813; Robert D. Priest, *The Gospel According to Renan: Reading, Writing, and Religion in Nineteenth-Century Europe* (Oxford: Oxford University Press, 2015).
19 See Stuart Clark, *Thinking with Demons: The Idea of Witchcraft in Early Modern Europe* (Oxford: Clarendon, 1997).
20 Robert Bartlett, *Why Can the Dead do such Great Things? Saints and Worshippers from the Martyrs to the Reformation* (Princeton: Princeton University Press, 2013), pp. 3–26.
21 For a seminal study, see Peter Brown, *The Cult of the Saints: Its Rise and Function in Latin Christianity* (Chicago: University of Chicago Press, 1982).
22 See Colleen McDannell, *Material Christianity: Religion and Popular Culture in America* (New Haven: Yale University Press, 1995); Robert Orsi, *The Madonna of 115th Street: Faith and Community in Italian Harlem, 1880–1950* (New Haven: Yale University Press, 2002); Margaret Cormack, *Saints and their Cults in the Atlantic World* (Columbia: University of South Carolina Press, 2007); Mary Heimann, 'Mysticism in Bootle: Victorian supernaturalism as an historical problem', *Journal of Ecclesiastical History*, 64 (2013), 335–56.
23 Eamon Duffy, *Saints, Sacrilege and Sedition: Religion and Conflict in the Tudor Reformations* (London: Bloomsbury, 2012), p. 33.
24 Karen Bruhn, 'Reforming Saint Peter: Protestant constructions of Saint Peter the Apostle in early modern England', *Sixteenth Century Journal*, 33, 1 (2002), 33–49.
25 Helen Parish, *Monks, Miracles and Magic: Reformation Representations of the Medieval Church* (Abingdon: Routledge, 2005), pp. 45–91.
26 *Ibid.*, pp. 92–118.
27 The literature on the medieval period, by contrast, is vast: see especially Patrick J. Geary, *Living with the Dead in the Middle Ages* (Ithaca: Cornell University Press, 1994); Caroline Walker Bynum, *Christian Materiality: An Essay on Religion in Late Medieval Europe* (Cambridge, MA: MIT Press, 2011).
28 Gal. 4: 10. Judith Maltby, *Prayer Book and People in Elizabethan and Early Stuart England* (Cambridge: Cambridge University Press, 1998), pp. 38–9.
29 Francis Procter, *A New History of the Book of Common Prayer with a Rationale of its Offices*, rev. W. H. Frere (1901; London: Macmillan, 1910), pp. 334–41.
30 Brian Cummings (ed.), *The Book of Common Prayer: The Texts of 1549, 1559, and 1662* (Oxford: Oxford University Press, 2011), pp. 790–3.
31 See 'The Prig' [Thomas de Longueville], *How to Make a Saint; or, the Process of Canonization in the Church of England* (London: Henry Holt, 1887).
32 E.g. Brooke Foss Westcott, 'The Communion of Saints' (1880), in Westcott, *The Historic Faith: Short Lectures on the Apostles' Creed* (London: Macmillan, 1883), pp. 250–1.
33 John Maiden, *National Religion and the Prayer Book Controversy, 1927–1928* (Woodbridge: Boydell Press, 2009).

34 Alec Ryrie, *Being Protestant in Reformation Britain* (Oxford: Oxford University Press, 2013), pp. 457–9.
35 But see Damian Nussbaum, 'Reviling the saints or reforming the calendar? John Foxe and his "Kalendar" of martyrs', in Susan Wabuda and Caroline Litzenberger (eds), *Belief and Practice in Reformation England* (Aldershot: Ashgate, 1998), pp. 113–36.
36 Irena Backus, *Historical Method and Confessional Identity in the Era of the Reformation* (Leiden: Brill, 2003).
37 Simon Ditchfield, 'Thinking with saints: sanctity and society in the early modern world', in Françoise Meltzer and Jaś Elsner (eds), *Saints: Faith Without Borders* (Chicago: Chicago University Press, 2011), pp. 160, 175–7.
38 Peter B. Nockles, 'The nineteenth-century reception' and Vivienne Westbrook, 'Mid-Victorian Foxe', *The Unabridged Acts and Monuments Online* (Sheffield: HRI Online Publications, 2011), www.johnfoxe.org, accessed 5 January 2015.
39 E.g. Margo Todd, *The Culture of Protestantism in Early Modern Scotland* (New Haven: Yale University Press, 2002), pp. 328–31; Bridget Heal, *The Cult of the Virgin Mary in Early Modern Germany* (Cambridge: Cambridge University Press, 2007), pp. 64–147; Joseph Leo Koerner, *The Reformation of the Image* (Chicago: Chicago University Press, 2008).
40 Alexandra Walsham, 'Skeletons in the cupboard: relics after the English Reformation', in Walsham (ed.), *Relics and Remains* (Oxford: Oxford University Press), pp. 132–3.
41 R. W. Scribner, 'Incombustible Luther: the image of the reformer in early modern Germany', *Past and Present*, 110 (1986), 38–68.
42 Ulinka Rublack, 'Grapho-relics: Lutheranism and the materialisation of the world', in Walsham (ed.), *Relics*, pp. 144–66.
43 Walsham, 'Skeletons', p. 134. See also Alexandra Walsham, *The Reformation of the Landscape* (Oxford: Oxford University Press, 2011), pp. 471–554.
44 Andrew Atherstone, 'The Martyrs' Memorial at Oxford', *Journal of Ecclesiastical History*, 54 (2003), 278–301.
45 Alexander Robertson, 'The work of reform in Spain', *Evangelical Christendom, Christian Work, and the News of the Churches*, 47 (1893), 111.
46 Alexander F. Mitchell, *The Scottish Reformation* (Edinburgh: Blackwood, 1900), p. 34.
47 See pp. 162, 201–3.
48 See e.g. Jan Golinski, *British Weather and the Climate of Enlightenment* (Chicago: Chicago University Press, 2007).
49 Jane Shaw, *Miracles in Enlightenment England* (New Haven: Yale University Press, 2006), pp. 1–20.
50 Robert Bruce Mullin, *Miracles and the Modern Religious Imagination* (New Haven: Yale University Press, 1996), pp. 9–30.
51 See Ditchfield, 'Thinking'; Paul Koudounaris, *Heavenly Bodies: Cult Treasures and Spectacular Saints from the Catacombs* (London: Thames and Hudson, 2013).
52 Elisa Andretta, 'Anatomie du Vénérable dans la Rome de la Contre-réforme: les autopsies d'Ignace de Loyola et de Philippe Neri', in Maria Pia Donato and Jill Kraye (eds), *Conflicting Duties: Science, Medicine, and Religion in Rome, 1550–1750* (London: Warburg Institute, 2009), pp. 275–300.
53 Clare Haynes, *Pictures and Popery: Art and Religion in England, 1660–1760* (Aldershot: Ashgate, 2006).

54 J. A. Hilton, 'The science of the saints: the spirituality of Butler's *Lives of the Saints*', *Recusant History*, 15 (1979–81), 189–93.
55 Jeremy Gregory, '*Homo religiosus*: masculinity and religion in the long eighteenth century', in Tim Hitchcock and Michèle Cohen (eds), *English Masculinities, 1660–1800* (London, 1999), pp. 85–110.
56 Eamon Duffy, 'Wesley and the Counter-Reformation', in Jane Garnett and Colin Matthew (eds), *Revival and Religion since 1700: Essays for John Walsh* (London: Hambledon Press, 1993), pp. 1–19.
57 George Lavington, *The Enthusiasm of Methodists and Papists Compared*, 3 vols (1749–51; London: J. and P. Knapton, 1754), I: pp. 14–20.
58 John Walsh, '"Celebrity" and "Holy Man": some contemporary perceptions of John Wesley' (unpublished paper).
59 'The life and experience of Richard Moss, one of the first Methodist preachers', *Methodist Magazine*, 21 (1798), 7.
60 George Eliot, *Adam Bede*, 3 vols (Edinburgh: William Blackwood and Sons, 1859), I: pp. 38–9.
61 Luke Tyerman, *The Life and Times of the Rev. John Wesley*, 3 vols (London: Hodder and Stoughton, 1870–71), III: p. 656.
62 E. G. Harmer, 'The Museum of Methodist Antiquities', *Wesleyan Methodist Magazine*, sixth series, 18, 12 (1889), 933–7.
63 Rosemary Sweet, *Antiquaries: The Discovery of the Past in Eighteenth-Century Britain* (London: Hambledon, 2004), pp. 231–76; Roy Strong, *And When Did You Last See Your Father?* (London: Thames and Hudson, 1978).
64 See pp. 112–26.
65 John Henry Newman, 'Note D. Series of saints' lives of 1843–4', in Newman, *Apologia Pro Vita Sua*, ed. Frank M. Turner (New Haven: Yale University Press, 2008), p. 390.
66 Alexander Forbes, *Kalendars of Scottish Saints* (Edinburgh: Edmonston and Douglas, 1872), p. l.
67 *Ibid.*, pp. xlvi–xlvii.
68 Rowan Strong, *Alexander Forbes of Brechin: The First Tractarian Bishop* (Oxford: Clarendon, 1995), pp. 233–7; Susan Mumm, *Stolen Daughters, Virgin Mothers: Anglican Sisterhoods in Victorian Britain* (London: Leicester University Press, 1999).
69 See Nick Groom, *Union Jack: The Story of a Flag* (London: Atlantic, 2006), pp. 154, 176–255.
70 Frances Arnold-Forster, *Studies in Church Dedications*, 3 vols (London: Skeffington and Son, 1899). For similarly Anglican projects, see Sabine Baring-Gould, *The Lives of the Saints*, 15 vols (London: J. Hodges, 1872–77); William Holden Hutton, *The Influence of Christianity upon National Character Illustrated by the Lives and Legends of the English Saints* (London: Wells Gardner, Darton and Co., 1903).
71 For an excellent survey, see Elizabeth Macfarlane, 'Cultures of Anglican Hagiography c. 1840–c. 1940 with Especial Reference to the Diocese of Truro' (DPhil thesis, University of Oxford, 2012).
72 G. A. Bremner, *Imperial Gothic: Religious Architecture and High Anglican Culture in the British Empire, 1840–1870* (New Haven: Yale University Press, 2013); Joseph Hardwick, *An Anglican British World* (Manchester: Manchester University Press, 2014), pp. 205–38.

73 John Edward Bowden, *The Life and Letters of Frederick William Faber* (London: Thomas Richardson and Son, 1869), pp. 328–9, 342–58.
74 *Ibid.*, pp. 346–7.
75 Mary Heimann, *Catholic Devotion in Victorian England* (Oxford: Clarendon, 1995), pp. 5–10.
76 Bowden, *Faber*, p. 329.
77 Heimann, *Catholic Devotion*, pp. 163–4.
78 See Jessica Martin, *Walton's Lives: Conformist Commemorations and the Rise of Biography* (Oxford: Clarendon Press, 2002).
79 Peter B. Nockles, *The Oxford Movement in Context: Anglican High Churchmanship, 1760–1857* (Cambridge: Cambridge University Press, 1994); [John Henry Newman], *Tracts for the Times*, No. 75 (London: J. G. and F. Rivington, 1835–36), pp. 135–45.
80 Frank M. Turner, *John Henry Newman: The Challenge to Evangelical Religion* (New Haven: Yale University Press, 2002), pp. 474–526.
81 Sir James Stephen, *Essays in Ecclesiastical Biography*, 2 vols (London: Longmans, etc., 1849), II: p. 373.
82 See Wheeler, *Old Enemies*; Janes, *Victorian Reformation*; Devon Fisher, *Roman Catholic Saints and Early Victorian Literature* (Aldershot: Ashgate, 2012).
83 Eileen Janes Yeo, 'Protestant feminists and Catholic saints in Victorian Britain', in Yeo (ed.), *Radical Femininity: Women's Self-Representation in the Public Sphere* (Manchester: Manchester University Press, 1998), pp. 127–48; Mary Heimann, 'St Francis and modern English sentiment', in Simon Ditchfield (ed.), *Christianity and Community in the West* (Aldershot: Ashgate, 2001), pp. 278–93.
84 Turner, *Newman*, pp. 488–9.
85 Stephen, *Ecclesiastical Biography*, I: p. 431.
86 *Ibid.*, II: p. 501.
87 Charles F. G. Masterman, *Frederick Denison Maurice* (London: A. R. Mowbray and Co., 1907), p. 202; Charles Kingsley, *Frederick Denison Maurice, a Sermon* (London: Macmillan, 1873), p. 5.
88 A. P. Stanley, 'Richard Baxter', *Macmillan's Magazine*, 32 (1875), 389–92.
89 Gareth Atkins, '"Idle reading"? Policing the boundaries of the nineteenth-century household', in John Doran, Charlotte Methuen and Alexandra Walsham (eds), *Religion and the Household*, Studies in Church History, 50 (Woodbridge: Boydell, 2014), pp. 331–42. Heimann, *Catholic Devotion*, p. 163n.
90 Cited in [George Mogridge], *Sarah Martin, The Prison Visitor of Yarmouth: A Story of a Useful Life* (London: Religious Tract Society [1872]), pp. 167–8.
91 'Ascetic saints', *The Eclectic Review*, 14 (June 1868), 482.
92 Brian Stanley, '"An ardour of devotion": the spiritual legacy of Henry Martyn', in Richard Fox Young (ed.), *India and the Indianness of Christianity* (Grand Rapids: Eerdmans, 2009), pp. 108–26.
93 *Ibid.*, p. 109.
94 E.g. George Smith, *Henry Martyn: Saint and Scholar* (London: Religious Tract Society, 1892), p. 530.
95 Samuel Wilberforce (ed.), *Journals and Letters of the Rev. Henry Martyn*, 2 vols (London: R. B. Seeley and W. Burnside, 1837), I: p. 470.

96  E.g. William Pakenham Walsh, *Heroes of the Mission Field* (London: Hodder and Stoughton, 1879); Emma Raymond Pitman, *Heroines of the Mission Field* (London: Cassell, Petter and Galpin, 1880).
97  Olive Anderson, 'The growth of Christian militarism in mid-Victorian Britain', *English Historical Review*, 86 (1971), 46–72; Graham Dawson, *Soldier Heroes: British Adventure, Empire and the Imagining of Masculinities* (London: Routledge, 1994), pp. 77–165.
98  Martin Harrison, *Victorian Stained Glass* (London: Barrie and Jenkins, 1980); Jim Cheshire, *Stained Glass and the Victorian Gothic Revival* (Manchester: Manchester University Press, 2004).
99  'Some remarks on glass painting, No. IV', *The Ecclesiologist*, 19, 124 (February 1858), 1–8.
100  F. W. B. Bullock, *The History of Ridley Hall, Cambridge*, 2 vols (Cambridge: Cambridge University Press, 1941), I: pp. 261–4, 296–7.
101  Barbara Britton, *A Brief Guide to St Jude's Hampstead Garden Suburb* ([London: privately printed?], 1979), pp. 3–5.
102  Gordon Ray (ed.), *The Letters and Private Papers of William Makepeace Thackeray*, 4 vols (London: Oxford University Press, 1945–46), I: p. 581; J. W. Cross (ed.), *George Eliot's Life*, 3 vols (Edinburgh: Blackwood, 1885), I: pp. 193–4.
103  J. A. V. Chapple and Arthur Pollard (eds), *The Letters of Mrs Gaskell* (Manchester: Manchester University Press, 1966), pp. 87–8.
104  Isabel Giberne Sieveking (ed.), *Memoir and Letters of Francis W. Newman* (London: Kegan Paul, Trench, Trübner, 1909), pp. 345–9.
105  Gladstone famously dubbed Mill 'the saint of rationalism'. See John Morley, *The Life of William Ewart Gladstone*, 3 vols (London: Macmillan, 1903), II: p. 544. See also David Stack, 'The death of John Stuart Mill', *Historical Journal*, 54 (2011), 167–90.
106  Janet Browne, *Charles Darwin: The Power of Place* (London: Pimlico, 2003), p. 383.
107  T. R. Wright, *The Religion of Humanity: The Impact of Comtean Positivism on Victorian Britain* (Cambridge: Cambridge University Press, 1986), pp. 37–8, 82–4, 99, 108.
108  William James, 'The energies of men', *The Philosophical Review*, 16 (1907), 1–20.
109  Mrs Humphry Ward, *Robert Elsmere* (London: Macmillan, 1888), pp. 227–8, 573–82, 603–4.
110  Ernest Renan, *Poetry of the Celtic Races and Other Essays* (London and New York: Walter Scott, 1896), pp. 163, 176–7.
111  *Ibid.*, pp. 184–5.
112  Mrs Jameson, *Sacred and Legendary Art*, 2 vols (London: Longman, etc., 1848), I: pp. xvii, xix–xxi.
113  James A. Froude, 'The lives of the saints', in Froude, *Short Studies on Great Subjects* (2nd edn, London: Longmans, 1867), pp. 363–83, at 366.
114  *Ibid.*, p. 367.
115  John R. Seeley, 'The Church as a teacher of morality', in W. L. Clay (ed.), *Essays in Church Polity* (London: Macmillan, 1868), pp. 266–7.
116  Timothy Larsen, *The Slain God: Anthropologists and the Christian Faith* (Oxford: Oxford University Press, 2014), pp. 17–18.
117  Edward. B. Tylor, *Primitive Culture: Researches into the Development of Mythology, Philosophy, Religion, Language, Art and Custom*, 2 vols (London: John Murray, 1871), II: pp. 110–12.

118 James G. Frazer, *The Golden Bough: A Study in Magic and Religion*, abridged edition (New York: Macmillan, 1922), p. 135.
119 *Ibid.*, pp. 74–5.
120 Larsen, *Slain God*, pp. 30–2; see also George W. Stocking, *After Tylor: British Social Anthropology, 1888–1951* (London: Athlone Press, 1995), pp. 47–83, 124–78.
121 Richard H. King, 'Religion, sociology, and psychology: William James and the re-enchantment of the world', in Martin Halliwell and Joel D. S. Rasmussen (eds), *William James and the Transatlantic Conversation* (Oxford: Oxford University Press, 2014), pp. 49–64.
122 William James, *The Varieties of Religious Experience* (London: Longmans, 1902), p. 331.
123 *Ibid.*, p. 271.
124 *Ibid.*, pp. 286–7, 361, 317.
125 *Ibid.*, pp. 339–78.
126 David A. Hollinger '"Damned for God's glory": William James and the scientific vindication of Protestant culture', in Wayne Proudfoot (ed.), *William James and a Science of Religions* (New York: Columbia University Press, 2004), pp. 9–30.
127 James, *Varieties*, p. 354.

# 1

# Paul

*Michael Ledger-Lomas*

IN FEBRUARY 1873, THE art critic and historian John Addington Symonds (1840–93) took an unusually traumatic trip to the dentist. As the laughing gas and chloroform kicked in, he became conscious of 'utter blankness' then 'flashes of intense light' and then suddenly of the presence of God, 'manifestly dealing with me, handling me, so to speak, in an intense present personal reality. I felt him streaming in like light upon me, and heard Him saying in no language, but as hands touch and communicate sensation, "I led you, I guided you; you will never sin, and weep, and wail in madness more; for, now, you have seen Me."' Symonds told God that while others had been convinced of His existence by miracles or spirit-rapping, this new experience had won him over. God agreed: did Symonds really think he had got a toothache for no purpose? Soon though, the anaesthetic started to wear off and with it this new assurance of God's existence. '"It is too horrible, it is too horrible, it is too horrible"', Symonds shrieked over and over in his dream. He flung himself on the ground, 'and at last awoke covered in blood, calling to the surgeons (who were frightened), "Why did you not kill me? Why did you not let me die?"' How devastating it was to learn that this 'long dateless ecstasy of vision of the very God' was 'after all ... no revelation, but that I had been tricked by the abnormal excitement of my brain'. 'Tell me what you think of it', Symonds asked his correspondent, the moral philosopher and celebrated agnostic Henry Sidgwick (1838–1900). 'If this had happened to a man in an uncritical age, would it not have carried conviction, like that of Saul of Tarsus, to his soul? A violent deepening of despair – a sense of being mocked and cheated – remains with me.'[1]

Saint Paul was ubiquitous in nineteenth-century religious thought, not only preoccupying Christian theologians but also fascinating those like Symonds who had broken with Christian belief. For Protestants, he was an icon of a faith that was not just ecclesiastical or historic but demanded a profoundly personal connection to Jesus Christ. Protestant scholars reminded popular audiences that he was peculiarly theirs: Catholics might venerate his relics, but their religion was derived from his words, with the Reformation and (for its sympathisers) the Evangelical Revival presented as the rediscovery of his long ignored message. For biblical critics, preachers and Sunday-school children, Paul was a historical person, whose physiognomy, character, early life or voyages could be known with more confidence than many of the murky figures who made up the canon of Roman Catholic saints, or the fantastical English saints discussed elsewhere in this volume.[2] At the same time, 'Paul' could mean not a distinct person but rather, like 'Deuteronomy' or 'the Psalmist', a majestic outcrop of a Bible understood to speak with equal, inspired authority throughout. His epistles could be quarried for individual verses and then tessellated with other proof texts into the dogmatic patterns that suited Church parties or theological traditions. Pauline phrases were lynchpins in complex, interminable arguments about the atonement or justification. Encountered in Bibles or tracts, they might trigger a religious crisis or even be inscribed on bodies: the tattoos of anchors sported by transported convicts recalled the 'hope' that was the 'anchor of the soul' (Heb. 6: 19).[3]

Pauls proliferated throughout the nineteenth century, just as churches did. This chapter concentrates though on the problem to which Symonds was led by his decayed tooth: the struggle to make sense of his supernatural and visionary experiences. Why did Protestants worry about them? The first reason was conversion. For evangelicals in particular, Paul's life showed how Christ's grace intervened directly in human lives.[4] Though 'superior', trilled Hannah More (1745–1833) in 1805, Paul's experience was 'not solitary; the change, though miraculous in this case, is not less certain in others'. Paul was an 'exemplification of the great Scripture doctrine which he taught – Faith made him, emphatically, *a New Man*'.[5] Evangelicals always differed among themselves and from other Protestant traditions over whether Christians required a conversion experience and of what kind. Yet conversion narratives as well as Christian pneumatology were modelled on Pauline words and narratives, so that their reality was bound up with the truth of Paul's conversion experience.[6] The second reason was Protestant apologetics. If Paul had seen the risen Jesus on the road to Damascus, the miracle confirmed the miracle of the resurrection and therefore the truth of the gospel against cavillers.

Protestants refused to see any saint as a spiritual acrobat whose feats should be applauded but not emulated. Saints were exemplary of emotions and virtues which all Christians should emulate, even if which saints and which virtues counted was always controversial. While Paul resembled other saints in this respect, his apparently miraculous conversion and vision of Jesus on the road to Damascus (Acts 9: 1–19; 22: 1–12, 26: 12–19), his claim to have 'seen Jesus Christ our Lord' (1 Cor. 9: 1) and to have had the Son revealed 'in me' (Gal. 1: 16), his voyage to the third heaven (2 Cor. 12: 2) and his speaking in tongues stood apart, not merely because they involved direct contact with the supernatural but also because they formed part of the New Testament, which vouchsafed them but was also dependent on their truth. If it was doubtful that Paul had received a revelation, then the New Testament's status as revelation was fragile. Yet supernatural experience had long been a hair in the mouth for Protestants. If Paul had personally communicated with the risen Jesus, why could Protestant sectaries or Catholic saints not do likewise? Enlightened divines had regarded naturalising scepticism about supernatural experience as a means of establishing that miracles ceased with the New Testament, thus preserving the latter as a unique source of revelation.[7] Yet such scepticism spread to its pages, creating a historical puzzle and an apologetic headache. Was it possible to reduce Paul's vision of Christ to an event in his mind rather than in the air without casting its truth into doubt? The impact of that question would be deepened by the growing insistence of biblical critics that the Acts of the Apostles, the only source for an objective vision on the road to Damascus, was a less reliable source for Paul's life than the epistles.

While all Protestants fretted about these problems, liberal Protestant scholars and thinkers did so more than most. The high views of scriptural inspiration espoused by evangelical and High Church writers until the later nineteenth century tempered their sense of Paul as an individual wrestling to convey his experiences. For the High Churchman Christopher Wordsworth (1807–85), 'the Divine Being Who inspired the Apostle, is a God of Order' who 'does every thing by counsel, measure, number and weight'. Therefore his epistles were not 'disjointed and fugitive essays, thrown out extemporaneously on the spur of the moment' but were 'designed by the Holy Spirit of God' to form 'a glorious building, complete in all its parts and proportions, and perfectly composed, harmonized and adorned, in solidity, symmetry, and beauty'.[8] Precisely because they could not share this complacency, were reluctant to concede a supernatural element in the New Testament and accepted that a scientific theology must be a radically historicised one, liberal Protestants developed a more sceptical, intense relationship to Paul.[9] They wished to access what Symonds called his experience of 'undemonstrable but irrefragable certainty of God' while questioning his interpretation of it. The answer lay in a phenomenological approach to past experience, which recognised the 'almost infinitely diversified forms' it had taken, while seeking to 'realise the states of mind in which they arose … to live them over again [and] to reproduce their movement in living imagination'.[10] Experience was a 'blessed word' in liberal Protestant apologetics.[11] A range of apologists found in appeals to experience a means of shoring up Christianity as other evidential props toppled. As the aborted conversion of Symonds showed, even agnostics remained open to experiential evidence that the God of Christianity existed. The 'careful study of psychologic fact' promised to reconcile science and religion, showing that discredited doctrines retained their value as a 'direct rendering in intellectual terms of religious experience'.[12] This chapter therefore concentrates on the liberal Protestant endeavour to reconcile an insistence that Paul's experiences were exemplary for modern Christians with a scientific explanation of how they had come about.

## A 'man of quick thought': Paul and enlightened apologetics

Most early nineteenth-century clerics and Christian apologists presented Paul as a reasonable man, the course of whose life had been changed by a supernatural revelation, which he was able to communicate lucidly to modern readers. This view was a bequest from Britain's Protestant and clerical enlightenment. One of its cornerstones was John Locke's *Paraphrase and Notes on the Epistles of Paul* (1705–07). Locke sought in this work to deny that the simple faith outlined in his *The Reasonableness of Christianity* (1696) rested on calculated neglect of Paul's epistles. In the 'Essay for the Understanding of St Paul's Epistles by Consulting St Paul Himself' that preceded the *Paraphrase*, Locke argued that a presuppositionless reading of the epistles would convert them from a jumbled store of Calvinist proof texts into communications from a 'Man of quick Thought, warm Temper, mighty well vers'd in the Writings of the Old Testament, and full of the doctrine of the New'. Like an Apostolic Tristram Shandy, Paul had a genius for 'Large Parentheses' and for 'Plenty and Vehemence'. Yet a careful reading of the epistles engendered admiration for a 'Train of Reasoning, proceeding on regular and cogent Argumentation from a Man rais'd above the ordinary pitch of Humanity to an higher and brighter way of Illumination.' That 'Light from Heaven' blazoned a simple message: accepting the risen Jesus as our Messiah was the way to salvation.[13] Numerous eighteenth-century divines would imitate Locke's method and conclusions in their studies of the epistles, especially heterodox Dissenters who were unhappy with the quotation of the epistles to support Calvinist or Trinitarian doctrine and who felt that Paul would emerge as a more liberal figure if they were instead read as idiosyncratic but reliable reports on his experience.[14]

The acme of this interpretation would be the translation of the epistles (1824) by the Unitarian polemicist Thomas Belsham (1750–1829), who was anxious to demonstrate that his co-religionists were not 'Socinian' enemies of Christ but candid investigators who simply attended to Paul's information. Belsham claimed that in his 'sacred interviews' with the risen Jesus, Paul learned that his disciples should not worship him but rather live as he had done. While these disclosures must be received as of inspired authority, that did not mean that Paul was inspired. He might have gone awry in 'his reasonings … his illustrations … his narratives of fact … his typical and figurative arguments from the Old Testament … his application of scriptural language … his application of scripture language … his interpretations of the sacred writings … his appropriation of Jewish prophecy'.[15] Belsham's list exposed him to allegations of 'disrespect' from orthodox critics, who viewed any qualification of Paul's authority as an arrogant attempt to judge him by modern standards. It was though a sincere attempt to argue that Paul's saintliness resided not in his reasoning but in his experiences. Belsham's commentary on the epistles presented them as materials for a history,

> exhibiting a very fair and most interesting representation of the character, the views, the feelings, and the exertions of one of the principal leaders and teachers of the new religion, of the very extraordinary circumstances in which he was placed, and of the integrity, the zeal, the courage, the fortitude, the patience, the prudence, and the perseverance, which he manifested in the discharge of his mission, and the labours which he undertook, in the dangers which he encountered, and in the sufferings which he endured.[16]

In arguing that Paul's character demonstrated that he had neither lied about nor invented his revelation of Christ, Belsham echoed a legalistic strain in Protestant apologetics, which had defended the New Testament as a set of unimpeachable witness statements.[17] One foundation of this tradition was George Lyttelton's *Observations on the Conversion and Apostleship of St Paul* (1747), which pleaded for the truth of the Christian revelation by arguing that an appearance of the risen Jesus to Paul was the only explanation of why an enemy of Christianity should become its ardent apostle. It was 'morally impossible' for Paul to have fabricated his conversion on the road to Damascus because the other apostles would have exposed him. Nor could Paul's vision have been a 'mere enthusiastical fancy' because his subsequent life passed tests that enthusiasts had failed. He had not boasted about his visions, especially for power or gain; his life was free from the 'extravagant Mortifications, such as the *Bramins* ... the Monks of *La Trape*, and other melancholy Enthusiasts, inflict on themselves'.[18] The second foundation of this argument, which quoted from Lyttelton and Benson, was *Horae Paulinae* (1790) by the Anglican apologist William Paley (1743–1805). A forensic demonstration that Acts and the epistles agreed with and verified one another in every particular, Paley's *Horae* closed by restating Lyttelton's case, arguing that Paul was a man of 'liberal attainments' whose endurance of 'incessant fatigue', 'stripes and stoning' and the risk of 'violent death' could only be explained on the supposition that he had personally received his apostleship from Christ.[19] As Paley's epigones explained, this was an argument from human nature to the reality of supernatural causation, in which Paul's strengths of character witnessed to a power beyond him.[20] In presenting Paul as a candid disputant and a hardy traveller, Lyttelton and Paley's apologetics also distanced him from the stereotype of the Popish saint etiolated by his private raptures and sufferings, just as British art of this period presented him as the bluff plaintiff of William Hogarth's *Paul before Felix* (1747) or the sturdy voyager of Benjamin West's *St Paul Shaking off the Viper* (1786), an altarpiece set before congregations of retired sailors in the chapel at Greenwich Hospital.

While Paley's Paul had an enlightened, even heterodox parentage, he was then popular across the Protestant spectrum. New editions and epitomes of Paley's *Horae*, many for use in universities, Dissenting colleges and Sunday schools, proliferated until the last quarter of the nineteenth century and were particularly attractive to evangelicals. The Anglican T. R. Birks (1810–83) produced a new edition of the *Horae* in 1850, crammed with fresh proofs, just as the Congregational polemicist Henry Rogers (1806–77) supplied a laudatory preface to a new edition of Lyttelton's *Observations* as late as 1868. Evangelicals may have rejected Belsham's Unitarianism as second only to deism, but they shared his and Paley's trust that it was possible to establish the truth and rationality of Paul's witness by careful rehearsal of probabilities. Evangelicals might think that an 'intellectual conviction' of the genuineness of Paul's writings counted for little if one did not appropriate their 'saving doctrines', but they still thought it was possible and important to defend such a conviction.[21] Their confidence that Paul spoke lucidly and reliably of his revelation in authentic epistles was part of a wider initiative to extract evidence from ancient chronology, topography and archaeology that would establish his heroic life as no less historical than any other phenomenon in the ancient world.[22]

Polar opposites in terms of doctrine, evangelicals and Unitarians stuck to this evidential reading of Paul's mind and experience because of the threat from freethinkers, who denied that the New Testament was or contained a historical revelation at all. Freethinkers agreed that Paul ought to have been a rational, candid witness, but denied that he was. Thomas Paine's *The Age of Reason* (1794–95) inverted Lyttelton's case, arguing that Paul's credibility was undermined by his fanaticism. Once Paul was exposed as a fanatic by his initial persecution of the Christians, then what happened outside Damascus was explicable enough. He had been hit by lightning, a 'stroke' that changed only the direction of his fanaticism.[23] If Paine was blunt in dismissing Paul's vision of Christ, then Jeremy Bentham (1748–1832) attacked Paul's integrity in *Not Paul, but Jesus* (1823). Writing as 'Gamaliel Smith', Bentham alleged that Paul faked his conversion to gain profitable control over the Christian movement and concluded his review of the narratives of Paul's vision on the way to Damascus by asking whether 'on such evidence ... any Judge [would] fine a man a shilling?'[24] He kicked up a swarm of Paleyan rebuttals, suggesting that both Paul's defenders in the Churches and his adversaries agreed that either his visions had an objective cause or he belonged in the Bedlam of fanatics and 'enthusiasts' that had begun at some point in sub-apostolic times.[25]

Yet it was easier to insist on the difference between scriptural saints and modern fanatics than to police it in practice. Conservative opponents of the radical prophets unleashed by the wars against revolutionary and Napoleonic France and of evangelical revivals denied that a Christian's contact with divine grace required 'extra-natural impulses, or sensible shocks upon the intellectual system' and harped on the lessons of what the dryly evangelical Isaac Taylor (1787–1865) called *The Natural History of Enthusiasm*.[26] Their scepticism was amplified from mid-century by medical men and psychologists, whose conviction that pathological experience explained the normal workings of the brain encouraged them to identify visions and voices as symptoms of religious mania and insanity.[27] Although the demolition of claims to supernatural experience was intended to safeguard the unique status of the experiences recorded in the New Testament, they too invited such diagnoses. In *Natural Causes and Supernatural Seemings* (1881), the psychiatrist Henry Maudsley (1835–1918) suggested that Paul's visions were symptoms of epilepsy. The parallel between religious visions and the symptoms of epilepsy was by then familiar in the medical literature and was often used for instance to explain the visions of Mohammed. Why not, Maudsley asked, extend it to Paul?[28]

## The 'language of ecstasy': Paul and higher criticism

Maudsley was a positivist rationalist who wished to show that there could never be admissible evidence for revelation. Yet if theologians need not accept his pathological Paul, developments in their own discipline also undermined the idea that the Apostle had been a rational Protestant gentleman. German higher critics of the New Testament and Church historians in the early nineteenth century sought to understand the development of apostolic Christianity as an immanent process, governed by the uniform causation which also applied to secular history. This scheme would be disrupted by miraculous interventions from without and so even pious critics such as August Neander (1789–1850) presented Paul's vision of Jesus and his subsequent conversion as psychological occurrences, allowing only that an external event such as thunder and lightning could have triggered a change of heart.[29] For Neander, that change could still be understood as a miracle in the head, but this emphasis disappeared for Ferdinand Christian Baur (1792–1860) and other Tübingen critics, who argued that Paul's conversion needed no outside cause. They understood it as a flash of intellectual lightning, the moment at which Paul realised that in dying on the cross Jesus had abrogated Judaism and established a universal spiritual religion. Paul's epistles presented his communications with Jesus as purely internal: the accounts in Acts of an encounter with Jesus on the road to Damascus were clumsy fictions which perverted or forgot Paul's intellectual revolution even as they wrote him up as a saint.[30] Though leading German scholars of Paul after Tübingen did not retain its broader interpretation of apostolic Christianity, they largely agreed that Paul's conversion involved a momentous thought about Jesus rather than a communication from him.[31] These suggestions were not at first even entertained by most British Protestants. William John Conybeare and John Saul Howson's *Life and Epistles of Saint Paul* (1852), perhaps the most sophisticated and influential portrait of a heroic, Paleyan Paul, rejected even Neander's mediating argument. It was for them uncomfortably reminiscent of Paine's argument that Paul had suffered a lightning strike, not received a revelation. Not until Frederic William Farrar's *The Life and Work of St Paul* (1874) did a widely read, avowedly reverent Life suggest reticently that Paul's vision and conversion may have been wholly internal.[32]

To find an energetic engagement with Baur's approach we have to look to churchmen with idealist leanings, who considered Paul's experiences as a form of flawed thought about Jesus, enabled but limited by his now archaic metaphysics. The Oxford don Benjamin Jowett (1817–93) suggested in his commentary on Paul's epistles (1855) that Paul's claim to have heard the voice of Jesus was written in a 'language of ecstasy' that did not respect modern divisions between internal and external, mind and world. What Paul called a revelation, Jowett added in his second edition, found a 'faint approximation' in 'intuitions of the mind respecting matters of conduct, or ... the suddenness of thought itself'.[33] For Jowett's critics, these arguments were poisonously condescending. Conybeare began his infamous review article on Jowett's work by associating him with the German professor who had shocked an Oxford common room by exclaiming: 'Paul! Paul was a clayver man, but he had his fancies. His letters I have read, but not often I agree with him.'[34] Conybeare saw that Jowett's arguments militated against the hope that Paul's experiences could be a template for our own. When Jowett questioned whether moderns who no longer experienced the world as Paul did could still say that 'Christ liveth in me', Conybeare replied that 'we thought and hoped that there had been hours and hours in the life of every true Christian when he could say this; and that the difference was rather, that St Paul realized perpetually that which, in most of his followers, is but intermittent.'[35] Yet as other critics less condemnatory of Jowett realised, his tone was less condescending than melancholy: while we could still aspire to the 'love of Christ', we must recognise that we could no longer know him as Paul had done.[36] It was significant that one of the first writers to hail Jowett's approach would be a Unitarian in revolt against his denomination's complacent rationalism: James Martineau (1805–1900), whose review of the work scorned Paley and Belsham's attempts to squeeze Paul into modern clothes and welcomed Jowett's emphasis on his radical otherness, which he hoped would help to end lazy assumptions about the authority of the New Testament over modern lives.[37]

Jowett had not meant to give a pathological reading of Paul. Yet one of his greatest offences was to distinguish Paul's neurasthenic personality from the 'general image of heroism, or knowledge, or power, or goodness' familiar from Protestant preaching and the iconography of Raphael and Benjamin West.[38] Jowett's friend Arthur Penrhyn Stanley (1815–81) wrote from Canterbury to report on a visiting preacher who had crossly proved 'by arguments of his own that S. Paul was a tall, strong, healthy and active man'.[39] The preacher had been provoked by Jowett's suggestion that Paul was not a man of 'resolute will, of untiring energy, of logical mind, of classic taste' but a palsied old dreamer. Jowett's Paul was not Lyttelton's man of timeless 'good sense', his faculties irradiated but unchanged by Christ, but a holy introvert with 'the same withdrawal from the things of earth, the same ecstasy, the same consciousness of the person of Christ' as the 'saints of the middle ages'.[40] Jowett could argue like this because he considered that the origin of Paul's experiences mattered less than their impact. Younger writers trained at Jowett's Balliol, such as T. H. Green (1836–82) and Edward Caird (1835–1908) were more willing to push Jowett's emphasis on historicising apostolic experience into a more overtly teleological direction. They argued that it was the movement of spiritual and intellectual progress initiated by Jesus and to which Paul had contributed which now made it possible to see the limitations of his experience. Given a teleological understanding of Christian history as a movement towards the highest truths of philosophy, the New Testament enjoyed only a relative rather than an absolute value.[41]

An idealist reading of Paul could therefore historicise his experience on the grounds that the history of the world tended towards the absolute realisation of truths first announced in the New Testament. Yet the emphasis on the points of contact between Paul's personality and those of other saints and dreamers could also be employed by historians of religion to question the uniqueness of Christianity. The most provocative attempt to subject Paul to purely naturalistic study came in Ernest Renan's *Les Apôtres* (1866) and *Saint Paul* (1869). A lapsed Catholic with no love for Luther's favourite saint, Renan (1823–92) brought an ironical eye to Paul.[42] He made short work of a conversion narrative invalidated by the assumption that miracles did not happen. If a physical resurrection was impossible, apparitions of Jesus must be delusions, leaving science to explain their origins. Mary Magdalene's vision of Jesus was an expression of her love for him, while the fever that characterised all embattled religious movements from the Huguenots to the Irvingites explained why her visions spread. These visions retained a whiff (*parfum*) of the human Jesus, but Paul's claim to share them began the betrayal of his memory by one who had never known him. Renan offered several naturalistic explanations of what had happened outside Damascus. Paul was one of those 'hommes ardents' common in the Orient, who switch from one faith to another in a trice; his vision was the projection of his remorse about persecuting Christians; or it was induced by thunder and lightning, which Hebrews took to be the voice of God; or perhaps the chilly, shady outskirts of Damascus had induced in Paul the feverish hallucinations from which Renan had suffered during field work in Syria.[43]

Renan's British readers did not need to share his hostility to Paul to emulate his frankly psychological and comparative treatment. When Matthew Arnold's *Saint Paul and Protestantism* (1869) adopted Renan's sceptical assumption of uniformity in supernatural experience, he aimed not to bury Paul but to praise him. By likening his vision of Christ to those of credulous 'Cornish revivalists', Arnold suggested that it was as banal as the poetry with which he celebrated Christian ethics was glorious.[44] Yet the hostile reaction to both Renan's and Arnold's writings showed that psychological accounts of Paul's conversion were unwelcome to most British readers if this entailed positing wholly immanent causes for it. Their argument that purely psychological or pathological explanations of Paul's conversion did not make psychological sense of his change of heart expressed the deeper fear that they turned Pauline Christianity into a mistake and robbed them of their own access to the risen Christ. Critiques of Arnold and Renan which did accept the argument for uniformity in religious experience reversed its charge, appealing from the felt reality of their own conversions under the influence of the 'living Christ' to Paul's.[45] As Arthur Cayley Headlam (1862–1947) and William Sanday (1843–1920) put it in their edition of the epistle to the Romans, the 'thousands and tens of thousands of Christians who have lived and died in the firm conviction' of 'supersensual realities' and notably of the possibility of real contact with the risen Christ afforded an 'indirect verification' of Paul's experiences and language.[46] Similarly, the spectacular encounters with Jesus promoted by nineteenth-century evangelical revivalists gave even sophisticated observers pause for thought: however they were explained, such experiences showed that human nature was 'adapted to receive divine inspiration as the lightning-rod is capable of transmitting electricity'.[47]

## Paul and the varieties of religious experience

Protestant theologians of a liberal bent would then concede that the supernatural experiences of Paul and the other apostles were not unique but uniform with those in other times and places only if they could give that concession an apologetic tweak. They were assisted by their growing interest in the theological uses of spiritualism, occultism and psychical research.[48] The richer understandings of the human personality that they promoted invited their apologetic application to the New Testament. A vital mediating role was played here by the Society for Psychical Research (SPR), which echoed spiritualists and occultists in insisting that supernormal experience was not plotted along a curve that drooped along the axis of civilisation but was scattered evenly throughout cultures and across time. Though science emphasised that supernatural experiences were hallucinations, psychical investigators were familiar with '*veridical* hallucinations' which carried messages from a super-sensory world.[49] Frederic Myers (1843–1901), a founder of the SPR as well as a classicist and agnostic who had first risen to notice with an agonised long poem on *Saint Paul* (1867), appropriated psychological theory to establish telepathy, clairvoyance and automatic writing as phenomena that cohered in the very nature of the (divided) self.[50] Myers thus urged that ecstatic trances and encounters were not necessarily pathological conditions but might serve to mark the 'Rubicon' between parts of the self.[51] He condemned Renan's assumption that biblical criticism must assume a 'permanent or immovable barrier' between 'the sensible and the super-sensible, the seen and unseen'. False to present 'experience', this issued in a reading of the New Testament no more credible than the miraculous one it replaced. How absurd was Renan's view of the apostles as 'hysterical monomaniacs', convinced that Jesus had appeared to them 'because there was an accidental noise, or a puff of air'. Visions of Jesus might be 'indications of laws' that 'in a sense unite, the seen and the unseen worlds' and evidence for their occurrence must be assessed in this spirit.[52]

The promise of Myers's psychology was realised by the American philosopher and psychologist William James (1842–1902). His *Varieties of Religious Experience* (1902) offered a taxonomy of experiences of the supernatural, ranging from Paul's conversion to Symonds's trip to the dentist. He invoked Myers to suggest that even the most morbid of these experiences hailed from a 'subliminal region' that opened onto an unseen world. James established Paul's conversion as the paradigmatic case in which a personality's triumph over its divisions occluded the line between the natural and the divine.[53] Protestant readers of James were heartened that they could now approach the Bible on the principle that 'there was in personality *possibility* which consciousness does not exhaust'.[54] Theologians and biblical critics who cited James were none too scrupulous in respecting the line between psychology and psychical research. They rummaged the SPR's reports for phenomena that in resembling the New Testament's supernatural experiences normalised and vindicated the latter. Maybe Jesus had made contact with his disciples and with Paul after death through hallucination and telepathy, just as the SPR's researches showed that phantasms of the living or apparitions of the dead might do?[55] Leading Anglican modernists argued that if psychology admitted 'the logic of the whole personality' it could show that Paul's language about Christ's revelation to and within him agreed with an understanding of personality's boundaries as porous membranes, not fixed barriers.[56]

The transfer of Paul from the theologians to the psychologists did not please everybody. Critics of James anticipated modern commentators in thinking that his psychological handling of religious experiences evaded the question of their objective truth.[57] To group Paul with other disturbed 'cases' invited the challenge of what a theology based on inferences from morbid experiences was worth.[58] James had recognised that

Paul's religious experience might be dismissed as the result of an epileptic seizure without demonstrating why this explanation should be ignored. Idealist theologians stung by James's open contempt for overintellectual defences of theism seized on his excessive trust in feeling and sensation. They preferred to think of religious experience not as an alternative to thought but rather as a form of compressed thought whose assessment called for 'metaphysicians', not psychologists.[59] As their wariness indicated, the truce between psychology and the Churches remained fragile.[60] Clerical writers nervously confined psychology to the description rather than the explanation of religious experience, their caution reflecting the fact that empirical studies of experiences such as conversion invited reductive explanations by correlating them with biological processes, particularly sexual urges.[61] Modernist biblical critics who used psychology to describe the supernatural experiences of Paul and the other apostles stressed that it was a neutral instrument, which neither impaired nor established their divine origin.[62]

This prospecting for the 'ancient stem' of Pauline experience was subject to countervailing scholarly pressures.[63] Theologians anxious to discover the historical Jesus were aware that 'Saint Paul's conception of the Christ' might be just a tissue of conventional representations rather than an expression of unmediated experience.[64] The painstaking archaeology by British and German historians of religion of intertestamental Judaism, of the oriental religions from which it had supposedly borrowed and of the mystery cults with which Paul came into contact all suggested that his experiences were embedded in a radically alien thought world, one stranger than Jowett had contemplated.[65] As Matthew Arnold's niece Mary Ward (1851–1920) commented in 1895, the 'sympathetic realism' with which scholars recreated the 'sources and foundations' of Paul's mind provoked the question: 'what is all this now worth?'[66]

The answer for some prominent liberal Protestant writers lay in locating Paul's greatness not in the content of his experiences but the use that he made of them. The classicist and Anglican modernist Percy Gardner (1846–1937) urged that *The Religious Experience of St Paul* (1911) would be 'appreciated best by those who have felt the strong breeze which is driving modern thought in the direction of pragmatism'. Paul anticipated William James in recognising that the value of experience lay not in 'perpetual converse with a divine power' than in 'working with it on the world'.[67] If his experiences could be likened to those of mystics in all ages and if they adopted the forms of late antique religion, then he nonetheless stood out in urging early Christians that such experiences should spur them to work together for the moralisation of the world. If only drug-induced delirium could bring Symonds into the mind of Paul, it is striking how many Protestant thinkers in the early twentieth century clung to an enlightened faith in his innate good sense.

## Notes

1 Horatio Brown, *John Addington Symonds: A Biography*, 2 vols (London: Smith, Elder, 1895), II: pp. 78–80.
2 See pp. 245–61.
3 Hamish Maxwell-Stewart and Ian Duffield, 'Skin-deep devotions: religious tattoos and convict transportation to Australia', in Jane Caplan (ed.), *Written on the Body: Tattoos in European and American History* (London: Reaktion, 2000), p. 125.
4 See e.g. Henry Blunt, *Twelve Lectures on the History of Saint Paul* (London: J. Hatchard, 1832–33), chs 1–2; Charles John Vaughan, *The Church of the First Days* (1874; London: Macmillan, 1890), part ii, ch. 1.
5 Hannah More, *An Essay on the Character and Practical Writings of St Paul*, 2 vols (1815; London: Cadell and Davies, 1819), I: pp. 93, 89.
6 See Bruce Hindmarsh, *The Evangelical Conversion Narrative: Spiritual Autobiography in Early Modern England* (Oxford: Oxford University Press, 2005).
7 Bruce Mullin, *Miracles and the Modern Religious Imagination* (New Haven: Yale University Press, 2005); Jane Shaw, *Miracles in Enlightenment England* (London: Yale University Press, 2006).
8 Christopher Wordsworth, *The Epistles of St Paul, in the Original Greek, Arranged in Chronological Order* (London: Rivingtons, 1859), p. vii.
9 See Johannes Zachhuber, *Theology as Science in Nineteenth-Century Germany: From F.C. Baur to Ernest Troeltsch* (Oxford: Oxford University Press, 2014) on science and historicism.
10 Edward Caird, *The Evolution of Religion*, 2 vols (1893; Glasgow: James Maclehose, 1894), I: pp. 19–20.
11 Hastings Rashdall, 'The validity of religious experience', *Modern Churchman*, 8 (1918–19), 302; Wayne Proudfoot, 'From theology to a science of religions: Jonathan Edwards and William James on religious affections', *Harvard Theological Review*, 82 (1989), 149–68; Ann Taves, *Fits, Trances and Visions: Experiencing Religion and Explaining Experience from Wesley to James* (Princeton: Princeton University Press, 1999); Martin Jay, *Songs of Experience: Modern American and European Variations on a Universal Theme* (London: University of California Press, 2005), ch. 3.
12 Percy Gardner, 'James's Gifford lectures', *Hibbert Journal*, 1 (1902–03), 186; Gardner, *Exploratio Evangelica* (London: Adam and Charles Black, 1899), p. 9.
13 John Locke, *A Paraphrase and Notes upon the Epistles of St Paul*, ed. Arthur W. Wainwright, 2 vols (Oxford: Oxford University Press, 1987), I: pp. 104, 111–12.
14 See e.g. George Benson, *A Paraphrase and Notes on the Epistles of St. Paul to Philemon, 1st Thessalonians, 2nd Thessalonians, 1st Timothy, Titus, 2nd Timothy: Attempted in Imitation of Mr. Locke's Manner* (London: Richard Ford, 1731–34).
15 Thomas Belsham, *The Epistles of Paul the Apostle Translated with an Exposition and Notes*, 4 vols (London: R. Hunter, 1822), II: p. 624; I: p. xxxi.
16 *Ibid.*, pp. lii–liii.
17 See Jan-Melissa Schramm, *Testimony and Advocacy in Victorian Law, Literature and Theology* (Cambridge: Cambridge University Press, 2000).
18 George Lyttelton, *Observations on the Conversion and Apostleship of St Paul, in a Letter to Gilbert West* (1747; London: R. and J. Dodsley, 1754), pp. 99, 73.

19 William Paley, *Horae Paulinae: Or, the Truth of the Scripture History of St Paul* (1790; London: J. Johnson, 1810), pp. 379–81.
20 Henry Hart Milman, *Character and Conduct of the Apostles Considered as an Evidence of Christianity* (Oxford: Oxford University Press, 1827), p. 361; Richard Whately, *Essays on Some of the Difficulties in the Writings of St Paul, and in Other Parts of the New Testament* (London: B. Fellowes, 1828), pp. 290–7.
21 T. R. Birks, 'Preface', in William Paley, *Horae Paulinae*, ed. Birks (London: Religious Tract Society, 1850), p. vi.
22 See Michael Ledger-Lomas, 'Shipwrecked: James Smith and the defence of biblical narrative in Victorian Britain', *Angermion*, 1 (2008), 83–109.
23 Thomas Paine, *The Age of Reason: Being an Investigation of True and Fabulous Theology* (1793; London: Barrois, 1794), p. 3; *The Age of Reason: Part the Second* (London: H. D. Symonds, 1795), pp. 89–90.
24 'Gamaliel Smith' [Jeremy Bentham], *Not Paul, but Jesus* (London: R. Taylor, 1823), p. 50.
25 See e.g. Thomas Smart Hughes, *A Defence of the Apostle St. Paul Against the Accusation of Gamaliel Smith, Esq. in ... 'Not Paul, but Jesus'* (Cambridge: Richard Newby, 1823–24).
26 Ian McCalman, 'New Jerusalems: prophecy, dissent and radical culture in England, 1786–1830', in Knud Haakonssen (ed.), *Enlightenment and Religion: Rational Dissent in Eighteenth-Century Britain* (Cambridge: Cambridge University Press, 1996), pp. 312–35; Mullin, *Miracles*; Shaw, *Miracles*; Taves, *Experience*, chs 1 and 2; Isaac Taylor, *Natural History of Enthusiasm* (London: Holdsworth and Ball, 1829), p. 63.
27 Leigh Schmidt, *Hearing Things: Religion, Illusion and the American Enlightenment* (Princeton: Princeton University Press, 2002), ch. 4. On psychology, see Leslie Hearnshaw, *A Short History of British Psychology, 1840–1940* (London: Methuen, 1964), chs 2, 5; Rick Allen, *Victorian Psychology and British Culture, 1850–1880* (Oxford: Oxford University Press, 2000).
28 Henry Maudsley, *Natural Causes and Supernatural Seemings* (London: Kegan Paul, Trench, 1886), pp. 170–6; James C. Howden, 'The religious sentiment in epileptics', *Journal of Mental Science*, 19 (1873), 483; William Ireland, 'The hallucinations of Mahomet and others', *Journal of Mental Science*, 20 (1873), 561–72. Robert Priest, '"After the God and the man, the patient": Jules Soury's psychopathology of Jesus and the boundaries of the science of religions in the early Third Republic', *French History*, 27 (2013), 535–56 shows how French thinkers applied this approach to Jesus himself.
29 See Wilhelm M. L. De Wette, *Lehrbuch der historisch-kritischen Einleitung in die Bibel Alten und Neuen Testamentes*, 2 vols (1817–26; Berlin: G. Reimer, 1833–34), II: p. 173; August Neander, *Geschichte der Pflanzung und Leitung der christlichen Kirche durch die Apostel*, 2 vols (Hamburg: Friedrich Andreas Perthes, 1832–33), I: pp. 105–15.
30 See e.g. Ferdinand Christian Baur, *Paulus der Apostel Jesu Christi: Sein Leben und Wirken, seine Briefe und seine Lehre* (Stuttgart: Becher & Müller, 1845), p. 4; Albert Schwegler, *Das nachapostolische Zeitalter in den Hauptmomenten seiner Entwicklung*, 2 vols (Tübingen: Ludwig Friedrich Fues, 1846); Eduard Zeller, *Die Apostelgeschichte nach ihrem Inhalt und Ursprung kritisch untersucht* (Stuttgart: Mäcken, 1854); Carl Holsten, *Zum Evangelium des Paulus und des Petrus: Altes und Neues* (Rostock: Stiller, 1868), ch. 1.
31 Otto Pfleiderer, *Der Paulinismus: Ein Beitrag zur Geschichte der urchristlichen Theologie* (Leipzig: Fues, 1873), pp. 14–16.

32 See William John Conybeare and John Saul Howson, *The Life and Epistles of Saint Paul*, 2 vols (London: Longmans, 1852), I: ch. 3; Frederic William Farrar, *The Life and Work of Saint Paul* (London: Cassell, 1874), ch. 10.
33 Benjamin Jowett, *The Epistles of St Paul to the Thessalonians, Galatians, Romans, with Notes*, 2 vols (London: John Murray, 1855), I: p. 225; Jowett, *Epistles*, 2 vols (2nd edn, London: John Murray, 1859), I: p. 265.
34 [W. J. Conybeare], 'The Neology of the cloister', *Quarterly Review*, 98 (1855), 148. To be fair to the German in question, Heinrich Ewald, he thought the dons had been discussing the theologian Heinrich Paulus.
35 *Ibid.*, p. 157.
36 Jowett, *Epistles* [1855], II: pp. 94–9, 237.
37 [James Martineau], 'St Paul', *National Review*, 2 (1855), 472.
38 Jowett, *Epistles* [1859], I: p. 353.
39 Balliol College, Oxford, MSS 403, Stanley to Jowett, [n.d.] 1855.
40 Jowett, *Epistles* [1855], I: pp. 298–9, 303.
41 Thomas Hill Green, 'Lectures on the New Testament', in *Works of Thomas Hill Green*, ed. R. L. Nettleship, 3 vols (London: Longmans, Green, 1885–88), III: p. 189; Edward Caird, *Evolution*, II: pp. 195, 202, 264. See too Caird, 'Saint Paul and the idea of evolution', *Hibbert Journal*, 2 (1903–04), 3, 17.
42 For this contrast, see François Laplanche, *Entre mythe et critique: la Bible en France* (Paris: A. Michel, 1994), pp. 152–8.
43 Ernest Renan, *Les Apôtres* (1866), in *Histoire des origines du Christianisme*, 2 vols (Paris: Laffont, 1995), I: pp. 314, 323, 338, 362, 303, 409–11, 326, 329.
44 Matthew Arnold, *Saint Paul and Protestantism: With an Essay on Puritanism and the Church of England* (1869; London: Smith, Elder, 1870), p. 74.
45 Robert William Dale, *The Living Christ and the Four Gospels* (London: Hodder and Stoughton, 1890); T. R. Glover, *Jesus in the Experience of Men* (London: Student Christian Movement, 1921), p. 16.
46 William Sanday and Arthur Cayley Headlam, *A Critical and Exegetical Commentary on the Epistle to the Romans* (Edinburgh: T. and T. Clark, 1895), p. xlvi.
47 Percy Gardner, *Exploratio Evangelica: A Brief Examination of the Basis and Origin of Christian Belief* (London: Adam and Charles Black, 1899), p. 20; William Boyd Carpenter, *The Witness of Religious Experience* (London: Williams and Norgate, 1916), p. 3.
48 Alex Owen, *The Place of Enchantment: British Occultism and the Culture of the Modern* (London: University of Chicago Press, 2004), pp. 27–8.
49 'Theory of apparitions', *Proceedings of the Society of Psychical Research*, 2 (1884), 168.
50 Ann Taves, 'The fragmentation of consciousness and *The Varieties of Religious Experience*: William James's contribution to a theory of religion', in Wayne Proudfoot (ed.), *William James and a Science of Religions* (London: Columbia University Press, 2004), pp. 48–72.
51 Frederic Myers, *Human Personality and Its Survival of Bodily Death*, 2 vols (London: Longmans, Green, 1903), I: pp. xli, 108–9, 123.
52 Frederic Myers, 'Ernest Renan', in *Essays, Modern* (1883; London: Macmillan, 1897), pp. 222–3.
53 Taves, 'Fragmentation'.
54 Alfred Garvie, 'Personality in God, Christ, man', *Hibbert Journal*, 5 (1906–07), 562 and

see similarly Percy Gardner, 'The psychology of religious experience', *Modern Churchman*, 8 (1918–19), 203.

55 Kirsopp Lake, *The Historical Evidence for the Resurrection of the Lord Jesus Christ* (London: Williams and Norgate, 1907), ch. 7; Lake, *The Stewardship of Faith: Our Heritage from Early Christianity* (London: Christophers, 1915), pp. 270–6; J. Arthur Hill, 'Psychical research as bearing on veracity in religion', *Hibbert Journal*, 5 (1906–07), 113–18; B. H. Streeter, 'The historic Christ', in *Foundations: A Statement of Christian Belief in Terms of Modern Thought* (London: Macmillan, 1912), p. 140; John Huntley Skrine, *The Survival of Jesus: A Priest's Study in Divine Telepathy* (New York: Constable and Company, 1917), chs 14–17.

56 William Sanday, *Christology and Personality: Containing: I: Christologies Ancient and Modern, II. Personality in Christ and in Ourselves* (Oxford: Clarendon Press, 1911), pp. 135–50; William Inge, *Christian Mysticism* (London: Methuen, 1899), p. ix.

57 Richard Rorty, 'Some inconsistencies in James's *Varieties*', in Proudfoot (ed.), *James*, pp. 86–97.

58 Hastings Rashdall, 'William James, *The Varieties of Religious Experience*', *Mind*, 12 (1903), 250.

59 Rashdall, 'Validity', pp. 302–15; W. R. Inge, *Faith and its Psychology* (London: Duckworth, 1909), ch. 4.

60 Graham Richards, 'Psychology and the churches in Britain, 1919–1939: symptoms of conversion', *History of the Human Sciences*, 13 (2000), 57–84.

61 Frank Granger, *The Soul of a Christian: A Study in Religious Experience* (London: Methuen, 1900), p. 2; W. R. Matthews, 'The psychological standpoint and its limitations', in E. J. Bicknell *et al.* (eds), *Psychology and the Church* (London: Macmillan, 1925), pp. 1–17; H. M. Relton, 'The psychology of prayer and religious experience', in *ibid.*, pp. 57–8, 65; David Hay, 'Psychologists interpreting conversion: two American forerunners of the hermeneutics of suspicion', *History of the Human Sciences*, 12 (1999), 55–72.

62 Kirsopp Lake, *Landmarks in the History of Early Christianity* (London: Macmillan, 1920), p. 44; Lake, *Evidence*, pp. 271–9; Lily Dougall, 'God in action', in B. H. Streeter (ed.), *God and His Relation to Man: Considered from the Standpoint of Philosophy, Psychology and Art* (London: Macmillan, 1919), pp. 23–67.

63 Auguste Sabatier, *Outlines of a Philosophy of Religion Based on Psychology and History* (London: Hodder and Stoughton, 1897), p. 4.

64 See e.g. David Forrest, *The Christ of History and of Experience* (Edinburgh: T. and T. Clark, 1901); David Somerville, *Saint Paul's Conception of the Christ: Or the Doctrine of the Second Adam* (Edinburgh: T. and T. Clark, 1897).

65 See Suzanne Marchand, *German Orientalism in the Age of Empire: Religion, Race, and Scholarship* (Cambridge: Cambridge University Press, 2009), ch. 6.

66 Mary Ward, 'Preface', in Adolf Hausrath, *A History of the New Testament Times: The Time of the Apostles* (London: Williams and Norgate, 1895), p. xxiii. See similarly Joseph Estlin Carpenter, *Christianity in the Light of Religious Experience* (Manchester: H. Rawson, 1906), p. 16.

67 Percy Gardner, *The Religious Experience of St Paul* (London: Williams and Norgate, 1911), pp. 227–8, 254.

# 2

# The Virgin Mary

*Carol Engelhardt Herringer*

Both historically and architecturally, the Brompton Oratory is a remarkable building. Built between 1880 and 1884 for the Congregation of the Priests of the Oratory of St Philip Neri, whose London community was founded by the flamboyant, controversial, and popular Catholic convert-priest Frederick William Faber (1814–63), this richly adorned Italianate church is a striking testimony to Roman Catholic confidence only a few decades after the restoration of the hierarchy in England. Officially named the Church of the Immaculate Heart of Mary, it reflects not just Faber's own exceptionally sentimental devotion to the Virgin, but also the increase in Marian devotion that characterised English Catholicism in the Victorian era. Beyond the official name of the Oratory, this devotion is manifested in two statues of the Virgin Mary. Atop the church the statue of a simply clad woman gazes downward, her arms open to the worshippers entering below. This welcoming image, depicting the Immaculate Heart of Mary, was erected as part of the south façade in 1893 following the design of Herbert Gribble (1847–94), a recent convert who had won the architectural contest to design the church. Inside, on the altar of the Lady Chapel, just to the right of the main altar, is 'Our Lady of Victories' (figure 4), which dates back to the earliest days of the Oratory when it was in King William Street, just off the Strand. In contrast to the simplicity of the statue atop the south façade, this Madonna has since at least the 1880s been clothed in cope and crown, and worshippers approach her and the infant son she holds to offer prayers and thanksgiving.[1]

The church and the statues are markers of the Marian devotion that characterised late Victorian Catholicism. To many Catholics they signified a return to practices that had flourished in medieval England. Before the Reformation, churches, chapels, and religious orders were dedicated to the Virgin Mary; supposed Marian artefacts were venerated and used for protection; and the devout made regular pilgrimages to Marian shrines, the most popular of which was that of Our Lady of Walsingham, which had been supported by English monarchs from Henry III onwards.[2] England was 'Mary's dower'. However, these popular forms of devotion were almost completely destroyed during the Tudor Reformations. Although Henry VIII had been both a patron of and pilgrim to the shrine at Walsingham, his Injunctions of 1538 led to its destruction, as well as of 'virtually the entire external manifestation of the cult of saints'.[3] Other

4  *Our Lady of Victories*, statue, mid nineteenth century.

Marian shrines and statues were destroyed (or at least removed) during the remainder of Henry's reign and especially during the reign of his son, Edward VI.[4] While Marian devotion was revived along with other Roman Catholic practices during the brief reign of Mary (1553–58), its public expression was decisively abolished under Elizabeth, although some of its language was transferred to the queen.[5] Nevertheless, its legacy remained. The most common Anglican dedication, including that of the two university churches in Oxford and Cambridge, was some version of her name, and statues of the Virgin and Child still marked the exteriors of some buildings, albeit not without controversy.[6] Major churches – including Westminster Abbey, and Bristol and Gloucester Cathedrals – retained their medieval Lady Chapels. Traditions of Marian devotion also survived in the writings of some High Church Anglicans and in the *Garden of the Soul* (1740), by the leading recusant Richard Challoner (1691–1781).[7]

Nevertheless, until the last decades of the nineteenth century Marian devotion was quite controversial, although by the time the Brompton Oratory was built these controversies had largely although not entirely subsided and the Virgin Mary's prominence among Catholics was firmly established. This mirrors broader developments across the global Catholic Church: in Britain, as in Europe and the Americas, there was a sharp upswing in Marian devotion in our period. This essay focuses on English manifestations of that broader phenomenon. It first describes the multivalent processes by which the Virgin Mary was 'remade' as a saint in a variety of genres and venues, including devotional manuals, sermons, public debates, poetry, paintings, and statues. It then considers the various motivations for this, suggesting that the shape of Marian devotion must be understood in the context of the Woman Question that was such a defining feature of mainstream Victorian culture. Finally it considers the extent to which perceptions of Mary as 'Queen of Heaven' were shaped by questions about female power and maternal nature, questions that were all the more pressing due to the presence of a queen on the English throne.[8]

## The Catholic Virgin Mary

Although it had earlier beginnings, the remaking of the Virgin Mary as a saint began in earnest in the 1830s, when Roman Catholics, along with Tractarians and more broadly defined ritualist groups in the Church of England (who after about 1850 can be jointly described as Anglo-Catholics) began to revive the English tradition of Marian devotion.[9] This was was a complex, deliberate process that required leadership and the active participation of the laity. Among the most prominent participants in the process were the three leaders of the Oxford Movement: John Keble (1792–1866), the beloved Anglican poet and priest; the scholar and eventual Roman Catholic convert John Henry Newman (1801–90); and the Regius Professor of Hebrew and Canon of Christ Church, Edward Bouverie Pusey (1800–82). Within this trio, Keble's Marian devotion was the most circumspect, in keeping with his gentle, non-confrontational personality. Professor of Poetry at Oxford from 1831 to 1841, he had already published 'The Annunciation of the Blessed Virgin' in *The Christian Year* (1827), his bestselling collection of devotional poetry. In 1844 Keble followed this depiction of the Virgin Mary as Jesus' closest companion who deserved praise that stopped short of adoration with 'Mother out of Sight' in *Lyra Innocentium*, his second volume of poems. However, the sharp rise of anti-Catholicism meant that at this time his plea for an increase in Marian devotion was deemed too dangerous by some of his friends, who feared that it signalled a sympathy towards Romanism, and so it was not finally published until 1868.[10] Pusey was a more forceful defender of the Virgin Mary as the *Theotokos*[11] in sermons and scholarly works. He was certain that she had an exceptionally close relationship with her son, that she freely chose to bear him and that she continued to intervene for those on earth. However, like many Tractarians, he was wary of more effusive continental Marian devotion, and in *The Church of England a portion of Christ's One Holy Catholic Church ... An Eirenicon* sought to distinguish between beliefs that the Council of Trent had decreed to be 'de fide', with which he agreed, and practices that went beyond this, and in so doing unhelpfully alienated English observers. This led to a series of sharp published exchanges with his friend Newman. The second phase of the Eirenicon controversy, as it is known, was Newman's response, *A letter addressed to the Rev. E. B. Pusey, D.D., on occasion of his Eirenicon* (1865). As an Anglican priest, Newman had delivered several sermons praising the Virgin as a faithful disciple and role model, and, now a Catholic, he went further, defending not just official doctrine but more popular practices and pamphlet literature. Newman's entry into the debate was unsurprising, given that, after his 1845 conversion, he had become more outspoken in articulating a view of the Virgin Mary as Jesus' most faithful disciple and one who would draw people to her son.[12] Undeterred, Pusey continued the argument in his *First letter to the very Rev. J. H. Newman, D.D., in Explanation Chiefly in Regard to the Reverential Love due to the Ever-Blessed Theotokos, and the Doctrine of her Immaculate Conception* (1869), which renewed and expanded his complaints about continental devotion as leading Christians away from Jesus to Mary.[13] The Eirenicon controversy was a key moment in the remaking of Mary as a saint in Victorian England, as it showed the divisions, which were stylistic as much as theological, among Victorian Catholics as well as the broad agreement that she was the pre-eminent Christian and a model for the faithful. By the end of the nineteenth century, this kind of dispute had largely disappeared, as Marian devotion was more accepted by, and less fraught for, Anglo-Catholics.

Newman's follower, fellow convert, and eventual antagonist Frederick Faber was one of the most emotional English devotees of the Virgin Mary. He recommended that Catholics address her as 'Mamma', and he published many poems and hymns that celebrated Mary as the ideal mother who was deeply connected to her son throughout his earthly life and even in heaven. Other prominent Catholic clergymen also held up the Virgin Mary as a saint for England. When Cardinal Nicholas Wiseman (1802–65) returned to England in 1850 as its first cardinal since Reginald Pole (1500–58), he announced his intention to restore Marian devotion, while the Redemptorist priest Thomas Edward Bridgett (1829–99) revived the designation of England as 'Our Lady's dower' in his history of Marian devotion in England, *Our Lady's Dowry* (1875).[14] These and other clergymen provided many of the textual explanations and defences of the image of the Virgin Mary as a saint for England. Although some Roman Catholic clergymen were more fervent than others, and some Tractarian, Ritualist, and Anglo-Catholic clergymen more hesitant about such developments, such works were instrumental in re-establishing Mary as central to the practice of Catholic Christianity in Victorian England.

Roman Catholic and Anglican women who joined the burgeoning religious orders were also key figures in the remaking of Mary as a saint. They often took Mary's virginity and obedience as the pattern for their own lives, and they frequently dedicated their orders to her: indeed, for Anglican sisterhoods established between 1845 and 1900, the second most common dedication was to the Virgin Mary.[15] In their daily lives they often had reminders of her on their persons, in their communities, and in their prayers. The seal designed in 1849 for Community of St Mary the Virgin, Wantage, which became the largest Anglican sisterhood, depicted the Virgin and Child, and the sisters wore crosses designed for them in 1875 by the Anglo-Catholic architect and designer William Butterfield (1814–1900), on which was inscribed Mary's reply to the angel, 'Ecce Ancilla Domini Fiat Mihi Secundum Verbum Tuum' (Behold the handmaid of the Lord; be it unto me according to thy word, Luke 1: 38).[16] Images of the Virgin Mary in sisterhoods and convents, such as the framed one that Priscilla Lydia Sellon (1821–76) placed a on the altar of the chapel of the Sisters of Mercy in Devonport, the first order she founded, were further reminders of her example. The Hail Mary and the Rosary (a medieval devotion that had been sustained in the recusant period and in which the 'Hail Mary' was central) were standard forms of prayer in the Roman Catholic tradition, while Anglican sisters often said at least the scriptural first half of the Hail Mary, or sang it to a chant that the sisters at St Margaret's, East Grinstead, found in their prayer book, based on the medieval Sarum Missal.[17] More remarkably, given the association of the Rosary with Rome, each sister in the Society of the Holy and Undivided Trinity, an Anglican sisterhood based in Oxford, received one as part of the limited personal possessions she was allowed.[18] The many varieties of public ministry undertaken by Catholic nuns and sisters, including teaching and nursing, meant that their devotion to the Virgin Mary could find a wider audience among the laity. For example, Margaret Mary Hallahan (1802–68), foundress of the Third Order of St Dominic of the English Congregation of St Catherine of Siena, insisted that a statue of the Virgin was one of the necessary aids to devotion when she established a community in Coventry, where she also began a Rosary circle among factory workers.[19] Catholic and Anglican sisterhoods and the activities around them undoubtedly added significantly to what Susan O'Brien refers to as 'the sum total of Marian devotion in England'.[20]

Members of the laity, especially Roman Catholics, were also instrumental in reviving Marian devotion. One of the best known was the patron of Pugin and aristocratic landowner Ambrose March Phillipps de Lisle (1809–78), who believed that the Virgin Mary encouraged his youthful conversion to Roman Catholicism in 1825. Many Catholics meditated daily on the life and virtues of the Virgin Mary. The Rosary was one of the two most popular church-based devotions among Roman Catholics in the Victorian period.[21] They also used devotional manuals that included the Hail Mary and other traditional Marian prayers, among them the Litany of Loretto, the *Ave Maris Stella*, and the *Stabat Mater*. Still the most popular devotional manual was Challoner's *Garden of the Soul*, which was reprinted throughout the nineteenth century, but they could also turn to other devotional manuals, including reprints of Challoner's *The Key of Heaven*, as well as more recent works like *The Golden Manual* (1850) and *The Rosary of the Most Blessed Virgin Mary: With the Litany of Loretto, and Other Devotions* (1849), by the convert-priest Willia Lockhart (1819–92).[22] Although English Catholics were generally more moderate in their devotions than their continental counterparts, they could also purchase translations of continental devotional works, such as the *Raccolta*, and they could use works such as Faber's *The Devout Child of Mary: A Novena in Honour of the Most Blessed Virgin Mary* (1852) to say Novenas, nine days of prayers for specific intentions. While Anglicans did not usually embrace these medieval devotions, some, including the Tractarian Alexander Penrose Forbes (1817–75), Bishop of Brechin, did defend the practice of praying to the saints, and many, including Keble, the author Charlotte Yonge (1823–1901) and the priest and future convert Henry Oxenham (1829–88), thought that it was acceptable to pray at least the first half of the Hail Mary.[23] Other High Anglicans were more ambivalent: Christina Rossetti (1830–94) portrayed the Virgin as a role model for Christians while rejecting any devotion that could be termed 'Mariolatry'.[24]

Similar asymmetries characterised the invocation of Mary in collective worship. In both Roman Catholic and Anglican churches, the congregation recited the Magnificat (Luke 1: 46–55), Mary's song commemorating the Annunciation, in their daily services, and they celebrated the Feast of the Annunciation on 25 March. For Catholics, contemplating the Annunciation was another occasion to celebrate Mary's unique role in salvation history. Anglicans who considered the Church of England to be Protestant interpreted Mary's role at the Annunciation more conservatively, identifying her as a pious and humble virgin who was worthy of emulation but not worship. While the leadership of the clergy was essential in placing Mary so centrally in Catholic Christianity of all varieties, the process could not have been accomplished without daily, repetitive invocations of her by the laity, either in the pews or in their own homes.

Mary's status as a saint for the Victorian era was both signalled and encouraged by the growing number of public devotional statues, such as those at the Brompton Oratory. Before mid-century, most Marian images were either private ones in homes or statues of her with the infant Jesus on the exteriors of Anglican churches. Oxford's only Roman Catholic Church – St Clement's Chapel, located unfashionably on the 'wrong' side of the Magdalen Bridge – was a plain yellow building that probably had no statues.[25] As the nineteenth century progressed, however, more statues and other images of the Virgin that reflected and encouraged Marian devotion appeared in Catholic churches. The first public statue, in Chelsea, was placed there thanks to a laywoman, the Hon. Laura Petre ('Sister Mary of St Francis') and against the wishes of the parish priest, while Margaret Hallahan brought the first public statues of the Virgin to Bristol.[26] Women were the producers as well as the champions of these images. Copies of the *Mater Admirabilis* – a fresco depicting the Virgin Mary as a contemplative, solitary young woman surrounded by symbols of purity, work, and knowledge, painted in 1844 in Rome by Pauline Perdrau (1815–95), a novice of the Religious of the Sacred Heart of Jesus order – soon began appearing in England.[27] Images of the

Virgin abounded at the Church of the Immaculate Conception, the London Jesuit church popularly known as Farm Street (consecrated 1849). Over the main entrance was a carved image of the Assumption of the Virgin, and inside were multiple statues, including a crowned statue of Our Lady of Farm Street presiding over the communion rail. Behind the high altar, designed by A. W. N. Pugin (1815–52) were two mosaics, one depicting the Annunciation and the other the Coronation of the Virgin. Seasonal creche scenes, designed to encourage devotion to Mary as a mother, became popular in Roman Catholic convents and schools in the second half of the century.[28] Another common image was that depicted on copies of the 'miraculous medal' depicting the apparition of the Virgin Mary that Catherine Labouré (1806–76) had reported seeing in her convent in the Rue de Bac, Paris, in 1830.[29]

The new doctrine of the Immaculate Conception, proclaimed in 1854 by Pope Pius IX (1792–1878), also provided inspiration for images even before it was officially promulgated. In 1843 French Sacred Heart nuns newly arrived in England decorated their church with embroidered lilies for the Feast of the Immaculate Conception. As soon as the doctrine was proclaimed, the Faithful Companions decorated Our Lady's Altar with lamps, candles and silver foliage: 'a grove of dazzling whiteness', according to one of them.[30] Thereafter, more permanent shrines were erected, such as the chapel dedicated to Our Lady of Lourdes (1882) at the Farm Street Church in London.[31]

Whilst the great majority of these images were in Roman Catholic churches and homes, Marian statues also began to appear in Anglo-Catholic churches, where new or restored rood screens often included an image of the Virgin, such as the one at St Augustine, Kilburn (consecrated 1880). Edward Burne-Jones (1833–98) created two Annunciation scenes, one in the 1860s as part of a triptych intended for the Anglo-Catholic St Paul's, Brighton, and another in 1876–79. Images of the Mother and Child were included in church windows, including that of of Milton Abbey, Dorset, designed by Pugin in 1847, and one of the central windows placed at the east end of Great St Mary's Church, Cambridge in 1872, demonstrating the newfound acceptability of such images to middle-of-the-road Anglicans.[32] Saint Saviour's, Leeds, funded anonymously by Pusey and consecrated in 1845, depicted in its three centre clerestory windows the Virgin Mary flanked by her parents. Further indications of Anglican Marian devotion were in the Lady Chapels that were restored at Wells Cathedral, Gloucester Cathedral, and St John the Baptist, Frome, Somerset, as well as in the new ones constructed amid the nineteenth-century church-building boom: a Lady Chapel was added at St Stephen's Church, South Kensington, for example, in around 1889.[33]

The process of re-envisualising the Virgin Mary was also conducted in more 'secular' spaces, in paintings by leading artists such as Dante Gabriel Rossetti (1828–82) and William Dyce (1806–64), a Scottish Episcopalian who painted many biblical subjects and produced the reredos for All Saints', Margaret Street, deemed the model church by the High Church *Ecclesiologist*.[34] Dyce painted two versions of the Madonna and Child, one c. 1827–30 and the other in 1845 for Prince Albert.[35] The earlier version is more overtly sentimental than the later one, in which Mary holds a Bible that is the focus of the gazes of both mother and child. Although he is not often thought of as an Anglo-Catholic, Dante Gabriel Rossetti painted images of the Virgin Mary twice and began writing the poem 'Ave' (originally called 'Mater Pulchrae Delectionis') during the period in which he and his family attended Christ Church, Albany Street, a Tractarian church in whose parish Park Village, the first Anglican sisterhood was established. Whilst *The Girlhood of Mary Virgin* (1848–49) depicts a passive young woman, the depiction of the Virgin in *Ecce Ancilla Domini* (1849–50) is a striking departure from the norm, as it shows the Virgin recoiling from the angel in a way that underscores her free will to the viewers who knew the ending of the story: this woman was shocked and even fearful, and yet she still freely agreed to bear the child.[36] Whilst these paintings were part of the fashion for painting biblical subjects in the nineteenth century, they also made a case for Mary's significance in secular as well as religious spaces.[37]

The work and lives of these many Catholics, Roman and Anglican, lay and vowed, men and women, combined to make the Virgin Mary into a saint for their times. One culmination of this process was the gradual revival of the shrine at Walsingham, which began in 1897 with a Roman Catholic pilgrimage from a chapel modelled on the Holy House of Loretto in King's Lynn to the Slipper Chapel at Houghton St Giles, traditionally the last chapel before arrival in Walsingham.[38] Anglican pilgrimages began shortly thereafter. Whilst advanced Anglicans were always more moderate in their descriptions of Mary's virtues and power than Roman Catholics, their mental picture of her as the sinless mother of Jesus, his constant companion and guide through his adolescence, his first and most faithful follower who stayed with him at the Cross, met him after the resurrection, continued her maternal relationship in heaven, and was a role model for all Christians was shared on both sides of the confessional divide. At the same time, the growth of more extravagant claims about Mary's queenship and her role as an intercessor provoked violent opposition. Such ideas were adamantly rejected by most Nonconformists, and by those who considered the established Church to be Protestant. Both groups saw Catholicism as semi-pagan.[39] As the Introduction to this book makes clear, Protestants of all stamps were wary of the potential of saints to detract from the life and salvific work of Christ. Their fears were magnified in his mother's case because of claims made about her own uniqueness. Was she a saint, or did she stand in a category of her own? Many argued that the cult of the Virgin was an echo of pagan goddess-worship, an idea that was advanced in public lectures, sermons, periodicals, and even, in the case of Anna Jameson's *Legends of the Madonna*, art history.[40] All this notwithstanding, Marian devotion among Catholics increased throughout the nineteenth century. In fact, Protestant–Catholic cut-and-thrust may well have contributed to Mary's high regard: Catholic responses reiterated the theological, historical, and personal justifications for treating her as an elevated figure, and in doing so rendered devotion to her even more important as a mark of allegiance.

## Queen Victoria and the Virgin Mary

Whilst the Victorians who promoted Marian devotion were primarily interested in the religious health of England, this last section explores how the status of the Virgin Mary could be affected by social and cultural forces that were less obviously related to Christianity. Understanding the ways in which the secular and the religious intersected in images of the Virgin underscores the broader significance of Marian representations in Victorian England, reminding us, too, of the permeability of religious and secular spheres.

Marian devotion was, as mentioned already, central to Catholicism not just in Victorian England but across Europe and the Americas, as Catholics asserted a distinctive feature of their tradition, both to encourage converts and also to combat Protestantism and secularism.[41] However, Marian devotion both in England and elsewhere in western Christianity, crucially, addressed the spiritual needs of Catholics. As noted above, many Catholics viewed the Virgin Mary as a model Christian whom they should emulate, and a smaller but still significant group viewed her as a saint who personally interceded for them. For them, the revival of Marian devotion was linked to the continuities that validated the truth of Catholicism: they rooted Catholicism in English history, and had the potential to inoculate believers against secularism. Most profoundly, then, the remaking of the Virgin Mary as a saint occurred because it addressed the religious needs of Catholics.

Yet the status of the Virgin Mary as a saint was also part of two secular conversations that sought to define the nature of womanhood. It is possible that her renewed prominence in the nineteenth century was partially a response to the dominant feminine ideals expressed in conduct manuals, medical books, novels, poetry, and paintings, as well as being enforced in parliamentary legislation. These ideals were expressed in a variety of ways, but they revolved around the valorisation of motherhood, moral purity and care for others. Mary and the Holy Family more generally were often presented in idealised, domestic terms as models for Christian households, both Protestant and, especially, Catholic ones.[42] However, the Virgin Mary as Catholics imagined her also had the potential to subvert such safe portrayals. She was Jesus' most faithful disciple, and maintained a close relationship with him into eternity, a relationship that allowed her still to intervene with him. As mother, Mary was useful in articulating gender ideals, but as monarch she was deeply problematic. Hence her centrality not just to theological debate but to the broader cultural context of interconfessional competition and rivalry.

To understand another factor that may have informed attitudes to the Marian devotion that was promoted at the Brompton Oratory, one must turn from the Oratory to its near neighbour on Cromwell Road, the Victoria and Albert Museum, and to the very different female figure that greets visitors who seek secular rather than theological enlightenment. This slim, assured, and regal stone Queen Victoria is flanked by Saints George and Michael and positioned above her husband, son, and daughter-in-law, looking out confidently across the street. This statue, designed by the museum's architect Aston Webb (1849–1930) and executed by Alfred Drury (1856–1944) in the early twentieth century, wears a crown and carries the symbols of her office, the sceptre and an orb. Whereas the images of the Virgin Mary at the Brompton Oratory represent virginity, maternity, and Catholicism, the image of Queen Victoria represents marital bliss and fecundity, imperial power, and a Protestant Church of England, established by law and with a female monarch as its Supreme Governor.

The Virgin Mary's rise to prominence in English devotional life coincided with the reign of a female monarch. In a sense the identification was a natural one: during the reign of Queen Elizabeth, for instance, as Helen Hackett has detailed, Marian imagery was appropriated by Elizabeth I and her courtiers to create a monarchical image that would be familiar to her subjects in a country that was only slowly becoming Protestant.[43] In Victorian England, when Catholicism was reviving instead of declining, it is possible that the process worked in the other direction. I would like to suggest that invoking the Virgin Mary may well have been a way of critiquing rather than supporting a queen who faced significant challenges in shaping a workable monarchical image.

Like her sixteenth-century predecessor, Victoria faced a number of challenges in shaping a monarchical image. One was cultural: feminine ideals did not sit straightforwardly with the exercise of political and public authority. This tension is clear in images of the very young Princess Victoria, which, as Susan Casteras comments, 'are identical in content and feeling with representations of almost any other well-bred female child. Invariably they show a sweet and chaste girl, often with the semi-mandatory accessory of flowers.'[44] After a brief interlude of depictions of her as an independent and lively young adolescent, the approach of adulthood saw the restoration of conventional portrayals of femininity.[45] These continued to predominate in the early years of her reign, most famously in reports of her accession to the throne in 1837. While she herself expressed her readiness to assume the throne, she was often incorrectly characterised as weeping when she learned of it.[46] One of the most interesting depictions of Victoria's early years is Henry Tanworth Wells's painting *Victoria Regina* (1880), showing the young Victoria receiving the news of her accession following her uncle's death.[47] Clothed in white bedclothes and with her hair undone (an indication of her virginal status), she recoils slightly from the formally clothed man – Francis, Marquess Conyngham (1797–1876) – who kneels before her to deliver the news and to signal his obedience. While Margaret Homans sees this image as a reference to the chivalric mode Victoria loved, and while her recoiling may be read as regal, the painting also echoes countless versions of the Annunciation scene, in which another young woman receives the news that will elevate her above all others.[48] Victoria is illuminated and almost haloed by the rays of early morning light that stream in through the palace windows. However, these conventionally feminine images were at odds with the image a monarch needed to project.

Victoria's marriage to her beloved Prince Albert made the difficulty of reconciling her reality to the feminine ideal even more obvious. As a wife, she was supposed to be subservient to her husband, but as a monarch she was subservient to no one. Anxieties about the implications of this conflict were popularly expressed around the time of her marriage in street ballads and images portraying Victoria asserting authority over her new husband, sometimes literally wearing the trousers.[49] Depictions of Victoria as a loving wife exacerbated this anxiety, for she was at the same time her husband's sovereign. Images of the couple offer ambiguous representations of the distribution of power, as Homans notes: 'Victoria's sitting or standing [in portraits with Albert] … can represent, simultaneously and ambiguously, her power as sovereign and her subordination as wife.'[50] This image of the Queen as a middle-class wife and mother was designed to underline her monarchical power while not challenging existing norms that allowed a woman to exercise influence only in submission to her husband. Yet when she adhered to this image, as in her decades of mourning for Albert after his death in 1861, her subjects chafed at her refusal to fulfil her public duties, and her popularity plunged. Additionally, as Victoria's subjects knew, she was not an ideal mother in an age that decreed that motherhood was women's primary function. Victoria acknowledged that Albert was the better parent, and her contemporaries often criticised her parenting, beginning when she refused to breast-feed her infants and continuing as her children matured.[51] Although Victoria may have been justified in giving her heir – who like his brother Alfred was a notorious drinker, gambler, and womaniser – no real responsibilities, some of Victoria's subjects blamed her for causing his extended adolescence.[52] Thus it is clear that 'her oxymoronic role as feminine dependent and supreme ruler' gave her a task that was difficult if not impossible: 'to function simultaneously as wife, mother, and queen fitted no Victorian conventions – for those place women either on a domestic or a heavenly throne'.[53]

Whereas the stone Queen Victoria is a single coherent image, a monarch more than a wife and mother, the struggle to harmonise her conflicting roles resulted in a series of images that were so complex and contradictory that scholars refer to 'the existence of many Victorias' and 'the various Victorias', and even liken her to a Russian Doll, a large image made up of many smaller images.[54] Homans argues that 'paradoxical representations of Victoria (as monarch on the one hand, as wife on the other)' were an important phase in England's transition to parliamentary democracy.[55] The comparison between Victoria and the Virgin Mary is an intriguing one. As Hackett notes regarding the iconography of female monarchy in the sixteenth century, 'an opposition has to be grounded in similitudes in order for differences to be clearly delineated'.[56] Perhaps invoking the Virgin Mary may have been a way to respond, obliquely, to the uneasiness generated by the queen. Both were mothers, wives, and powerful women – but whereas the Queen's attributes were often in tension with one another, Mary assured Catholics that female power was extensive, benevolent, and maternal, but only so long as it was contained in one unique figure.

## Conclusion

Susan O'Brien has argued that 'a distinctive Catholic space' was created in our period. 'By the end of the nineteenth century a Roman Catholic space, whether it was church or home, school or convent, was recognisable to insiders and outsiders through the images and artefacts on display.'[57] This statement is also true of Anglo-Catholic spaces, thanks in large part to an increasing level of comfort with images of the Virgin. These defined spaces signalled that Catholics had made the Virgin Mary a saint for their time: a mother whose unique relationship to the divine made her worthy of devotion.

Mary's conquest of English Catholicism continued into the twentieth century. On the parish level, the Marian statues that were expected in Roman Catholic churches became increasingly evident in Anglo-Catholic churches, too. In the first decades of the twentieth century they were introduced in St Stephen's, South Kensington; All Saints', Margaret Street; St John's, Tuebrook; and St Saviour's, Leeds, among others, while figures of the Virgin Mary and the favourite disciple were added to the rood screen when the congregation accumulated sufficient funds at St Peter's, London Docks.[58] Further testimony to the Anglo-Catholic acceptance of Marian devotion were the Lady Chapels that proliferated in the early twentieth century, including several in London, at St Barnabas', Pimlico; All Saints', Margaret Street; and St Mary Magdalene, Munster Square. Later in the century, the growth of Marian devotion among Anglo-Catholics created the opportunity for a formal consideration of similarities and differences that were addressed in two documents produced by the Anglican-Roman Catholic International Commission (ARCIC): *Authority in the Church II* (1981) and *Mary: Grace and Hope in Christ* (2004). Interdenominational co-operation has also been evident between the Anglo-Catholic and Roman Catholic shrines dedicated to Our Lady of Walsingham, both of which were well established by the 1930s and began co-operating in the 1980s.[59] This level of cohesion may make it seem as though Marian devotion is simply a necessary part of Catholicism, but, as this chapter has shown, this important aspect of Catholic devotional life rose to its current prominence in England only relatively recently and quite rapidly, within two or three generations.

## Notes

I wish to express my thanks to the participants at the colloquium in Cambridge that was the inspiration for this book for their astute questions and helpful observations, to the anonymous reader of an earlier version of this essay, and to my colleagues in the Dayton area – Rick Incorvati, Barry Milligan, Chris Oldstone-Moore, Tammy Proctor, and Laura Vorachek – for their rigorous and helpful reading of a later version.

1  E-mail communication with Amanda Siravo, PA to the Provost of the Brompton Oratory, 22 June 2012.
2  For information on the tradition of English Marian devotion, see Eamon Duffy, *The Stripping of the Altars* (2nd edn, New Haven: Yale University Press, 2005), pp. 256–65; Christopher

Haigh, *English Reformations: Religion, Politics, and Society under the Tudors* (Oxford: Clarendon Press, 1993), ch. 1; Gary Waller, *Walsingham and the English Imagination* (Farnham: Ashgate, 2011), chs 1–3.

3 Duffy, *Stripping*, p. 407.
4 *Ibid.*, pp. 407–23; Waller, *Walsingham*, pp. 93–7.
5 See Helen Hackett, *Virgin Mother, Maiden Queen: Elizabeth I and the Cult of the Virgin Mary* (London: Macmillan, 1995).
6 Archbishop Laud's installation of a statue in the porch of St Mary the Virgin, Oxford was interpreted by his opponents as yet another indication that he was a crypto-Catholic, and was one of the charges filed against him at his 1644 trial.
7 For Anglican traditions of Marian devotion before the nineteenth century, see A. M. Allchin, *The Joy of All Creation: An Anglican Meditation on the Place of Mary* (London: New City, 1993), esp. chs 2–5, and Roger Greenacre, *Maiden, Mother and Queen: Mary in the Anglican Tradition*, ed. Colin Podmore (Norwich: Canterbury Press, 2013), chs 11–14.
8 For a more detailed examination of Catholic views of the Virgin Mary in the Victorian period, see my *Victorians and the Virgin Mary* (Manchester: Manchester University Press, 2008), esp. ch. 2.
9 Because the latter defined the Church of England as a branch of the universal Catholic Church, claimed a Catholic identity while disavowing a Protestant one, and sought to revive Catholic practices, they are here grouped with Roman Catholics as undifferentiated 'Catholics'.
10 J. T. Coleridge, *A Memoir of the Rev. John Keble* (2nd edn, Oxford and London: James Parker, 1869), pp. 289–91.
11 Roman Catholics interpreted this as 'Mother of God'; Pusey preferred to interpret it as 'Christ-bearer'.
12 See Mary Heimann, *Catholic Devotion in Victorian England* (Oxford: Clarendon, 1995).
13 For further details, see Mark D. Chapman, *The Fantasy of Reunion: Anglicans, Catholics, and Ecumenism, 1833–1882* (Oxford: Oxford University Press, 2014), pp. 68–130.
14 Edward Norman, *The English Catholic Church in the Nineteenth Century* (Oxford: Clarendon, 1984), p. 146.
15 The most popular dedication was to Jesus. See Susan Mumm, *Stolen Daughters, Virgin Mothers: Anglican Sisterhoods in Victorian Britain* (London: Leicester University Press, 1999), Appendix 1. Many of the Irish and continental Catholic orders that opened convents and other institutions in this period were dedicated to Mary, as were new, more English orders. See Susan O'Brien, 'French nuns in nineteenth-century England', *Past & Present*, 154 (1997), 150, 155, 156, 171–2; Sister A. F. Norton, 'A History of the Community of St. Mary the Virgin, Wantage: Foundation and Early Development 1848–1858' (MA thesis, University of Durham, 1974), p. 31.
16 Norton, 'History', p. 18; *A Hundred Years of Blessing within an English Community* (London: Society for Promoting Christian Knowledge, 1946), p. 10.
17 Sisterhood of St Margaret's, *Breviary Offices from Lauds to Compline Inclusive* (London: J. T. Hayes, 1874), p. 212. The Sarum Missal had been used throughout much of England, Wales, and Ireland, and was revived in the second half of the nineteenth century by Anglo-Catholics keen to quarry an 'English' rather than a 'Roman' liturgy.
18 Mumm, *Stolen Daughters*, p. 31.

19 Susan O'Brien, 'Making Catholic spaces: women, décor, and devotion in the English Catholic Church, 1840–1900', in D. Wood (ed.), *The Church and the Arts*, Studies in Church History, 28 (Oxford: Blackwell, 1992), p. 456.
20 O'Brien, 'French nuns', 170.
21 Heimann, *Catholic Devotion*, p. 42.
22 Editions of Challoner's *Garden* were published in London in 1800, 1844, 1845, 1854, 1856, 1872, 1873, 1877, 1878, 1883, 1884 and 1899. Other editions were published at Wolverhampton (1801), Manchester (1818), Birmingham (1844), Dublin (1854, 1892) and Edinburgh (1874).
23 See Herringer, *Victorians*, pp. 60–2.
24 See Kathryn Ready, 'Reading Mary as reader: the Marian art of Dante Gabriel and Christina Rossetti', *Victorian Poetry* 46 (2008), esp. 163–5.
25 Peter F. Anson, *Building up the Waste Places: The Revival of Monastic Life on Medieval Lines in the Post-Reformation Church of England* (Leighton Buzzard: The Faith Press, 1973), p. 34.
26 O'Brien, 'Making Catholic spaces', 456–7.
27 *Ibid.*, 458.
28 *Ibid.*, 459–60.
29 Labouré herself was canonised by Pius XII in 1947.
30 O'Brien, 'French nuns', 170–1.
31 For more detailed discussion of the Victorian reception of the doctrine of the Immaculate Conception, see Herringer, *Victorians*, ch. 4.
32 June Osborne, *Stained Glass in England* (1981; rev. edn, Stroud: Sutton, 1997), p. 86; Norton, 'History', p. 18; W. D. Bushell, *The Church of St Mary the Great: The University Church at Cambridge* (Cambridge: Bowes and Bowes, 1948), ch. 13.
33 George Peirce Grantham, *A History of St Saviour's, Leeds* (London: Joseph Masters; Leeds: Harrison and Son, [1872]), p. 46. The medieval Lady Chapel at St Patrick's Cathedral, Dublin, which had until the early nineteenth century been used as a church in its own right by French Huguenots, was also restored in the Victorian period.
34 Artists who defined themselves as Protestant also painted the Virgin Mary. See Nancy Davenport, 'William Holman Hunt: layered belief in the art of a pre-Raphaelite Realist', *Religion and the Arts*, 16 (2012), 29–77.
35 For a discussion and reproduction of the 1845 image, see Michaela Giebelhausen, *Painting the Bible: Representation and Belief in Mid-Victorian Britain* (Aldershot: Ashgate, 2006), pp. 80–2.
36 For the influence of Anglo-Catholicism on Rossetti's work in the 1840s and early 1850s, see D. M. R. Bentley, 'Rossetti's "Ave" and related pictures', *Victorian Poetry*, 15 (1977), 32–5, and Sharon Smulders, 'A breach of faith: D. G. Rossetti's "Ave", Art-Catholicism, and "Poems"', *Victorian Poetry*, 30 (1992), 63–74.
37 See T. S. R. Boase, 'Biblical illustration in nineteenth-century art', *Journal of the Warburg and Courtauld Institutes*, 29 (1966), 349–67 and Giebelhausen, *Painting*.
38 The Slipper Chapel, which tradition held was where pilgrims left their shoes before proceeding to the Shrine of Our Lady of Walsingham, was purchased in 1894 by the wealthy convert Charlotte Boyd (1837–1906) and donated to the monastery at Downside Abbey to help revive Benedictine life. See Sean Gill, 'Marian revivalism in modern English Christianity: the example of Walsingham', in Robert N. Swanson (ed.), *The Church and*

*Mary*, Studies in Church History, 39 (Woodbridge: Boydell Press, 2004), 349; Waller, *Walsingham*, p. 168.
39  For more on the Protestant view of the Virgin Mary, see Herringer, *Victorians*, ch. 3.
40  Although Jameson herself was far from being blindly hostile to Catholicism *per se*. For an interpretation of Mary as an empowering figure for Protestant women, see Kimberley van Esveld Adams, *Our Lady of Victorian Feminism: The Madonna in the Work of Anna Jameson, Margaret Fuller, and George Eliot* (Athens: Ohio University Press, 2001).
41  See Robert A. Orsi, *The Madonna of 115th Street: Faith and Community in Italian Harlem, 1880–1950* (New Haven: Yale University Press, 1985); David Blackbourn, *Marpingen: Apparitions of the Virgin Mary in Nineteenth-Century Germany* (New York: Alfred Knopf, 1994); Sandra Zimdars-Swartz, *Encountering Mary: From La Salette to Medjugorje* (Princeton: Princeton University Press, 1991); Barbara Corrado Pope, 'Immaculate and powerful: the Marian revival in the nineteenth century', in Clarissa W. Atkinson, Constance H. Buchanan and Margaret R. Miles (eds), *Immaculate and Powerful: The Female in Sacred Image and Social Reality* (Boston, MA: Beacon Press, 1985), pp. 173–200.
42  See, for example, Sally Cuneen, *In Search of Mary: The Woman and the Symbol* (London: Random House, 2010), p. 256; Adams, *Our Lady*, p. 89.
43  Nicola J. Watson, '*Gloriana Victoriana*: Victoria and the cultural memory of Elizabeth I', in Margaret Homans and Adrienna Munich (eds), *Remaking Queen Victoria* (Cambridge: Cambridge University Press, 1997), pp. 79–104, explores another way in which Victoria's reign was the inverse of Elizabeth's, arguing that the earlier queen's perceived flaws were emphasised in order to highlight Victoria's virtues.
44  Susan P. Casteras, 'The wise child and her "offspring": some changing faces of Queen Victoria', in Homans and Munich (eds), *Remaking*, p. 183.
45  Casteras, 'Wise child', pp. 185–9.
46  Margaret Homans, '"To the Queen's private apartments": royal family portraiture and the construction of Victoria's sovereign obedience', *Victorian Studies*, 37, 1 (1993), 1–41, p. 15.
47  11 Wells later painted a larger version of the painting, which was exhibited at the Royal Academy in 1887 and purchased by Victoria. For a reproduction of the first version, see Casteras, 'The wise child', p. 196.
48  12 See Homans, '"To the Queen's private apartments"', p. 15; Alison Booth, 'Illustrious company: Victoria among other women in Anglo-American role model anthologies', in Homans and Munich, *Remaking*, p. 64. For other Victorian representations of this scene, see Watson, '*Gloriana Victoriana*', p. 80.
49  See Adrienne Munich, *Queen Victoria's Secrets* (New York: Columbia University Press, 1996), pp. 61–3; Homans, '"To the Queen's private apartments,"' pp. 11–12. An 1841 *Punch* cartoon depicts him as an unemployed Cupid; see Lytton Strachey, *The Illustrated Queen Victoria* (1921; London: Bloomsbury Publishing, 1987), p. 83.
50  Homans, 'Queen's private apartments', p. 15. The ambiguities of these portraits are discussed in detail on pp. 14–16.
51  Herringer, *Victorians*, p. 39.
52  *Ibid.*, pp. 93–4.
53  Booth, 'Illustrious company', p. 6; Munich, *Victoria's Secrets*, p. 20.
54  Homans and Munich, *Remaking*, p. 2; Booth, 'Illustrious company', p. 60; John Plunkett, *Queen Victoria: First Media Monarch* (Oxford: Oxford University Press, 2003), p. 2.

55 Homans, 'Queen's private apartments', p. 2.
56 Hackett, *Virgin Mother*, p. 5.
57 O'Brien, 'Making Catholic spaces', 452.
58 In the early twentieth century, rood screens were added at St Barnabas', Pimlico and at St Stephen's, South Kensington.
59 For an analysis of twentieth-century versions of the shrines, see Gill, 'Marian revivalism', and Waller, *Walsingham*, esp. ch. 7. Dominic Janes documents ongoing Protestant hostility to the shrine in *Victorian Reformation: The Fight over Idolatry in the Church of England, 1840–1860* (Oxford and New York: Oxford University Press, 2009).

3

# Claudia Rufina

*Martha Vandrei*

THE CHURCH OF ST Llonio, named for a sixth-century Welsh saint, stands atop a small hill, against which the houses and gardens that make up the village of Llandinam are snugly nestled. Llandinam is best known as the home town of the Victorian industrialist David Davies. A roadside statue of Davies commemorates not only the iron bridge he built across the nearby River Severn, but also his contribution to national economic development during the middle to late nineteenth century. In this sense, Llandinam has an illustrious past of recent heritage: Davies's railways and collieries shaped the modern, industrial landscape of south Wales. But, inside St Llonio's Church, one can find a past of much greater antiquity.

The south aisle of St Llonio's is dominated by three stained-glass windows designed and commissioned by Elinor Powell in 1897 (figure 5). Powell was the daughter of a local landowner, and she placed the windows in memory of her mother and father. Each window depicts a scene from the early history of Christianity, but not, perhaps, ones familiar to the modern observer. The viewer might recognise Caractacus but the other figures depicted here are less easily placed. What to make of the window on the far left, in which a woman and a man, identified as Claudia and Pudens, are shown at their marriage ceremony? Elinor Powell gave this description of the scene: 'The marriage of Pudens and Gladys – or Claudia. Pudens to be a very fine type of Roman nobility in the most splendid uniform of a Roman soldier. Gladys to be very fascinating and beautiful, and simply clad in a loose soft white Grecian robe – edged with gold device.'[1] But who were Claudia and Pudens, and why were they so important to the daughter of a Victorian landowner in rural Wales?

The 'Gladys or Claudia' referred to here was purportedly a British princess who lived sometime in the 50s and 60s AD, and said to be the daughter of either Caractacus or another, less well-known first-century king, Cogidunus (or Cogidubnus). Variously cast as a hostage or a refugee from war-torn Britain, forced out by the rebellion of Queen Boudica in 61, Claudia, it is said, married Pudens, who was either a centurion or a Roman senator, or both. Although almost entirely unknown to twenty-first-century audiences, the story of Claudia Rufina was once held to have profound implications for the very early history of the Christian religion, not in Rome, but in Britain. According to this story, she was purportedly converted to Christianity by none

5 *The marriage of Pudens and Claudia; Paul explaining the Gospel to Caractacus and Bran the Blessed; Sts Prasside and Pudenziana*, three-light window, 1897, Church of St Llonio, Llandinam, Powys.

other than Saint Paul and subsequently became the matriarch of a powerful Christian family, and possibly the first Christian Briton. The main points at issue in Claudia's life were her identity as a Briton, her Christianity, and her association, explored at length below, with Saint Paul, all of which had crucial implications for debates about very early Christianity in Britain.

Also important were her often confused familial connections. Her marriage to Pudens is itself a matter of conjecture predicated on the assumption that scattered ancient references to a first-century Claudia all allude to the same woman. A man called Pudens almost certainly did live in first-century Rome at the head of a large household.[2] He was said to have been married to Savinella, though even one recent authority notes the possibility that his wife was in fact called Claudia.[3] Tantalisingly, it was often thought that Saint Peter had been sheltered in Pudens's home, and that the Vatican's 'St Peter's Chair' had been a gift from Pudens to the first Bishop of Rome.[4] Pudens was also said to have been the father of a number of children who were later canonised, most notably Saint Pudentiana, from whose church in Rome Cardinal Wiseman took his title of Cardinal.

But Catholic commentators, Wiseman among them, rarely referred to Claudia, and she was never canonised by the Catholic Church. It has been noted elsewhere that Claudia's candidacy for sainthood was in fact mooted and rejected.[5] However, she is still associated in some Catholic circles with 7 August and 19 May.[6] Perhaps coincidentally, 19 May was also the feastday of Saint Pudentiana, before she, like many others, was deprived of the status of saint by the Roman Catholic Church in 1969.[7] Yet Claudia is far more significant as part of a complex history that was especially relevant within the established Church of England. Unlike the Roman conception of sainthood, Claudia's importance in the Anglican tradition was not dependent on her as an object of especial divine favour, and did not give birth to a cult of devotion. Rather, the details of her life carried profound implications for one particular aspect of ecclesiastical historical argument: when and by whom had the British Isles come to be converted to Christianity? This essay will begin by recounting the early modern story of Claudia Rufina's importance to that question, before moving on to discuss how those earlier strands of argumentation were taken up in the nineteenth century.[8] In the course of this essay, it will become clear that Claudia became a key nexus in which to explore the place of historical evidence in Anglican theology and ecclesiology. Claudia allowed Anglicans to put forward an exceptionalist argument, and she did so in two ways. First, and most obviously, she supported a version of history in which Britain had maintained a pristine and independent form of episcopal Christianity from the time of the apostles. Secondly, because the evidence for Claudia's story was so deeply embedded in the esoteric works of ancient and medieval writers and in little-known archaeological finds, her story could be used to demonstrate the extent to which the beliefs of the established Church could be tested by historical, philological and antiquarian research. On the one hand this differentiated the established Church from Protestant sects that rejected the authority of tradition, while it also allowed Anglicans to claim an impeccably factual pedigree on the authority of antiquity. On the other it could be contrasted with the image of Catholicism as founded on assertion, coercion, and gradual degradation. Exactly how, by whose agency, and in which form Christianity first came to Britain was a matter of serious historical-antiquarian debate, on which all the evidence of traditional, classical, and medieval sources was brought to bear.

## Early modern Protestant antiquarianism

Bede's *Ecclesiastical History* credited the mission of Saint Augustine, undertaken at the behest of Pope Gregory in the sixth century, with securing a foothold for Christianity in the British Isles, and in particular among the pagan Anglo-Saxons. But during the Reformation Bede's narrative, in which English Christianity originated in Rome, became problematic for Protestant reformers seeking to divest themselves of Rome's claims to authority. Catholic polemicists were quick to point out that Bede, a most avowedly English historian, was also a devout Catholic and a monk whose history was proof of Rome's importance in Britain's past.[9] For sixteenth- and seventeenth-century papal apologists, the Roman Church had been God's benison to men, and to reject its authority was to reject the one true Church. They sneered at Protestantism as a recent innovation: 'where was your Church before Luther?' As Tony Claydon has described, Protestant responses took divergent forms and played to sometimes contradictory sensibilities.[10] Yet most reformers in Britain agreed on one key point: that Christianity must have arrived in the British Isles long before Augustine's mission, possibly even within a few decades of Christ's death. To show this, early modern scholars turned to patrology, coupled with the careful compilation of Roman and British source material.[11] There was more than one answer to be gleaned from such a vast corpus, and thus a number of ways to conceive of the British Church's independence from Rome.

One legend, traced to William of Malmesbury, told of Joseph of Arimathea's journey to Britain in the first century, when he and his associates settled in Glastonbury and began converting the locals.[12] Another told of evangelising missions by the Apostle Simon Zealotes, while similar stories claimed that Saint James, or even Saint Peter, had come to Britain as missionaries.[13] Yet another popular tale, which was also retold by Bede in the *Ecclesiastical History*, told of the second-century Lucius, a British king who had begged the Pope to send bishops to help him convert to Christianity.[14] The Pope's missionaries made the journey to Britain, converted King Lucius, and then set to work on the rest of the native British population. Bede's story suggested that the Britons *and* the Anglo-Saxons owed their Christianity to Rome, an insinuation which, even well into the nineteenth century, Protestant, and especially Welsh, commentators continued to decry as a popish fatuity.[15]

But perhaps the most widely discussed conversion story involved Saint Paul's agency in bringing Christianity to Britain in the years following Christ's death. There were two versions of this story. The first posited that, while in Rome, Paul had met British migrants there. These Britons were either already Christians or were converted by their intercourse with Paul, and it was at Paul's behest that they then returned to their native land to spread the new faith. The second, slightly altered version, which took place within a similar timeframe, held that Paul had voyaged to Britain personally after he had met with sympathetic Britons in Rome. Either way, Paul would have consecrated bishops to follow in his footsteps, thus laying one possible foundation for apostolic succession in Britain.

Paul's role in the conversion of Britain was said by many to have been supported in the works of the Church Fathers, including Clement of Rome, Jerome, and Theodoret, all of whom lived within the first six centuries of the Christian era. The testimony of the ancients, however, was often vague, referring only to Paul's activities in 'the utmost bounds of the west' or 'the isles that lie in the ocean'.[16] Nevertheless, eminent sixteenth- and seventeenth-century scholars such as Matthew Parker (1504–75), William Camden (1551–1623), James Ussher (1581–1656), and William Cave (1637–1713) drew on ancient writers to endorse the view that British Christianity was of Pauline origin.[17] Although they admitted, to varying degrees, that the benighted pagan Anglo-Saxons had been led by the guiding hand of Augustine, the Celtic and British Church, it was argued, had sustained a native form of Christian worship from time immemorial. The part played by this native Church had been suppressed by Anglo-Saxon chroniclers such as Bede and his monkish supporters. However, there was enough extant evidence from antiquity, the reformers maintained, to clear the Roman stain from the complexion of British Christianity, while also legitimating the British ecclesiastical establishment as sanctified by the accepted tradition of a primitive and universal Church inherited lineally from the apostles.[18]

Claudia was not mentioned by the Church Fathers, nor was there any direct reference to her (only to an unnamed daughter of Caractacus) by classical historians, particularly Tacitus, whose *Annals*, written in the second century, was one of the main sources for the life of Caractacus.[19] Nevertheless, Claudia was often thought to have been one of the Britons affiliated with Paul in Rome, and much intellectual energy was expended over the course of almost four centuries in rationalising that belief. Perhaps the most important early work in this regard was Edward Stillingfleet's *Origines Britannicae* (1685). Stillingfleet (1635–99) explained and endorsed the most important elements of the Claudia story, addressing her status as a British princess, her marriage to a Roman senator, and her identity as a Christian in Rome at great length. Stillingfleet was read well into the nineteenth century, and Claudia's later reputation owes a great deal to him. Like many before him, Stillingfleet accepted the chronology elucidated by the sixth-century British writer Gildas, who believed that the introduction of Christianity in Britain had occurred between the last years of Tiberius's reign in 37 and the 'fatal victory' of Suetonius Paulinus over Queen Boudica, in 61.[20] The dates for these events, and that of Paul's discharge from Roman captivity, were much disputed. Stillingfleet gave the date of Paul's release as the fifth year of Nero; Boudica's rebellion, by his reckoning, had happened in the seventh or eighth. This left a two- to three-year period in which Paul might have undertaken a mission to Britain.

Adding yet more colour to these eventful decades, the rebellion of Caractacus, King of the Silures, had ended in c. 50 with Caractacus's capture and extradition to Rome – accompanied, it is said, by his family, including a daughter. Based on this coincidence, Stillingfleet reasoned that, moved by her father's eloquence, the Roman Emperor Claudius adopted Claudia and gave her his name. Stillingfleet then averred that it was this child of British nobility, adopted into Roman royalty as Claudia Rufina, who encouraged Saint Paul to go to Britain and personally evangelise to the kinsmen she had left behind. Caractacus and Paul were being held captive in Rome at the same time and it seemed entirely plausible, to Stillingfleet at least, that the British royal family would have encountered the Apostle to the Gentiles, who then converted them to the new faith. 'If this Claudia were St. Paul's Disciple, why might not she excite that Apostle to go into her Country, to plant Christianity there, as he had done with so much Success in other Places?'[21] Extrapolating from this tradition, Stillingfleet, and later John Inett (1647–1717), who provided a continuation of the former's history in *Origines Anglicanae* (1704), posited a jointly British and apostolic origin for native

Christianity; Inett extended this to underpin a Celtic origin for English Christianity, arguing that Augustine was merely duplicating existing efforts.[22]

But, as we have seen, there was no direct evidence to support the conclusion that Caractacus's daughter had been called Claudia. To make this claim, Stillingfleet turned to two first-century sources and once again used the coincidence of dates as the basis for his argument. Each of these sources mentions a Claudia and connects her with a man called Pudens, but neither explicitly confirms that these two Claudias were the same person, and only one of the sources notes that she was a British émigrée. The first witness to place a Claudia in Rome with Pudens was Saint Paul himself in his Second Epistle to Timothy. The letter ended with 'Eubulus greeteth thee, and Pudens, and Linus, and Claudia'. The second source was the epigrammatist Martial (c. 40–104), who named a 'Claudia Rufina' in two of his verses. This Claudia Rufina was said by Martial to have been married to Pudens, evidence that Stillingfleet pounced on as proving that these were Paul's associates. Martial praised Claudia's beauty and charm, qualities he admits were undimmed, despite her being of foreign rather than Roman stock, in Book IV epigram 13, published in AD 91 on the occasion of her marriage to Pudens.[23] He later wrote to celebrate the birth of a child to Pudens and Claudia, in Book XI, epigram 53, published in 96; here he referred to Claudia as 'descended from woad-stained Britons'.[24]

There was enough circumstantial evidence to sustain scholarly interest in Claudia's association with Paul in the years after the Reformation. In the nineteenth century, scholars continued to chew over old debates about early Christianity in Britain, often relying on the same ancient sources as their predecessors. Claudia did not always enter into their arguments, but Paul's mission to Britain remained a hot topic. Thomas Burgess (1756–1837), Bishop of St David's, wrote extensively on the subject of Paul's involvement in the earliest history of Christianity in the British Isles, using the authority of the ancient writers Clement, Eusebius, Jerome, and Theodoret to demonstrate that true religion came directly and personally from Saint Paul on his journey around Europe and the 'Western parts'.[25] But, like the British travels of Paul, Claudia remained within the realm of tradition – that is to say, her story rested on the foundation of apostolic and patristic writing from the sixth decade up to the sixth century. It was in defence of this traditional evidence, and in defence of the Church of England's reliance on it, that Claudia came to be employed in the nineteenth century.

## The Anglican Claudia of the early nineteenth century

Fears of creeping Romish incursion and of the seductive power of radical Protestantism were a growing Anglican preoccupation in the period after 1800. Anxieties increased with the repeal of the Test and Corporation Acts in 1828, followed quickly by Catholic Emancipation in 1829, and the reinstatement of a Catholic hierarchy in Britain in 1850, the so-called 'Papal Aggression'.[26] In such an atmosphere, Claudia's story had perennial valence as part of a narrative of the established Church's independence from

Rome. Robert Southey gave it some credence in his *Book of the Church* (1824). Francis Thackeray (1793–1842), a Hertfordshire curate and the uncle of the more famous W. M., included discussion of Claudia in his posthumously published *Researches into the Ecclesiastical and Political State of Ancient Britain under the Roman Emperors* (1843).[27] James Yeowell (1803?–1875), an antiquary and indexer, was convinced of the story's merits and repeated it in his *Chronicles of the Ancient British Church* (1847). Yeowell drew extensively on the first pamphlet dedicated solely to examining Claudia Rufina's role in early Christian history, William Lisle Bowles's *Pudens and Claudia of St. Paul*, the third edition of which was published in 1839.[28]

As chaplain to the Prince Regent from 1818, and Canon Residentiary at Salisbury Cathedral, Bowles (1762–1850) was devoted to promoting popular understanding of the established Church, its tenets and its history, within a highly fraught confessional atmosphere.[29] It is likely that Bowles chose the story of Claudia and Pudens chiefly because it supported British independence from papal Catholicism, as well as being a romantic tale which he could flavour with dramatic twists. Bowles examined the evidence in minute detail and presented it in emphatic and descriptive language. Beginning with Caractacus's capture and extradition to Rome with his wife and children and the family's audience before the Emperor Claudius, Bowles revelled in the theatre of the event. As he described it, when faced with Caractacus's little daughter, and, 'struck perhaps by the child's innocence and beauty, in such a scene; ... Claudius might then have adopted her ... and how much must the interest increase, if we think that through her ... the rage of the lion, "from whose mouth Paul was delivered," became calm at the voice of innocence, and a British-born virgin!'[30] Bowles elaborated further, describing Claudia's encounters with Saint Paul while an unwilling resident at Nero's court. 'Being first interested in the fate of the poor prisoner, and afterwards converted', Claudia 'witnessed his constancy and faith, when "the Lord delivered him out of the mouth of the lion".'[31] Bowles went on to claim that the persecution of the Christians famously pursued by Nero was a characteristically violent reaction to the discovery of a Christian cell, led by Claudia, in his own household. Somehow, Claudia and her fellow converts escaped the persecution and made their way back to Britain, and thus it was 'through her' that 'the Isles afar off should see the Lord's glory'.[32]

Although buoying Claudia's historicity in the public imagination was one of Bowles's motives, the overriding intent behind the pamphlet was to strike a blow against the forces of popular ignorance, of which Catholicism was only one of the most ruthless agents. Ignorance, Bowles claimed elsewhere, was also bred by 'the general superficial diffusion ... of that kind of knowledge, which veers this way or that according to the Magazine and Tracts, that direct it'.[33] For Bowles, forms of Protestant Dissent which deified individual private judgement were as opposed to the acquisition of knowledge as the authoritarian superstitions of Roman Catholicism.[34] Bowles's work demonstrates that by the 1830s and 1840s Claudia's story was no longer confined to the musings of theologians at a lofty disconnect from ordinary worshippers. Rather, there was a strong sense among Anglican scholars who supported the Claudia legend that they were constructing a convincing history that would put paid to the claims of radical Protestants and Roman Catholics to being the saviours of British souls.

One way of looking at this would be to see it as part of or at least in parallel with the reflex towards tradition that drove Tractarian-inspired High Churchmen to restore 'Catholic' forms, to revisit the Church Fathers, and to excavate stories of saints from their own land, as Elizabeth Macfarlane shows elsewhere in this volume. There is some truth in this, for as the Church in Wales took on an increasingly Anglo-Catholic flavour it sought to establish a canon of Welsh and British saints, of whom Claudia was one, appearing for instance in *Baner y Groes*, a Welsh-language periodical edited by the cleric, antiquary, and Eisteddfod revivalist John Williams or 'ab Ithel' (1811–62) as part of the anti-papal but pro-Catholic story it tried to tell.[35] Williams was one of the founders of the Cambrian Archaeology Association (1846), whose house journal, *Archaeologia Cambrensis*, would in coming decades provide an important venue for speculation about early Christianity in Wales. He also began the *Cambrian Journal* and was a leading light in the Welsh Manuscripts Society and, alongside Richard Williams Morgan or 'Mor Meirion' (c. 1815–89) and several others, combined antiquarian folklorism and bardic pageantry with being an Anglican clergyman. Morgan's *The British Kymry, or Britons of Cambria* (1857) purported to trace the history of the Welsh from the biblical flood to the nineteenth century. In combining churchmanship with nationalism, figures like Williams and Morgan built enthusiastically and sometimes imaginatively on the work of those such as Bowles and of the Reverend William Hales (1747–1831), Rector of Killesandra in Ireland. Hales employed Claudia's story to add a sense of historical legitimacy to a popular Welsh legend surrounding 'Bran the Blessed' – yet another variation on the first-century conversion stories centred on Paul. Hales did this in response to Bishop Burgess, who had attributed the Britons' conversion to Paul himself, without mentioning Britons such as Caractacus or Claudia.[36] Hales reintroduced the Welsh leader as part of his evidence, once again noting that Caractacus had been taken to Rome, accompanied by his children. But he added a key detail: that Caractacus's father, Bran, had also been taken hostage. This was why he acquired the appellation 'the Blessed': Hales thought it likely that that Bran met with Paul in Rome, was converted by him, and returned to Britain to proselytise his kinsmen.[37]

Hales appealed to the documentary record of Welsh antiquity for evidence of this story. One oft-employed source was the Welsh Triads, a series of manuscripts relating to ancient Welsh legends, including heroes and saints of the early Church, compiled in the late thirteenth century.[38] Although of medieval origin, the Triads had suffered disfigurement at the hands of the enthusiastic antiquary Edward Williams, famous as Iolo Morganwg (1747–1826), whose commitment to Welsh cultural nationalism was unhampered by any attachment to historical reality. It was difficult even for the astute antiquary to distinguish between some of Morganwg's eighteenth-century forgeries and the genuine medieval article, especially if, as in Hales's case, they belied a frustratingly scant source base. It is unclear whether Hales or his colleagues were aware of it, but it was probably through the intervention of Iolo Morganwg that Welsh scholars came to believe that Caractacus had a daughter called Eigen.[39] Hales, citing Peter Robert's *Collectanea Cambrica* (1811), which was itself not above suspicion, argued that Eigen was one and the same with the Claudia of Martial and Paul, simply called by a different name.[40] Thus the spread of Christian teachings had begun with the return from Rome of a group of native Britons, among them Bran and Eigen. The new religion then passed from Wales to Ireland, and there would have been a steady exchange of the faithful thereafter, which ensured the conversion by native Christians of successive waves of migrants to Britain. However dubious the Welsh sources were, Hales argued, they seemed to be corroborated by the Bible and the testimony of antiquity. Even those sympathetic to narratives of Welsh exceptionalism remained unconvinced, however.[41]

## Was Claudia Welsh?

Aside from a desire to construct a more convincingly Welsh history of Britain's conversion, there is a second possible reason why the Paul/Claudia story was taken up by Welsh writers. As noted above, worries about a decline in traditional learning and theology formed a significant spur for antiquarian research among Anglican clergymen. And there were few places in Britain more threatened by radical Protestant disdain for extra-biblical tradition than Wales. Alarm among Welsh Anglican clergy was palpable. By 1861 Morgan had supplemented his grand narrative with an exhaustively researched book on Paul's conversion of the Britons, and he blamed the English establishment for alienating Welsh Anglicans by appointing monoglot Englishmen to lead Welsh-speaking congregations.[42] One simple remedy, Morgan argued, was to appoint more Welsh-speaking bishops. When an Englishman, Vowler Short, who demonstrated no desire to learn Welsh, was consecrated Bishop of St Asaph, Morgan was furious, and doubly so due to his conviction that the rightful recipient of the office should have been his own uncle, the Archdeacon of Cardigan, John Williams (1792–1858).[43]

Williams was himself a proponent of Welsh-language preaching, a prominent schoolmaster, and a friend of the novelist Walter Scott (1771–1832), not to mention the onetime protégé of Burgess, to whom he owed his appointment as Vicar of Lampeter in 1820. By no means a Tractarian like his North Wales namesake, Williams was nevertheless a keen historian, a churchman, and a Welsh patriot, and he took up his pen in defence of Claudia Rufina in order to argue for the utility of tradition in the battle for the hearts and minds of worshippers.

> Among those who pride themselves on being called Christians according to the Bible, and the Bible alone, there has practically prevailed a wish to make a sad disruption, between the Bible History itself, and the historical traditions, which connect that history with the actual events which immediately succeeded its inspired termination. In proof of this, I can bring no more striking example than the fact that it remained for me to embody, in one Essay, the details of my present subject.[44]

The times called for a new investigation of the traditions around Claudia, which, Williams noted, had not progressed since Stillingfleet's admittedly highly astute study.[45] Williams's book was an impressive attempt to reconcile the different trajectories of Claudia's story. He drew on the legends around Paul, around Lucius, and even rationalised that Claudia's curious absence from the Welsh Triads, which Hales had sought to explain away as a case of mistaken identity, was in fact proof that her family had been blacklisted by the ancient British writers, who viewed her father – who Williams believed to have been Cogidunus, not Caractacus – as a Roman collaborator.

Williams was attempting to unify the traditionary record in order to cement the story's transcendent truth: Claudia had been a British princess, she had been an active Christian in Paul's Rome, and she and her associates had been responsible, directly or indirectly, for the conversion of the ancient Britons. Once again, English Christianity was given a Celtic, or British, origin, and, furthermore, Williams's imagined English reader was confronted with the shocking notion that the ancient Britons had been a civilised and respectable people, a far cry from the primitive tribesmen imagined by generations of English writers. Williams was sensitive to what he perceived to be the novelty of his position, stating in his preface that 'my line of argument will have far more opposition to encounter from the long-cherished prejudices of the English people respecting the social and intellectual state of our British Ancestors, than from any failure in the moral demonstration'.[46] Like many others before him, Williams bewailed the 'suicidal' belief among Anglicans that Augustine was the founder of English Christianity: it was through the stories of ancient British heroes and saints that the English could be rescued from any lingering sense that they owed their faith to Rome.[47]

From this perspective, one might expect Williams to have emphasised Claudia's long-established geographical connection to Wales as the daughter of Caractacus. However, Williams argued that Claudia was not the daughter of the indisputably Welsh Caractacus, but of the much less well-known King Cogidunus, who ruled the area around Chichester in Sussex. She was, Williams claimed, a British princess, but one with a geographical link to modern-day England. Williams called attention to the discovery by the antiquaries Roger Gale (1672–1744) and William Stukeley (1687–1765) of a mysterious Roman inscription in Chichester in 1723.[48] Using evidence from the inscription (which seemed to suggest a transaction of land between Cogidunus and someone with the name of Pudens) Williams reasoned that Claudia must have been sent to Rome by Cogidunus to protect her during Boudica's uprising, and that she had met Pudens, who had himself served in Britain, while there. As a client king of the Romans, Cogidunus would have been considered a traitor by Boudica and the Iceni, and his child would have been removed to the safe hands of his Roman allies – hence Claudia's excision from the Welsh Triads.[49]

Williams's pamphlet was more ambitious than a simple recital of old evidence with an admixture of his own novel analysis. He used the Claudia story as a case in point to demonstrate that ecclesiastical historians should be willing to embrace traditional beliefs and treat them as worthy of historical enquiry in their own right, in order to make their work meaningful for laypeople. Williams possessed an unwavering belief that even the most critical scrutiny of the historical record would yield independent testimony to his own faith position. That being the case, Williams urged his fellow clergymen, antiquaries, and scholars of ecclesiastical history to look outside the New Testament for legends and traditions that might be drawn upon to 'reconstruct for the Protestant believer, a probable history of the first centuries of Christianity', a history whose verifiability would make it a powerful weapon in the battle for hearts, minds, and souls.[50]

> If this be not done, we shall certainly in our disputes with Romanism, be worsted in a most important field of controversy; and if worsted on this ground, the time will come when the denial of such important facts, as may hereafter be authentically proved, will recoil upon our own heads, shake the faith of our most judicious followers in the soundness of our system, and induce them to regard us as predetermined sceptics, anxious for no other evidence that may serve to confirm us in our own preconceived opinions, however slight their foundation on facts may be, however contrary to probable testimony they may be proved to be.[51]

Protestants keen to establish lines of descent, in other words, could tend towards over-keen archaeology, scraping off and discarding the very strata that would cement their connection to the bedrock of apostolic truth.

Williams was sincere in subjecting Claudia to a rigorous historical examination, but to those outside the Anglican establishment, and even to some within it, every return visit to the Claudia story was but a regurgitation of the tired fatuities of earlier generations. Individual uses of Claudia's story too easily resembled attempts by Newman and his coterie to appropriate the Church Fathers and medieval 'English Saints' and in so doing to 're-catholicise' the Church of England. And if Dissenting writers were increasingly suspicious of the works of Eusebius, Tertullian, and the rest, they were similarly sceptical about Anglican appropriations of Paul and Claudia. In 1852, William Lindsay Alexander (1808–84), a Scottish Congregationalist minister, systematically dismantled the evidence for Claudia Rufina's very existence, let alone her purported status as the first British Christian and the bearer of Paul's apostolic bequest. He did not limit his scrutiny to Claudia and Pudens. Alexander declared that all attempts to establish the means by which Christianity first came to Britain were 'either the deliberate inventions of mendacious chroniclers, or traditional corruptions of imperfectly remembered facts'. Instead, a gleeful Alexander announced the impossibility of ever arriving at a conclusion.[52] This lacuna in historical knowledge was to be celebrated rather than lamented; ignorant of the identities of these first missionaries, British Christians of the nineteenth century were free from the lure of idolatry, and could build their religion instead on the firmer foundations of biblically prescribed facts and practices.[53]

These confessional battles were not the only means by which Claudia became part of the historical-cultural complexion of nineteenth-century Britain. In literature, Claudia's romantic life story could be used as a vehicle to teach readers about the horrors of paganism and immorality, and to suggest, if not prove, one possible narrative of early Christian history. The world of the first century, redolent with pagans, Jews, Christians, heroes, and villains, and rich with didactic potential, was a popular subject in Victorian historical fiction.[54] Although there was undoubtedly an element of subversive titillation in lurid depictions of Roman decadence, not to mention the ghoulish details of early martyrdom, substantive antiquarian and theological arguments could also be explored within these fictionalised histories. Two novels published in the 1890s gave fairly large roles to Claudia and her lover, Pudens: F. W. Farrar's *Darkness and Dawn* (1891), and A. J. Church's *The Burning of Rome* (1892).[55] Both used the Claudia story to explore the role of Britons in spreading the faith during its earliest and most dangerous years. They did so by deliberately eliding fact and fiction. As Farrar put it, 'the history of the preceding pages has told, and the fiction has illustrated, the truths which it was [the author's] object to set forth'.[56]

In *Darkness and Dawn*, Claudia is the uncorrupted flower of British virginity amidst a tangle of Roman divorcees and mistresses, a maiden 'before whose beautiful personality the tinsel compliments of her many admirers seemed to sink into shamed silence'.[57] Farrar's Claudia had been a Christian before coming to Rome, another factor which accounts for her maidenly charm, and which immediately embeds her amidst the group of stalwart believers in Rome. Her relationship with the Roman Pudens provides the narrative arc to her story, but it is the Roman rather than the Briton who finds himself abandoning paganism for the teachings of Paul. Claudia and Pudens eventually return to Britain where, it is implied, they are able to practise and preach their newfound faith in peace.

Church's *The Burning of Rome* was effectively a dramatisation of Tacitus's *Annals* — not at all surprising, given that Church had published a translation in 1869.[58] However, because Tacitus had never actually mentioned Claudia by name or explored her story in any detail, Church confected his account with details gleaned from outside Tacitus. Once again, the British princess and Pudens, the Roman citizen, were the chief romantic protagonists, and the scene of Claudia's marriage to Pudens appeared as the novel's frontispiece and acted as its denouement.[59] But Church chose to follow John Williams in making Claudia the daughter of King Cogidunus, sent from her native land to escape the wrath of Boudica and the rebellious Britons who viewed her father as a traitor. The story ends happily, with Nero's death, and the reunion between Claudia, by then in hiding, and Pudens, who had been sent far away in his capacity as a centurion. The reunion is brought about by the agency of none other than the poet Martial, one of many real characters to whom Church gave dramatic imagined roles. Again, Pudens, the pagan Roman, comes to Christianity through his association with his wife and her British Christian friends.

Both novelists focused on Claudia's eventful life before and immediately after her marriage, showing little interest in the minute details of imagined happily-ever-afters.

Claudia's quiet life as a wife and mother was not exactly an inspiring subject for novelists, quite aside from the lack of evidence. Antiquaries were similarly reluctant to make conjectures about the identities or activities of Claudia's children. Only John Williams had given the subject serious consideration, postulating that Claudia had borne between three and six children.[60] Elsewhere, resting on the authority of Ussher, Williams named two girls, Pudentiana and Praxedes (Prassedes), and two boys, Timotheus and Novatus.[61] But aside from these brief notices, there was little to go on, making it all the more interesting that Elinor Powell's stained-glass window presents such an elaborate romantic portrayal of Claudia, her children, and their role in early Christian history (figure 5). Her scheme melded together elements of the various legends surrounding the family, while discounting some others. We have already seen that the first window portrays Claudia, or 'Gladys',[62] and Pudens's Christian marriage ceremony, an event at least partially supported by the ancient writers. The central light shows the Apostle Paul preaching to Caractacus and Bran, an event supported only by conjectural readings of the Welsh Triads, a story that Powell seemed to embrace with patriotic enthusiasm. As she described the central figures, Caractacus was to have 'Welsh features, with a noble heroic countenance and the dress of a distinguished British General. His father Bran to have an intellectual enthusiastic face, and majestic saintly garments.'[63]

The third and final light shows two female figures, one upright, holding a vase, the other on her knees, sponge in hand, mopping up puddles of blood. A male figure and his assistant can be seen in the background lifting the lifeless body of a martyr. The women are here called Prasside and Pudenziana; the male figure, Powell's note reveals, is Linus, their brother. This scene is an amalgamation of the traditions around Claudia that make her the mother of Prassedes and Pudentiana, but with the addition of Linus, rather than Timotheus or Novatus. Linus was sometimes identified with the man who became Bishop of Rome after the martyrdom of Saint Peter – which would make Claudia the mother of the second Pope, and that Pope of British extraction. So much for Rome converting Britain! In this window it is the other way round. Powell must have constructed this version of events through a study of modern antiquarian works, where she would have found more than one presentation of the varied evidence. Rather than privileging one, this was to be her own idiosyncratic interpretation which reconciled them all, and placed Wales, specifically Llandinam, at its heart.

## Conclusion

The earliest years of Christian history in Britain are still shrouded in mystery, and are likely to remain so. Claudia's part in that history is likewise part of that mystery, and the facts of her life will remain elusive. But Claudia's existence, a composite formed from Paul, Martial, and the anonymous daughter of Caractacus mentioned by Tacitus, suggested an alternative history of British religion that proved hugely useful and influential for Protestants after the Reformation, and which gained new impetus in our period. Her life suggested that the Britons' part in bringing Christianity to their own shores had been drastically underestimated, or even deliberately overlooked. This claim had particular valence within the established Church, keen to stress both its Protestant nature but also its apostolic inheritance in an increasingly sectarian Wales. By the later nineteenth century, High Church historical scholarship stressing continuities between the medieval and post-Reformation Churches, and arguing that the Church of England had always been both Catholic and Reformed, made such narratives less important. Claudia and her coadjutors were not forgotten, but they did become the property of nationalist and racially inflected semi-scholarly subcultures, joining a host of other real and imagined figures in the mythology of British Israelism, for example.[64]

This shift helps in part to explain both Claudia's purchase for nineteenth-century Anglican antiquarians, but also her modern neglect. For much of the period in question, Claudia's story was one front on which to fight for the legitimacy of tradition as a source for history, belief, and practice. Historical reconstruction was therefore key to her use, from the work of Edward Stillingfleet, to that of John Williams, and even to the stained-glass windows of Elinor Powell.[65] Yet Claudia serves also to show the extent to which the lines between supposition and evidence, between amateur antiquarianism and scholarly history, and between faith and fiction, remained as they always had been, blurred. It was only with the rise of history as a profession, in the later nineteenth century, that boundaries were drawn more firmly. Even so, novels still projected evidence against an imagined background, and in some circles at least, embellishment could still take the place of historical reasoning. Fact, fiction, and faith were combined and recombined in various iterations, none of which was ever refined into the authoritative version of Britain's Christian antiquity. It was this very lack of authority that gave Claudia's story purchase. If for some the search for origins and solid data to back them up was of paramount importance, Claudia tells a somewhat different story, about how tradition, local and regional identities, nationalism, and scholarship intersected; how scraps of ancient evidence could be used to construct a liminal narrative suspended between fact and fiction, but built solidly on faith.

## Notes

I wish to thank the parishioners of St Llonio's church for their assistance and for permission to photograph the stained-glass windows. Jeremy Pryce of Llandinam kindly sent photocopies of the original memorandum in which Powell describes her desired designs, for which I am grateful.

1  Memorandum by Elinor Powell held by Jeremy Pryce.
2  J. H. Parker, 'The House of Pudens in Rome', *Archaeological Journal*, 28 (1871), 41–9.
3  M. M. Schaeffer, *Women in Pastoral Office: The Story of St Prassede, Rome* (Oxford: Oxford University Press, 2013), p. 15, n. 43.
4  N. Wiseman, 'Remarks on Lady Morgan's statements regarding St Peter's chair', *Essays*

*on Various Subjects*, 3 vols (London: Dolman, 1853), III: p. 304. I am grateful to Dr Brian Murray for this information.

5 C. D. Williams, *Boudica and her Stories: Narrative Transformations of a Warrior Queen* (Newark: University of Delaware Press, 2009), p. 176.
6 See www.catholic.org/saints/saint.php?saint_id=609, accessed 2 April 2014.
7 See Schaeffer, *Women*, pp. 3–5.
8 For more on this, see S. Goldhill, *The Buried Life of Things* (Cambridge: Cambridge University Press, 2015), pp. 34–5.
9 N. J. Higham, *(Re-)Reading Bede: The Ecclesiastical History in Context* (London: Routledge, 2006), pp. 32–40.
10 T. Claydon, *Europe and the Making of England, 1660–1760* (Cambridge: Cambridge University Press, 2007), ch. 2.
11 J.-L. Quantin, *The Church of England and Christian Antiquity: The Construction of a Confessional Identity in the Seventeenth Century* (Oxford: Oxford University Press, 2009).
12 W. L. Alexander, *The Ancient British Church* (1852; London: Religious Tract Society, 1889), p. 67.
13 J. Yeowell, *Chronicles of the Ancient British Church* (London: J. Gladding, 1847), pp. 14–16.
14 For an overview see F. Heal, 'What can King Lucius do for you? The Reformation and the early British church', *English Historical Review*, 120 (2005), 593–614.
15 J. Williams (Ab Ithel), *The Church of England Independent of the Church of Rome in All Ages* (London: W. E. Painter etc., 1836), p. 4.
16 These arguments are summarised in W. T. Gidney, *History of the London Society for Promoting Christianity among the Jews* (London, 1908), pp. 14–15, and in Alexander, *British Church*, p. 34. See also Yeowell, *Chronicles*, pp. 17–28.
17 Gidney, *History*, p. 14.
18 See Claydon, *Europe*, pp. 284–93.
19 For Caractacus's capture, see Tacitus, *The Annals*, trans. A. J. Church and W. J. Brodribb (1869; Mineola: Dover Publications, 2006), pp. 264–7.
20 E. Stillingfleet, *Origines Britannicae, or, the Antiquities of the British Churches* (London: Henry Mortlock, 1685), p. 4.
21 *Ibid.*, p. 28.
22 Claydon, *Europe*, pp. 110–15.
23 R. M. Soldevila, *Martial, Book IV: A Commentary* (Leiden: Brill, 2006), p. 41.
24 N. M. Kay, *Martial, Book XI: A Commentary* (London: Duckworth, 1985), p. 185.
25 T. Burgess, *Christ, and not St Peter, the Rock of the Christian Church; and St Paul, the Founder of the Church in Britain* (Carmarthen: J. Evans, 1812).
26 M. Wheeler, *The Old Enemies: Catholic and Protestant in Nineteenth-Century English Culture* (Cambridge: Cambridge University Press, 2006), ch. 1.
27 F. Thackeray, *Researches into the Ecclesiastical and Political State of Ancient Britain under the Roman Emperors* (London: Thomas Cadell, 1843).
28 W. L. Bowles, *Pudens and Claudia of St. Paul: On the Earliest Introduction of the Christian Faith to These Islands, through Claudia, certainly a British Lady, Supposed Daughter of Caractacus* (3rd edn, Bristol: [n.p.], 1839).
29 J. W. Marston, rev. Leon Litvack, 'Bowles, William Lisle (1762–1850)', *Oxford Dictionary of National Biography* (Oxford: Oxford University Press, 2004), online edition.

30 Bowles, *Pudens and Claudia*, p. 9.
31 *Ibid.*, pp. 4–5.
32 *Ibid.*, p. 10.
33 W. L. Bowles, *The Plain Bible, and the Protestant Church in England* (Bath: Richard Cruttwell, 1818), p. 38.
34 *Ibid.*, p. 81.
35 *Baner y Groes*, 1 (1855), 109. For Welsh Tractarianism, see John Boneham, 'Isaac Williams and Welsh Tractarian theology', in Stewart J. Brown and Peter B. Nockles (eds), *The Oxford Movement: Europe and the Wider World, 1830–1930* (Cambridge: Cambridge University Press, 2012), pp. 37–55.
36 'Memoir of William Hales, D.D.', *British Magazine*, 1 (1832), 554.
37 W. Hales, *An Essay on the Origin and Purity of the Primitive Church of the British Isles* (London: Rivingtons, 1819).
38 R. Bromwich (ed.), *Trioedd Ynys Prydein* (Cardiff: University of Wales Press, 1961).
39 T. Williams (ed.), *Iolo Manuscripts, a Selection of Ancient Welsh Manuscripts… from the collection made by the late Edward Williams, Iolo Morganwg…* (Llandovery: The Welsh MSS. Society, 1847), p. 538 mentions Eigen as a daughter of Caractacus, but the provenance of the manuscript is questionable.
40 Hales, *Essay*, p. 104.
41 R. Rees, *An Essay on the Welsh Saints of the Primitive Churches* (London: Longmans, etc., 1836), p. 79. However, Rees did not fully accept that the Bran story was 'a modern forgery'.
42 R. W. Morgan, *St Paul in Britain; or the Origin of British as Opposed to Papal Christianity* (Oxford and London: J. H. Parker, 1861).
43 For Morgan's increasingly unorthodox beliefs see R. L. Brown, *Parochial Lives: A Study in the Nineteenth-Century Welsh Church* (Llanrwst: Gwasg Carreg Gwalch, 2002), pp. 131–64.
44 J. Williams, *Claudia and Pudens, an Attempt to Show that Claudia, Mentioned in St Paul's Second Epistle to Timothy, was a British Princess* (Llandovery: William Rees, 1848), p. 39.
45 *Ibid.*, p. 27.
46 *Ibid.*, p. viii.
47 *Ibid.*, p. 56.
48 R. Hingley, *The Recovery of Roman Britain 1586–1906* (Oxford: Oxford University Press, 2008), p. 185.
49 Williams, *Claudia*, p. 25.
50 *Ibid.*, p. 40.
51 *Ibid.*, p. 41.
52 Alexander, *British Church*, p. 111.
53 *Ibid.*, p. 113.
54 See R. W. Rhodes, *The Lion and the Cross: Early Christianity in Victorian Novels* (Columbus: Ohio State University Press, 1995); M. Ledger-Lomas, 'First-century fiction in the late nineteenth century', *Nineteenth-Century Contexts*, 31 (2009), 59–72.
55 A. J. Church, *The Burning of Rome, a Story of Nero's Days* (London: Seeley, 1891); F. W. Farrar, *Darkness and Dawn, or Scenes in the Days of Nero, an Historic Tale* (London: Longmans, 1892).
56 Farrar, *Darkness*, p. 568.

57 *Ibid.*, p. 76.
58 Tacitus, *Annals*, trans. Church and Brodribb.
59 Church, *Burning*, p. 75.
60 Williams, *Claudia*, p. 52.
61 *Ibid.*, pp. 42–3. Williams suggested that Timotheus proselytised in Britain.
62 This is another Welsh variation on her name. See 'Claudia, or Gwladys Ruffina', in T. J. Llewelyn Prichard, *The Heroines of Welsh History* (London: W. and F. G. Cash, 1854), pp. 175–8.
63 Powell, private memorandum.
64 See Jasmine Donahaye, *Whose People? Wales, Israel, Palestine* (Cardiff: University of Wales Press, 2012).
65 See M. Vandrei, 'A Victorian invention? Thomas Thornycroft's "Boadicea Group" and the idea of historical culture in Britain', *Historical Journal*, 57 (2014), 485–508.

4

# Patrick

*Andrew R. Holmes*

SCHOLARSHIP ON THE INTERPRETATION of Ireland's patron saint in the nineteenth century has focused exclusively on Catholic or Church of Ireland historians.¹ This is entirely understandable as both sets of writers used Patrick as a means of demonstrating, for instance, apostolic succession and the right of either Church to describe itself as the true Church of Ireland. It ought to be remembered that Catholics made up around 75% of the Irish population whereas the minority Church of Ireland was the Church as by law established until January 1871, its membership largely drawn from the descendants of English settlers in the early modern period. By contrast, Presbyterians in Ireland were not part of the established Church, rejected diocesan episcopacy and apostolic succession, and traced their origins to the influx of Scottish settlers to the northern province of Ulster in the seventeenth century, an area that remained their heartland and where they constituted the majority of Protestants.² Throughout the nineteenth century, an Irish-Scottish identity was asserted by Presbyterians as a means of promoting religious reform, fostering denominational pride, and asserting their loyalty to the United Kingdom.³

These comments suggest that Presbyterians should not have been concerned with Patrick and the early Irish Church. However, from the 1830s onwards, a variety of Presbyterian writers grappled with Ireland's patron saint and in so doing used Patrick as a means of contributing to contemporary debates about historical scholarship, Church organisation, missionary activity, and identity politics. A study of Presbyterian interpretations of Patrick in the nineteenth century offers a suggestive perspective on the broader theme of this volume by examining a community that had no tradition of discussing saints before the 1830s. As demonstrated below, in comparison with Catholic and Church of Ireland writers, Presbyterians were relaxed in their reading of Patrick but were nevertheless keen to demonstrate that their Patrick was different from those offered by other Churches. Following the eminent Church of Ireland scholar of the seventeenth century, Archbishop James Ussher (1581–1656), they rejected Catholic claims that Patrick had a papal commission and the popular devotions that surrounded sainthood. This 'Protestant' Patrick was essential to the effort to convert Catholic Ireland to evangelical Christianity in the nineteenth century by showing that evangelicalism was the true descendant of the early Irish Church rather than the increasingly Roman Catholic Church of Victorian Ireland. Yet though Presbyterians accepted Patrick's independence from Rome and his essentially evangelical doctrine, they rejected the notion that Patrick was a diocesan bishop and the High Church claim of apostolic succession. As a consequence, the interpretation of Patrick raises a number of important issues about what mattered to Irish Presbyterians in the nineteenth century. It also offers a means of assessing their multiple identities and especially the balance between their origins in seventeenth-century Scottish immigration and their Irish identity. Indeed, Scottish interest in Patrick will be an important theme in what follows.

To address these themes, the following chapter is divided into three sections. The first begins by describing interpretations of Patrick by Protestant and Catholic writers in the early modern period and how the rise of evangelicalism in the early nineteenth century stimulated scholarly interest in the saint. Evangelicalism also revived Presbyterian self-confidence and denominational identity, and section two charts the development of a distinctive Presbyterian interpretation of Patrick. As demonstrated in the final section, this effort did not remain the preserve of scholars but was closely connected with the attempt to bring about the conversion of Irish Catholics, an endeavour that was fitfully supported by Scottish Presbyterians.

## The early modern Patrick and James Seaton Reid

The religious revolution of the sixteenth century transformed the understanding of sainthood and the popular devotion that surrounded individual saints. In response to the Protestant challenge, Catholic writers described Patrick as a Moses-like patriarch and emphasised the perpetual loyalty of the Irish to the papacy, thus creating a coherent vision of faith and fatherland by the early seventeenth century. As a consequence of their efforts, Patrick's feast day (17 March) was included in the Roman breviary of 1631 and the revised Roman calendar of 1632.[4] In response, Ussher sought to demonstrate that the minority Protestant Church of Ireland was not a colonial Church but the legitimate descendant of the early Irish Church, which had only finally succumbed to Roman influence in the twelfth century. Like Edward Stillingfleet (1635–99) in Martha Vandrei's chapter on Claudia Rufina, Ussher claimed that the 'aboriginal' Church in Ireland pre-dated not just later papal missions, but the papacy itself as an institution. In *A Discourse of the Religion Anciently Professed by the Irish and Brittish* (1622), he argued that early Irish Christianity was Bible-based and its theology grace-centred, while the Church was independent of both the papacy and Britain.[5] Ussher's work would dominate Patrician scholarship for the next 150 years, though the eighteenth century witnessed a less polemical approach to Patrick and he became 'one of the few historical figures to command the respect of both the Catholic and Protestant religious communities in Ireland' between 1750 and 1800.[6]

Throughout the seventeenth and eighteenth centuries, Patrick was ignored by Presbyterian writers with only two exceptions. Andrew Stewart (d. 1671), the

Minister of Donaghadee between 1646 and 1671, offered an extended Ussher-esque discussion of Patrick in a largely forgotten manuscript that was only partly published in 1866, and there was a brief mention of the saint in William Crawford's *History of Ireland* (1783).[7] Irish Presbyterians were instead more concerned with modern events, especially the arrival of Scottish ministers in Ulster from 1613 and the formation of the first presbytery on Irish soil in June 1642. The most influential discussion of this theme was offered by Patrick Adair (1625?–94) in his manuscript history of Presbyterianism from 1623 to 1670. Adair had been installed as Minister at Cairncastle in east County Antrim in May 1646 and fulfilled a variety of important roles for Presbyterians, including leading delegations that welcomed William of Orange to England in 1689 and to Ireland in 1690. His so-called 'True Narrative of the rise and progress of the Presbyterian Church in Ireland' sought to demonstrate that Scottish Presbyterians were the providential means of converting and improving Ireland.[8] Though an edition of this work was not published until 1866, it was well known to late seventeenth-century Presbyterians and was used extensively by James Kirkpatrick (c. 1676–1743) in his 1713 work, *An Historical Essay upon the Loyalty of Presbyterians*.[9]

Scholarly interest in Patrick was stimulated by the upheaval of the 1790s. Within European culture more generally, writers appealed to tradition and history in response to the threat or reality of revolution. Amongst Irish Protestants, the politicisation of the 1790s and the bloody rebellion of 1798 acted as a catalyst for the growth of evangelicalism. Conversionist religion was seen as a panacea for the problems of Irish society and stimulated Church of Ireland interest in Patrick as a means of engaging Catholics in order to convert them.[10] The rapid expansion of evangelicalism deeply affected Presbyterians.[11] Indeed, the most important contribution to Protestant historiography in this period was James Seaton Reid's *History of the Presbyterian Church in Ireland*, volume one of which was published in 1834. This remains the standard work on the subject and reflected the growing self-confidence that evangelicalism gave to Presbyterians. Reid (1798–1851) was successively Minister of the Synod of Ulster (1819–37), Professor of Ecclesiastical History, Church Government, and Pastoral Theology for the denomination (1837–41), and Regius Professor of Ecclesiastical and Civil History at the University of Glasgow (1841–51).[12] Reid devoted little more than a page to the early Church in Ireland as he was concerned at the outset with contrasting the failure of the English Reformation in Tudor Ireland and the comparative success of Scottish Presbyterianism in Ulster. Yet his comments established some of the principal themes of Presbyterian interpretations of Patrick. Despite the controversies of the early modern period, Reid maintained that there was 'considerable unanimity' amongst scholars that the early Irish Church, 'though not free from error, differed most materially and for a length of time, from that of Rome'.

> The free and commanded use of the Scriptures – the inculcation of the doctrines of grace and of the efficacy of the sacrifice and intercession of Christ, without any allusion to the mass, to transubstantiation, purgatory, human merit or prayers for the dead – the

diversity in the forms of celebrating divine worship – the rejection of the papal supremacy – the marriage of the clergy – the scriptural character of the early bishops, each having the charge of only one parish, and being labourers 'in word and doctrine' – the Presbyterial order of the Culdees and their singular piety and zeal – all these important points of doctrine and discipline which were maintained and practised in the ancient Irish Church, clearly indicate its opposition to the papal system.[13]

According to Reid, this initial purity and independence were gradually undermined until the Irish Church was completely assimilated by Rome in the twelfth century, an event presided over by an English Pope, Adrian IV, and accompanied by the Norman invasion of Ireland.

Reid's interpretation was based on Ussher's *Discourse*, but it also drew upon John Jamieson's *Historical Account of the Ancient Culdees of Iona* (1811). Jamieson (1759–1838) was a minister of one of the Presbyterian secession Churches in Scotland, a devoted evangelical, and a significant scholar and philologist.[14] The use of Jamieson draws attention to Reid's attempt to use the Scottish origins of Irish Presbyterianism in the seventeenth century as a blueprint for the reform of the Synod of Ulster in his own day and as a means of creating Presbyterian unity amongst his co-religionists on either side of the North Channel.[15] Following Adair rather than Stewart, it was Presbyterian ministers such as Robert Blair (1593–1666) and John Livingstone (1603–72) who were model pastors and missionaries, not Patrick. This attempt to return to seventeenth-century Presbyterian values was a key component of the movement for religious reform from the late 1820s onwards. It led to the unification of the Synod of Ulster and the Secession Synod to form the present-day General Assembly of the Presbyterian Church in Ireland in 1840 and to the remarkable revival of religion that swept Presbyterian Ulster in 1859.

## Patrick and Presbyterian historians

Despite this focus on the seventeenth century, Reid's concern with historical scholarship, coupled with the more general interest in mission and identity, led Presbyterian writers to consider Patrick and the early Irish Church in more detail. An important stimulus came in the late 1830s when Archibald Boyd (1803–83) and other High Church episcopalians in north-west Ulster attempted from the pulpit and in print to unchurch Presbyterians. This High Church assault drew forth a series of responses from Presbyterian ministers, including *Presbyterianism Defended* (1839) and the more substantial *Plea of Presbytery* (1841).[16] The controversy was important in stimulating Presbyterian self-confidence against the established Church and their own Scottish Presbyterian identity.[17] It also encouraged Irish Presbyterians to offer a more extensive interpretation of the early history of the Church that would lead to significant statements on Patrick. In *Presbyterianism Defended*, W. D. Killen (1806–1902) claimed that early Irish bishops were not the same as diocesan bishops and had only authority over a local congregation. Following Jamieson and Ussher, Killen stated 'that the gospel was first preached in Ireland by presbyterian ministers' and suspected that Patrick himself was a Presbyterian.[18]

At the time of publication, Killen was Minister of Raphoe in County Donegal, but in July 1841 he was unanimously appointed as Reid's successor as Professor of Church History, Ecclesiastical Government, and Pastoral Theology for the General Assembly.[19] He spent the rest of his career in Belfast and became President of the Presbyterian College, which was opened in 1853. He published a series of works on the history and constitution of the Church, some of which became standard texts for Presbyterians on both sides of the Atlantic – *The Ancient Church: Its History, Doctrine, Worship, and Constitution* (1859), *The Old Catholic Church* (1871), *The Ecclesiastical History of Ireland* (1875), *The Ignatian Epistles Entirely Spurious* (1886), and *The Framework of the Church* (1890). Killen's interest in the early Irish Church was shared by other Presbyterian historians, most notably Thomas Witherow and James Heron. Witherow (1824–90) was a Presbyterian evangelical, Professor of Church History at Magee College, Derry, between 1865 and 1890, and author of many well-known historical works, including *Derry and Enniskillen* (1873).[20] His contribution to Patrician studies was through substantial articles in the *British and Foreign Evangelical Review* and the *British Quarterly Review*.[21] Heron (1836–1918) had been a minister in various parts of Ulster before becoming Professor of Church History at the Presbyterian College, Belfast, in 1889. Before his death in 1918, he published several works on Church history, including *The Celtic Church in Ireland* (1898), *A Short History of Puritanism* (1908), and *The Evolution of Latin Christianity* (1919).[22]

All three writers asserted the need to employ contemporary sources, such as Patrick's autobiographical 'Confession', rather than using the subsequent lives of Patrick produced from the seventh century onwards. Killen stated that these bore 'abundant evidences of their monkish origin. They exhibit such credulity, such a want of common sense, such chronological blundering, and such recklessness of assertion, that they are nearly worthless as historical documents'.[23] With tongue firmly in cheek, Witherow remarked that it was 'quite evident that the farther we depart from Patrick's own time, the more is known about him'.[24] A commitment to primary sources and scepticism about tradition are characteristics of modern historical method, but it is clear in the case of Killen that denominational concerns controlled his interpretation and that the Derry controversy was a formative experience for him.[25] Writing in 1897 the American writer Charles Casey Starbuck (1827–1909) described Killen as 'a presbyterian High Churchman' and 'one of the most thorough grain'.[26] Witherow and Heron were less strident than Killen. Witherow believed that the disinterested pursuit of the truth was vital in the study of Patrick.

> Historical criticism alone can restore to us the real Patrick of the fifth century. The moss of ages needs to be removed with the chisel and the mallet, that we may look once more on the bare unadorned monument of a great name. In the legendary past he stands out as a mythical personage grandly dim – a magician rather than a minister; but this more critical age will prefer to look at him in the true light of a humble Christian and a successful

missionary, whose doctrine and life and heart were sound in the main, and whose errors were the errors of his times.[27]

Witherow applied the same criticisms to the description of Colum Cille / Columba in *The Monks of the West from St. Benedict to St. Bernard* (1860–77), by Charles Forbes René de Montalembert (1810–70). Montalembert's interpretation was condemned by Witherow because he did not meet the demands of modern historical criticism – he was 'deficient in accuracy'; he failed to 'draw the line between fact and fiction with a stern and a firm hand'; much of his material was derived from later and unreliable writers; 'his very facts are presented through a coloured medium which did not originally belong to them; and the product is sent out to the world as if it were a record of recognised and admitted truth'.[28] An unbiased interpretation of the facts was also a constant theme in Heron's *The Celtic Church in Ireland*, the most extensive treatment of Patrick offered by an Irish Presbyterian. 'But ... to treat the facts thus – to ignore them when they are inconvenient and do not suit our theory, or to twist and colour them to make them conform to our modem Church patterns – is not to write history, but to pervert it, and to make real insight into ancient affairs and institutions impossible.'[29] As several other chapters in this volume show, such denunciations were characteristic of Protestant scholars who, while sometimes averse to canonisation in principle, nevertheless pared away layers of 'monkish' accretion in their curiosity about the remarkable individuals that gave rise to later mythmaking.[30]

As suggested by these quotations, Presbyterian writers were openly critical of aspects of the early Irish Church, including the use of the sign of the cross, celibacy, asceticism, auricular confession, the administration of eucharist, and the invocation of the saints.[31] On the basis of a self-confessed commitment to critical scholarship, Presbyterians concluded that Patrick was probably evangelical in doctrine and the early Irish Church similar to Presbyterianism in organisation. The prominent Presbyterian antiquarian and historian W. T. Latimer (1842–1919) summarised the views of Presbyterians on Patrick's doctrine in his *History of the Irish Presbyterians* (1902):

> In Patrick's writings there is no allusion to Mary-worship, or to Purgatory, or to Transubstantiation. They contain no prayers to saints; and they appeal to the Scriptures as the only standard of faith and of morals. The necessity of possessing a renewed heart and enlightened understanding is pointed out with great distinctness, and Christ is shown to be the only Mediator between God and man.[32]

In terms of the status and polity of the early Irish Church, Presbyterian writers were agreed that Patrick did not have a papal commission and that the Irish Church was the last in western Christendom to succumb to Roman influence. Heron considered that the question of whether Patrick received a commission from Rome was 'not one of any vital importance' and that no one 'should change his Church principles in consequence'. Though vital issues were at stake, 'it is a matter to be determined solely in the light of the evidence available on the subject. Prejudice in favour of some particular Church cannot justify one-sided treatment of the evidence. The one question is, In what direction does the weight of the evidence point?' On that basis, Heron concluded that the evidence clearly demonstrated that 'the independence of the early Irish Church with respect to Rome is one of the most indubitable facts of history'.[33]

Heron also claimed that 'in no modern Church have we an exact transcript of the organisation of the old Celtic Church', and his comments reflected the relaxed attitude of Presbyterians in general to the polity of Patrick's Church.[34] Yet this attitude concealed a conviction that their Church organisation better reflected the practice of Patrick and his Church than those of Episcopalians and Catholics. Indeed Presbyterian writers were especially scathing in their criticism of any interpretation that upheld apostolic succession and unchurched Presbyterians. For Presbyterians the distinction between the visible Church and the invisible Church of the elect in Christ remained fundamental, and so too did the final authority of the Bible in determining the organisation of the visible Church. The Presbyterian minister and future President of Queen's College, Belfast, Thomas Hamilton (1842–1926) noted in 1886: 'It is the Church which conforms to the pattern laid down there, and not the Church which corresponds most nearly to the Church of St. Patrick, which is the true apostolic Church. The authority or example of a Paul or a Peter is worth ten thousand times more than those of all the saints in the Romish calendar.' Immediately, however, Hamilton pointed out that if 'any stress is to be laid upon Patrick's teaching, or upon the Church organization which he set up, it is plain that neither Romanism nor Protestant Episcopacy can claim the benefit of either'.[35]

The idea of a primitive, proto-Presbyterian Church that was subsequently overrun by Roman envoys and practices was attractive to nineteenth-century Presbyterians in both Ireland and Scotland. For many Presbyterian evangelicals in Scotland, the 'achievements of the Reformation represented the return to a native or national tradition, the rejection of an alien tyranny that had suppressed ... Scotland's true character as a Presbyterian nation enjoying the benefits of civil and religious liberty'.[36] What they had in mind was the mission established by Columba at Iona and the subsequent spread of Christianity through the Culdees of the seventh to eleventh centuries. For Presbyterian scholars in the nineteenth century, these communities of clergy who differed in organisation and ethos from later monastic orders were further evidence of the similarity between early Christianity in Ireland and Scotland and later Presbyterianism. This interpretation of the character of the Celtic Church was an important aspect of Presbyterian identity in global terms. At the first meeting in 1877 of the Alliance of the Reformed Churches holding the Presbyterian System (later the World Alliance of Reformed Churches), Peter Lorimer (1812–79), a Presbyterian professor in London, noted 'that the early Church of St. Patrick, Columba, and Columbanus, was far more nearly allied in its fundamental principles of order and discipline to the Presbyterian than to the Episcopalian Churches of modern times'. In his contribution to the same debate on the desirability of studying the history of Presbyterianism, Thomas M'Lauchlan (1816–86) stated: 'Through the Scoto-Irish Church they could trace the principles of Presbyterianism further back in Scotland and Ireland than in any other part of the world.' M'Lauchlan was eager to inform foreign delegates that Scottish Presbyterianism was not a product solely of the Reformation and that 'they could trace back the principles that governed the Presbyterian Churches to the seventh century'.[37] M'Lauchlan was a prominent Free Church scholar who was Minister of St Columba's Gaelic congregation in Edinburgh. In *The Early Scottish Church* (1865), M'Lauchlan followed Ussher's interpretation of Patrick as a British-born missionary who had no papal commission and did not establish a hierarchical Church.[38] McLauchlan's work was received with acclamation as 'the completest and most satisfactory history ever yet produced of "The Early Scottish Church"'.[39]

## Patrick and Presbyterian missions

In addition to these theological and ecclesiological issues, Patrick was described by Presbyterians as a model missionary and was employed as a means of encouraging support for the conversion of Catholic Ireland. Once again, issues of identity were to the fore and there was a significant Scottish-Irish dimension to this endeavour. Though fulsome in its praise for Reid in general, his *History* was criticised by Presbyterian evangelicals in Scotland for devoting so little attention to the early Church in Ireland. An anonymous reviewer embarked on a lengthy discourse about the Celtic Church in order to address popular prejudices against Presbyterianism and to promote evangelism amongst Irish Catholics. The review concluded by recognising the contradiction between the purity of Patrick's Church and the religion of the Catholic majority in Ireland in the nineteenth century.[40] Another Scottish writer observed in 1835 that God had recently reminded British Protestants of their 'long neglect' of Ireland by making 'these unreclaimed lands a continual source of enmity and embarrassment'. They should not expect peace in Ireland 'till the light of the Reformation has been fully carried into every parish and hamlet of that country'.[41] The desire of Scottish evangelicals to convert and civilise Catholic Ireland was eagerly seized upon by Irish Presbyterians. The Home Mission of the Synod of Ulster sent an address to the members of the Church of Scotland in 1833 asking for funds, individual ministers undertook fundraising trips later in the decade, societies were established in Scotland to support the Irish missions in the 1840s, and financial contributions from there constituted a significant proportion of the funds available to missions in Ireland.[42] At a special meeting of the Synod to discuss missionary activity in September 1833, speeches on missionary work amongst Catholics in Ireland were delivered by two Church of Scotland ministers, Duncan Macfarlane of Renfrew (1793–1853) and Norman McLeod of Campsie (1812–72), the noted Gaelic scholar.[43]

The concern of Presbyterians in Ireland and Scotland to promote the evangelisation of Irish Catholics meant that Presbyterian scholarship on Patrick was communicated to a wider audience. Patrick seemed to embody the missionary ideals that Presbyterians believed would win Irish Catholics to the evangelical version of Christianity. Witherow noted that Patrick's credentials as a missionary were not based on learning, piety, position or supposed miracles: 'Humility, unselfishness, zeal for God, burning love for human souls, and a courage that does not quail in sight of death, show themselves everywhere throughout the writings of this fine old Christian missionary.'[44] For Killen, Patrick was a simple man called by God to faithfully convert the Irish from paganism to Christianity. 'Though destitute of the advantages of a finished education, he was mighty in the Scriptures; he had an excellent command of the native language; he had a heart to feel and a hand to relieve; he was wholly devoted to his work; and his natural eloquence soon enchained crowds of admiring auditors.'[45] Irish Presbyterian writers referred to a vision attributed to Patrick by Jocelin of Furness in the twelfth century about a light of salvation rising in Ulidia – that is, the northern province of Ulster in which Presbyterians where overwhelmingly concentrated. 'May Patrick's vision be realised in our time. May there go forth from Ulidia (from Ulster) to Munster, from the north to the south – not spreading clouds of darkness, but the very light of life; not hate, but love; not notes of war, but peace through the Prince of peace.'[46] Witherow made telling reference to this vision in a public lecture at Magee College, Derry, in November 1866. The lecture was entitled 'St Patrick and Missions to Ireland' and he sought to apply lessons from a study of Patrick to contemporary Presbyterian missionary activity amongst Irish Catholics. He identified as one of the principal obstacles to the success of such activity the 'want of sympathy with our fellow countrymen' and noted that 'two hundred and fifty years should have naturalised us on Irish soil, yet to this hour most of us feel as if we were only Scots in Ireland'. He continued: 'We ought to remember that Ireland, not Scotland, is our-birth spot and our home. We are not Scots, but Irishmen. Without casting from us the traditions of our origin – traditions of which no great people ever can be ashamed – let us rather strive to engraft upon them the traditions of that other country which we have added as our own and which has nourished us at its breast.'[47]

In this context, Patrick was a key means by which Presbyterians sought to demonstrate their Irish identity. Specifically, Presbyterians wanted to demonstrate to Irish Catholics that Presbyterian evangelicalism best reflected the doctrine and practice of Patrick and the early Irish Church. Such interpretations were mediated through the General Assembly's Mission to Roman Catholics, which gradually became known as the Irish Mission.[48] This organisation was responsible for evangelistic strategy and publicising the work of the mission, both of which involved the distribution through colporteurs of cheap literature in the form of tracts, pamphlets, and periodicals such as *Plain Words Spoken in Behalf of the Ancient Apostolic Faith*, *The Key of Truth*, and *The Christian Irishman*. Especially significant in this literary endeavour was Hamilton Magee (1824–1902), who was born in Belfast but spent his entire ministerial career in the south of Ireland, first as the Minister of Killala in Mayo from 1849 and then as Superintendent of the Dublin Mission from 1854.[49] Magee attempted to indigenise Presbyterianism in Ireland by drawing attention to a Patrick who was neither a Romanist nor a ritualist, but a type of evangelical who presided over a non-hierarchical Church, teaching doctrines that were eventually carried to Iona by Colum Cille and diffused by the Culdees. Protestants ought to observe 17 March in prayer as 'it enables Scriptural Protestants to put in, before the country and the world, their indisputable claim to be the true inheritors and representatives both of St Patrick's Scriptural creed and of his Christian patriotism'.[50]

Magee edited the Mission's periodicals, which partly aimed at educating Presbyterians and Irish Catholics in this interpretation of the early Irish Church, and the Irish Mission also published a number of pamphlets on Patrick.[51] Those who wrote for the Irish Mission had a naive confidence in the ability of objective historical analysis to bring peace to Ireland and to promote the conversion of Catholics. For instance, W. B. Kirkpatrick (1802–82), Minister of Mary's Abbey congregation in Dublin, contributed a series of short articles on 'facts' of Irish history to *Plain Words*, revised versions of which were published as *Chapters in Irish History* (1875).[52] In the preface, Kirkpatrick observed that to the lack of historical knowledge 'are to be traced many of those prejudices and animosities which have proved so long and so unhappily obstructive to social order, and to national progress'. Though he suggested that a form of self-government for Ireland could be beneficial, his interpretation of Irish history was not nationalist.[53] The 'facts' that Kirkpatrick identified included the independence of the ancient Irish Church from Rome, that Ireland had been given to England by Pope Adrian IV, that Cromwell had the best interests of Ireland at heart, and that William of Orange upheld the rights of individual conscience. Confidence in intellectual preparation for conversion was shared by Samuel Andrews (d. 1901), Minister of a congregation in Portadown and later of Westport in County Mayo. Andrews welcomed the development of a 'science of history' and believed that the 'genuine materials of history collected by disinterested scholars, shall in future be possessed by the Irish people, causing both the discontent arising from misconception and the arrogance of which is fed on falsehood, to vanish from our land'.[54] All Presbyterians were confident in the ultimate conversion of Irish Catholics to evangelical religion, a confidence based on an optimistic vision of the eventual conversion of the entire world.[55]

There was a transatlantic interest in evangelistic work in Catholic Ireland that was stimulated in large measure by the unparalleled emigration of Irish Catholics in the wake of the Famine. The English members of the Evangelical Alliance decided to hold a day of prayer for the evangelisation of Ireland in March 1873.[56] Later that year, the Minister of Lurgan congregation, Lowry E. Berkeley (1823–82), delivered an address on the topic to the Sixth General Council of the Alliance in New York. Berkeley declared that 'Ireland was once full of the Gospel', that Irish missionaries such as Colum Cille 'held forth the light of truth in multitudes of places as well as in Iona', and though Ireland had eventually submitted to the papacy, 'the day of its redemption draweth nigh'.[57] The day of prayer seems to have been popular and another was arranged for St Patrick's Day, 17 March 1874. Magee was hopeful that it would be even more successful owing to the recent evangelistic missions of D. L. Moody and I. D. Sankey in Britain and Ireland. Magee firmly believed, 'If our Roman Catholic countrymen were all to come back to the creed of St. Patrick, the "religious difficulty" would have vanished for ever in Ireland: there would be no place for the religious dissensions which have been the weakness and disgrace of our country.' Magee addressed the concerns of some Protestants that they would be praying to Patrick by pointing out that they would instead be praying 'to the God who in great mercy sent St. Patrick to our shores; and who can raise up, as it pleases Him, not one but many St Patricks to bear the torch of the old Evangel over all the land, that once more "the people which walk in darkness may see a great light"; and that "they that dwell in the land of the shadow of death, upon them may the light shine".'[58] Two public meetings were held in the Metropolitan Hall, Dublin, on 17 March. The chair was taken by the Master of Chancery in Ireland, William Brooke (1796–1881), a Church of Ireland evangelical. The meetings were addressed by various Irish members of the Evangelical Alliance – including Brooke, who spoke on 'St Patrick and the old religion of Ireland'.[59] According to the *Christian Irishman*, the tradition of a day of prayer on 17 March sponsored by the Evangelical Alliance continued into the new century.

Scottish–Irish links were again prominent in this missionary activity, and the mutual indebtedness of both countries for their conversion to the gospel was a recurring theme – Scotland was converted through Colum Cille while the hope of Ireland rested on the descendants of Scottish Presbyterians who came to Ireland in the seventeenth century. In his review of Killen's *Ecclesiastical History of Ireland*, A. F. Mitchell (1822–99), Professor of Ecclesiastical History at St Andrews, asked, 'Why, when we have our days of special prayer for missions to the heathen, should we have no season of special intercession for those who are bound to us by so many endearing associations from the days of Patrick and Columba to those of Ussher and Bedell, of Blair and Livingstone?'[60] For Magee, Scottish supporters of the evangelisation of Ireland were 'repaying an ancient and almost forgotten debt' and he reminded readers that the 'kindly light of Iona was kindled by the hands of Irishmen'. Magee argued that evangelical Protestants, and Presbyterians certainly, should not feel ashamed of celebrating the life and legacy of Patrick because the Scottish Reformation 'consisted largely in the shaking off, as of a deadly incubus, by the giant hand of a quickened and united people, the accumulated superstitions of ages, and a return to the scriptural faith and simple polity of the Culdees, whose influence had never quite died out of the national heart'.[61] In 1883 the Scottish Association for Irish Missions was formed and raised £3,584 10s. 11d. in its first year.[62] To support the aims of the Scottish Association, Magee published a pamphlet, *Scotland and Ireland* (1887), in which he highlighted the providential role of Irish Presbyterianism in the extension of the gospel to all the inhabitants of Ireland, discerning that this had been God's intention when he had brought representatives of the Columban Church of Scotland back to Ireland in the early seventeenth century.[63] In 1887 a letter from the Free Church of Scotland to the Irish General Assembly claimed 'that the Irish Presbyterian Church is the bulwark of Christian truth for the North of Ireland, and worthy of the sympathy of the Protestant Churches everywhere'.[64]

Despite such efforts, it seems that Scottish support for Presbyterian missions in Ireland fluctuated over the course of the nineteenth century. In 1897 a similar communication from the Free Church expressed regret for the lack of support the Irish Church had received from Scottish congregations.[65] By the 1880s, there was significant tension between Scottish and Irish Presbyterians owing to the spread of critical attitudes towards the Bible in the Free Church. This was compounded by the ambivalent attitude of that denomination towards Home Rule for Ireland, a policy that was almost universally rejected by Irish Presbyterians.[66] This specific development reminds us that Presbyterian interpretations of Patrick in the nineteenth century were shaped by the symbiotic, sometimes antagonistic, relationship between their Irish identity and Scottish origins. Patrick was important in terms of adjudicating denominational rivalries, prompting scholarly research, and as a means of encouraging the conversion of Catholic Ireland to evangelical religion. But for Presbyterians, Patrick was always eclipsed by the memory of their seventeenth-century forebears. This account of their origins was of much more value because it was better able to articulate the principles that mattered to them in the nineteenth century – evangelical Calvinism, the Presbyterian origins of religious and civil liberty in Britain and Ireland, and the distinctiveness of Ulster-Scots within the United Kingdom. In some respects, Patrick was too Irish for them. Unlike the patron saint who was not born in Ireland but became more Irish than the Irish, the problem for Presbyterians was that many believed they were in Ireland but not of it.

## Notes

1 Daniel A. Binchy, 'Patrick and his biographers ancient and modern', *Studia Hibernica*, 2 (1962), 7–173; Fergal Grannell, 'Early Irish ecclesiastical studies', in Michael Hurley (ed.), *Irish Anglicanism 1869–1969: Essays on the Role of Anglicanism in Irish Life* (Dublin: A. Figgis, 1970), pp. 39–50; Jacqueline R. Hill, 'The Church of Ireland and perceptions of Irish Church history, c.1790–1869', in Terence Dooley (ed.), *Ireland's Polemical Past: Views of Irish history in Honour of R. V. Comerford* (Dublin: University College Dublin Press, 2010), pp. 9–31.

2 The best overview of the history of Irish Presbyterians remains R. F. G. Holmes, *Our Irish Presbyterian Heritage* (Belfast: Publications Committee of the Presbyterian Church in Ireland, 1985).

3 Andrew R. Holmes, 'Presbyterian religion, historiography and Ulster Scots identity, c. 1800 to 1914', *Historical Journal*, 52 (2009), 615–40; 'Irish Presbyterian commemorations of their Scottish past, c. 1830 to 1914', in James McConnel and Frank Ferguson (eds), *Ireland and Scotland in the Nineteenth Century* (Dublin: Four Courts Press, 2009), pp. 48–61; 'The Scottish Reformations and the origin of religious and civil liberty in Britain and Ireland: Presbyterian interpretations, c. 1800–1860', in Peter Nockles and Vivienne Westbrook (eds), *Reinventing the Reformation in the Nineteenth Century*, Special Issue of the Bulletin of the John Rylands Library, 90 (2014), 135–54.

4 Bernadette Cunningham and Raymond Gillespie, '"The most adaptable of saints": the cult of St Patrick in the seventeenth century', *Archivium Hibernicum*, 49 (1995), 82–104.

5   Alan Ford, *James Ussher: Theology, History, and Politics in Early-Modern Ireland and England* (Oxford: Oxford University Press, 2009), pp. 119–32.
6   Clare O'Halloran, '"The island of saints and scholars": views of the early Church and sectarian politics in late-eighteenth century Ireland', *Eighteenth-Century Ireland*, 5 (1990), 7. See also Bridget McCormack, *Perceptions of St Patrick in Eighteenth-Century Ireland* (Dublin: Four Courts Press, 2000).
7   A modern edition of Stewart's history has been prepared for publication: Robert Armstrong, Andrew R. Holmes, Scott Spurlock, and Patrick Walsh (eds), *Presbyterian History in Ireland: Two Seventeenth-Century Narratives by Patrick Adair and Andrew Stewart* (Belfast: Ulster Historical Foundation, 2016). William Crawford, *A History of Ireland from the Earliest Period to the Present Time: In a Series of Letters Addressed to William Hamilton, Esq.*, 2 vols (Strabane: John Bellew, 1783), I: pp. 60–3.
8   *A True Narrative of the Rise and Progress of the Presbyterian Church in Ireland (1623–1670) by the Rev. Patrick Adair, Minister of Belfast. Also, the History of the Church in Ireland since the Scots were Naturalized*, ed. W. D. Killen (Belfast: Aitchison, 1866).
9   James Kirkpatrick, *An Historical Essay upon the Loyalty of Presbyterians in Great-Britain and Ireland from the Reformation to this Present Year 1713* ([Belfast], 1713).
10  For evangelicalism more generally, see David Hempton and Myrtle Hill, *Evangelical Protestantism in Ulster Society 1740–1890* (London: Routledge, 1992); for Church of Ireland writers, Hill, 'Church of Ireland', pp. 13–22.
11  Andrew R. Holmes, *The Shaping of Ulster Presbyterian Belief and Practice, 1770 to 1840* (Oxford: Oxford University Press, 2006).
12  Robert Allen, *James Seaton Reid: A Centenary Biography* (Belfast: W. Mullan, 1951).
13  James S. Reid, *History of the Presbyterian Church in Ireland*, ed. William D. Killen, 3 vols (2nd edn, Belfast: Mullan, 1867), I: p. 2.
14  T. W. Bayne, rev. J. D. Haigh, 'Jamieson, John (1759–1838)', *Oxford Dictionary of National Biography* (Oxford: Oxford University Press, 2004), online edition.
15  Holmes, 'Presbyterian religion', 625–8.
16  *Presbyterianism Defended, and the Arguments of Modern Advocates of Prelacy Examined and Refuted, in Four Discourses, by Ministers of the Synod of Ulster* (Glasgow, 1839); *The Plea of Presbytery in Behalf of the Ordination, Government, Discipline, and Worship of the Christian Church, as Opposed to the Unscriptural Character and Claim of Prelacy. In a Reply to the Rev. Archibald Boyd, A.M., by Ministers of the General Synod of Ulster. Second Edition – Improved and Enlarged* (Belfast: William M'Comb, etc., 1841).
17  Thomas Croskery and Thomas Witherow, *Life of the Rev. A. P. Goudy, D.D.* (Dublin: Humphrey and Armour, 1887), pp. 71–87; Andrew R. Holmes, 'Covenanter politics: evangelicalism, political liberalism and Ulster Presbyterians, 1798–1914', *English Historical Review*, 125 (2010), 349–50.
18  *Plea of Presbytery*, pp. 68–9, 27.
19  T. Hamilton, rev. F. Holmes, 'Killen, William Dool (1806–1902)', *Oxford Dictionary of National Biography*.
20  *The Autobiography of Thomas Witherow 1824–1890*, ed. G. Mawhinney and E. Dunlop (Draperstown: Ballinascreen Historical Society, 1990).
21  For example, Thomas Witherow, 'St Patrick, the apostle of Ireland', *British and Foreign Evangelical Review*, 13 (1864), 661–77.

22 Robert Allen, *The Presbyterian College Belfast 1853–1953* (Belfast: W. Mullan, 1954), pp. 232, 313.
23 William D. Killen, *The Ecclesiastical History of Ireland*, 2 vols (London: Macmillan, 1875), I: p. 84.
24 T. Witherow, 'St Patrick', *British Quarterly Review*, 92 (1867), 462.
25 William D. Killen, *Reminiscences of a Long Life* (London: Hodder and Stoughton, 1901), pp. 81–7.
26 Charles C. Starbuck, 'Did the Gaelic church revive presbyterial ordination?', *Methodist Review*, 79 (1897), 365.
27 Witherow, 'St Patrick', 463.
28 T. Witherow, 'Montalembert on St Columba', *British and Foreign Evangelical Review*, 17 (1868), 449–77, at 475.
29 James Heron, *The Celtic Church in Ireland: The Story of Ireland and Irish Christianity from the Time of St. Patrick to the Reformation* (London: Service and Paton, 1898), p. 162.
30 See esp. chapters by Vandrei, Atkins and Macfarlane, in this volume.
31 For example, see the comments of Witherow in 'Montalembert', 468–75 and 'The Culdees, and their later history', *British Quarterly Review*, 75 (1882), 57–8.
32 William T. Latimer, *A History of the Irish Presbyterians* (2nd edn, Belfast: Cleeland, 1902), p. 5.
33 Heron, *Celtic Church*, pp. 84, 86.
34 *Ibid.*, p. 381.
35 Thomas Hamilton, *History of the Irish Presbyterian Church* (2nd edn, Edinburgh: T. & T. Clark, 1887), p. 13.
36 James J. Coleman, 'The Double-Life of the Scottish Past: Discourses of Commemoration in Nineteenth-Century Scotland' (PhD thesis, University of Glasgow, 2005), p. 200.
37 John Thomson (ed.), *Report of Proceedings of the First General Presbyterian Council Convened at Edinburgh, July 1877* (Edinburgh: Thomas and Archibald Constable, 1877), pp. 253, 257.
38 Thomas M'Lauchlan, *The Early Scottish Church: The Ecclesiastical History of Scotland, from the First to the Twelfth Century* (Edinburgh: T. & T. Clark, 1865), pp. 92–9.
39 'The Culdean Church', *British and Foreign Evangelical Review*, 15 (1866), 171.
40 'Dr Reid's Ulster Church', *Presbyterian Review*, 5 (1834), 606–8, 645–6.
41 'Renewed communion with the Synod of Ulster', *Presbyterian Review*, 6 (1835), 326, 327.
42 Holmes, 'Presbyterian religion', 622–3; Robert J. Rodgers, 'Presbyterian Missionary Activity among Irish Roman Catholics in the Nineteenth Century' (MA thesis, Queen's University Belfast, 1969), pp. 259–61.
43 *Missionary Sermons and Speeches Delivered at a Special Meeting of the General Synod of Ulster, held in the Scots Church, Mary's Abbey, Dublin, in September, 1833* (Belfast: William McComb; Dublin: W. Curry jun. & Co.; Edinburgh and Glasgow: Waugh & Innes, etc., 1834), pp. 134–41, 151–9.
44 Witherow, 'St Patrick', 445.
45 William D. Killen, *The Old Catholic Church: Or, the History, Doctrine, Worship, and Polity of the Christians Traced from the Apostolic Age to the Establishment of the Pope as a Temporal Sovereign, A. D. 755* (Edinburgh: T. & T. Clark, 1871), p. 314.
46 Heron, *Celtic Church*, p. 128.

47 'Opening of the Session of the Magee College, Londonderry', *Weekly Northern Whig* (17 November 1866), p. 6.
48 Robert J. Rodgers, 'Vision unrealised: the Presbyterian mission to Irish Roman Catholics in the nineteenth century', *Bulletin of the Presbyterian Historical Society of Ireland*, 20 (1991), 12–31.
49 John M. Barkley (ed.), *Fasti of the General Assembly of the Presbyterian Church in Ireland 1840–1910*, 3 vols (Belfast: Presbyterian Historical Society, 1986–87), I: p. 58; Hamilton Magee, *Fifty Years in 'the Irish Mission'* (Belfast: Religious Tract and Book Depot, 1902).
50 H. Magee, *Ireland and Saint Patrick*, Lectures for the Times, 5 (Dublin: Robertson and Co. [1878]), p. 3.
51 See the list of titles in Magee, *Fifty Years*, pp. 208–10.
52 For example, William B. Kirkpatrick, 'Facts in Irish history which Protestants and Catholics alike should know', *Plain Words* (April 1866), 33–6, (May 1866), 49–51; 'The study of Irish history', *Plain Words* (September 1874), 225–7.
53 William B. Kirkpatrick, *Chapters in Irish History* (2nd edn, London: S.W. Partridge & Co. [1875]), p. iv.
54 Samuel Andrews, 'Irish history', *Plain Words* (April 1875), 85.
55 Andrew R. Holmes, 'The uses and interpretation of prophecy in Irish Presbyterianism, 1850–1930', in Crawford Gribben and Andrew R. Holmes (eds), *Protestant Millennialism, Evangelicalism, and Irish society, 1790–2005* (Basingstoke: Palgrave Macmillan, 2006), pp. 144–73, esp. pp. 156–9.
56 'Day of prayer for Ireland', *Plain Words* (February 1873), 51.
57 L. E. Berkeley, 'Evangelisation in Ireland', in Philip Schaff and S. Irenaeus Prime (eds), *History, Essays, Orations, and Other Documents of the Sixth General Conference of the Evangelical Alliance, held in New York, October 2–12, 1873* (New York: Harper & Brothers, 1874), p. 515.
58 'Day of prayer for Ireland', *Plain Words* (March 1874), 59.
59 'The late day of prayer for Ireland', *Plain Words* (April 1874), 94–5. William Brooke, 'St Patrick and the old religion of Ireland', *Plain Words* (April 1874), 87–90.
60 A. F. Mitchell, 'The ecclesiastical history of Ireland', *British and Foreign Evangelical Review*, 25 (1876), 741.
61 Magee, *Ireland and Saint Patrick*, pp. 15, 16.
62 *Scottish Association for Irish Missions under the Care of the General Assembly of the Presbyterian Church in Ireland. Inauguration Meeting, November 20th, 1883* (Dublin: Assembly's Irish Mission Office, 1883); Thomas Croskery, *Irish Presbyterianism: its History, Character, Influence, and Present Position* (Dublin: Humphrey and Armour, 1884), p. 57.
63 Hamilton Magee, *Scotland and Ireland: Their Mutual Indebtedness in the Gospel* (Edinburgh: Religious Tract and Book Society, 1887).
64 *Minutes of the General Assembly of the Presbyterian Church in Ireland*, 8 (1887), 378.
65 *Minutes of the General Assembly of the Presbyterian Church in Ireland*, 9 (1897), 366.
66 Holmes, 'Presbyterian religion', 636–40.

# 5

# Thomas Becket

*Nicholas Vincent*

Questions are sometimes more revealing than the answers they elicit. The questions posed in Michaelmas 1866 to those taking Oxford University's examinations in law and history were of particular significance. This was the first time that a paper devoted to 'modern' (as opposed to ancient) history had been set for the newly independent Law and History School. Just as important, the exam papers reflected the interests of William Stubbs (1825–1901), newly appointed Regius Professor and arguably Victorian England's greatest medievalist.[1] Amongst a variety of topics 'pass' candidates were asked: 'What has been the part taken generally by the Popes in the struggles of the English people for political liberty? Give exceptions.' Note the twist in the tail here: ever the downfall of the pass-degree man. For those seeking honours, the question was phrased differently: 'Trace the fluctuation of popular feeling in England with regard to the papacy in the twelfth and thirteenth centuries; and say at what point was its moral influence highest.' Those taking the special subject on William of Malmesbury (whose chronicles Stubbs was in the process of editing) were additionally required to: 'Sketch the rise, policy, and fall of Bishop Roger of Salisbury, and compare his career with those of Becket and Wolsey.'[2] No candidate, 'pass' school or honours, could have omitted the name of Thomas Becket.

I cite these long-forgotten examinations not as examples of the quaint, but as an introduction to what the Victorians really thought about Thomas Becket, archbishop and martyr. As we shall see, they did indeed think long and hard about him, and their thoughts tended to run along not one but a multitude of lines. State versus Church, King versus Pope, England versus Europe, Puritan versus papist, amateur history versus scholarly professionalism, all of these topics and more are comprehended within the broader theme of the Victorian view of Becket. In essence, between the 1830s and the 1860s, something very significant happened to Becket's image. From having been dismissed as an agent of Rome and the red rag of popery, by 1860 Thomas could be seen not only as a great Englishman but a great patriot, even as a great democrat. By 1855, indeed, the Catholic *Dublin Review*, convinced of his sanctity, was seeking to crown Becket as the true author of Magna Carta: as the initiator of that process by which the powers of the English Crown were first challenged and then brought under proper control.[3] A few years later, Edward Augustus Freeman (1823–92) could suggest that Saint Thomas of Canterbury, for all his faults, and whether or not a 'saint' in the accepted interpretation of that term, was 'fairly entitled to a place among the worthies of whom England is proud'.[4]

## The inherited Becket: Protestant villain, romantic icon

As is so often the case, university students came late to facts and opinions already divulged to school children. Let us begin in the antediluvian world of the 1830s, in whose popular histories Becket continued to be set down in entirely negative terms. *Little Arthur's History of England* (1835), by Lady Callcott (1785–1842), gives some idea of received opinions. Little Arthur was left in no doubt that Thomas Becket was one of the 'bad things' that had happened in the reign of King Henry II. This was because of an even more dreadful person, the bishop of Rome, who had started calling himself 'Pope'. These bishops of Rome 'said that the clergymen were their servants, and that neither the kings nor judges of any country should punish them ... without the pope's leave. This was foolish and wrong.' The King thought that, because some clergymen were wicked, they ought to be judged and punished as other men. 'But the Archbishop of Canterbury, whose name was Thomas Becket, thought differently. This Becket wanted to be as great a man as the King ... At last, one day, after a very great dispute, Henry fell into a violent passion, and said he wished Becket was dead.' Four knights duly answered this request, for which consequence of his bad temper the King was truly sorry. This was indeed 'one of the very bad things in Henry's life'. Even worse, however, was his marriage to Eleanor of Aquitaine, who was 'very ill-tempered [and] in all ways a bad woman', having been married before, to the King of France, who had 'sent her away' ('divorce' being a term too shocking for the ears of Little Arthur).[5]

Lady Callcott's cousin 'Mrs Markham' (Elizabeth Penrose, c. 1779–1837) told a similar story in her *History of England* (1823): a less than perfect marriage of essay and light chit-chat. First the essay. Having been expected to assist the King against 'church tyranny', Becket entirely changed his way of life: 'The ostentation of affected sanctity made him take a satisfaction in inflicting on himself the severest penances.' After a great deal of disagreement, the intricate particulars of which Mrs Markham spared her readers, the King lost his temper. Users of *Questions on Markham's History of England* (1845) were specifically asked: 'What did the King do in a moment of great irritation?' Four 'gentlemen' of the royal household duly rode to Canterbury, where Becket was persuaded to flee into his cathedral, 'thinking the sanctity of the place would protect him'. It did not, and for this, the King was once again very sorry.[6]

It is only at this point that we arrive at the peculiar joy of Markham's *History*, each dull catechism being followed by a dialogue between the authoress and her children, 'Richard', 'George' and 'Mary':

> George: 'How I should like to have seen Thomas à Becket in all his state and magnificence!' ...

Mary: 'And then, mamma, how shocking it was that the poor man should be so barbarously murdered!'

Mrs Markham: 'Murder was not then considered so great a crime as in reality it is. The lawlessness of the times, and the continued wars, made men savage and hard-hearted.'[7]

The negative portrayal of Becket had persisted for at least three centuries. It was to survive for some time afterwards, not least because it was from Markham's *History* that Charles Dickens (1812–70) was to fashion his own *Child's History of England* (serialised 1851–53).[8]

As for the pattern itself: having been accepted after his death in 1170 as England's greatest martyr, Thomas Becket had been eclipsed from the 1530s onwards as a result of his too close association with the Pope. Henry VIII and the reformers had not only cleansed Canterbury and all England of Becket's shrine and cult but had deliberately blackened his reputation, portraying him not as a martyr but a traitor to king and realm.[9] A reaction against this blackening of Becket's name can be traced from the 1790s onwards. It had a number of sources, traced in recent years by Clare Simmons.[10] To begin with, there were the efforts of Catholic writers, especially of Joseph Berington (1743–1827) and John Lingard (1771–1851). Both were writing in deliberate reaction to the most influential of the eighteenth-century Protestants or agnostics, Lord Lyttelton (1709–73) and David Hume (1711–76), who between them had concluded that Becket was not only an instrument of popery, but, worse, a self-deluded hypocrite.[11] According to Lyttelton, whose *History of the Life of King Henry the Second* was first published in 1767, but whose prejudices lived on for many years thereafter, Becket had been 'guilty of a wilful and premeditated perjury ... [and was] in the highest degree ungrateful to a very kind master ... His good qualities were so misapplied that they became no less hurtful to the public weal of the kingdom than the worst of his vices.'[12] It was as an upstart who threatened to place England under the papal heel that he continued to appear in popular engravings that portrayed his early life. As late as the *Picture History of England* (1861), for example, he is shown as epicene and hatchet-faced, riding under a papal baldachin.[13] The Pope here bears a striking resemblance to that most cadaverous of Victorian Catholics, Henry Manning (1808–92), future Cardinal Archbishop of Westminster.[14]

By contrast, from the 1790s we begin to glimpse quite another image of Thomas, no longer as young fanatic but as Lear-like elder, struck down by brute assassins on the flagstones of Canterbury Cathedral.[15] In the shadow of the guillotine, which had despatched so many Catholic monks and nuns on the Continent, not to mention a French king, Lingard was inclined to allow the saintly and heroic to take precedence over the more negative side of Becket's career. Although even he was forced to admit that the balance, for and against, was hard to determine: 'Thus, at the age of fifty-three, perished this extraordinary man, a martyr to what he deemed to be his duty, the preservation of the immunities of the Church.'[16]

In tandem with this came a rediscovery of Becket no longer as Ultramontane conspirator but as an activist sprung from the middle classes of London who was committed to the wellbeing of the common people. It was thus that he was presented by the Tory radical William Cobbett (1763–1835) in his *History of the Protestant Reformation* (1824–27), and subsequently by members of the Oxford Movement, beginning with Richard Hurrell Froude (1803–36).[17] Even after the calming of the 'condition of England' question, aspects of this reinvented Becket as Everyman lived on. By the 1890s, indeed, Becket's rise from humble beginnings, via merit and hard work, was being presented as something straight out of the world of Samuel Smiles's *Self Help*.[18]

Thirdly, in an age of scepticism and the machine, Becket offered a return to that romanticised 'gloomth' of the Middle Ages so beloved by Horace Walpole (1717–97), Walter Scott (1771–1832) and their successors. The most sophisticated literary expression of this new reverence occurs late in our story, in Tennyson's verse drama *Becket*, written in 1876, published in 1884 and, after 1891, a leading vehicle for the great Henry Irving (1838–1905).[19] It is from a performance of Tennyson's *Becket*, staged at Windsor Castle in 1893, that we gain our one certain proof that Queen Victoria took a personal interest in Becket's story. The Queen-Empress enjoyed the performance but deprecated some of the 'disagreeable and coarse' language assigned by Tennyson to the scenes between Rosamund and Queen Eleanor.[20]

## The Victorians and the cult of Saint Thomas

If some aspects of the Becket story were too red-blooded for Windsor, the bewildering nineteenth-century also found the cult that had surrounded his relics. Medieval pilgrims to Becket's shrine in Canterbury had known very well what was expected of them: miracles worked through drinking, or at the very least the payment for vessels containing, portions of Becket's blood.[21] William Gladstone (1809–98), by contrast, visiting Naples in May 1832, expressed particular disgust for the liquefaction of the blood of Saint Gennaro, a ritual that, in his telling, as of many Protestant travellers, became a symbol for Catholic corruption.[22] Others enjoyed exposing the credulousness that invested purported miracles with such significance. William Buckland (1784–1856), Oxford dinosaur hunter, neighbour of Dr Pusey and future Dean of Westminster, who on his honeymoon to Palermo is said to have exposed the relics of Saint Rosalia as those of a goat, visited another foreign cathedral, 'where was exhibited a martyr's blood – dark spots on the pavement ever fresh and ineradicable. The professor dropped on the pavement and touched the stain with his tongue. "I can tell you what is is; it is bat's urine".'[23] Of the more exuberantly 'Mediterranean' aspects of Becket's cult, the Victorians were understandably shy. The oozing, viscous, androgynous aspects of sanctity were not to all tastes. Even so, there were elements to the medieval cult of relics that, although undoubtedly strange, retained their appeal.

One such was pilgrimage. To an age obsessed with the new possibilities opened up by trains, tramways and bicycles, pilgrimage was itself part of the Victorian world picture, even if the keener sort of Protestant frowned upon it as 'Romish'. In July 1873, questions were asked in the House of Commons over the throng of Catholic 'pilgrims', led by a Jesuit priest, said to have attended Canterbury Cathedral on the feast of Thomas's translation (7 July), a feast that, like that of his martyrdom (29 December), was in theory banished from the Anglican calendar.[24] Yet in other Anglican circles, pilgrimage was increasingly not just tolerated but encouraged. Treading in the footsteps of Christ, or saints closer to home, could supply answers to questions that 'Germanisers' and Tübingen dry-as-dusts could never hope to fathom. 'Let them at least enjoy the delusion, say benevolent persons; the prayers of the saint may have no power to save her child, but still the mother may as well fancy that they have', ventriloquised one reviewer in the ultra-Tractarian *British Critic*, lamenting the English abandonment of pilgrimage and procession. 'Who knows what might have happened had Saint Thomas's bones remained undisturbed at Canterbury? Who knows that the dead faith of some slumbering churchman might not have been warmed by their vicinity just as the dead man was raised to life by contact with the bones of Elisha.'[25] As in the Middle Ages, of course, there was no easy dividing line between pilgrimage and holiday.[26] As Dean Stanley (1815–81) noted in the 1850s, by which time Canterbury was drawing large numbers, medieval pilgrimage was a phenomenon that had 'swept into its vortex all the classes who now travel together in excursion trains, or on Rhine steam-boats'.[27] Tennyson made pilgrimage to Canterbury in August 1877, visiting 'each separate scene of Becket's martyrdom'.[28]

For those keen to bring the past alive, Canterbury had not one but two claims to Becket, both as the place of the archbishop's martyrdom and as the destination of Chaucer's pilgrims, themselves 'the Holy Blissful Martyr for to seek'. Even the most Protestant of authorities were prepared to acknowledge Chaucer's greatness, and if Chaucer was great, then so, by implication, was the saint whose fame he celebrated. Even F. D. Maurice (1805–72) could not explain Chaucer to his students without first explaining Becket.[29] With his determination to cover every topographical angle, Stanley was perhaps the first writer in English to attempt to reconstruct the precise itinerary and timetable of Chaucer's pilgrims, from the Talbot Inn (then the 'Tabard') at 75 High Street, Borough Road, at dawn on the morning of 28 April, through to their arrival at Canterbury, which he assigned to just after 4pm the following day.[30] Stanley's *Memorials* represent the high-water mark of Victorian Becket worship, being deeply endowed with that sense of place and topography that was the hallmark both of Victorian tourism and of the Victorian pursuit of religious truth. They can be read like a detective story, with a crime, a victim (Becket), a locked crime scene (the cathedral) and a master detective (Stanley himself). Reconstructing Becket's final moments was not without its difficulties. Stanley had somehow to communicate the savagery of the events and speeches at Canterbury in December 1170, without causing his readers offence:

> Those ... who, in the curious change of feeling that has come over our age, are inclined to the ancient reverence for St Thomas of Canterbury, as the meek and gentle saint of

holier and happier times than our own, may, perhaps, be led to modify their judgment by the description, taken not from his enemies, but from his admiring followers, of the violence, the obstinacy, the furious words and acts, which deformed even the dignity of his last hour, and well nigh turned the solemnity of his 'martyrdom' into an unseemly brawl.[31]

Stanley cited the word 'leno' (pimp) that Becket had hurled at Reginald Fitzurse, but only in a footnote and in Latin, preferring in his English text to refer to it as 'a coarse epithet' translated as 'profligate wretch'.[32] Most writers sidestepped this problem altogether, referring to Becket's use of an 'ill name' (Dickens), or his 'fierce words' (Kate Norgate).[33]

Besides its allure as travelogue, the Becket story exerted another strong appeal to Victorian sensibilities. Writing for an audience of children, and drawing on Hume's account, Mrs Markham had recorded that Becket: 'Affected the greatest austerities; he wore sack-cloth, which he never changed till it was full of dirt and vermin, next his skin; he ate nothing but bread and drank water in which fennel had been steeped to make it nauseous; he lacerated himself with continual scourging.'[34] The historian James Anthony Froude (1818–94), arguing against the 'fact idolators' who would dismiss as lies what were merely imaginative or mythic retellings of reality, allowed that the hair shirt of Becket and his other penances were incontestable prodigies.[35] Nevertheless, he would in 1877 pen a study of Becket so polemically charged against both its subject's character and the absurdities of his cult that Freeman condemned it as an attack on Froude's long-dead brother, Hurrell, an avid proponent of Becket worship.[36] The emphasis laid upon beating in virtually all of the accounts of Becket, by women as by men, perhaps tells us something significant about Victorian understandings of medieval Catholicism, and about the acceptance of violence as a potentially religious impulse. Freeman had referred in 1860 to Becket as a fine example of 'muscular Christianity',[37] and as Thomas Hughes's Tom Brown was only too aware: 'Every one who is worth his salt has his enemies who must be beaten, be they evil thoughts and habits in himself, or spiritual wickedness in high places, or Russians, or Border-ruffians, or Bill, Tom or Harry, who will not let him live his life in quiet till he has thrashed them'.[38] As was so often the case with descriptive prose, it was A. P. Stanley (perhaps Arnold of Rugby's most famous protégé) who offered the most vivid account, reporting Becket's hair shirt ('of unusual roughness') and the 'hair drawers' down to the knees, 'the whole so fastened together as to admit of being readily taken off for his daily scourgings, of which yesterday's portion was still apparent in the stripes on his body'. Worse than this: 'The marvel was increased by the sight – to our notions so revolting – of the innumerable vermin with which the haircloth abounded – boiling over with them, as one account describes it, like water in a simmering cauldron.'[39]

This brings us to another aspect of the Victorian Becket cult. A 'Romish doctrine' specifically condemned in Article XXII of the Church of England, the veneration of relics was one of those sticking points that John Henry Newman (1801–90) had greatest difficult smoothing over in Tract 90. Most Protestant writers were unimpressed by his casuistry. Dickens, viewing the relics of Saint Charles Borromeo at Milan in 1844, preferred to describe what he saw as something from the gothic horrors of Mrs Radcliffe or 'Monk' Lewis:

> A windlass slowly removes the front of the altar; and, within it, in a gorgeous shrine of gold and silver, is seen, through alabaster, the shrivelled mummy of a man: the pontifical robes with which it is adorned, radiant with diamonds, emeralds, rubies: every costly and magnificent gem. The shrunken heap of poor earth in the midst of this great glitter, is more pitiful than if it lay upon a dunghill. There is not a ray of imprisoned light in all the flash and fire of jewels, but seems to mock the dusty holes where eyes were, once. Every thread of silk in the rich vestments seems only a provision from the worms that spin, for the behoof of worms that propagate in sepulchers [sic].[40]

Yet for those living in an age in which the past had increasingly to be preserved against the march of Gradgrindian statistics and blue books, what surer proof of God's continuing providence than the rediscovery of relics long thought lost? This was, after all, the age that collected everything, from Napoleon's penis, to the heart of Louis XIV, shrivelled to the size of a small nut, eventually swallowed by Dean Buckland in a fit of omnivorous curiosity.[41] It also witnessed the rediscovery of large numbers of saints' relics in France and Bavaria supposedly destroyed by the revolutionaries of the 1790s, now salvaged and translated to new shrines in the full glare of journalistic speculation.[42]

The Jesuit historian John Morris (1826–93), writing in the 1880s, refers to a great treasury of Becket relics, including chasubles and other vestments at Courtrai, Dixmude and Sens, an amice at Erdington near Birmingham, and another mitre, obtained by Cardinal Wiseman from Sens, and today in the Victoria and Albert Museum. Bones were still, according to Morris, to be seen at Rome, Liège, Veroli and Marsala.[43] Perhaps the most remarkable of the objects Morris listed was that half of the altar stone originally preserved at Sens on which Becket is said to have celebrated mass, obtained by the Catholic bishop James Gillis (1802–64). Gillis used it to make an altar for his domestic chapel in Edinburgh. At its foot he placed what he believed to be the heart of Henry II, obtained as a gift from the mayor of Orleans.[44] In 1888, three years after Morris's inventory, the Dean and Chapter of Canterbury disinterred a skeleton in the crypt that for a while at least was proclaimed to be that of Becket. The discovery was nationally and internationally reported. An attempt was made to provoke a 'miracle' by bringing the bones into contact with a blind boy from Margate. Very soon, the furore died down, the rumours were denied and the 'relics' reburied.[45] Morris played a significant role in ensuring the triumph of scepticism and common sense.[46] It is no coincidence, however, that such acts of faith should have shone forth in age of self-conscious modernity.

## Becket and the constitution

Mid-Victorian fears were expressed over the creeping growth of the state and over the dangers posed to English 'liberty' by the prerogatives of Parliament, Privy Council and 'shopocracy'. The story of Becket had a unique resonance here, not least in its use in debates about the relationship between Church and state. In 1844 Sir Frederick Hervey-Bathurst erected a stone commemorating the site of Clarendon Palace, in Wiltshire. He commissioned a local stonemason to inscribe the following message:

> The building of which this fragment once formed a part was long a favourite residence of the English monarchs, and has been historically connected with many important transactions and distinguished characters ... Here were enacted the Constitutions of Clarendon,– the first barrier raised against the claims of secular jurisdiction by the See of Rome. The spirit awakened within these walls ceased not to operate till it had vindicated the authority of the laws and accomplished the reformation of the Church of England.[47]

If not everyone agreed, attitudes to Clarendon remained a touchstone of Protestant orthodoxy. Henry Manning, attempting in the 1840s to bolster his childhood Anglicanism against the onset of Roman Catholic doubts, found himself reading the Constitutions as a medicinal exercise.[48] Far from purging him of his Catholicism, they helped drive him across the great divide into the welcoming arms of Rome.

Becket, then, remained central to Victorian political narratives. He appears in the novels of Anthony Trollope (1815–82), being cited in *Phineas Redux* (1874) by Trollope's fictitious Young Englandist Mr Daubeny in a debate over the relations between Church and state:

> On the subject of the Church [Mr Daubeny] was rather misty but very profound. He went into the question of very early Churches indeed ... The gist of his argument was to show that audacity in Reform was the very backbone of Conservatism. By a clearly pronounced disunion of Church and state the theocracy of Thomas à Becket would be restored, and the people of England would soon again become the faithful flocks of faithful shepherds.[49]

For Trollope's Mr Daubeny, read the real-life Mr Disraeli (1804–81), whose real-life nemesis, Mr Gladstone, knew almost as much about Becket as he did about the struggles between Church and state. Gladstone is to be found reading Becketiana in the 1830s, in Hurrell Froude's *Remains*; in 1854, in Stanley's *Memorials*; in 1859, in Canon Robertson's *Life*; in 1876, in Aubrey de Vere's verse epic; in 1884 and again in 1893 in the poem by Tennyson.[50] In 1854, perhaps inspired by the publication of his friend Stanley's 'Murder of Becket', Gladstone had paid what seems to have been his first visit to Canterbury, being shown around the cathedral where Becket met his death.[51] Canterbury by this time was already the subject of numerous guidebooks, all of which placed Becket squarely at the centre of things.[52]

Becket's reputation also crossed the English Channel. From the 1820s onwards, as part of a Catholic revival just as intense as that of Oxford, France became convulsed by debates over Christian Socialism and Gallican detachment from Rome. Relations between the Gallican hierarchy and the Ultramontane Pope Pius IX (1792–1878) came increasingly to resemble the situation following the 1164 Constitutions of Clarendon, when Henry II attempted to wrest power from Pope Alexander III. In 1848, and again in 1871, archbishops of Paris were martyred, if not with swords before the high altar of Notre Dame, then with muskets fired by the Paris mob.[53] No wonder, then, that there was a keen French appetite for the Becket story, together with French editions and translations of Latin and English authorities. Sens, Pontigny and Lyons, already interwoven into Becket's legend, became significant destinations on the Victorian Pilgrims' Way.[54] John Allen Giles's *Life of Thomas à Becket* (1846) was, appropriately enough, translated in 1858 by Georges Darboy (1813–71), leading advocate of Gallicanism, future archbishop of Paris, and himself in 1871 a martyr to revolutionary violence.[55] 'J'accepte l'augure', he is supposed to have said, when entrusted with Becket's cross by an admirer.[56]

Underlying the rediscovery of Becket lay a vast substratum of materials, Catholic and Protestant, scholarly and popular, reliable and otherwise. More than a dozen book-length biographies were published in Victoria's reign. There was fierce debate in the periodicals.[57] Figures as disparate as John Keble (1792–1866), Thomas Carlyle (1795–1881), Frederick Faber (1814–63) and Herbert Hensley Henson (1863–1947) defended Becket's reputation, or, in the case of both Freeman and Stubbs, dreamed of writing his biography.[58] Becket also found a place in popular fiction. Long before Tennyson's *Becket* (1884), he is mentioned at least twice in Walter Scott's *Ivanhoe* (1820), in many ways the foundation charter of Victorian medievalism. Scott's Sir Maurice de Bracy swears his oaths 'by the bones of Thomas à Becket', and Scott's Waldemar Fitz Urse is himself the son of one of Becket's murderers.[59]

Either one was for Saint Thomas, in which case one was likely to be branded Catholic or crypto-Catholic, with a love for saints and relics and ritual. Or one was against him, in which case one wrote not of Saint Thomas but of (Thomas) Becket, and risked being branded a Low Church Protestant, out of tune with the medieval. In either case, Thomas remained combustible stuff. Many hundreds of images of him were scattered across the newly built Catholic and Anglo-Catholic churches not just of nineteenth-century England, but of Ireland and the English-speaking world. In 1840, for example, Daniel O'Connell (1775–1847) purchased a vast canvas exhibited at the Royal Academy, *The Martyrdom of Thomas à Becket*, for display in St Andrew's, Westland Row, Dublin. It still hangs there above the high altar.[60] The message it conveys is a highly political one. The ruffian knights of Henry II, here shown plunging their swords into the martyred archbishop, were the same as, or close cousins of, those who had followed King Henry to Ireland two years after Becket's death. There began the centuries-long tradition of English oppression and brutality. Saint Thomas's murder was thus the spur to an atrocity even more extreme: the martyrdom of the entire Catholic people of Ireland. O'Connell himself was proclaimed a new Saint Thomas, who 'strove and suffered for the liberties of his country and his church'. This comparison was noticed, resentfully, in Protestant circles. Stanley, whose *Memorials of Canterbury* did more than any other modern book to stir up interest in Becket and the circumstances of his martyrdom, pointed out, with unaccustomed venom, that the O'Connell comparison was 'true in another sense' than that in which it was intended. In other words, like Becket, O'Connell was more famed as brawler than as peacemaker.[61]

For much of the nineteenth century, the classic Catholic biography of Saint Thomas remained Morris's *Life and Martyrdom of Saint Thomas Becket* (1859), reissued in an expanded edition in 1885. Morris was an Old Harrovian, born in India. His conversion to Catholicism in 1846, whilst still an undergraduate at Trinity College, Cambridge, excited outrage in *The Times* and the disgrace of his tutor, Frederick Paley (1815–88). Morris entered the English College at Rome before taking charge of the Mission of St Thomas of Canterbury at Fulham. As a future personal secretary to cardinals Wiseman and Manning, he was close to the Catholic hierarchy. Allowing for its obvious confessional bias – the 1859 frontispiece shows Saint Thomas attended by the heavenly host – Morris's biography was perhaps the first properly to harmonise the lives and letters now made available in scholarly editions by his Anglican contemporaries. Its expansion between 1859 and 1885 was in part because of Morris's new contacts with the Jesuits and in particular with the Bollandists of Brussels: our first indication of a tendency to adopt a European outlook towards Becket that was to transcend what had previously been the narrowly Anglocentric.

As this should remind us, Becket himself remained if not untouchable then very hard for Protestants to handle. As late as 1895, following his installation as Dean of Canterbury, Frederic William Farrar (1831–1903) preached an inaugural sermon in which he referred to the martyrdoms of archbishops Sudbury, Alphege and Laud, quite deliberately excluding Saint Thomas.[62] Mandell Creighton (1843–1901) judged Thomas, like Hildebrand, to have been one who had worked in 'man's way' rather than in God's.[63] Of course, this did not prevent Victorian writers from reinventing Becket in their own image. Like Gordon and Havelock, those men of religion and the Gatling gun, Becket's fighting on the side of right was regarded by many Victorians as a thoroughly good thing. His command of troops on the Toulouse campaign of 1159, or his unhorsing of a French opponent in single combat were further proofs of manliness. Becket was no 'man milliner' of the High Church variety derided in Tom Brown's Oxford.[64] For a generation inclined to equate celibacy or ritualism with the corrupt or effete, Becket could be portrayed as a full-blooded English gentleman.[65] The Catholic author Mrs Hope (1809–87) described him as 'very tall and handsome, with a large quick eye, a slightly aquiline nose, and a calm, gentle countenance'. On campaign outside Toulouse in 1159, '[Becket] led [his men] into battle, encouraging them, pointing out the path to glory, and directing their movements by signals on a small trumpet'.[66] Robert Hugh Benson (1871–1914), Catholic brother of A. C. and E. H., specifically denied that Thomas was 'in the least like the kind of colourless dummy of which foolish people think that a Catholic Saint and hero is made.'[67] On the contrary, he was 'a tall, long-limbed lad – far above the average in height – with an aquiline nose and very bright, large eyes'. Benson's Thomas was 'extremely fond of outdoor sports, and extremely competent at them', albeit that, like the captain of the First XI, 'He loved too to dress well, and make a fine appearance.'[68]

It was to sturdy Tom Brown that the Rev W. D. Bushell (1838–1917), himself an assistant master at Harrow, turned for comparisons in describing life in a medieval archbishop's household. Under Archbishop Theobald, Bushell suggests:

> [Becket's] first Term, as we now might call it, does not seem to have been a happy one. New boys still have their trials ... Readers of 'Tom Brown' will find that life in an Archbishop's Household was not altogether different in some respects from life in a Public School. We find at least the villain of the piece, the Flashman, the inevitable bully, in the person of a certain Roger of Bishopsbridge, Roger de Pont l'Evêque, who knowing that Thomas had come to Harrow with the Hatchetbearer Ralph, gave him the name of Thomas Baillehache, or the Hatchet-clerk ... What Tom Brown found in Arthur and in East, [Becket] found in Roger of Neustria and in John of Canterbury.[69]

What the Flashman of the piece did not do, either in Bushell's retelling or in any other of the Victorian denigrations of Roger de Pont l'Évêque, was to seduce a male serving boy, who was then blinded and hanged to avoid exposure of the crime. This appalling allegation, laid against Roger in one of the letters of John of Salisbury, was no doubt exaggerated (perhaps derived from Suetonius on the emperor Nero).[70] By the Victorians it was left cloaked in the penumbra of a learned language.

## Thomas Becket's place in religious and scholarly controversy

In Newman's *Loss and Gain* (1848), the imminent conversion of his alter ego, Charles Reding, is signalled when Charles takes a night-time walk and meditates upon a wayside crucifix overhanging a well sacred to Saint Thomas the Martyr. He kneels to kiss the wood of the cross, and 'then rose and turned to the cold well; he took some water in his palm and drank it'.[71] What happens thereafter can be read as a consequence of this physical encounter with Saint Thomas: the first, halting admission of Catholic truth. Others went further, none further than Frederick Faber. In February 1846, plunging to Rome as one of Newman's first imitators, Faber chose to travel to Italy via the cathedral at Sens, specifically so that he and his fellow convert, Antony Hutchison (1822–63), could venerate the relics of Saint Thomas. 'What interested me most was the priest's dress of St Thomas of Canterbury; I kissed the glass of the window through which I was allowed to see them.'[72] Rather like any later 'outing' or rite of passage, Faber's physical prostration before relics was intended as irrevocable proof of his conversion.

Meanwhile, to Anglicans, let alone to Nonconformists, an un-sainted Becket deserved no place in Protestant commemorations. Hence the questions asked in Parliament in the 1870s over Catholic visitors to Canterbury. Hence also the continued exclusion of Becket from the Anglican Prayer Book.[73] From the 1820s onwards, Catholic churches in large number were dedicated to Saint Thomas of Canterbury, most provocatively in the 1880s, in the case of the parish church of St Thomas of Canterbury in Burgate, built just outside the precincts of Canterbury Cathedral, with lavish imagery and a display of relics.[74] To an extent that has seldom been recognised, Becket, or rather 'St Thomas', became in the mid nineteenth century a figurehead for the Oxford Movement, for Anglican ritualists, and for the revived English Roman Catholic establishment.

Denied *new* churches dedicated to Saint Thomas, Anglo-Catholics had to content themselves with the rediscovery of dedications concealed, since the 1530s, by rededications to Saint Thomas the Apostle, and with echoes of earlier veneration, such as the fact that the Quarter Sessions of the Eastern division of Kent continued to meet on the Tuesday after the feast of Saint Thomas of Canterbury.[75] The slum parish of St Thomas behind Oxford railway station was in the 1840s stridently reattributed to Saint Thomas the Martyr. It was there that the chasuble, that reddest of red popish rags, was first reintroduced to Anglican worship, and the Tractarian rector, Thomas Chamberlain (1810–92), founded a sisterhood dedicated to 'St Thomas Martyr', devoted to the care of the poor.[76] For the first post-Reformation dedication to Saint Thomas Becket of an Anglican place of worship we have to wait until 1892, when a private chapel at Teignmouth was 'dedicated and formally opened' by the Archdeacon of Zanzibar acting under licence from the Bishop of the Universities Mission to Central Africa.[77] Becket might be of use in Africa, to potential Anglican martyrs striving against heathen and over-mighty kings. To those nearer home, he remained too large a gnat to swallow.

All of this Anglican sound and fury had first been signalled as early as the 1830s. It was symbolically apt that Becket played a central role in the first meeting between Wiseman, Gladstone and Manning, at the English College in Rome on 29 December 1838, a meeting deliberately timed to coincide with the feast of the martyrdom of Saint Thomas (29 December), the College's patron saint.[78] As this suggests, Becket was already significant in the first encounters between the Oxford Movement and Rome.

In successive issues of the *British Magazine* for 1832–33, Richard Hurrell Froude (1803–36), Fellow of Oriel, had published a remarkable survey of Becket, viewed not from a biographical perspective but via the shifting prismatic of Becket's letters. Of these Latin letters, Froude translated nearly fifty.[79] Here he turned not just to the 1682 edition by Christian Wolf ('Lupus') of the *Quadripartites*, mostly written by four of Becket's contemporaries, but to a search for manuscripts. A few brief steps from Oriel, Froude had access to the Cave manuscript of Gilbert Foliot's letters in Bodley.[80] He also sought out more exotic things. Attempting to escape the English climate and his own tuberculosis, he encouraged Newman to accompany him on an expedition to Rome. There together in 1833, they sought out the Roman church of St Thomas.[81] Via Wiseman, Froude applied for access to the Vatican collections. The request seems to have been granted.[82] It was a request of momentous significance, both as the occasion for the first meeting between those Victorian titans, the future Cardinals Wiseman and Newman, and as evidence for that dawning awareness on behalf of English historians that a large part of the materials for English history were to be found in the libraries of Italy and France.

Froude's 'Becket' might have vanished without trace but for the untimely circumstances of Froude's own death and the decision of his friends and literary executors, Newman and John Keble (1792–1866), to publish a two-volume collection of his *Remains*. As Lytton Strachey (1880–1932) phrased it, with feline insinuation, 'When Froude succeeded in impregnating Newman with the ideas of Keble, the Oxford Movement began.'[83] Arguably it was in Froude's *Remains* that Newman and Keble first struck the spark that was to light so great a pyre. The second volume was dominated by a translation, adapted and continued by Newman, of a large portion of the Becket Correspondence.[84] Not only did the polemic of the 1160s become common currency for the most polemical of nineteenth-century theologians, but Becket played no small part in launching Newman on his voyage from the harbour of Anglicanism into the stormier seas of Rome. The Becket lives and letters, now circulated in a variety of modern editions, invited a synoptic harmonisation that itself resulted in a 'Quest for the Historical Thomas', roughly contemporary with the work of Strauss, albeit with rather different aims, and a decade or more in advance of that of Renan, Seeley and Farrar on the historical Jesus.[85]

By the 1840s, Becket and the Becket letters stood at the very forefront of modern religious controversy. The notorious Gorham Case of 1850, specifically the actions of the Judicial Committee of the Privy Council in overruling the Bishop of Exeter's refusal to institute the evangelical George Cornelius Gorham (1787–1857) to a living, on grounds of his denial of baptismal regeneration, was decried by High Churchmen as unwarranted erastian interference.[86] If spiritual decisions were to be challenged in secular courts, truly the days of Clarendon and Henry II were come again. Within a week of the 'Gorham Judgment', Cardinal Wiseman preached a sermon praising the resistance to secular power led by Saint Thomas and other Catholic archbishops of Canterbury.[87] It was Gorham that forced Manning into the arms of Rome.[88] And it was Gorham that was signified in 1855, when Anthony Trollope, in the first volume of his Barchester Chronicles, described the bookcases of the Archdeacon Grantley at Plumstead Episcopi, surmounted by 'the busts of the greatest among the great: Chrysostom, St Augustine, Thomas a Becket, Cardinal Wolsey, Archbishop Laud, and Dr Philpotts [sic]', Henry Phillpotts (1778–1869) being the bishop who had tried to thwart Gorham.[89] Dean Stanley approved neither of Phillpotts's hectoring authoritarianism nor of evangelical dogmatism, but it is interesting nevertheless to find in his *Memorials of Canterbury* an acknowledgement of the Rev. George Gorham, 'now Vicar of Bramford Speke', for his 'courtesy and profound antiquarian knowledge' in identifying the castle of Gorron in Maine, to which Henry II had retired after Becket's death, and from which the Gorham family claimed to originate.[90]

Gorham also played its part in a wider enterprise to which I can refer here only in outline. What we know of the life and posterity of Becket comes to us chiefly from the writings of half a dozen twelfth-century biographers, from Becket's own correspondence with contemporaries, lovingly collected after his death, and from the two great collections of miracles compiled at his shrine. Together, these 'Becket Materials' constitute one of the greatest dossiers of source materials ever collected for a medieval saint. They were generally sneered at by eighteenth-century writers, Hume foremost among them.[91] Froude's work began a significant shift in taste. The lead was taken up by his contemporary, John Allen Giles (1808–84).[92] Giles established himself in the 1840s as one of the most prolific (and slapdash) editors of Latin texts, both classical and medieval, that England has ever produced.[93] He compiled a vast edition of Becket's *Lives and Letters*, published between 1844 and 1848 from Giles's own printing press in Oxford. This was an enterprise of vast proportions, extreme inaccuracy and immediate appeal. It involved Giles himself in travel to numerous French and Belgian libraries, in search of manuscript materials. For this he deserves grateful commemoration, since his discoveries, however poorly processed, contributed to a a new openness to European themes, and a curiosity for continental archival exploration. Unfortunately for Giles, in 1854 disaster struck, when he conducted an illegal marriage. The crime was in fact an act of mercy, and at least in part the result of obsessive determination to spend time at his editiorial work, but it led to disgrace and three months' imprisonment.[94]

From this flowed further consequences for the Victorian study of Becket. Giles's inaccuracies had been immediately apparent. Others now proposed to correct his errors. One was the great William Stubbs. Another was the Anglican clergyman, James Craigie Robertson (1813–82). Robertson was an anti-Catholic rationalist, of a very different stamp from the romantically sceptical Giles.[95] In 1859, he published a life with the significantly bald title *Becket, Archbishop of Canterbury*. His book poured scorn on Giles's works, edited 'as you edit waggon-loads of rubbish, by turning the waggon upside-down'. With venomous intent, it even alluded to Giles' recent imprisonment.[96] It earned Robertson a canonry in Canterbury Cathedral and, in 1864, an invitation to re-edit for the Rolls Series materials that Giles had first put into circulation twenty years before.[97] Giles objected to the infringement of what he considered copyright. To overcome this, Robertson chose to open what was in essence a re-edition with the one major source that Giles had overlooked: a collection of miracles, written by a monk named William of Canterbury. The manuscript of this had only come to light in 1854, rediscovered in the library of Winchester College by the Catholic antiquary and eccentric Francis Baigent (c. 1831–1918).[98] As I have described elsewhere, Robertson's decision to begin his collection with miracles, and the publication of the Winchester manuscript before properly establishing whether other manuscripts survived in continental libraries, had significant consequences.[99] Not the least of these was the new emphasis placed upon Becket as miracle worker. This was to draw another controversial figure into Becket's orbit. Edwin Abbott (1838–1926), Headmaster of the City of London School, was a scientific rationalist who in 1891, the year after Newman's death, published a bitter assault on Newman's work on miracles.¹⁰⁰ Turning his guns against the Becket cult, in 1898 Abbott published a two-volume study. These applied the same techniques of criticism that the Germanisers had previously applied to the Gospels. More than a century later, they remain more or less the only attempt to turn the Becket miracles into English.¹⁰¹

## Epilogue

For all of these reasons, Becket retained his potency. Let us end, though, on a more picturesque note. Visiting Tournai in 1886, and travelling incognito, Edward White Benson (1829–96), Archbishop of Canterbury, was shown a chasuble said to have belonged to Becket. There, in his own words,

> An odd thing happened. The sacristan was pleased evidently by all our interest, and while expounding it (vestment) and the 'martyrdom while saying the office' together, he gathered it up saying, 'Vous mettrez la tête par là', and suddenly put it over my head, and there I stood dressed from head to foot (it is very long and fell quite to my feet) in the first chasuble I ever had on, and being the first Archbishop of Canterbury, I suppose, who ever had it on since Thomas himself. As he did it he said 'Il était archevêque, vous savez, de Cantorbéry' … and it sounded (if ever omen was) like a bidding to do something or leave something undone.¹⁰²

Benson's willingness to cloak himself in vestments at which his Anglican predecessors would have shuddered should remind us of the great distance travelled by the nineteenth-century Church, not least in the reinvention of medieval saints. By 1889 we find Robert Anchor Thompson (1821–94) writing from a staunchly Protestant perspective (although with less than perfect syntax) to defend Becket from any charge of treachery:

> No Englishman was ever more beloved in life, none has been so long or so fervently honoured after his death, as the man who, for three and a half centuries and more, was worshipped in England and the Christian world, and, in ignorant parts of it, is worshipped still – not as he was, and will be yet be known with higher honour than before, and more his own, 𝕿𝖍𝖔𝖒𝖆𝖘 𝕭𝖊𝖈𝖐𝖊𝖙, 𝕿𝖍𝖊 𝕱𝖎𝖗𝖘𝖙 𝕲𝖗𝖊𝖆𝖙 𝕻𝖆𝖙𝖗𝖎𝖔𝖙 𝖔𝖋 𝕿𝖍𝖊 𝕾𝖊𝖈𝖔𝖓𝖉 𝕰𝖓𝖌𝖑𝖆𝖓𝖉, but as St Thomas of Canterbury.¹⁰³

The contrast here, not least between manly Protestant capital, and Catholic gothic lettering, tells us a great deal about the image of Thomas Becket. It also offers no small insight into the Victorian mindset.

## Notes

What follows represents a highly condensed selection of materials that in due course will appear as a monograph on *Becket and the Victorians*. For references that I might otherwise have missed, I am indebted to Simon Bailey, Arthur Burns, Peter Crooks, Colin Haydon, Michael Ledger-Lomas, Sarah Monks, Mark Whittow, Cressida Williams and George Woudhuysen.

1 See Reba N. Soffer, 'Modern history', and Barry Nicholas, 'Jurisprudence', in M. G. Brock and M. C. Curthoys (eds), *The History of the University of Oxford VII: Nineteenth-Century Oxford, Part 2* (Oxford: Clarendon, 2000), pp. 363, 389–90; John Kenyon, *The History Men: The Historical Profession in England since the Renaissance* (2nd edn, London: Weidenfeld and Nicholson, 1993), pp. 150–1, 171.
2 Papers from the University of Oxford archive: Oxford, Bodleian Library 2626 d.8. See also E. H. Cordeaux and D. H. Merry, *A Bibliography of Printed Works Relating to the University of Oxford* (Oxford: Clarendon, 1968), no. 2241.
3 'St Thomas of Canterbury', *Dublin Review*, 38 (1855), 355–413, esp. 409.
4 E. A. Freeman, 'St Thomas of Canterbury and his biographers', *Historical Essays* (London: Macmillan, 1871), p. 113.
5 Maria, Lady Callcott, *Little Arthur's History of England* (1835; London: Murray, 1936), pp. 65–8.
6 Mrs Markham, *A History of England: From the First Invasion by the Romans to the end of the Reign of George III* (1823; rev. edn, London: T. J. Allman, 1878), pp. 83–6.
7 Markham, *History*, pp. 91–2.
8 See Charles Dickens, *A Child's History of England*, 3 vols (London: Bradbury and Evans, 1852), I: pp. 136–70.
9 See Helen L. Parish, *Monks, Miracles and Magic: Reformation Representations of the Medieval Church* (London: Routledge, 2005), esp. pp. 92–105; Arthur F. Marotti, *Religious Ideology and Cultural Fantasy: Catholic and Anti-Catholic Discourses in Early Modern England* (Notre Dame: Notre Dame University Press, 2005), pp. 16, 213–14 n. 28.
10 Clare A. Simmons, *Reversing the Conquest: History and Myth in Nineteenth-Century British Literature* (New Brunswick: Rutgers University Press, 1990), esp. pp. 113–39.
11 *Ibid.*, pp. 114–17.
12 George, Lord Lyttelton, *The History of the Life of King Henry the Second*, 4 vols (1767; Dublin: J. Faulkner, 1768–72), II: pp. 644–6.
13 'Passage of À Becket through France', in *The Picture History of England in Eighty Beautiful Engravings* (London and New York: Cassell, etc., 1861), p. 37.
14 'The Pope between the kings of France and England', in *ibid.*, p. 35.
15 See, for instance, John Opie's *The Murder of Thomas a Becket* (1792–1800), much reproduced; see also *Picture History*, p. 39; and *Cassell's History of England: The Jubilee Edition*, 8 vols (London: Cassell, c. 1887–95?), I: p. 197.
16 John Lingard, *The History of England*, 8 vols (London: J. Mawman, 1819–30), II: p. 89.
17 Simmons, *Reversing the Conquest*, pp. 124–32.
18 See Lewis B. Radford (1869–1937), winner of Cambridge University's Prince Consort Prize: *Thomas of London Before his Consecration* (Cambridge: Cambridge University Press, 1894).
19 For the poem's evolution, see Hallam Tennyson, *Alfred, Lord Tennyson: A Memoir* (London: Macmillan, 1899), pp. 580–5, 635.
20 Arthur Ponsonby, *Henry Ponsonby: Queen Victoria's Private Secretary, His Life from His Letters* (London: Macmillan, 1942), pp. 82–3.
21 Arthur Penrhyn Stanley, *Historical Memorials of Canterbury* (2nd edn, London: J. Murray, 1855), pp. 72–4, 76, 83.

22 M. R. D. Foot and H. C. G. Matthew (eds), *The Gladstone Diaries*, 14 vols (Oxford: Clarendon Press, 1968–94), I: pp. 489–90.
23 William Tuckwell, *Reminiscences of Oxford* (London: Cassell, 1900), p. 40. For the goat bones, see Elizabeth O. Gordon, *The Life and Correspondence of William Buckland, D.D., F.R.S.* (London: J. Murray, 1894), pp. 95–6.
24 'Canterbury Cathedral – alleged "pilgrimage" – questions', *House of Commons Debates*, 217 (18 July 1873), cols 603–5.
25 'M. Rio's La Petite Chouannerie', *British Critic*, 32 (1842), 283.
26 John Pemble, *The Mediterranean Passion: Victorians and Edwardians in the South* (Oxford: Clarendon, 1987), pp. 67–70, 210.
27 Stanley, *Memorials*, p. 166.
28 Tennyson, *Lord Tennyson*, p. 580.
29 Frederick Maurice, *The Life of Frederick Denison Maurice*, 2 vols (3rd edn, London: Macmillan, 1884), I: p. 300.
30 Stanley, *Memorials*, pp. 169–71.
31 *Ibid.*, p. 94.
32 *Ibid.*, p. 67.
33 Dickens, *Child's History*, I: p. 156; Kate Norgate, 'Thomas, known as Thomas à Becket (1118?–1170)', from the original *Dictionary of National Biography*, available at www.oxforddnb.com/view/olddnb/27201, accessed 7 November 2014.
34 Markham, *History*, p. 85; see also Dickens, *Child's History*, I: p. 144.
35 James A. Froude, 'The lives of the saints', in *Short Studies on Great Subjects: First Series* (2nd edn, London: Longmans, 1867), p. 367.
36 James A. Froude, 'Life and times of Thomas Becket', in *Short Studies on Great Subjects: Fourth Series* (London: Longmans, 1883), pp. 1–230; E. A. Freeman, 'Mr Froude's "Life and times of Thomas Becket"', *Contemporary Review*, 31, 821–42; 32, 116–39, 474–500; 33, 213–41 (all 1878).
37 Freeman, 'St Thomas', p. 102.
38 Thomas Hughes, *Tom Brown's Schooldays* (1857; London: Macmillan, 1869), p. 282.
39 Stanley, *Memorials*, pp. 75–6. The Magdeburg Centuriators had long before singled out the vermin in Becket's belt as a subject for mockery, much to the indignation of the Catholic apologist Antoine-Frédéric Ozanam, *Deux Chanceliers d'Angleterre: Bacon de Vérulam et S. Thomas de Cantorbéry* (Paris and Lyon: [n.p.], 1836), p. 206n.
40 Charles Dickens, *Pictures from Italy*, ed. K. Flint (London: Penguin, 1998), p. 95; Dominic Janes, 'Dickens and the Catholic corpse', in M. Hollington and F. Orestano (eds), *Dickens and Italy: 'Little Dorrit' and 'Pictures from Italy'* (Newcastle: Cambridge Scholars, 2009), pp. 170–86.
41 Augustus J. C. Hare, *The Story of My Life*, 6 vols (London: George Allen, 1896), V: p. 358.
42 Not least the relic of Christ's foreskin 'rediscovered' in 1855 by Ursuline nuns at Charroux, for which, see Philip Spencer, *Politics of Belief in Nineteenth-Century France* (London: Faber, 1954), pp. 177, 206.
43 John Morris, *The Life and Martyrdom of Saint Thomas Becket Archbishop of Canterbury*, 2 vols (London: Burns and Oates, 1885), II: pp. 510–19. For the relics displayed in Wiseman's private chapel, see Wilfrid Ward, *The Life and Times of Cardinal Wiseman*, 2 vols (London: Longmans, Green, 1897), I: p. 507.

44  Gillis was given the heart in thanks for a panegyric preached in honour of Joan of Arc. Morris, *Life*, II: p. 514.
45  John Butler, *The Quest for Becket's Bones: The Mystery of the Relics of St Thomas Becket of Canterbury* (New Haven and London: Yale University Press, 1995), esp. p. 40.
46  *Ibid.*, pp. 40, 52–3.
47  T. B. James and A. M. Robinson, *Clarendon Palace: The History and Archaeology of a Medieval Palace and Hunting Lodge* (London: Society of Antiquaries of London, 1988), pp. 50, 91, and plate IIa.
48  D. Newsome, *The Parting of Friends* (1966; Leominster: Gracewing, 1993), p. 329.
49  Anthony Trollope, *Phineas Redux*, ed. John C. Whale (1874; Oxford: Oxford University Press, 1983), p. 297.
50  *Gladstone Diaries*, II: p. 355 (15 August 1838); IV: p. 643 (25 August 1854); V: p. 456 (15 January 1860); IX: p. 140 (12 July 1876); XI: p. 257 (10 December 1884); XIII: p. 208 (25 February 1893).
51  *Ibid.*, IV: p. 633 (14 July 1854); p. 648 (18 September 1854).
52  See, e.g., *The Canterbury Guide: Containing an Account of Whatever is Curious or Worth Observation in that Ancient City* (Canterbury: R. Colegate, 1845).
53  Austin Gough, *Paris and Rome: The Gallican Church and the Ultramontane Campaign 1848–1853* (Oxford: Clarendon, 1986).
54  As early as 1833, Hurrell Froude was planning such a trip: Charles S. Dessain, *et al.* (eds), *The Letters and Diaries of John Henry Newman*, 32 vols (London: Thomas Nelson and Sons; Oxford: Clarendon, 1961–2008), III: p. 291.
55  John A. Giles, *The Life and Letters of Thomas à Becket, Now First Gathered from the Contemporary Historians*, 2 vols (London: Whittaker, 1846); Giles, *Saint Thomas Becket, Archêveque de Cantérbury et Martyr*, trans. G. Darboy, 2 vols (Paris: Ambroise Bray, 1858).
56  Joseph-Alfred Foulon, *Histoire de la Vie et des Oeuvres de Mgr Darboy, Archevêque de Paris* (Paris: Librairie Possielgue Frères, 1889), pp. 176–80.
57  See Simmons, *Reversing the Conquest*, pp. 125–39. See also Robert Anchor Thompson, *Thomas Becket: Martyr and Patriot* (London: Kegan Paul, 1889); Elizabeth M. Stewart, *The People's Martyr* (London: D. Stewart, 1872); William Holden Hutton, *Thomas Becket, Archbishop of Canterbury* (London: Pitman, etc., 1910); Susan Cunnington, *The Story of Thomas Becket, Archbishop of Canterbury* (London: George G. Harrap, 1914).
58  Thomas Carlyle, *Past and Present*, ed. G. K. Chesterton (1843; Oxford: Oxford University Press, 1909), pp. 157, 245, 248, 254–5; J. T. Coleridge, *A Memoir of the Rev. John Keble*, 2 vols (Oxford and London: J. Parker, 1869), II: p. 408; Owen Chadwick, *Hensley Henson* (Oxford: Clarendon, 1983), p. 17. For Freeman's verse-epic on Becket, written at the age of 17, see W. R. W. Stephens, *The Life and Letters of Edward A. Freeman* (London: Macmillan, 1895), I: p. 38. For Stubbs, proud to have been born at Knaresborough with its Becket connections, see William H. Hutton (ed.), *Letters of William Stubbs* (London: Archibald Constable, 1904), pp. 4, 93–4, 179, 182.
59  Walter Scott, *Ivanhoe* (1820; London: Everyman, 1906), pp. 231, 336–7. For similar stuff, see John George Edgar, *Runnymede and Lincoln Fair* (1866; London: J. M. Dent, 1908), p. 66; Charles Grindrod, *The Shadow of the Raggedstone* (London: Simpkin, etc, 1888).
60  The painter, Alfred Elmore (1815–81), was in general better known for anti-Catholic themes.

61 Stanley, *Memorials*, pp. 94–5 n., citing Ozanam, *Deux Chanceliers*.
62 Reginald Farrar, *The Life of Frederic William Farrar* (London: Nisbet, 1905), pp. 313–14.
63 William G. Fallows, *Mandell Creighton and the English Church* (London: Oxford University Press, 1964), p. 116.
64 See Thomas Hughes, *Tom Brown at Oxford* (1861; London: Macmillan, 1889), esp. p. 79; see also Norman Vance, *The Sinews of the Spirit: The Ideal of Christian Manliness in Victorian Literature and Religious Thought* (Cambridge: Cambridge University Press, 1985).
65 David Hilliard, 'Unenglish and unmanly: Anglo-Catholicism and homosexuality', *Victorian Studies*, 25 (1982), 181–210.
66 Anne Fulton Hope, *The Life of S. Thomas à Becket of Canterbury* (London: Burns and Oates, 1868), pp. 31, 49.
67 See Introduction, pp. 13–17, and Macfarlane's chapter 14, pp. 245–61, in this volume.
68 R. H. Benson, *The Holy Blissful Martyr St Thomas of Canterbury* (London: Macdonald and Evans, 1908), pp. 15–16, 21.
69 William D. Bushell, 'St Thomas of Canterbury at Harrow: a lecture delivered before the Harrow branch of the London Diocesan Church Reading Union', in *Harrow Octocentenary Tracts*, 14 vols (Cambridge: Macmillan and Bowes, 1893–1914), VIII: p. 11.
70 W. J. Millor and C. N. L. Brooke (eds), *The Letters of John of Salisbury: Volume Two (The Later Letters, 1163–1180)* (Oxford: Clarendon Press, 1979), pp. 746–9, n. 307.
71 John Henry Newman, *Loss and Gain: The Story of a Convert*, ed. A. G. Hill (Oxford: Oxford University Press, 1986), p. 201.
72 John E. Bowden, *The Life and Letters of Frederick William Faber* (London: Thomas Richardson and Son, 1869), pp. 270–3.
73 See Walter H. Frere, *Some Principles of Liturgical Reform* (London: John Murray, 1911), pp. 21–39, 56–7. The 1928 Prayer Book allowed the restitution of the feast of St Thomas on 29 December but not that of his translation on 7 July.
74 E.g. Newport, Isle of Wight (c. 1791); Fairford, Gloucestershire (1845); Fulham (1847); St Thomas of Canterbury and the English Martyrs, Preston, Lancashire (1864); Northampton Cathedral, dedicated to Our Lady Immaculate and St Thomas of Canterbury (1864), these last three by Pugin; Woodford Green (1896).
75 Frances Arnold-Forster, *Studies in Church Dedications*, 3 vols (London: Skeffington and Son, 1899), I: pp. 356–61, 36; III: pp. 450–1.
76 William C. E. Newbolt, *Years that Are Past* (London: W. Gardner, Darton, 1921), p. 69.
77 Arnold-Forster, *Studies*, I: p. 361.
78 Ward, *Wiseman*, I: pp. 271–2; E. S. Purcell, *Life of Cardinal Manning Archbishop of Westminster*, 2 vols (London: Macmillan, 1896), I: pp. 155–6; *Gladstone Diaries*, II: p. 542. Macaulay had visited the College a month before: George O. Trevelyan, *The Life and Letters of Lord Macaulay*, 2 vols (London: Longmans, 1876), II: pp. 30–1.
79 'Thomas a Becket', *British Magazine*, 2 (1832), 233–43, 453–9; 3 (1833), 31–8, 150–47, 399–411, 525–34; 4 (1833), 255–60, 376–82, 607–11; 5 (1834), 11–15, 655–8.
80 Froude, 'Becket', *British Magazine*, 2 (1832), 235–6; 3 (1833), 35–6, 399–402.
81 Newman, *Letters and Diaries*, III: pp. 92–3, 96, 190, 284, 291.
82 Louise I. Guiney, *Hurrell Froude: Memoranda and Comments* (London: Methuen, 1904), pp. 98, 103. For evidence that Froude did indeed inspect the manuscript, see John Henry

Newman and John Keble (eds), *Remains of the Late Reverend Richard Hurrell Froude*, 4 vols (London: J. G. and F. Rivington, 1838–39), IV: p. 196.
83   Lytton Strachey, *Eminent Victorians* (London: Chatto and Windus, 1918), p. 16.
84   Guiney, *Froude*, pp. 132, 159–60. For Newman and Keble's editorial additions, see *Remains*, IV: pp. vii–viii, 12–13.
85   The parallel between the Becket lives and the synoptic Gospels was noted by Freeman in 1860: Freeman, 'St Thomas', pp. 91–2.
86   Owen Chadwick, *The Victorian Church*, 2 vols (London: Adam and Charles Black, 1966–70), I: pp. 250–71.
87   Ward, *Wiseman*, I: p. 519.
88   Purcell, *Manning*, I: pp. 500–628.
89   Trollope, *The Warden* (1855; London: Oxford University Press, 1952), p. 160.
90   Stanley, *Memorials*, pp. 87–8.
91   David Hume, *The History of England*, 8 vols (1761; London: T. Cadell, 1786), I: pp. 417–18.
92   David Bromwich, *The Diary and Memoirs of John Allen Giles* (Taunton: Somerset Record Society, 2000).
93   Nicholas Vincent, 'William of Canterbury and Benedict of Peterborough: the manuscripts, date and context of the Becket miracle collections', Edina Bozóky (ed.), *Hagiographie, Idéologie et Politique au Moyen Âge en Occident* (Turnhout: Brepols, 2012), pp. 349–57, and Vincent, 'John Allen Giles and the Three Thomases', M. Staunton (ed.) *The World of Herbert of Bosham* (Woodbridge: Boydell, forthcoming).
94   Vincent, 'John Allen Giles'.
95   See Vincent, 'William of Canterbury', pp. 352–3.
96   James C. Robertson, *Becket, Archbishop of Canterbury: A Biography* (London: J. Murray, 1859), esp. pp. 169–72.
97   J. R. Green to E. A. Freeman, April/May 1864, in Leslie Stephen (ed.), *The Letters of John Richard Green* (London: Macmillan, 1901), pp. 144–5.
98   Vincent, 'William of Canterbury', pp. 354–5.
99   *Ibid.*, pp. 356–87.
100  Edwin A. Abbott, *Philomythus: An Antidote Against Credulity* (London: Macmillan, 1891).
101  Edwin A. Abbott, *St Thomas of Canterbury: His Death and Miracles*, 2 vols (London: A. and C. Black, 1898).
102  Arthur C. Benson, *The Life of Edward White Benson, Sometime Archbishop of Canterbury* (1898; London and New York: Macmillan, 1901), p. 307.
103  Thompson, *Becket*, pp. 313–14.

# 6

# Thomas More

*William Sheils*

THIS CHAPTER DERIVES FROM a longstanding if somewhat fitful engagement with the posthumous reputation of Thomas More (1478–1535), and especially as it was construed among the English cultural and intellectual elites. At times of political change or social crisis from the 1580s to the 1930s and beyond, More's reputation and writings have been appealed to, sometimes by opposing parties, but often also in ways that cut across such divisions. He has acquired some unsuspecting advocates. Among the earliest was the Puritan John Hoddesdon (fl. 1650), whose life of More, based heavily on the Latin life of 1588 by the priest Thomas Stapleton (1535–98), was published in 1652 during the birthpangs of the English republic.[1] It is, however, another of those periods of constitutional crisis which provides the context for this paper. That is, the debate on Catholic Emancipation – an issue which became a crucial, if not a defining feature of British political discourse following the Act of Union of 1801 – and the consequent absorption of large numbers of Roman Catholic subjects resident in Ireland into the British state. This is not the place in which to trace that history, but the cause gathered dramatic momentum in 1823 when Daniel O'Connell (1775–1847) and Richard Sheil (1791–1851) founded the Catholic Association in Ireland (soon to be followed by a mainland equivalent), and after the failure in the following year of a bill designed to outlaw such associations.[2] In this environment scholarly rivalries soon transformed themselves into political ones, or at least enhanced their overt political content. At the centre of this was the Poet Laureate, Robert Southey (1774–1843), already excoriated as an apostate from his radical past following the publication of his poem on the death of George III, and named as 'the first man to be hanged' by the radical journalist William Cobbett (1763–1835) once the Radicals came to power.[3]

This chapter argues that, in their writings on More, Southey and Cobbett represent one stage in a characteristic trend in English literary and historical culture, beginning almost from the moment of More's execution, which periodically looked to his life and death as an expression of all that was perceived to be best in the Christian and in English life. This is a tradition which endures to the present day, notwithstanding the presence of some powerful dissenting voices, most recently that of the Booker Prize winning novelist, Hilary Mantel.[4] In the 1820s More, whilst not yet officially a saint of the Roman Church, had long been considered both saint and martyr by his English co-religionists, and his memory had been kept alive by relics, by his published writings, and by manuscript biographies which circulated among the recusant and exile communities. The first published biography, *Tres Thomae*, written in Latin by the exile priest Thomas Stapleton, had clearly signalled his claim to sainthood by linking his life with those of two saints called Thomas, one the Apostle, and the other another martyr of the English Crown, Becket. Stapleton had underlined More's sanctity by stressing his universal appeal and incorporating the approving comments of Protestant humanists such as More's friend Simon Grynaeus (1493–1541) into the narrative.[5] Stapleton's cross-confessional focus meant that, by the end of the seventeenth century, More had also attracted supporters among English Protestants, especially among members of the established Church such as Gilbert Burnet (1643–1715), bishop, historian of the English Reformation, and in 1684 the translator of *Utopia*.[6] To the erastian Whig Burnet, More was the epitome of moderation, a Protestant reformer *avant la lettre*, and this was a view which gained currency in mid-eighteenth-century literary culture, with Jonathan Swift (1667–1745) declaring More to have been 'the person of the greatest virtue this kingdom ever produced'. That claim was echoed in Southey's work.

What follows also emphasises the ways in which the past became a key battleground in the war between radicals and the conservatives in the decades following the French Revolution. In the context of legislation proposing Catholic relief, attention was not surprisingly focused on the period of the Reformation. Debate was all the hotter when it came to the personalities of that period, for with Catholics and Protestants alike trying to elevate their own favourites and to topple those of their confessional rivals, figures such as Anne Boleyn, Erasmus, Cranmer, Fisher and of course More were praised or condemned almost whenever historical writers and their reviewers took up their pens.[7] In this context the publication of the *History of England* by the Catholic priest-scholar John Lingard (1771–1851), and especially that of volume five, in which the Henrician Reformation was discussed at length, made a significant impact. Lingard grounded his history securely in the primary sources, and produced an essentially political account of reform which challenged the confessional narratives which had hitherto dominated contemporary understanding, the received narrative of English religious history drawn from the pages of the martyrologist John Foxe's *Acts and Monuments* which, from the time of its publication in the 1560s, had provided the touchstone for mainstream Protestant accounts.[8] Lingard's *History* established the author as a scholar of European importance and secured for him a wide readership beyond Catholic circles in England, providing, for example, Cobbett with much of the material for his critical but not very critically researched *History of the Reformation*.[9] It also provoked a response from Robert Southey, and it is to Southey's case that I wish to turn, for it is in his account of the Reformation that the figure of More gets perhaps the most extensive treatment. Despite his radical youth, his early attraction to Unitarianism and his experimentation with pantisocracy, by the later 1810s Southey had become a stout defender of establishment, Poet Laureate, and, if not a very active member of the Church of England, an aggressive supporter of a Church and state policy.[10] Southey saw the defence of the Revolution settlement of 1689 as a crucial element in sustaining the stability and security of a society which he thought to be on the point of breakdown under the combined stresses of capitalism, manufacturing and urbanisation, the origins of which he deemed to be rooted in the Reformation. The saintly More, as we shall see, became a crucial vehicle for discussion and for critiquing these changes.

## The *Book of the Church*

In the course of the 1820s, Southey's religious principles and social conservatism came together in a form of patriotism labelled as 'romantic conservatism' by David Eastwood and others.[11] And Southey was not the only romantic poet addressing these issues; in rather more philosophical mode Samuel Taylor Coleridge (1772–1834) was putting together his famous and influential essay *On the Constitution of the Church and State* (1830), whilst in 1822 William Wordsworth (1770–1850) penned a series of sonnets on the English Church, a proposal which he had discussed with Southey and which Southey thought of as constituting an unintended collaboration with his own work.[12] In that sense Southey saw himself participating in a wider endeavour of the poetic imagination which, faced with the upheavals of industrial revolution at home and political revolution abroad, sought a realignment of the religious foundations of society.[13] It was in Southey, however, that the impulse to defend the Church was most clearly seen, and he embarked on the writing of two broadly historical works which would set out his political, social and ecclesiastical agenda. The publication in 1818 of *The End of Religious Controversy*, a learned defence of the loyalty of English Catholics and the truth of their Church's claims, by Bishop John Milner, Vicar General of the Midland district, provoked Southey into embarking on this project, for which he had high hopes.[14] The books were written contemporaneously and were designed to inform each other: in a letter of April 1821 Southey wrote: 'I am proceeding also with my Dialogues, and with the Book of the Church – two works by which I shall deserve well of posterity, whatever treatment they may provoke now from the bigoted, the irreligious and the fractious.'[15]

These remarks reflect the strength of feeling that existed on both sides in literary and political circles. Southey's judgement about his contemporary reception was entirely accurate, as we shall see, although not without its compensations if we can judge by the print runs and royalties that followed. But his assessment of the impact of these books on posterity was entirely misplaced. Read by scholars for the most abstruse of purposes, they are mentioned briefly in the most recent scholarly biography by Bill Speck and the monograph by David Craig, and have been given fuller treatment only in the recent study by Stuart Andrews.[16] What were these texts on which Southey vested so much time and energy? The *Book of the Church*, published in 1824 and reprinted twice within the year, was an essentially Foxean narrative of English Church history which responded to Lingard quite directly in that it continued the story up to the removal of

James II and the settlement of 1688–89. The thrust of its argument is best expressed in the author's own words, taken from his final paragraph:

> From the time of the Revolution the Church of England has partaken of the stability and security of the State. Here therefore I terminate this compendious, but faithful view of its rise, progress and political struggles. It has rescued us, first from heathenism, then from papal idolatry and superstition; it has saved us from temporal as well as spiritual despotism. We owe to it our moral and intellectual character as a nation; much of our private happiness, much of our public strength. Whatever should weaken it, would in the same degree injure the commonweal; whatever should overthrow it, would in sure and immediate consequence bring down the goodly fabric of that Constitution, whereof it is a constituent and necessary part.[17]

The most pressing threat to that state of affairs was the granting of civil emancipation to Roman Catholics, in the pursuit of which he claimed both Catholics and Dissenters to be in unholy alliance. It was to counter that alliance that Southey undertook the writing of the book.[18] In *Book of the Church* the Reformation formed a central part of the story, and within that narrative the figure of Thomas More acquired a more complex delineation, derived in part from Burnet, than that offered in Foxe's sixteenth-century account. Yet Southey could not escape dealing with More's involvement in the persecution of the early martyrs, nor indeed with his complicity in the falsification of the accounts in the record. Writing of the outspoken preacher Thomas Bilney (c. 1495–1531) and his alleged confession at the stake Southey concluded:

> For it was one of the pious frauds of the Romanists, to spread reports that their victims had seen and acknowledged their error, when too late to save their lives, and had asked pardon of God and man for their heresies, with their latest breath. This last wrong was offered to Bilney, and it would have been fatal to his good name on earth, the falsehood having been believed and published by Sir Thomas More, if Parker, in whose primacy the Church of England was afterward established by Elizabeth, had not attended at his martyrdom, for the love which he bore to the martyr, and established the truth by his unquestionable testimony.[19]

Southey then turned to the heroism of the Protestant martyrs, focusing on the controversy between More and William Tyndale (c. 1494–1536) over the vernacular Bible as a centrepiece of the narrative. In his account of the martyrdom of the lawyer and reformer James Bainham (d. 1532), he recalled the martyr's defiant gesture: 'The book which Bainham held up in the church, when he proclaimed his repentance, and his readiness to die for the truth, would alone have been sufficient to draw upon him enquiry and persecution. It was Tindal's translation, now one of the rarest volumes in the collections of the curious: and in its effect upon this nation, the most important that ever issued from the press.'[20] Southey then recounted Tyndale's life and his career, praising the translator who 'perceived that it was impossible to establish the people in any truth, except the Scriptures were laid plainly before them in their mother tongue, that they might see the process, order, and meaning of the text. The Romanists understood perfectly well how little the practice of their Church was supported by Scripture: and that if the Ark of the Covenant was admitted Dagon must fall.' There followed an account of the Tyndale Bible and its impact: 'A spirit had been roused, which no persecution could suppress. Dangerous as it was to possess the book, it was eagerly sought for; and of those persons who dispersed it, some were punished by penance and heavy fines; others, who preached and avowed its doctrines, by the flames.'[21] The campaign against the Bible brought Southey back to More and the literary controversy with Tyndale, in which he concluded that More, in the context of polemic, quickly 'degenerated into the worst forms of controversy, and its worst temper'.[22]

So far, so good and, in Foxean terms, entirely predictable, but at this point the narrative broke off from its Foxean moorings. Notwithstanding Southey's acknowledgement of More's active role in both persecuting Protestants and undermining the vernacular translation, he embarked on a lengthy defence of More's actions, depicting him as a victim of the age in which he lived, and as a strong defender of establishment and, thus, of stability. The passage is worth considering at some length:

> Sir Thomas More is represented by the Protestant martyrologists, as a cruel persecutor; by the Catholics, as a blessed martyr. Like some of his contemporaries he was both. But the character of this illustrious man deserves a fairer estimate than has been given it, either by his adorers or his enemies. It behoves us ever to bear in mind, that while actions are always to be judged by the immutable standard of right and wrong, the judgement which we pass upon men must be qualified by consideration of age, country, situation, and other incidental circumstances; and it will then be found, that he who is charitable in his judgement is generally the least unjust. Sir Thomas More would, in any age of the world, have ranked among the wisest and best of men. One generation earlier, he would have appeared as a precursor of the reformation, and perhaps have delayed it by procuring the correction of grosser abuses, thereby rendering its necessity less urgent. One generation later, and his natural place would have been in Elizabeth's council, among the pillars of the Church of England. But the circumstances wherein he found himself were peculiarly unpropitious to his disposition, his happiness, and even his character in aftertimes. His high station compelled him to take an active part in public affairs, in forwarding the work of persecution he believed that he was discharging not only a legal, but a religious duty.[23]

This passage touches the crux of those issues which have engaged every generation writing about More and his part in the persecution of heresy, a part he was proud of and listed prominently among those achievements he recorded on the epitaph he composed for his own tomb, describing himself as 'yet to thieves, murderers, and heretics grievous'.[24] This aspect of More's life has often been overlooked by his defenders, and it remains unacknowledged on the Vatican's website in the *Motu Proprio* of John Paul II proclaiming More as the patron saint of statesmen and politicians.[25] The defenders of More's actions against heretics have generally come from two diametrically opposing directions which one can define broadly as 'liberal', as in placing the individual conscience above the dictates of policy, and 'conservative', as prioritising good order and stability.[26] It was this conservative defence which characterised Southey's account: for Southey it was the zeal of the reformers which threatened the order and stability of society, and it was More who recognised the importance of that stability. In responding to the Protestants 'he saw that they tended to subversion, not of existing institutions alone, but of civil society itself; the atrocious frenzy of the Anabaptists in Germany confirmed him in this apprehension'.[27] But there was a further issue at stake: the nature of society itself. More's response stemmed not only from an aversion to the threat of civil breakdown, but also from a deep attachment to the medieval Church which, in what we might today describe as its 'Duffyesque' manifestation, sought to uphold the sacramentalism through which the Church sustained both individual piety and social harmony.

> He [More] was contented with it as it stood, and in the strength of his attachment to its better principles, loved some of its errors and excused others. Herein he was unlike his friend Erasmus ... More was characteristically devout: the imaginative part of Catholicism had its full effect on him; its splendid ceremonials, its magnificent edifices, its alliance with music, painting and sculpture; its observances, so skilfully interwoven with the business, the festivities, and the ordinary ceremony of life ... [I]n these things he delighted ... and all these the reformers were for sweeping away.[28]

## Sir Thomas More: Or, Colloquies on the Progress and Prospects of Society

This encomium to More and to what Southey saw as 'the best' of the medieval Church is crucial when we come to consider the other text which Southey was writing at this time. This was a critique of contemporary society, framed within the form of a dialogue between a younger man, a fictional representation of Southey himself, called Montesinos, and an unlikely partner: the ghost of Thomas More. Southey had been engaged on the book from at least 1817, and it finally appeared in two volumes in 1829 under the title *Sir Thomas More: Or, Colloquies on the Progress and Prospects of Society*.[29] The volumes contained fifteen conversations between the protagonists, located at different sites throughout the Lake District and illustrated by engravings after the watercolourist William Westall (1781–1850). These engravings, designed to heighten the timeless qualities of the romantic Lakeland landscape were themselves part of the message to the literary and professional classes which were the intended audience for the book. The colloquies covered a range of topics: the feudal system (good, if not always so in practice), manufacturing (bad, in that it offered false promises), economic improvement (well-intentioned but mostly wrongheaded), population growth (bad in its moral and social consequences), and the American Revolution (just plain bad). It centred on the most pressing political and religious questions of the day, dealing with Catholic Emancipation (which passed the same year), the Reformation, and Church establishment.[30]

Southey explicitly likened the problems facing humanist reformers in the early sixteenth century to those faced by conservative social commentators in his own day. How to protect civil and ecclesiastical institutions in a period of rapid economic and social change? He expressed this succinctly in a letter to his friend John Rickman (1771–1840), founder of the national census and a fellow conservative reformer: 'I shall put together a good deal of historical matter in these interlocutions, taking society in two of its critical periods – the age of the Reformation, and this in which we live.'[31]

For Southey, as for his political opponent William Cobbett, the crucial event of the Reformation in socio-political terms was the dissolution of the monasteries. Ignoring somewhat the dictates of chronology More's ghost is led to say of that process: 'I beheld a system of profligate robbery, a transfer of property from religious establishments to knaves and courtiers', to which Montesinos/Southey responds: 'the system of spoliation we have seen renewed in these days, as the first effect of the French Revolution, wherever it extended'.[32] Out of the Reformation there had emerged a class of greedy capitalists who had, over the succeeding three centuries, led contemporary society into the divisive conditions which Southey lamented. Furthermore, the Reformation also removed those very institutions best suited to ameliorating the lives of those victims left behind by the onward march of progress: hospitals, almshouses and the like. The discussion that followed took the reader through what by now was familiar territory: the failure to maintain the Church as an institution led to political instability which, in turn, undermined true faith so that without establishment the people were not brought up in proper understanding of religion. More's ghost concluded: 'In men thus prepared the propagandist of Atheism and the Jesuit both find facile converts ... Indeed the transition between Popery and infidelity is in either direction short and easy.'[33] Putting these words into More's mouth, expressing as they did an assumption which had been a commonplace of Protestant polemic since the sixteenth century, detached More from the post-Tridentine Church which claimed him as its martyr. It was a Church to which Southey had been a consistent enemy ever since his radical youth when in 1795 he visited Spain and Portugal, where 'in a lovely country, a paradise of nature' he saw a people 'kept in ignorance and poverty by the double despotism of church and state'.[34]

The contemporary lesson for England, however, was that the failure of the political establishment to support the established Church, and the Church's consequent failure to provide spiritual sustenance to the laity, had created a vacuum into which Methodists and Dissenters had stepped, with their love feasts, their music and their outdoor meetings, modes of religious expression which More's ghost compared unfavourably with the medieval Church, declaring that these were 'better provided by the Roman Church, in fraternities, and processions and festivals'. Noting that the growth of Methodism was most pronounced in the larger towns, and the failure of the established Church to provide clergy in those areas, More's ghost recalled another medieval precedent, the mendicant orders, commenting that 'such places were better supplied, methinks, when the Convents sent forth itinerant preachers throughout the country'.³⁵ Thus was the perceived contemporary conspiracy between Catholics and Dissenters explained in cultural terms through the agency of voluntary association in matters of religion, an agency which both parties espoused. It was the failure of politicians to defend the established Church that gave them their opportunity.

Notwithstanding the praise of the medieval Church implicit in More's comments, it is important to remember that the discussion remained robust on the question of contemporary Catholicism, with Montesinos/Southey forcefully articulating traditional suspicions about papal 'tyranny', from which the Reformation saved the nation, and of institutions such as nunneries, which 'are connected with the worst corruptions of popery, being at once nurseries of superstition and of misery. In their least objectionable point of view they serve as Bedlams'.³⁶ Similar examples of Southey's vigorous anti-Catholicism appear throughout the text, but they are usually tempered by More's ghost. In their discussions of the process of the Reformation it was he who retained the final word, ventriloquising Southey's conclusion that 'ecclesiastical establishment – that, and that alone can preserve the social body from putresence and dissolution'.³⁷ Thus, just as the Catholic martyr More emerged in the *Book of the Church* as a creator and defender of the Elizabethan Settlement *avant la lettre*, so, in the *Colloquies*, his ghost donned the mantle of a Georgian 'Church and state' Anglican.

The discussion of Southey's 'romantic conservatism' on social issues, as described by David Eastwood and others, has largely ignored the importance accorded to the Reformation and to ecclesiastical history in the formation of that view.³⁸ Putting together this social commentary and the *Book of the Church* makes it clear that for Southey these were two sides of the same coin. The career and character of Thomas More played a key role in fusing them together. But how did Southey come upon him? Southey had no substantial biography of More to consult, and his chief source, beyond the characterisation of More as the persecutor of Protestants in Foxe, was the edition of *The Complete English Works* published in the reign of Queen Mary, which he consulted after much searching in London.³⁹ In addition, the secular writings of More, especially *Utopia* in Burnet's translation, were readily available, and these no doubt had a significant influence on the early radicalism of Southey when, as young men in the 1790s inspired by the revolutionary events in France, he and his friend Coleridge devised a blueprint for a utopian society, pantisocracy, which they planned to found in the new American Republic.⁴⁰ Indeed, that early radicalism may well have informed Southey's choice of More, for he recognised that, just as sixteenth-century humanists and nineteenth-century reformers faced similar socio-political challenges, so he and More shared a trajectory from early radicalism to a mature conservatism. More's ghost makes this clear on being first recognised at the start of the *Colloquies*:

> You apprehend me. We have both speculated in the joy and freedom of our youth upon the possible improvement of society: and both in like manner have lived to dread with reason the effects of that restless spirit ... By comparing the great operating causes in the age of the Reformation, and in this age of revolutions, going back to the former age, and

looking at things as I then beheld them, perceiving wherein I judged rightly and wherein I erred, and tracing the progress of those causes which are now developing their own tremendous power, you will derive instruction.[41]

Of course, Southey's defence of the medieval Church through More has to be demarcated from his views of the contemporary Catholic Church, which he regarded as autocratic and idolatrous, an 'incurably and restlessly intolerant' institution which, from his experiences abroad, he castigated for keeping its people in ignorance.[42] Catholics were in thrall to a priesthood committed, in Southey's eyes, to the overthrow of the British state. For Southey, therefore, the incorporation of large numbers of Catholic Irish within the British state since 1801, which so exercised his discussion of emancipation, threatened its civil and religious foundations. In answer to a series of questions from More's ghost, Montesinos replies: 'what greater error could a government commit than that of conferring political privileges upon a class of freeholders who had no expectations of them, no pretensions to them upon any grounds of common policy ... and giving encouragement to a priesthood, who are the confederated and sworn enemies of that religion which is the cornerstone of the British constitution'. More's ghost has no answer to this except the weary generalisation that 'religion is the only foundation of society, and governments which have not this basis are built upon sand'.[43] More could thus be deployed as an effective defender of social stability and of medieval religion whilst simultaneously being held at arm's length from the modern Roman Church and its adherents, who claimed him as a martyr.

## Responses and reactions

To the Whig historian Thomas Babington Macaulay (1800–59), writing in the *Edinburgh Review*, the format of the *Dialogues* and their contents were 'mere rubbish'. Montesinos, Macaulay snorted, initially mistakes the ghost of More for an American tourist, the two ridiculously romanticising 'rose-bushes and poor-rates' instead of 'steam-engines and independence' as the cure for present-day woes. What purported to be a dialogue, Macaulay pointed out sarcastically, was in fact a conversation 'between two Southeys, equally eloquent, equally angry, equally unreasonable, and equally given to talking about what they do not understand'.[44] Such derision was understandable.[45] Yet Southey was not alone in seeking More as a companion and interlocutor. His fiercely radical opponent Cobbett, also a proud Protestant, enlisted More in his polemical *History of the Protestant Reformation* (1824–27), in which he was equally vehement in condemnation of the Henrician reforms, but with very different contemporary targets in mind:

> We now come to that copious source of blood, the suppression of the Pope's Supremacy. To deny the King's supremacy was made high treason, and to refuse to take the oath acknowledging that supremacy was deemed a denial of it. Sir Thomas More who was Lord Chancellor and John Fisher who was bishop of Rochester, were put to death for

refusing to take the oath. Of all the men in England, these were the two most famed for learning, for integrity, for piety, and for long and faithful service to the king and his father. It is no weak presumption in favour of the pope's supremacy that these two men, who had exerted their talents to prevent its suppression, laid their heads on the block rather than accept that suppression. But knowing as we do, that it is the refusal of our fellow Catholic subjects to take this same oath, for which More and Fisher died, knowing that this is the cause of all that cruel treatment which the Irish people have so long endured, and to put an end to which they are now so arduously struggling ... consider whether it be favourable, or otherwise, to true religion and civil liberty, to grant them their rightful place in society.[46]

Thus it was that the radical journalist drew diametrically opposed conclusions to those of Southey from More's execution. In so doing, Cobbett's casual treatment of the historical record would have embarrassed Lingard, the historian whose work inspired his polemic, but Cobbett's position won the day and Catholic Emancipation was passed in 1829.[47] This deployment of More's reputation for sanctity by a variety of Protestant antagonists has gone largely unnoticed until now.

What does this tell us of the uses to which saints and questions of sanctity were put in nineteenth-century England? Stapleton's polemical claim that More's life had attracted the admiration of some Protestant reformers while he lived and in the generations after his death was vindicated by the way in which his personality, and the manner of his death, became a central motif in the arguments over Catholic Emancipation. To draw the conclusions he did, Southey needed to counter the claim put forward by Cobbett: that the examples of More and Fisher justified the demands of contemporary Catholics to freedom of worship and the removal of other civil restrictions. To do this, Southey associated More with the heroic churchmen of the early English Reformation. We have already noted the way in which, in the *Book of the Church*, More was depicted as a precursor of the founders of the Elizabethan Church. In the *Colloquies* More's ghost aligned himself with Cranmer, admitting that as both persecutors and persecuted, they were products and victims of the age in which they lived.[48] In acknowledging this, however, Southey was emphatic in distancing More from the persecutions of the later Marian bishops. As the saint's ghost was to declare, 'Bonner was a monster of barbarity: Stephen Gardiner a time-serving politician, with a hard head and a harder heart.'[49] These of course were Southey's views and, whatever the fates of Bonner and Gardiner, the earthly conflicts of More and his Protestant opponents were finally resolved in death. From his heavenly home the ghost of Thomas More assured his companion Montesinos that these old enmities had been cast off: 'Luther and I are friends and associates now, and Frith and Bainham have forgiven me.'[50]

Such ecumenical generosity was not exhibited so readily in the England of the mid- and later Victorian period. The changes of the 1830s and 1840s led to an enhanced Catholic presence in Parliament and the magistracy, and created a national educational programme in Ireland which removed control of religious education from the Church of Ireland and increased the authority of the Catholic clergy.[51] These policies, and the conversions to Rome of a number of highly educated Anglicans, following that of John Henry Newman (1801–90) in 1845, caused anxiety to British Protestants of all persuasions, their concerns being given greater, and more popular, expression following the influx of about 250,000 poor Irish immigrants into England fleeing the potato famine of the late 1840s. The pastoral needs of this new Catholic population, located chiefly in the capital and the indusrtrialising cities, led to restoration of the Catholic hierarchy in England in 1850, in the face of opposition from the Whig government, which had been traditionally supporters of Catholic claims.[52] Neither the revived Catholicism of the converts nor the imported faith of the Irish poor had any place for the reformed, benignly patriarchal, and essentially English Catholicism epitomised in the characterisations of Southey and Cobbett.[53] The new brands of Catholicism were, by contrast, more Roman than Rome, and their appeal to the medieval past was not so much to the social values of a feudal order as to the aesthetics and rituals of a world in which the miraculous was ever present.[54]

The rising confessional temperature meant that the past was again brought into play. A popular history of the English Reformation to challenge that of Lingard, *The History of England from the Fall of Wolsey to the Death of Elizabeth*, was produced in twelve volumes by James Anthony Froude (1818–94) between 1856 and 1870. Froude was later appointed Regius Professor of History at Oxford, and his *History*, later amended to finish with the defeat of the Spanish Armada, came to dominate Protestant understandings of the English Reformation for the rest of the century.[55]

Yet if Froude's story of intellectual and commercial rebirth retained much of the Protestant flavour of earlier accounts, he also represented a significant shift in opinion. Since 'Protestant' now stood less for particular doctrines or ecclesiology as for freedom of conscience, free trade and unfettered exploration, it made less sense to dismiss a More or a Fisher on the grounds of their beliefs. Character mattered more than creed, and while there remained plenty of Protestant hardliners prepared to condemn More, for many others, he and his family were part of the Reformation-as-drama; a pageant in which human interest stories figured more highly than dusty dogmas.[56] Hence, perhaps, the proliferation of vivid paintings drawing on William Roper's eyewitness account of More bidding farewell to his daughter Margaret (Roper's own wife) by John Rogers Herbert (1844), Edward Matthew Ward (1840s) and W. F. Yeames (1872).[57] There were also versions of Margaret rescuing her father's head, by Charles Landseer (c. 1832) and Lucy Maddox Brown (1873); and of More posing in Holbein's studio, by John Evan Hodgson (1861). Catholic or not, by the early twentieth century there was a sense that More had been on the right side of the argument in many of the things that mattered. He appears twice at the Palace of Westminster, celebrating enlightened learning in Frank Cadogan's *Thomas More and Erasmus Visit the Children of King Henry VII at Greenwich in 1499* (1910), and defending the constitution in Vivian Forbes's *Thomas More Defending the Liberty of the House of Commons* (1927).

Catholics too shared the family drama of More's life, expressed most clearly in *The*

*Life and Writings of Sir Thomas More* by Father Thomas Bridgett (1829–99), published in 1891.[58] But as far as More's reputation among the hierarchy was concerned, he was placed decisively among the ranks of the English martyrs, alongside those Elizabethans, mostly seminary priests and Jesuits, executed by the Crown after 1558. For the Roman Church he was unequivocally a saint, and was set upon that path, as Lucy Underwood's chapter in this volume shows, in the beatification process of 1886.[59] More's connection to the later Catholic martyrs had, of course, no place in the accounts of Southey or Cobbett, and was to be uncoupled from them again in 1935 when More and Fisher were canonised. Most of the Elizabethan martyrs had to wait until 1970 for their elevation, and some of them have yet to achieve it.

## Conclusion

So it is with saints: we construct them in our own image or, more accurately, in the image that we wish to foster. This was as true in the 1820s as at any other time, and More's acknowledged sanctity, among Catholics, Protestants and, though they would not perhaps own that description, non-believers, has continued to see his life appropriated for political purposes. Just as Southey and Cobbett could construct that life as a model of conservatism or radicalism to suit their political purposes, so at the time of the canonisation in the 1930s the meanings of More's life were hotly contested by liberal and conservative advocates, both Catholic and Protestant.[60] From Gilbert Burnet in the 1690s to Tony Blair in the 1990s, More has been wheeled out to rhetorical effect by those seeking what they imagine to be the higher ground.[61] The debates of the 1820s, stimulated by the question of Catholic Emancipation, form only one chapter in a long story. It suggests that the response of Protestant commentators to an English saint was more complex than that suggested by the literary scholar Anne Lake Prescott in her recent study of More's afterlives. Neither Southey nor Cobbett stressed the persecutory polemical More; rather, they celebrated his moral courage.[62]

## Notes

1 John Guy, *Thomas More* (London: Arnold, 2000), pp. 1–20; Anne Lake Prescott, 'Afterlives', in George M. Logan (ed.), *The Cambridge Companion to Thomas More* (Cambridge: Cambridge University Press, 2011), pp. 265–87.
2 The fullest account of this is found in G. I. T. Machin, *The Catholic Question in English Politics 1820–1830* (Oxford: Oxford University Press, 1964); for the Catholic Association see pp. 43–64.
3 See William A. Speck, *Robert Southey, Entire Man of Letters* (New Haven and London: Yale University Press, 2006), pp. 169–207.
4 Robert Bolt's *A Man for All Seasons* was first performed on stage in 1960 at the then Globe Theatre, London, and influentially shaped positive views of More among mid- and later twentieth-century audiences. For a more sceptical portrayal, see Hilary Mantel, *Wolf Hall* (London: Fourth Estate, 2009).

5 William J. Sheils, 'Polemic as piety: Thomas Stapleton's *Tres Thomae* and Catholic controversy in the 1580s', *Journal of Ecclesiastical History*, 60 (2009), 74–94, esp. 85, 91.
6 Martin Greig, 'Burnet, Gilbert (1643–1715)', *Oxford Dictionary of National Biography* (Oxford: Oxford University Press, 2004), online edition.
7 See essays in Peter Nockles and Vivienne Westbrook (eds), *Reinventing the Reformation in the Nineteenth Century*, special issue of the Bulletin of the John Rylands Library, 90 (2014).
8 John Lingard, *History of England from the First Invasion by the Romans to the Accession of William and Mary in 1688*, 10 vols (London: Dolman, 1819–30). The work was specifically designed to challenge Foxe, and the history of the Reformation, treated in volumes four (1824) and five (1825), forms the core of the text. See Edwin Jones, *John Lingard and the Search for Historical Truth* (Brighton: Sussex Academic Press, 2001), pp. 198–207, and Jones, *The English Nation: The Great Myth* (Stroud: Sutton, 1998), pp. 168–217.
9 Rosemary O'Day, 'John Lingard: historians and contemporary politics', in Peter Philips (ed.), *Lingard Remembered* (London: Catholic Record Society, 2004), pp. 82–104.
10 Speck, *Southey*, pp. 42–82, 169–88.
11 David Eastwood, 'Robert Southey and the intellectual origins of romantic conservatism', *English Historical Review*, 104 (1999), 308–31.
12 Samuel T. Coleridge, *On the Constitution of the Church and State According to the Idea of Each*, ed. John Colmer (1830; London: Oxford University Press, 1976).
13 William Wordsworth, *Ecclesiastical Sketches: A Tale in Verse* (London: Longman, Hurst, 1822); Charles C. Southey, *The Life and Correspondence of Robert Southey*, 6 vols (London: Longman, Brown, Green, 1849–50), V: p. 65. For the influence of both see Stephen Prickett, *Romanticism and Religion: The Tradition of Coleridge and Wordsworth in the Victorian Church* (Cambridge: Cambridge University Press, 2008), and Kirstie Blair, *Form and Faith in Victorian Religion and Poetry* (Oxford: Oxford University Press, 2011).
14 Stuart Andrews, *Robert Southey: History, Politics, Religion* (London: Palgrave Macmillan, 2011), pp. 79–90.
15 Southey, *Correspondence*, V: p. 77.
16 Speck, *Southey*, pp. 195–7; David M. Craig, *Robert Southey and Romantic Apostasy: Political Argument in Britain 1780–1840* (Woodbridge: Boydell, 2007); Andrews, *Robert Southey*, pp. 101–20, 183–8. See also Jones, *English Nation*, pp. 162–5 and Sheridan Gilley, 'Nationality and liberty, Protestant and Catholic: Robert Southey's *Book of the Church*' in S. Mews (ed.), *Religion and National Identity*, Studies in Church History, 18 (Oxford: Basil Blackwell, 1982), pp. 409–32.
17 Robert Southey, *Book of the Church*, 2 vols (London: John Murray, 1824), II: p. 528. Southey's assertion of the importance of challenging papal idolatry and despotism was more pronounced in the second edition of 1825 and, in response to his Catholic critics, he produced a polemical defence, *Vindiciae Ecclesiae Anglicanae: Essays on the Romish Religion and Vindicating the Book of the Church* (London: Keating & Brown, 1826).
18 Southey, *Correspondence*, V: p. 122.
19 Southey, *Book of the Church*, II: p. 17.
20 *Ibid.*, p. 20.
21 *Ibid.*, pp. 22–4.

22  *Ibid.*, p. 28.
23  *Ibid.*, pp. 24–5. This theme was picked up by Rose Macaulay in an essay at the time of the canonisation process: see *The Spectator* (18 January 1935), p. 13.
24  The Latin text is engraved in Chelsea Old Church, More's parish church, and a translation is in Thomas Bridgett, *The Life and Writings of Sir Thomas More* (London: Burns and Oates, 1891), pp. 250–2.
25  See www.vatican.va/holy_father/john_paul_ii/motu_proprio/documents/hf_jp-ii_mo tu-proprio_20001031_thomas-more_en.html, accessed 14 October 2014.
26  Compare, for example, two biographies produced around the time of More's canonisation, both by supporters of the cause. Richard W. Chambers, *Thomas More* (London: Jonathan Cape, 1935), which inspired Robert Bolt, depicts More as a champion of freedom of conscience, while Christopher Hollis, *Thomas More* (London: Sheed & Ward, 1934) characterises him as a defender of order.
27  Southey, *Book of the Church*, II: pp. 26–7.
28  *Ibid.*, p. 27.
29  Robert Southey, *Sir Thomas More: Or, Colloquies on the Progress and Prospects of Society* (1829; 2nd edn, London: John Murray, 1831). See pp. 1–2 for the genesis of the book. It was published with a frontispiece engraving of the Holbein portrait of More.
30  *Ibid.* The titles of the colloquies dealing with these issues hint at Southey's sympathies: Colloquy X 'Crosthwaite Church – St Kentigern', I: pp. 303–89, having dwelt upon the permanence of the landscape around St Kentigern's Church, Crosthwaite, goes on to discuss the Reformation, linking it directly to dissent and to Methodism; while Colloquy XI, 'Infidelity', II: pp. 1–58, deals with the advantages of Church establishment.
31  Southey to Rickman, 28 January 1820, in Southey, *Correspondence*, V: p. 17, and see Southey, *Colloquies*, I: p. 18.
32  *Ibid.*, pp. 342–3.
33  *Ibid.*, p. 352.
34  Robert Southey, *Letters Written During a Short Residence in Spain and Portugal* (Bristol and London: Cottle, 1797), p. 59.
35  Southey, *Colloquies*, I: p. 368.
36  *Ibid.*, p. 339.
37  *Ibid.*, p. 389.
38  Eastwood, 'Southey'.
39  Aside from Stapleton's *Tres Thomae*, published in Leiden in 1588, Samuel Weller Singer had recently published *The Life of Sir Thomas More by his son-in-law William Roper Esq.* (London: R. Triphook, 1822). The other great monument to More's memory was a Marian publication, *The Workes of Sir Thomas More Knyght, Sometime Lorde Chauncellor of England, Written by him in the Englyshe Tonge* (London: Rastell, 1557). For Southey's pursuit of the *Workes* see *Correspondence*, V: pp. 16–17. It was also consulted by Coleridge while composing *On the Constitution of the Church and State*.
40  Speck, *Southey*, pp. 42–61; Richard Holmes, *Coleridge: Early Visions* (1989; London, Harper Perennial, 2005), pp. 59–88.
41  Southey, *Colloquies*, I: p. 19.
42  Southey, *Vindiciae*, pp. xiv–xv.
43  Southey, *Colloquies*, I: pp. 283–4.

44 [Thomas Babington Macaulay], 'Southey's *Colloquies on Society*', *Edinburgh Review*, 50, 100 (1830), 534, 536, 540.
45 For further reaction, much of it unfavourable, see David M. Craig, 'Subservient talents? Robert Southey as a public moralist', in Lynda Pratt (ed.), *Robert Southey and the Contexts of English Romanticism* (Aldershot: Ashgate, 2006), pp. 112–14.
46 William Cobbett, A *History of the Protestant Reformation in England and Ireland* (1824–27; Dublin: James Duffy, 1867), letter 3, paragraph 84.
47 O'Day, 'John Lingard', p. 103.
48 For a similar juxtaposition, see the Selwyn Divinity School in Cambridge (1879), which has statues of Cranmer and Fisher on either side of its front door. Gordon Rupp, 'A Cambridge centenary: the Selwyn Divinity School, 1879–1979', *Historical Journal*, 24 (1981), 417–28.
49 Southey, *Colloquies*, I: pp. 249–50.
50 *Ibid.*, p. 341.
51 J. P. Parry, 'Nonconformity, clericalism and "Englishness": the United Kingdom', in Christopher Clark and Wolfram Kaiser (eds), *Culture Wars: Secular-Catholic Conflict in Nineteenth-Century Europe* (Cambridge: Cambridge University Press, 2003), pp. 152–80, esp. pp. 155–7.
52 For a rich examination of confessional conflict in mid-century culture, see Michael Wheeler, *The Old Enemies: Catholic and Protestant in Nineteenth-Century English Culture* (Cambridge: Cambridge University Press, 2006).
53 Sheridan Gilley, 'The Roman Catholic Church, 1780–1940', in Sheridan Gilley and William J. Sheils (eds), *A History of Religion in Britain* (Oxford: Blackwell, 1994), pp. 345–62, esp. pp. 350–7.
54 For alternative Catholicising traditions that *did* link medieval religion with social concern, see Simon Skinner, *Tractarians and the 'Condition of England': The Social and Political Thought of the Oxford Movement* (Oxford: Clarendon, 2004).
55 Rosemary O'Day, *The Debate on the English Reformation* (London: Methuen, 1986), pp. 91–4; Ciaran Brady, *James Anthony Froude: The Intellectual Biography of a Victorian Prophet* (Oxford: Oxford University Press, 2013), ch. 7.
56 For more on the importance of Tudor figures in popular perceptions of the past, see Billie Melman, *The Culture of History: English Uses of the Past, 1800–1953* (Oxford: Oxford University Press, 2006) and, more generally, Tatiana C. String and Marcus Bull (eds), *Tudorism: Historical Imagination and the Appropriation of the Sixteenth Century* (Oxford: Oxford University Press, 2011).
57 For the description that provoked the paintings, see Singer, *Life of More by Roper*, pp. 90–1.
58 Bridgett, *Life and Writings of More*.
59 See pp. 144–8.
60 See, for example, 'St Thomas and St John', *The Times* (2 February 1935), p. 13.
61 See Gilbert Burnet, *History of the Reformation of the Church of England*, 6 vols (1679–1715; London: Priestley, 1820), V: p. 42. Note the date of this edition.
62 Prescott, 'Afterlives', p. 269.

# 7

# Ignatius Loyola

*Gareth Atkins*

'THERE IS NOT, AND there never was on this earth, a work of human policy so well deserving of examination as the Roman Catholic Church.' So wrote Thomas Babington Macaulay (1800–59) in a celebrated *Edinburgh Review* article on the *History of the Popes*, by Leopold von Ranke (1795–1886).[1] Revolutionary atheism, commercial progress and the march of mind had failed to kill it off, chiefly, Macaulay reflected, because centuries of experience had taught the papacy not to resist fanaticism but to harness it:

> The ignorant enthusiast whom the Anglican Church makes an enemy, and, whatever the polite and learned may think, a most dangerous enemy, the Catholic church makes a champion. She bids him nurse his beard, covers him with a gown and hood of coarse dark stuff, ties a rope round his waist, and sends him forth to teach in her name. He costs her nothing.

'In this way', he observed, 'the Church of Rome unites in herself all the strength of establishment, all the strength of Dissent. With the utmost pomp of a hierarchy above, she has all the energy of the voluntary system below.'[2] 'Even for female agency', Macaulay continued, 'there is a place in her system.' 'At Rome, the Countess of Huntingdon would have a place in the calendar as St. Selina, and Mrs. Fry would be foundress and first Superior of the Blessed Order of Sisters of the Gaols.'[3] Instead of driving such figures into separatism, Rome encouraged them.

> Place Ignatius Loyola at Oxford. He is certain to become the head of a formidable secession. Place John Wesley at Rome. He is certain to be the first General of a new society devoted to the interests and honour of the Church. Place St. Theresa in London. Her restless enthusiasm ferments into madness, not untinctured with craft. She becomes the prophetess, the mother of the faithful, holds disputations with the devil, issues sealed pardons to her adorers, and lies in of the Shiloh. Place Joanna Southcote [*sic*] at Rome. She founds an order of barefooted Carmelites, every one of whom is ready to suffer martyrdom for the Church: a solemn service is consecrated to her memory; and her statue, placed over the holy water, strikes the eye of every stranger who enters St. Peter's.[4]

Macaulay was clearly enjoying himself. But like many of his contemporaries in Britain and abroad he was intrigued by the resilience of the papacy amid revolution and counter-revolution. In particular, the suppression of the Society of Jesus in 1773 and its semi-miraculous resurrection in 1814 prompted an avalanche of commentary, most of it unfavourable, some of it hysterical, and all of it adding layers to the so-called 'Black Legend'. Had the removal of their restraining influence prompted the Revolution, as the Jesuits themselves claimed?[5] Or had they in fact secretly fomented it in order to bring down principalities and popes, and thus to enhance their own power?[6] Real and imaginary representatives of the Society supplied progressive thinkers across Europe with a cast of unblinking emissaries of papal dominion and implacable enemies of modern thought. In France, for instance, the historians Jules Michelet (1798–1874) and Edgar Quinet (1803–75) declared 'la guerre aux jesuites', while the intensely anti-Jesuit sensation novel *Le Juif errant* (1845) by Eugène Sue (1804–57) sold over 120,000 copies, was adapted for the stage in Paris and London, and rapidly became an international hit.[7] During the upheavals of 1848 the Society again fell foul of revolutionary anti-clericalism, being banished from Switzerland and the Habsburg dominions and fleeing Rome. They became deeply unpopular in Italy during the *Risorgimento*, and were expelled from Prussia in 1872, at the height of Bismarck's *Kulturkampf*, and from France in 1880.[8] In Britain too they loomed large on the pages of gothic novels[9] and lurid pamphlets, fuelling hysterical reactions whenever Jesuit asylum-seekers arrived from the Continent and prompting Protestant conspiracy theorists to blame papal fifth-columnists for everything from the Oxford Movement[10] and the Maynooth Grant[11] to the repeal of the Corn Laws and the Factory Education Bill.[12]

Macaulay was not merely peddling prejudices, however. His wry reflections emphasise how debates about the role of character, leadership and sanctity in religious movements came to preoccupy religious commentators in the middle decades of the century. Their reflections ranged freely over the ecclesiastical past, often with scant regard for confessional binaries. Catholic figures as much as Protestants provided food for thought. This trend, as we shall see, was particularly marked among liberal Protestants, but it was also noticeable among Protestants more generally, even those of a fairly conservative bent. One figure who fascinated them was Iñigo Lopez de Loyola (1491–1556), known to most British people as Ignatius Loyola. Loyola was a byword for everything that Protestants loved to hate: asceticism, eccentricity, improbable miracles, slavish allegiance to the Pope. Worst of all, he was a Jesuit; and not just any Jesuit, but the founder and first general of the Society. Yet although and perhaps because he was painted in such lurid terms, this chapter will argue that thinkers from across the confessional spectrum found his life and career deeply interesting. Students of psychology could not fail to notice that the wild-eyed enthusiast was also a shrewd judge of human nature. Proponents of Christian manliness could admire the self-discipline of the soldier-saint. Advocates of sober, single-minded holiness found eloquent evidence of this in his *Spiritual Exercises*. In short, while Loyola ticked most of the boxes for what Protestants found unsettling about Catholic saints, he also embodied attributes they held in high estimation.

This chapter, then, traces a crucial tension in Protestant understandings of sanctity, between the impulse to regard saints as normative figures, on the one hand, and a more historicised or even ironic awareness, on the other, that they were products of their times, their national cultures or indeed their mythographers. While Protestants were reluctant to abandon the idea that God worked through individuals, they were also aware that saints and the construction of their legends might reveal more about human nature than they did about divine intervention. Loyola allows us to examine that tension through three interwoven themes. One is the search for the historical Ignatius: how commentators sought to pare away the monkish fables that surrounded him in order to reveal the real man. Another is how Loyola was placed historically and culturally: like his near-contemporary, Teresa of Avila (1515–82), his Spanishness was invoked to explain his ardent Counter-Reformation religiosity and his imperious nature, twin attributes which were of a piece with his country's artistic, imperial and cultural achievements in the sixteenth century, but which also bore much of the blame for Spain's decline thereafter.[13] Third, and related to both of these, it considers how Loyola's personal magnetism and spirituality were dissected by writers keen to analyse or to appropriate his methods and charisma.

## The inherited Loyola

In the nineteenth century, as in every century since the sixteenth, the stories told about Ignatius were deeply polarised. His defenders and his detractors alike called upon the same sources and anecdotes, although they drew very different conclusions from them about his motives, his supposed visions and the reliability of the sources themselves. His early life is a case in point. Born to a Basque noble family in 1491, the young 'Ignacio' became page to a relative in Castile, modelling himself after the adventures of El Cid, the knights of Camelot and *La Chanson de Roland*. He loved martial exercises and longed for 'vainglorious' fame, fitting himself out in the latest fashions, fighting duels and placing himself at the centre of military actions. At the siege of Pamplona in 1521, however, a cannonball wounded one leg and smashed the other; and after several operations he was left lame for life. His enforced retirement provoked a spiritual crisis, which included intensive reading on the lives of the saints, concluding at the mountaintop Benedictine monastery of Santa Maria de Montserrat in Catalonia on 25 March 1522, when he hung up his sword and armour before the Black Madonna and dedicated himself to her service. All this could have been calculated to appeal to romantics who saw Spain through the eyes of Cervantes. Yet the elision of Christian commitment and knightly service to his damsel could cut both ways. While some commentators lapped up Loyola's chivalric sensibility, others thought him gullible in swallowing not just knightly fables but fanciful hagiographic accounts too. Either way, Montserrat was already on the tourist trail in the 1840s, thanks in part to its inclusion in probably the most popular 'Murray's Handbook for Travellers', the volume for Spain, written by the art connoisseur, essayist and traveller Richard Ford

(1796–1858).[14] What they found there prompted unfavourable commentary from sniffy British evangelicals, who dismissed the image venerated by so many as 'probably that of a negress and child' brought from North Africa by 'the Moors', and who exulted in the formation of a Protestant and purportedly indigenous episcopal Church in Spain to rival the 'alien' dominion of Rome.[15] 'When the pilgrimage season comes round, and thousands are climbing the steeps of Montserrat to adore the image on its summit, these Reformers stand by the way and put into the hands of the poor deluded people that which is fitted to turn them from their folly.'[16]

From Montserrat, Loyola went to nearby Manresa. Here the division between Loyola's champions and his debunkers became a chasm. For his Jesuit biographers his extreme austerities – standing for hours at a time to pray, sleeping in a cave and scourging himself three times a day – finally brought him close to heaven. Sceptics retorted that they brought him close to insanity: instead of consulting Scripture for words of truth, 'he ... lived entirely in ecstasies and contemplation', coming to mistake the voice of the Devil for the voice of God.[17] Nevertheless, Manresa set him on the road to self-denying austerity, quixotic pilgrimage to the Holy Land in 1523, self-imposed penury, street preaching, study at the University of Alcalá and then at Paris, where the Company of Jesus was formed in 1534, and finally Rome, where the Pope gave approval for the Company to become the Society in 1540. Loyola was chosen as the first superior-general; his *Spiritual Exercises* were published in 1548; and he died in Rome in July 1556. Protestant readers found his self-punishment particularly repulsive: he 'revelled in filth, and rendered to the sick, especially to such as were afflicted with ulcers, services of which it is impossible to read the account without a strong disposition to sickness', shuddered one.[18] If Catholic writers were less euphemistic, detailing with relish how he sucked beggars' sores, as well as deliberately rolling in briars, this was in part because overripe Counter-Reformation hagiographies continued to shape retellings of the story. The volumes on Saint Ignatius in Frederick William Faber's (1814–63) Oratorian *Saints and Servants of God* series (42 volumes, 1847–56),[19] for instance, were a translation of the life by Father Mariani (1680–1751), which in turn drew on what the saint had dictated to Luis Gonzales de Camara, on the early lives by Pedro de Ribadeneira (1527–1611) and by Giovanni Pietro Maffei (1533–1603), on the biography by the Italian historian of the Jesuit Order Niccolo Orlandini (1554–1606). The massive account in the Bollandists' *Acta Sanctorum*, first published in 1731, was based mostly upon Ribadeneira.[20] These, alongside the work of Daniello Bartoli (1608–85) and Luigi Carnoli, alias 'Vigilio Nolarci' (fl. 1680), continued to be retranslated, republished and excerpted throughout the nineteenth century.

Protestants, too, scoured these sources, albeit with a view to sending them up. Beneath the layers of polemic, however, was an experience that was deeply familiar to them: conversion. So while few approved Loyola's behaviour, they found it hard to dismiss him out of hand. In the words of the Principal of St Andrews, John Tulloch (1823–86), writing in the 1870s:

there was nothing unusual in the state of mind through which Loyola passed. The same spiritual tragedy is more or less repeated in every wakened conscience ... [I]t is more or less the experience of all who have come out of darkness into what they believe a marvellous light. In this respect Luther and Bunyan and Ignatius are all brethren, born to religious strength out of the same throes of spiritual birth.[21]

Tulloch was a Broad Church Scottish Presbyterian, but he was employing a set of comparisons that had long been made by controversialists on both sides of the confessional divide.[22] For the French philologist and ex-Catholic *enfant terrible* Ernest Renan (1823–92) the obvious parallel was with Calvin:

Careless of wealth, of titles, of honours, indifferent to pomp, modest in his life, apparently humble, sacrificing everything to the desire of making others like himself, I hardly know of a man, save Ignatius Loyola, who could match him in these terrible transports; but Loyola threw into them a Spanish ardour and a sweep of imagination.[23]

The more well-worn analogy, however, was with Luther. The internationally blockbusting *Histoire de la Réformation du seizième siècle* (1835–53), for example, by the Swiss historian Jean Henri Merle D'Aubigné (1794–1872), inverted Maffei in presenting Loyola and Luther as near-identical twins separated at the moment of spiritual birth.[24] The monks of Manresa and of Erfurt, D'Aubigné argued, each wrestled with a crisis for which the ordinances of the Church offered no succour.

Both were deeply sensible of the multitude of their sins. Both were seeking for reconciliation with God, and longed to have the assurance in their hearts. If a Staupitz with the Bible in his hand had appeared in the convent of Manresa, possibly Inigo might have become the Luther of the Peninsula. These two great men of the sixteenth century, these founders of two spiritual powers which for three centuries have been warring together, were at this moment brothers; and perhaps, if they had met, Luther and Loyola would have embraced, and mingled their tears and their prayers. But it was not to be. 'Luther turned towards Christ; Loyola only fell back upon himself.'[25]

The idea that Ignacio's choice between the Bible and the *Golden Legend* decided the course of the Counter-Reformation was a dramatic biographical device that may have drawn impetus from Ranke's presentation of the Counter-Reformation less as a form of decay than as what the Reformation looked like when refracted through a southern European lens. Out of eighteenth-century thought developed a lively interest in how a country's religion shaped national character, and how that in turn coloured the religiosity of individual men and women. Enlightenment writers such as David Hume (1711–76), Adam Smith (1723–90) and William Robertson (1721–93) were enthralled by the decline and fall of Spain, which they, like their later readers, blamed on the malign influence of priestcraft. Yet where they had been preoccupied with political economy, nineteenth-century readers were interested in character. The contrast between Loyola and Luther emblematised commonly held differences between the Catholic south and the Protestant north of Europe: pride, passion and romantic visions as against prudence, practicality and common sense. Artists like John

Frederick Lewis (1804–76) and John 'Spanish' Phillip (1817–67) painted a rickety but romantic Iberia peopled with scheming peasants, down-at-heel *hidalgos* and of course wily Jesuits.[26] It was by no means a negative vision, but it was one in which religion bore much of the blame for Spanish backwardness.[27] When the National Gallery acquired Zurbarán's macabre *St Francis in Meditation* in 1853 it served only to underline such prejudices.[28] After all, the gothic gloom of the cloister and the sunny world of Cervantes were opposite sides of the same coin. 'Spain never changes', proclaimed George Borrow (1803–81) in his 1843 bestseller, *The Bible in Spain*. Pride, he argued, had fuelled her rise, and it was pride that lay behind her present-day plight. 'For nearly two centuries, she was the she-butcher, *La Verduga*, of malignant Rome', too arrogant and aristocratic to see that she was tilting at windmills.

> It was by humouring her pride that she was induced to waste her precious blood and treasure in the Low Country wars, to launch the Spanish Armada, and to many other equally insane actions ... Flattered by the title of Gonfaloniera of the Vicar of Jesus, and eager to prove herself not unworthy of the same, she shut her eyes, and rushed upon her own destruction with the cry of 'Charge, Spain!'[29]

The slide from banner-bearer to banker and then to discard, Borrow concluded, had been as inevitable as it was humiliating.

Although it was easy, as Borrow did, to invoke Spain's most famous fictional creation, the inflexible ardour that Cervantes satirised in *Don Quixote* was anything but a laughing matter. It was this that animated the men of iron who made sixteenth-century Spain and her armies so fearsome; that impelled Hernan Cortes (1485–1547) and Francisco Pizarro (c. 1471/6–1541) to conquer the New World; that animated Bartolomé de las Casas (c. 1484–1566) to set his face against colonial slavery there; that directed Philip II (1527–98) against the enemies of Rome far and wide. Loyola was, then, a man of his time. 'In him the Spain of the sixteenth century found its truest and most complete representative', reckoned the prolific historian and essayist James Anthony Froude (1818–94). 'Careless of pleasure, careless of his life, temperate in his personal habits, without passion, without imagination, with nerves of steel, [he had] a supreme conviction that the duty of subjects was to obey those who were set over them.'[30] In fact the passage referred to the Duke of Alva (1507–82), whose rule in the Netherlands remained a byword for brutality, but it encapsulates what many thought about Ignatius. 'His will was a Spanish will,' explained one critic, 'which means a haughty, indomitable will, that would have bridged the Red Sea, if the waters had not parted.'[31] While Borrow believed that Rome had ruined Spain, for the poet Arthur Hugh Clough (1819–61), trapped in the Eternal City during the French siege of 1849, it was the other way around. In *Amours de voyage* he railed against the 'vile tyrannous Spaniards' who had 'fanaticized' Europe and who refused to release their 'choicest prey, Italy', damning their 'emasculate pupils', 'gimcrack churches', 'pseudo-learning and lies', 'confessional boxes and postures', 'metallic beliefs and regimental devotions'.[32] 'A bomb

I am thankful to say has left its mark on the facade of the Gesu', he told a friend. 'I wish it had stirred up old Ignatius.'[33]

## Searching for the Ignatius of history

Clough was unusual in describing Loyola himself in such disparaging terms. For amid the resurgence of Catholicism in mainland Britain and the burgeoning growth of evangelical Nonconformity, commentators were beginning to attend to what caused the rise and fall of religious movements. There was a growing emphasis on the idea that while providence operated through great religious leaders it did so less through supernatural means than via natural attributes: decision, foresight, personality. Robert Southey's 1820 *Life of Wesley*, for instance, discerned a close likeness between John Wesley (1703–91) and Loyola, arguing that they matched each other in absolutism, organisational genius, sincerity and 'enthusiasm',[34] observing maliciously that Wesley had published the lives of heretics and Catholics and found them virtuous, and quoting him on his alter ego: 'surely one of the greatest men that ever was engaged in the support of so bad a cause!'[35] Methodists did not enjoy the comparison, but 'Protestant Loyola' was an epithet that stuck, partly because of Wesley's autocratic style, but also because in an age that celebrated military heroes, Ignatius the soldier-saint fitted with the idea that Wesley had been the Wellington of the Methodist movement, a Generalissimo who inspired absolute obedience. Later on, when Thomas Henry Huxley (1825–95) wanted to criticise the founder of the Salvation Army, General William Booth (1829–1912), and in particular Booth's unguarded claims to authority over his 'troops', it was natural that he should label him a new Loyola with a despotism to match.[36]

Increasingly, however, such ideas were less polemical than they were heuristic: the challenge was to explain the success of such figures, not to question their sanity. Some of the most interesting and sustained early work on the psychology of religious leaders was by the Essex scholar and *littérateur* Isaac Taylor (1787–1865), whose *Natural History of Enthusiasm*, published in 1829, made his name as an authority on it, being followed by *Fanaticism* (1833), *Spiritual Despotism* (1835) and in 1849 and 1851 two individual studies, one of them *Loyola* and the other, predictably, *Wesley and Methodism*. Loyola appears throughout Taylor's output as a dauntless fanatic who, in building up a fund of 'supererogatory spiritual merit', was self-disciplined to the point of being superhuman; a papist Jeremy Bentham whose *Exercises* made windows into men's souls and who set up a 'labyrinth' of obedience which ensured that 'every Jesuit is a spy upon every Jesuit'.[37] If his near-contemporary Shakespeare could paint all moods of human nature, Loyola ruled them.[38] While Taylor clearly disliked Ignatius, his aim was to explain dispassionately the evolution of a machine 'constructed for grasping, and crushing, and converting to its own use, the most substantial things of earth'.[39] His subject's genius, he argued, was to free himself and those around him from the trappings of medieval monkery; to realise, like Luther, that the future lay in mobile, missionary Christianity, and to drag his Church into that new era. Taylor's Loyola was no obsessive self-punisher, but used asceticism in order to attract attention, encouraging his followers to use flagellation, iron girdles and rough shirts to demonstrate self-command and to gain a hearing rather than as ends in themselves.[40] The movement Loyola founded was deeply suspect, but its success bespoke a subtle grasp of the springs of human nature that warranted examination.

Taylor's attempt to distinguish Ignatius the man from the tall tales told about him flew in the face of an enormous volume of polemical literature that sought at once to sneer and to shiver at the Jesuits. Voltaire (1684–1778) had assumed that Loyola was both calculating and self-deluded; that he was not just bad but mad as well. If you want to be a saint, smirked the Sage of Ferney, calibrate your extravagances to prevailing prejudices: avoid being hanged and you might be canonised instead.[41] During the religious unease of the late 1840s this remained an easy tune to play. Andrew Steinmetz's sensational exposé of his time as a Jesuit novice suggested that the saint's insanity was matched only by those who followed him.[42] Steinmetz (1816–77) joked that the fables recounted about Ignatius resembled the Arabian Nights.[43] Others chortled that Loyola's lifelong limp gave the lie to reports of his miraculous healing in a dream: 'the therapeutic skill of St Peter was less perfect than might have been expected'.[44] The High Churchman R. C. Trench's influential *Notes on the Miracles of Our Lord* (1846) made a subtler point. Like many but not all Protestants, Trench (1807–86) thought that while miracles took place in the New Testament, they ceased once the early Church could survive without them.[45] Catholic cults were therefore not just untrue but derogated from the uniqueness of Christ, and in few places was this truer than in accounts of the early Jesuits:

> Upwards of two hundred miracles of Loyola were laid before the Pope, when his canonization was in question, – miracles beside which those of our Lord shrink into insignificance. If Christ by his word and look repelled and expelled demons, Ignatius did the same by a letter. If Christ walked once upon the sea, Ignatius many times in the air. If Christ, by his shining countenance and glistening garments, once amazed his disciples, Ignatius did it frequently, and, entering into dark chambers, could, by his presence, light them up as with candles.

Yet Trench was at pains to emphasise that the fault lay with later biographers more than with Loyola himself. Borrowing from the critical toolbox of the Pietist German biblical scholar August Tholuck (1799–1877), he insisted that accounts of miracles and visions did not feature at all in Ribadeneira's early biography and accreted only gradually thereafter: they were the fault of hagiologists rather than the man himself.[46] Taylor, too, sought to unravel the same mythical tangle. Given his emphasis on Loyola's hard-headed, hard-hearted understanding of human nature, he found accounts of self-imposed mendicancy not merely hard to stomach but hard to believe, dismissing the 'gigantic nonsense' of his begging cottiers for bread within half an hour's walk of his family seat as an unworthy fabrication.[47] To dismiss his prodigies, Taylor argued, made

Ignatius at once more credible and more worthy of study. 'The real Ignatius Loyola has been freed of a shining face and floating a foot off the ground.'[48]

While the evangelical *Christian Observer* doubted whether what Loyola experienced could really be called a 'conversion', it acknowledged the force of this argument.[49] More controversial was another 1849 book, *Essays in Ecclesiastical Biography*, a compilation of pieces published anonymously by Sir James Stephen (1789–1859) in the *Edinburgh Review* since the late 1830s. Stephen was a son of the Clapham Sect, but his reviews display a familiarity with mainstream French and German historical writing that went well beyond the bounds of narrow Protestant partisanship. His large-hearted portrayal of figures from across the Christian era as footsoldiers under the same divine banner did not please everybody. Several Anglicans charged him with abandoning the Thirty-Nine Articles, adding for good measure accusations of Gnosticism.[50] The Unitarian *Christian Reformer* chimed in in his favour, as did the Nonconformist *Eclectic Review* and the *Examiner*, which praised Stephen's 'large capability of sentiment'.[51] From the other side of the fence the Catholic *Rambler* lambasted him as the 'ex-mismanager' of the *Christian Observer*, rejoicing that the Clapham villa where the Bible Society had been mooted was now a Catholic chapel and condemning the *Essays* as patronising in their flattening out of doctrinal divisions.[52] Others, too, excoriated his ecumenism: 'he suggests the compilation of a new hagiology (which he is pleased to call *Protestant*)', spat one writer, 'including Popes, Jesuits, Monks, Nuns, Reformers, Presbyterians, Independents, and Methodists'.[53] This, of course, was Stephen's point. While saintliness expressed itself in different ways at different times, often admixed with lamentable failings, it was to be revered wherever it was to be found, even among 'the Founders of Jesuitism', the topic of an essay first published in 1842.[54] 'Unalluring, and on the whole unlovely as it is,' Stephen remarked, 'the image of Loyola must ever command the homage of the world', with its 'raptures', 'superhuman audacity' and single-mindedness.[55] Would that the missions, mitres, and meetings of the contemporary world, he mused, might absorb at least some of the white heat of Jesuit 'enthusiasm'. It was Loyola's prickly personal 'spell', after all, his nagging repetition of 'what does it benefit a man if he gain the whole world, and lose his soul', that impelled Francis Xavier (1506–52) to abandon family and comforts to proselytise in the East.[56]

## Liberal Protestant historicism

The mixed reception accorded Stephen's *Essays* was understandable. For while fantastical stories published by flamboyant Catholic converts like Faber were easily laughed off, in the era of Papal Aggression and Pius IX ecumenical attempts to rehabilitate Loyola were always likely to fall on stony ground. The mid- to late 1840s saw the publication of numerous analyses of the Society of Jesus which exposed unpalatable aspects of Ignatian thought, especially regarding education and spiritual training. Particularly disturbing was the insistence that members of the Society submit not just outwardly but inwardly too to the authoritative pronouncements of their superiors, acquiescing *perinde ac cadaverum* ('in the manner of a corpse'). 'If [the Church] shall have defined anything to be black which to our eyes appears to be white,' ran Ignatius's *Exercises* in a new edition, 'we ought in like manner to pronounce it to be black.'[57] Conspiracy theories about Jesuit brainwashing lurked behind Carlyle's semi-coherent rantings about Ignatius in his *Latter Day Pamphlets* of 1850, behind Kingsley's flailing attack on Newman in 1864 and behind Gladstone's flinty response to the Vatican Decrees a decade later, which famously referred to the Jesuits as 'the deadliest foes that mental and moral liberty have ever known'.[58] When the Oxford preacher and don H. P. Liddon (1829–90) was accused in 1867 of inserting unacknowledged passages from Ignatius into his sermons, evangelical journals accused him of papistry[59] and more liberal commentators charged him with plagiarism,[60] both finding Jesuitry hard to stomach, particularly given Liddon's influence over undergraduates.[61] At the same time, it was increasingly difficult to condemn Loyola unread. There was an outpouring of abridgements and annotated editions of the *Spiritual Exercises*, many of them by Catholic-minded Anglicans and Protestant antiquarians rather than paid-up Romanists.[62] That they could be cited by William James alongside yoga as a way of accessing deeper physiological and psychological 'energies' is suggestive of a cut-and-paste tendency in late-century spirituality, whereby 'techniques' could be decoupled from their contexts (and progenitors) and deployed to subtly different ends.[63] Florence Nightingale was a case in point.[64]

This process was helped by shifting opinions across a spectrum of liberal Christians, many of whom used history to argue that dogmatic squabbling obscured the fundamental unity of the divine message. Tulloch's articles in *Good Words* on Dominic, Francis of Assisi and Ignatius were one attempt to rehabilitate them from centuries of Protestant scaremongering.[65] Here too was evidence of the hunt for historical realities, for while the orders such figures founded came in for criticism, Tulloch was keen to emphasise that they themselves had been men of integrity and vision. More influential, perhaps, and certainly more controversial, was A. P. Stanley (1815–81), who visited Montserrat in 1858, and whose introductory lectures as Regius Professor of Ecclesiastical History, delivered in Oxford the previous year, mischievously warned Protestant hairsplitters that Christian history was populated by outlandish figures who made current controversies look laughably petty.[66]

> Pelagius lurks under the mitre of Chrysostom or the cowl of Jerome; Loyola will find himself by the side of Wesley; John Knox will recognise a fellow-worker in Hildebrand; the austerities of Benedict, the intolerance of Dominic, will find their counterpart at Geneva and in Massachusetts; the missionary zeal of the Arian Ulfilas, of the Jesuit Xavier, and of the Protestant Schwarz will be seen to flow from the same source.[67]

One did not have to be an out-and-out liberal to view Catholic figures in a favourable light. Stephen was one example of this; but it was no coincidence that in 1862 another second-generation Claphamite, the General Secretary of the Church Missionary Society Henry Venn (1796–1873), published a *Missionary Life and Labours* of *Francis Xavier*, which, while critical, lauded its subject's endurance and vitality.[68] Francis of Assisi, too, attracted growing attention, much of it positive: the popular biography by Mrs Oliphant (1828–97) treated him with near-devotion, stripping back legends, smoothing out eccentricities, and downplaying the role of the papacy to reveal a compassionate figure who might now make a good, if dreamy, Methodist domestic visitor.[69] The two Francises appeared increasingly frequently in the biographical compilations doled out as Sunday-school prizes, often being placed incongruously alongside Henry Martyn (1786–1812) or Dr Livingstone (1813–73).[70]

Ignatius featured less often, save in very Catholic collections, such as *Stories of the Saints for Children*, by the prolific Mary Seymour (fl. 1880–96), which pulled no punches in its aggressive defence of Jesuitism and indeed of disciplining the flesh.[71] For most writers self-mortification was a subject to be avoided, especially in an age where sport was fast becoming the acceptable outlet for excess male energies. 'Footer shorts', one hearty author opined, 'are far better than a hair shirt as a dress for a saint.'[72] There was a sense, moreover, that Ignatius was a better role model for men than for boys, especially among those who favoured holy hard men above plump philanthropists. This was undoubtedly the case for the restless freethinker Francis Newman (1805–97), whose autobiographical *Phases of Faith* (1850) described how during 'strivings after a more primitive Christianity' in Ireland he had come under the spell of the Calvinist future Brethren leader John Nelson Darby (1800–82). Darby had a beard, cared little for appearance, clothes or food, and tramped across rough country in all weathers to minister to his flock. The Catholics, Newman reported, saw him as a saint 'of the ancient breed': if half a dozen such men could be found, Ireland would become Protestant within weeks.[73] Most significant was his power to bend inferior wills to his own. While Newman came to disapprove of Darby, he well remembered the force of a one-sided, self-sacrificially ardent individual: 'such was Ignatius Loyola in his day'.[74] As Stanley pointed out in his 1855 commentary on 1 Corinthians, the Jesuits more than anyone else could claim to be following the advice of the Apostle Paul to discipline their bodies to make themselves fitter for the service of God.[75] From here to Christian militarism was only a short step; hence the otherwise scarcely credible letter from an Aldershot officer to Fanny Kingsley (1814–91) to the effect that Charles had taught him 'to respect both John Bunyan and Ignatius Loyola, the soldier priest!'[76]

Respect of a different kind caused Loyola to be included in the *Calendrier Positive* (1849), by Auguste Comte (1798–1857). The calendar was divided into thirteen lunar months, organised in order of ascending religious and moral truth, beginning with Moses, Aristotle and Archimedes and moving through the months of Saint Paul, Shakespeare and Descartes to the late eighteenth-century anatomist Bichat. Loyola appeared on the 22nd day of Saint Paul, but only in leap years, instead of Xavier.[77] Comte's Positivist 'saints' were not in heaven; their 'power' was in their contribution to human progress. Yet even if 'saint' connoted a set of character traits rather than divine inspiration, Loyola made for a fascinating case-study: psychologists enjoyed discussing his physiognomy and phrenology, agreeing that his bumps indicated a figure accustomed to decision and discipline and that his eyes were 'deep-set and full of fire'.[78] Granted, there remained ambivalence about the movement he had bequeathed. But when Renan collaborated with Max Müller (1823–1900) on the religion volume of *Portraits of the Hundred Greatest Men in History* (1879–80), Loyola was among the fifteen chosen, alongside Paul, Augustine, Luther and Wesley, and placed between Calvin and Bossuet.[79] By the end of the century it was possible to contextualise even his pedagogical ideas rather than condemning them out of hand. A dedicated volume appeared in Heinemann's 'The Great Educators' series, for instance, alongside Aristotle, Alcuin, Abelard, Pestalozzi, Bell, Lancaster and Arnold.[80]

## Conclusion

In 1892, in the autumn of his career, James Anthony Froude, now Regius Professor of History at Oxford, revised and republished an essay on Saint Teresa of Avila. In it he ventriloquised Macaulay on the Church of Rome's treatment of its 'enthusiasts'. 'She may employ them wisely while they are alive,' he added, 'but when they are dead she decks them out in paint and tinsel, to be worshipped as divinities. Their history becomes a legend. They are surrounded with an envelope of lies.' To reveal Teresa as she really was would be to dethrone 'the favourite idol of modern Spain'.[81] Froude was Carlyle's pupil and biographer, and such comments bear marks of the latter's preoccupation with heroes. Yet as Ciaran Brady has brilliantly shown, Froude's subtle dissections of character – especially religious character – both nuanced and went beyond those of his mentor.[82] Ever since his participation in Newman's *Lives of the English Saints* series he had returned repeatedly to holy men and women, and to the processes by which they came to be regarded as such. An 1862 essay on Teresa, while sympathetic, had explained her visions chiefly in terms of physical disorder.[83] Now he regarded her psychological state as fundamentally sane and therefore valuable, at once embodying and yet transcending the characteristic deficiencies of her time and place. Like Ignatius she was emphatically Spanish; she too breathed life for a time into a moribund religious system; and if she failed, she did so nobly and in a way that underlined rather than denied her humanity.

Yet Froude's Teresa, just as much as Taylor's Ignatius, was at the same time a parable about how saints could be misused.

> Teresa's image still stands in the Castilian churches. The faithful crowd about her with their offerings, and dream that they leave behind them their aches and pains; but her words were forgotten, and her rules sank again into neglect. The Church of Rome would have done better in keeping alive Teresa's spirit than in converting her into a goddess.

Froude was quick to anticipate readers who read such comments as unvarnished anti-Catholicism.

> When a great teacher dies who has told us truths which it would be disagreeable to act upon, we write adoring lives of him, we place him in the intellectual pantheon; but we

go on as if he had never lived at all. We put up statues to him as if that would do as well, and the prophet who has denounced idols is made an idol himself.[84]

For Froude, then, saints were those who challenged those around them to improve themselves, and to act on their beliefs. Idolatry, therefore, was not the property of Catholics but the reaction of the many, perhaps the majority, who would prefer their energy to be safely earthed rather than released.

Herein lay the grounds of the Protestant confusion about how to deal with Loyola. For if sanctity was about one's ability to inspire emulation rather than veneration, he more than anyone else plumbed the depths of idolatry while also scaling the heights of human endurance and organisation. Although some reacted by condemning him out of hand, from the 1840s onwards, as we have seen, he and other prominent figures from the turbulent sixteenth century came to be regarded less as proponents of dogmatic systems than as those who discerned the mighty social and cultural currents flowing round them and, in different ways, harnessed them. It was becoming possible, in other words, to revere both Luther and Loyola rather than having to choose between them. British visitors to the Gesu in the nineteenth century who ventured to visit Ignatius's rooms – open on Mondays, Wednesdays and Fridays from nine until eleven – might have been surprised to learn that the spiritual giant they had perhaps encountered in print was only 5'2" tall.[85] Yet it was precisely this gap, between the cult and the man, that made Ignatius Loyola so compelling.

## Notes

1 [Thomas Babington Macaulay], 'Ranke's *History of the Popes*', *Edinburgh Review*, 72, 144 (1840), 227–58.
2 *Ibid.*, 249.
3 *Ibid.*, 249–50.
4 *Ibid.*, 250.
5 Charles Robert Dallas, *New Conspiracy Against the Jesuits, Detected and Briefly Exposed* (London: J. Ridgway, 1815).
6 [John Poynder], *A Brief Account of the Jesuits … Tending to Establish the Danger of the Revival of that Order to the World at Large, and to the United Kingdom in Particular* (London: F. C. and J. Rivington, 1815); [Poynder], *A History of the Jesuits; to Which is Prefaced a Reply to Mr Dallas's Defence of that Order*, 2 vols (London: Baldwin, Cradock and Joy, 1816). That same year (1816) also witnessed a new translation of Blaise Pascal's *Provincial Letters, Containing an Exposure of the Reasonings and Morals of the Jesuits* (London: Gale and Fenner, 1816).
7 Maureen Moran, *Catholic Sensationalism and Victorian Literature* (Liverpool: Liverpool University Press, 2007), p. 73.
8 Roisin Healy, *The Jesuit Specter* [sic] *in Imperial Germany* (Leiden: Brill, 2003); Geoffrey Cubitt, *The Jesuit Myth: Conspiracy Theory and Politics in Nineteenth-Century France* (Oxford: Clarendon, 1993).
9 *Hawkstone: A Tale of and for England in 184–* (1845), by the High Church Oxford don William Sewell (1804–74) went through numerous editions.

10  *The Times* (9 March 1841), p. 6.
11  *Ibid.* (16 June 1845), p. 6.
12  See R. W. Overbury, *The Jesuits* (London: Houlston and Stoneman, 1846), p. 208; and, more generally, Henry Isaac Roper, *The Jesuits* (2nd edn, London: Houlston and Stoneman, 1848).
13  David Howarth, *The Invention of Spain: Anglo-Spanish Cultural Relations, 1770–1870* (Manchester: Manchester University Press, 2007), pp. 59–88.
14  [Richard Ford], *A Handbook for Travellers in Spain, and Readers at Home*, 2 vols (1845; 3rd edn, London: John Murray, 1855), I: pp. 419–26. For commentary on several such works, see [Nicholas Wiseman], 'Spain', *Dublin Review*, 18 (1845), 370–484.
15  Alexander Robertson, 'The work of reform in Spain', *Evangelical Christendom, Christian Work, and the News of the Churches*, 47 (1893), 110–12.
16  *Ibid.*, 112–13.
17  J. H. Merle D'Aubigné, *History of the Reformation of the Sixteenth Century*, trans. H. White, 4 vols (1838–53; New York, Robert Carter and Brothers, 1853), III: p. 119.
18  Sir James Stephen, 'The founders of Jesuitism', in Stephen, *Essays in Ecclesiastical Biography*, 2 vols (London: Longmans, etc., 1849), I: p. 159.
19  Antonio Francesco Mariani, *The Life of St Ignatius Loyola, Founder of the Jesuits*, 2 vols (London: Thomas Richardson and Son, 1848–49). See also Stewart Rose, *Ignatius Loyola and the Early Jesuits* (London: Longmans, Green, 1870).
20  *Acta Sanctorum VII, Iulii Tomus VII* (Antwerp and Brussels: Société des Bollandistes, 1731), pp. 409–853.
21  John Tulloch, 'Ignatius Loyola', *Good Words*, 18 (December 1877), 531.
22  See e.g. Isaac Taylor, *Loyola: And Jesuitism in Its Rudiments* (London: Longman, 1849), pp. 38–9. Assembling theological or spiritual blood-brotherhoods transcending time, space and confession was a speciality among Protestant historians: witness Joseph Milner's *History of the Church of Christ* (1794–1807), or August Neander's *Light in the Dark Places* (translated 1850).
23  Ernest Renan, 'John Calvin', in *Studies of Religious History and Criticism*, trans. O. B. Frothingham (New York: Carleton, 1864), p. 287.
24  D'Aubigné, *History*, III: pp. 116–17.
25  *Ibid.*, p. 118.
26  Christopher Baker, David Howarth and Paul Stirton, *The Discovery of Spain: British Artists and Collectors, Goya to Picasso* (Edinburgh: National Galleries of Scotland, 2009).
27  See e.g. Frederick Meyrick, *The Practical Working of the Church of Spain* (Oxford: John Henry Parker, 1851).
28  *Ibid.*, pp. 15–28.
29  George Borrow, *The Bible in Spain*, 3 vols (London: John Murray, 1843), I: pp. xiv–xv.
30  James Anthony Froude, *The History of England from the Fall of Wolsey to the Death of Elizabeth*, 12 vols (London: Longmans, 1856–70), IX, p. 318.
31  Andrew Steinmetz, *History of the Jesuits*, 3 vols (London: R. Bentley, 1848), I: p. 274.
32  B. Clough, *The Poems and Prose Remains of Arthur Hugh Clough*, 2 vols (London: Macmillan, 1869), II: p. 305.
33  Clough to Francis Turner Palgrave, 28 June 1849, in *Letters and Remains of Arthur Hugh Clough* (London: Spottiswoode, 1865), p. 136.

34　Robert Southey, *The Life of Wesley: And the Progress of Methodism*, 2 vols (2nd edn, London: Longman, Hurst, Rees, etc., 1820), II: p. 197.
35　*Ibid.*, pp. 193–6, esp. 193n.
36　*The Times* (1 December 1890), pp. 9, 13; (6 December), p. 5; (9 December), p. 13; (11 December), p. 13.
37　Taylor, *Loyola*, p. 296.
38　*Ibid.*, p. 15.
39　*Ibid.*, p. 14.
40　*Ibid.*, p. 98.
41　'Ignace de Loyola', in *Oeuvres completes de Voltaire*, ed. P. A. C. de Beaumarchais *et al.*, 70 vols (Kehl: De l'Imprimerie de la Société Littéraire-Typographique, 1785–89), XLI: p. 249.
42　Andrew Steinmetz, *The Novitiate: Or, a Year Among the English Jesuits* (London: Smith, Elder, 1846).
43　Steinmetz, *History*, I: p. 422.
44　Stephen, 'Founders of Jesuitism', p. 156.
45　See Introduction, pp. 9, 14–15.
46　Richard Chenevix Trench, *Notes on the Miracles of Our Lord* (London: John W. Parker, 1846), pp. 49–51n. See also August Tholuck, *Vermischte Schriften grössenteils apologetischen Inhalts* (Hamburg: F. Perthes, 1839), pp. 50–7. The care with which Ignatius's canonisation was conducted, and its circumspection regarding accounts of his miracles, is underlined in Simon Ditchfield, '"Coping with the *beati moderni*": canonization procedure in the aftermath of the Council of Trent', in Thomas M. McCoog (ed.), *Ite Inflammate Omnia* (Rome: Institutum Historicum Societatis Jesu, 2010), pp. 413–39.
47　Taylor, *Loyola*, p. 96.
48　*Ibid.*, p. 172.
49　*Christian Observer*, 49 (1850), 320–33.
50　William Bonner Hopkins, *Some Points of Christian Doctrine* (Cambridge: Deighton, 1849); Lucius Arthur, *Letter to Sir J. Stephen Threatening Proceedings Against Him* (c. 1852), Cambridge University Library, Rare Books Room, Cam.b.500.10, item 18.
51　*Christian Reformer*, 6 (1850), 1–16; *Eclectic Review*, new series, 26 (1849), 123; *Examiner* (9 June 1849), p. 356.
52　*Rambler: A Catholic Journal and Review*, 6 (1849), 308–9.
53　Hopkins, *Some Points*, p. 94.
54　Originally published unsigned as 'Ignatius Loyola and his associates', *Edinburgh Review*, 75, 152 (1842), 297–358.
55　Stephen, 'Founders of Jesuitism', p. 253.
56　*Ibid.*, pp. 187, 188, 237.
57　Charles Seager, *The Spiritual Exercises of St Ignatius Loyola* (London: Dolman, 1847), p. 180.
58　'Jesuitism', in Thomas Carlyle, *Selected Works, XIX: Latter-Day Pamphlets* (London: Chapman and Hall, 1870), pp. 353–403; Charles Kingsley, *What, Then, Does Dr Newman Mean?* (London and Cambridge: Macmillan, 1864); W. E. Gladstone, *The Vatican Decrees in their Bearing on Civil Allegiance* (London: John Murray, 1874), p. 58.
59　*Bulwark or Reformation Journal*, 17 (1867), 166–7.

60 C[harles] K[egan] P[aul], 'Liddon's sermons', *Theological Review*, 4, 19 (1867), 589–93; 'Note', *Theological Review*, 4, 20 (1867), 161–2.
61 J. O. Johnston, *Life and Letters of Henry Parry Liddon* (London: Longmans, Green, 1904), pp. 78–80.
62 See e.g. Orby Shipley, *Spiritual Exercises of S. Ignatius of Loyola* (London: Longmans, 1870).
63 William James, 'The energies of men', *The Philosophical Review*, 16 (1907), 1–20.
64 Gerard Vallée (ed.), *Florence Nightingale on Mysticism and Eastern Religions* (Waterloo, ON: Wilfred Laurier University Press, 2004), pp. 43–5, 522.
65 John Tulloch, 'St Dominic and his age', *Good Words*, 18 (December 1877), 161–8; 'St Francis', *ibid.*, 418–23, 449–52; 'Ignatius Loyola', *ibid.*, 531–6, 618–22; 'The Order of Jesuits', *ibid.*, 689–93; 'The Order of Jesuits. II', *ibid.*, 738–42.
66 Rowland Prothero, *The Life and Correspondence of Arthur Penrhyn Stanley*, 2 vols (New York: Charles Scribner's Sons, 1894), II: pp. 3–4.
67 A. P. Stanley, *Three Introductory Lectures on the Study of Ecclesiastical History* (Oxford: John Henry Parker, 1857), pp. 73–4. See also F. W. Farrar, *Saintly Workers* (London: Macmillan, 1878).
68 M. A. Smith, 'The missionary statesman and the missionary saint: Henry Venn's *Life of Francis Xavier*', in Smith (ed.), *British Evangelical Identities Past and Present* (Carlisle: Paternoster Press, 2008), pp. 238–52.
69 Mary Heimann, 'St Francis and modern English sentiment', in Simon Ditchfield (ed.), *Christianity and Community in the West* (Aldershot: Ashgate, 2001), pp. 285–7.
70 E.g. Mary E. Beck, *Turning Points, and Their Results in the Lives of Eminent Christians* (London: Hodder and Stoughton, 1888).
71 M[ary] F[rances] S[eymour], *Stories of the Saints, for Children* [first series] (London: R. Washbourne, 1874), pp. 134–40.
72 H. G. Tunnicliff, *Marching as to War: Talks on Soldiers of Christ's Empire* (London: Charles H. Kelly, 1917), p. 27.
73 Francis William Newman, *Phases of Faith* (London: John Chapman, 1850), pp. 27–8.
74 *Ibid.*, pp. 33–4.
75 A. P. Stanley, *The Epistles of St Paul to the Corinthians*, 2 vols (London: John Murray, 1855), I: pp. 214–25.
76 F. E. Kingsley, *Charles Kingsley: His Letters and Memories of His Life*, 2 vols (London: Henry S. King, 1877), II: p. 374.
77 Auguste Comte, *Calendrier positiviste, ou, Système général de commémoration publique* (Paris: L. Mathias, 1849).
78 See e.g. Taylor, *Loyola*, p. 20; Ernest Renan, 'Loyola', in Max Müller and Renan (eds), *Portraits of the Hundred Greatest Men in History, IV: Religion* (1879–80; London: Sampson Low, etc., 1885), p. 185.
79 *Ibid.*, pp. 183–6.
80 Thomas Hughes, *Loyola and the Educational System of the Jesuits* (London: W. Heinemann, 1892).
81 J. A. Froude, 'Saint Teresa', in *The Spanish Story of the Armada, and Other Essays* (London: Longmans Green, 1892), pp. 181–2.
82 Ciaran Brady, *James Anthony Froude: An Intellectual Biography of a Victorian Prophet* (Oxford: Oxford University Press, 2013), pp. 86–111, 321–51, 440–8.

83 [J. A. Froude], 'Saint Teresa: A Psychological Study', *Fraser's Magazine*, 65 (1862), 59–74.
84 Froude, 'Teresa', pp. 248–9.
85 K. Baedeker, *Italy: Handbook for Travellers, Second Part. Central Italy and Rome* (12th edn, London: Dulau, 1897), pp. 206–7.

# 8

# English Catholic martyrs

*Lucy Underwood*

IN JANUARY 1887, *The Times* published its response to the beatification by Leo XIII of fifty-four English Catholic martyrs of the Reformation era. It gave most space to Thomas More (1478–1535) and John Fisher (1469–1535), declaring itself 'gratified at any opportunity of recalling to the world the fame of two eminent countrymen'. As for this particular honour,

> Beatification and canonization meant more formerly than now. Sir Thomas More's most fervent admirers will hardly pray to him or implore for his mediation. Not even a new church is likely to be dedicated to him. It is not only that the obtusest mind would be sensible of the disgust which the object of adoration, one of the sanest natures which ever existed, would have felt at any such tribute; the current of sentiment itself in the Church of Rome has bent with the age, and no longer flows in that direction.[1]

This writer might have been disappointed had he seen the letter from Cardinal Manning (1808–92), Archbishop of Westminster, to John Morris (1826–93), the Jesuit priest whose efforts were largely responsible for Rome's recognition of these English martyrs: 'I thank God with you to have lived to see this *in diebus nostris* ... It is like the resurrection of the Witnesses whose bodies have lain so long in Babylon ... I have long invoked St Thomas More in secret, and now write him so for the first time.'[2] The *Times* journalist would presumably have been even more disappointed later that year, when a Catholic church dedicated to Our Lady of the Assumption and the English Martyrs was founded in Cambridge.[3]

The beatification of the English Martyrs has received little scholarly attention.[4] Yet the reception of the Reformation martyrs illuminates questions concerning the social and cultural development of Catholicism: how converts, longstanding Catholic communities, and the Irish immigrants who swelled Catholic ranks throughout the century related to each other, and how Catholic leaders responded to these changes.[5] It also relates to the appropriation of history: throughout the nineteenth century, rival versions of the Reformation informed cultural consciousness as well as occupying historians. If the 1886 beatifications were indicative of wider confessional conflicts, they impinged too on tensions internal to English Catholicism, between its 'Ultramontane' and its 'Cisalpine' or 'liberal' elements.[6] These involved questions of papal authority, intellectual freedom, and relations between civil and ecclesiastical governance, but also perceptions of national identity – as indicated by references to the Ultramontanists' opponents as 'English Catholics'.[7]

Some English Catholics had looked towards canonisation of the martyrs ever since the executions, when they compiled and disseminated accounts of their colleagues' deaths. The first systematic attempt to catalogue the 'English Martyrs' belongs to Richard Smith (1567–1655), appointed bishop with responsibility for English Catholics in 1627. Bishop Richard Challoner (1691–1781), Vicar Apostolic, published his *Memoirs of Missionary Priests* in 1741–42.[8] But for Rome to recognise these martyrs officially required the completion of a canonical process, which English Catholics lacked the resources and ecclesiastical organisation to initiate. The restoration of the Catholic hierarchy in 1850 made it possible to start the process with a diocesan commission, held in 1874. Twelve years later, a verdict from Rome's Sacred Congregation of Rites was not forthcoming, but the martyrs' advocates then found a piece of evidence which enabled them to fast-track some of the 309 martyrs under consideration. *Ecclesiae Anglicanae Trophaea* was a book of engravings published in 1584, commemorating as martyrs various Catholics executed by Henry VIII and Elizabeth I, which had been approved by the then Pope, Gregory XIII.[9] This was allowed as evidence that devotion to these individuals as martyrs had previously been authorised, and in December 1886 those fifty-four were beatified by 'equipollent' decree. In 1895, nine more martyrs were added. During the twentieth century, 221 more were beatified and 45 canonised. This study explores the beginnings of this process, examining the martyrs' role in Catholic–Protestant encounters in late Victorian England, as well as their place in the development of Catholic identity.

## The martyrs and the development of 'modern' English Catholic historiography

If nineteenth-century Catholic scholarship was rooted in early modern historiography, it was also formed by the creation of the 'modern' discipline of history from the late eighteenth century onwards. The groundbreaking work of John Lingard (1771–1851) – with its self-conscious emphasis on firsthand archival research – lay behind that of those who sought both Rome's recognition of the English Martyrs, and to vindicate them to non-Catholics.[10] The last quarter of the century witnessed an explosion in such scholarship. John Morris SJ was official postulator of the cause of the English Martyrs, and their advocate from the 1850s until his death in 1893. While presenting evidence to Cardinal Manning's diocesan commission, and having volumes of it translated into Latin for the Congregation of Rites, Morris also published scholarly works, mainly reproductions of primary sources with commentary.[11] Assisted by the nuns of the Bar Convent, York, and the Anglican James Raine (1830–96), Chancellor and Canon Residentiary at York Minster, Morris transcribed copious official records of the prosecution of northern Catholics,[12] as well as contemporary Catholic accounts of persecution.[13] Joseph Gillow (1850–1921) produced a *Biographical Dictionary of the English Catholics* (1885–1902),[14] and Henry Foley SJ (1811–91) compiled eight volumes of sixteenth- and seventeenth-century primary sources: *Records of the English Province of the Society of Jesus* (1875–83).[15] Francis Knox (1822–82) of the London Oratory edited the 'Diaries' of the English College, Douai, the seminary which trained English priests from 1568 until the French Revolution.[16]

Interestingly, their work received considerable recognition outside Catholic circles.[17] Morris's biographer could quote admiring reviews from non-Catholic publications: '[Morris] gives us his facts, produces his evidence, and leaves us to ourselves to make the best or worst of the case.' According to the *Athenaeum*, Morris 'never allowed himself' to be a 'controversialist'. 'The theological and polemical element is absolutely eliminated, the historical is not only in the ascendant, it is paramount.'[18] Foley's *Records*, on the other hand, got mixed reviews in the *Athenaeum*, which dismissed him as 'a person of the most extravagant and passionate credulity', censuring his apparent acceptance of the thaumaturgical accounts that he printed.[19] Foley's too-ready engagement with his subjects' sanctity opened him to the charge of being a bad historian. Awareness of non-Catholic reactions certainly influenced Catholic scholars' views of each other. Writing to Morris, his fellow Jesuit Richard Clarke (1839–1900) commented: 'I suppose you have seen the *Athenaeum* in which [Foley] was so unmercifully (& I think not unfairly) roasted?' Clarke continued: 'I hope the article will lead the superiors to stop the writing or at all events the publication of works, which seem to me to bring no honour to the society, rather the reverse.'[20] Clarke distanced himself and Morris from Foley's overt promotion of sanctity, but in a sense his motivation remained religious. The Society's Catholic mission would be jeopardised by its members' failure to conform to the expectations of scholarship.

Reactions to Catholic histories derived from debates dating from the era of the martyrdoms themselves. During the Reformation, each side regarded the other's 'martyrs' as 'pseudo-martyrs': they did not die for the truth, and therefore their courage, suffering or piety was irrelevant to claims of sanctity.[21] English Protestant regimes, however, also made the slightly different claim that Catholics were not executed for religion, but as traitors. Catholics argued this was true only in the narrowest legal sense, in that the government had widened the definition of treason to include practising the Catholic religion. Nineteenth-century Protestant commentary exploited this alleged distinction to construct persecution as something peculiar to (and inseparable from) Catholicism; it indicated that it was a false – and dangerous – religion. By implication, *not* persecuting was a manifestation of true, Protestant Christianity.[22] In this sense, the martyr-saint status of executed English Catholics was not merely unwelcome rival propaganda, it was a threat to Protestant identity.

Qualified recognition of 'rival' martyrs can reveal underlying antagonisms. There is a humanist slant to *The Times*'s praise of More and Fisher: the former's 'Romanism has been forgotten in his astounding humanity'. Both men's friendship with Erasmus (1466–1533) was praised, since 'All three exposed themselves to obloquy and disgrace as leaders against the ecclesiastical abuses of Rome'. 'Had their prime, such as it was, co-incided with the reign of Mary, they would have been fortunate had they escaped the tender attentions of a Bishop Bonner.' More and Fisher (as well as Erasmus) are construed here almost as Protestants *avant la lettre*. Erasmus's career indicated that 'the shafts which pierced a vent from which Protestantism was able to emerge let also light and air into the subterranean caverns of the Roman Communion'.[23] *The Times* wished to 'honour' two worthy English humanists without endorsing their Catholic sanctity.

The *Saturday Review* commented in similar vein that 'The compilers of the Decree have shown their discretion in placing at the head the two names which will at once commend themselves to the respectful memory of the great body of Englishmen, Cardinal Fisher and Sir Thomas More'.[24] This article accepted Fisher and More only to discount most of their companions: Henrician martyrs had opposed the Royal Supremacy in matters spiritual, and 'may justly on the Roman theory be regarded as martyrs'; but the Elizabethan martyrs, executed after Pope Pius V's excommunication of Elizabeth (1570), died for 'the deposing and dispensing power of the Pope, a tenet which is now generally abandoned, and which never was an article of faith'. The seminary priests were suspected of conspiring against the 'government and liberties' of England, and the Jesuits allegedly taught tyrannicide. The *Saturday Review*, therefore, could not 'on any intelligent principle rank them among "the noble army of martyrs"'.[25] Thus, while Henry VIII's reputation was sacrificed, England's Protestant settlement was preserved from the taint of having made martyrs.[26]

In 1880, a *Saturday Review* article reacting to the Catholic Union's petition to the Vatican to canonise the English Martyrs also admitted the Henrician martyrs, but argued that canonising them would endanger the progress of toleration. Evenhandedly criticising Foxe's 'book of martyrs', especially a recent 'Sunday-school edition of it', the *Review* opined that 'The faggots of Smithfield and the gibbets of Tyburn will prove equally available instruments to conjure with'. 'Those who prefer Christian charity to sectarian rancour may naturally prefer that both should be forgotten.' The *Review*'s contribution to this forgetting was to remind its readers of the power of the 'fires of Smithfield' in protestantising England, and to explain Elizabethan anti-Catholic legislation as 'reasonable alarm' against Catholic and papal conspiracy, such that 'the main responsibility for the blood of "the English martyrs" rests, not with the Queen but with … the reigning Pope … Leo XIII is asked to build the sepulchres of the prophets whom his predecessors slew'. As though aware of the paradox in this, the report added, 'We have glided half unconsciously into the language of the "Gunpowder Treason" service, only expunged within recent memory from the English Prayer Book in a spirit the reverse of that which prompts the proposed introduction of fresh controversial amenities into the ritual of Rome.'[27] The reference to 'ritual' (i.e. the liturgical commemoration of English Martyrs) again isolates saint-making as the problem. The effect is to maintain a historical/theological interpretation endorsing martyr status for Protestants while denying it to Catholic martyrs, and simultaneously to claim a superior commitment to 'Christian charity' in the present day.

The *Review*'s comment on the 'discretion' of heading the list of martyrs with More and Fisher hinted that they were being used to cover the beatification of a lot of shady characters,[28] an interpretation *The Times* raised explicitly regarding proposals to beatify Mary, Queen of Scots (1542–87). Among the original beati, 'The illustrious More and the learned Fisher' were 'the picked strawberries at the top of the basket, and nobody cared to scrutinise closely the exact quality of the merits of the accompanying crowd'. It is unsurprising that Protestant contemporaries derided the notion of canonising Mary Stuart, whose claims to sanctity in general and martyrdom in particular are debatable (her beatification never went ahead). Yet such attacks were used to criticise the beatification of English martyrs in general. 'The revived fashion of saint-making must have reached fever-heat when it is seriously proposed to beatify Mary, Queen of Scots', snorted *The Times*, which saw canonisation as regrettable regression for a Church that had been slowly becoming less objectionable. The main difference between Mary and those who made the cut was that 'Queen Mary occupies too wide a space in history to have her failings ... overlooked'.[29]

Sainthood and saint-making was what drew suspicion. This is paradoxical, in that the canonisation procedures, requiring multi-stage enquiry, documentary evidence, and proof of alleged miracles had been designed to raise the credibility of sainthood, as well as to control it: only individuals whose holiness had been historically verified would be honoured. Yet it was precisely this formalisation of sanctity that occasioned Protestant suspicions about historical distortion, and the ecclesiastical authoritarianism they discerned in it.

The treatment of More, Fisher and their companions illustrates how praising the virtues of 'martyrs' from across the confessional divide was distinct from acknowledging the status of 'martyrdom'. It was this tension which the Anglican schoolmaster-historian Augustus Jessopp (1823–1914) set out to negotiate in his biography of Henry Walpole SJ (1558–95).[30] He accorded his subject only qualified personal praise, describing how Walpole, under torture, gave information and offered to recant before recovering his resolve: Walpole 'aspired to be a hero and ... failed'.[31] But Jessopp justified Walpole's martyr status, insisting that 'religious persecution was no novelty on one side or the other'. While acknowledging the provocative politics of Elizabethan Catholics, he stated that 'whatever excuse may be found for the persecution by Elizabeth in the fierce attacks of Parsons and his fellows, is fairly to be allowed for the atrocities of Mary's reign in the abominable scurrilities of Becon and Knox'.[32] Emphasising that Walpole's 'creed was not my creed' and 'his character ... not without defects', Jessopp also argued that 'These men [Catholic martyrs] were of the same stuff that Latimer and Rowland Taylor were made of ... Surely, surely they deserve at least a portion of the same honour! Let us not grudge it them.'[33] Martyrs of rival creeds, then, were ultimately 'the same stuff'.

Jessopp intended to persuade non-Catholic readers; he couches his provocative defence in a conciliatory tone, and his title – *One Generation of a Norfolk House* – creates an expectation of family history rather than hagiography, in contrast to Morris's more confessional *Troubles of our Catholic Forefathers*. Jessopp knew Morris, and corresponded with Foley;[34] Morris noted of *One Generation* that 'the friendliness is far greater than could have been expected from a man in his position'.[35] His review took lengthy exception to Jessopp's criticisms of Walpole, apparently preferring a picture of unadulterated virtue. But Morris declared *One Generation* 'a great gain to the cause of right' – and forgave its faults because it would 'penetrate where no Catholic book would be admitted'.[36]

This raises the issue of how Protestant criticism affected Catholic campaigns to make the martyrs saints. One key question is whether controversial candidates were excluded – those whose inclusion would bolster accusations that 'martyrs' were really political dissidents. The beatification decrees of 1886 and 1892 may be compared with a list of martyrs compiled by the Oratorian priest Thomas Graves Law (1836–1904) in 1876.[37] Law omits, for example, John Felton, who had been executed for fastening a copy of the bull excommunicating Elizabeth to the bishop of London's gate in 1570. He also excluded Thomas Percy, Earl of Northumberland, who led the Northern Rising and was executed in 1572. That Felton was beatified in 1886 and Percy in 1892 underlines the significance of the 1584 engravings. Felton appears in *Ecclesiae Anglicanae Trophaea*; Percy is not named, but the 'quidam vir illustris' whose execution plate 30 depicts is probably him.[38] It seems that, despite potential awkwardness, certain martyrs were included because to exclude them would be to jeopardise the authority of the crucial text, perhaps delaying the entire cause indefinitely. When Bede Camm (1864–1942) compiled his *Lives* of the beatified martyrs, he felt the need for special justifications.[39] Percy was beatified because he had been offered a pardon for his treason on condition that he changed his religion, hence his refusal to apostatise actually sealed his fate.[40] Camm had equal difficulty with Blessed John Haile, who, indicted for criticising Henry VIII's second marriage and the Royal Supremacy, had pleaded guilty and apologised,[41] and with Felton's obviously political rejection of Elizabeth's right to rule.[42] Camm's preface discussed 'martyrs' who had denied the Queen's temporal power, and were vulnerable to the charge of having been traitors in the ordinary sense. His defence framed the familiar 'politics or religion' debate in terms which engaged Catholic definitions of martyrdom. The essential point, Camm argued, was whether a person was executed 'out of the motive of hatred of the faith'. Felton and Haile were killed in 'odium fidei', whatever the other details of their deaths. He also tried to insulate them from the cause of the martyrs in general by stressing that these 'exceptional' cases 'involve many more problems than the lives of the other martyrs do'. But Camm also deployed a justification which challenged the religion–politics dichotomy itself, appealing to patriotism and provocatively suggesting comparisons with John Hampden and other Civil War figures who 'are commonly belauded as champions of popular resistance to the encroachments of the Crown'.[43] Camm may have seriously intended to render his martyrs as defenders of English liberty, but his comparison also criticised what he perceived as inconsistencies in the criteria for inclusion in whiggish narratives of progress and patriotism. Camm's defence of his subjects' sanctity both narrowed it to canonical definitions that could be independent of political complexities and exploited the broader culture of commemoration which made secular 'saints' out of political heroes.

Some omissions were perhaps attributable to potential controversy. Law's 1876 list included Henry Garnet SJ, executed in 1606 for alleged complicity in the Gunpowder Plot. There were those at the time and afterwards who defended Garnet's innocence and regarded him as a martyr; but Garnet's case was among those 'delayed' by the Congregation of Rites as unproven, and was never reintroduced. Despite evidence in his favour, Garnet had a consistently bad press from non-Catholic historians, which due to the Gunpowder Plot connection found its way into popular perceptions, and perhaps it was felt that to beatify him would be imprudent.[44] Yet, on the whole, in selecting subjects for beatification, Rome proceeded according to her own rules, in serene disregard of ammunition she might give to Protestant commentators. English Catholics, for their part, were aware of the controversy which saint-making invited, but would not jeopardise recognition of the 'baptism of blood' they claimed for their heritage in order to avoid interconfessional confrontation.

## Pilgrimages, prayers, church dedications

In December 1886, shortly after the beatification, Morris lectured the pupils of Stonyhurst College on 'The English martyrs: why they died, what they suffered, what sort of men they were'. He opened by anticipating his audience's reaction: 'The English Martyrs! Who are they?' Morris alleged that 'not so very long ago ... there was not a boy in a Catholic college who was not quite at home with Challoner's *Missionary Priests*, and as that book tells all about most of the martyrs, every one then knew something about them. But nowadays Challoner is thrown on one side and the English Martyrs are in danger of being forgotten.' The recent beatification, Morris clearly hoped, would assist in dispelling this obscurity.[45] John Pollen (1820–1902), Morris's biographer, concurred: prior to the beatifications, the martyrs had been little talked about. Pollen suggested that this was partly because English Catholics were embarrassed by Protestant charges that their martyrs had been political dissidents. Rome's recognition, Pollen insisted, had cleared these doubts.[46]

It has been argued that the 1935 canonisation of John Fisher and Thomas More was not a response to popular devotion and that English Catholics had to be taught to integrate Fisher and More into their religious identity. This is attributed to the fact that the Catholic population was mainly working-class and ethnically Irish, with little affinity to any recusant heritage.[47] Since the demography of Victorian Catholicism was similar, perhaps the English Martyrs mattered mainly to those concerned to vindicate the 'Englishness' of English Catholicism, and to challenge Protestant historical narratives: converts, scholars, and people who prided themselves on recusant family pasts.[48] Morris and Pollen themselves suggested that beatifying the martyrs did not so much respond to popular demand as provide the opportunity to create it. But with ecclesiastical sanction secured, that opportunity was seized.

Morris's Stonyhurst lecture, given before 1886 was out, was quickly printed. Other means of fostering enthusiasm were also available. Pilgrimages to sites connected with English Martyrs were organised, as when 600 people joined a pilgrimage at York to venerate a relic of Margaret Clitherow, and then processed to the former site of York's gallows where various Catholic martyrs had died, while in September 1893 three thousand Catholics joined a pilgrimage to Barlow Hall in honour of the Lancashire martyr Ambrose Barlow. A pilgrimage to Glastonbury to honour its martyred abbot of 1539 was arranged during the Catholic Truth Society's conference in September 1895, with an indulgence offered to pilgrims. These events were reported in the local press without animosity, sometimes in language which suggests a Catholic reporter.[49]

Presumably to facilitate such devotions, in 1891 Morris produced a penny-pamphlet 'Litany' of the English Martyrs. The litany invoked ancient English saints before moving on to Reformation martyrs. The tag in each invocation summing up the cause or manner of that martyr's death indicates Morris's concern to raise awareness: 'Blessed Thomas Abel, Edward Powel and Richard Fetherston, defenders of the sanctity of marriage, *pray for us*' (they had opposed Henry VIII's first divorce); 'Blessed Everard Hanse, who in thy pains didst exclaim, O happy day…'.[50] While Morris's litany and Camm's *Lives* restricted themselves to those martyrs already beatified, pilgrimages did not always do so. Clitherow, executed in 1586, and Barlow, executed in 1642, could not appear in the 1583 engravings, nor (consequently) in the 1886 beatification decree: they were beatified in 1929. Hence pilgrimages commemorating them in the 1890s may reflect local traditions not wholly dependent on renewed promotion through the canonisation campaign. The advocates of the Reformation martyrs certainly wished to widen their audience, to make England's new saints a staple of religious life. And if three thousand people would attend a pilgrimage, they were not entirely failing.

Church dedications also promoted the martyrs. Our Lady and the English Martyrs, Cambridge, was not the first; English Martyrs Church, Preston, Lancashire was founded in 1867, and in 1887 commissioned sculptures of Lancashire martyrs as part of its rebuilding.[51] Another church dedicated to the English Martyrs opened at Tower Hill, London in 1876. Any gap between the interests of the Catholic population and the recusant preoccupations of a scholarly elite did not affect this church's founders: the *British Architect* reported that the church had been built 'to meet the spiritual necessities of 6,000 of the poorest Catholics of London'.[52]

These dedications raise intriguing questions concerning official sainthood. A fund-raising appeal described Tower Hill as 'a memorial of the holy martyrs whose blood flowed near the spot where the church is rising', comparing it to the Protestant Martyrs' Memorial in Oxford.[53] But since church dedications are restricted to officially recognised saints, it is difficult to see how these churches could be named for Reformation martyrs.[54] One possibility is that 'English Martyrs' did not necessarily refer to More, Fisher, and company: there were many long-canonised saints who fitted the bill, providing a dedication that simultaneously created space for eulogising Reformation martyrs. Manning's opening homily at Tower Hill discoursed on the Reformation martyrs in the context of 'a historical sketch' which praised medieval saints, including Thomas of Canterbury and Anselm, and linked the British protomartyr, Alban, to More and Fisher.[55] These churches therefore subtly promoted existing attachment to the Reformation martyrs, acted as a plea for their canonisation, and incorporated them into English Catholic hagiography.

Our Lady and the English Martyrs, Cambridge, was the first foundation since the beatification. Reformation martyr-iconography pervades, from the windows to the motifs decorating the pillars. On the baldacchino, an emblem of the Five Wounds of Christ recalls the banners of the 1536 Pilgrimage of Grace, when northerners rebelled against Henry VIII in defence of the 'old religion'. The church's design demonstrates awareness that constructing a landmark Catholic building in the university town historically connected with the Protestant Reformation was invested with significance: the location was a reason for the interest shown by eminent individuals such as Cardinal Newman and a justification for its grand scale.[56] The south aisle windows chronicle the life of Fisher, whose statue stands over the north door. Fisher had been Chancellor of the university, and his prominence embodied Catholic claims to a place in its history. It also engaged with other contemporary commemorations of early modern confessional heroes: in the 1874 Emmanuel Congregational Church on Trumpington Street, stained-glass windows portrayed martyred Elizabethan separatists and Oliver Cromwell. The Divinity School, built 1879, was designed to reconcile competing traditions in a comprehensive scheme: when its statues were installed in 1890, they included Fisher, Erasmus, and Thomas Cranmer.[57]

The windows of the Cambridge church displayed earlier martyrs alongside Reformation ones: Thomas of Canterbury in the North transept chapel; Alban, Edmund, Augustine, and others in the clerestory, including Pope Eleutherius and the mythical British King Lucius, whose ecclesiological significance had been hotly debated during the Reformation.[58] Like Manning's Tower Hill sermon, the purpose of this iconographical scheme was theological and historical. Against perceived Anglican usurpations, its claim was that the Catholicism maintained by Elizabethan recusants and their successors was the ancient Christianity of England.[59]

## The martyrs, Catholicism and Englishness

Hence this was also a narrative of national identity: a Catholic 'mythology' of England. Although the role of Protestantism, and concomitantly anti-Catholicism, in shaping English national identity has been repeatedly examined, Catholic perceptions of national identity have received less attention.[60] Yet Catholics, too, developed narratives of 'Englishness' which competed with and influenced Protestant ones.[61] This imagined England was invoked in a petition by the Catholic Union of Great Britain to the Vatican, seeking canonisation of the 'English Martyrs', which *The Times* published in January 1880.[62]

The Catholic Union outlined three 'motives' for its petition: first, the 'steadfast courage of that heroic band' which endured persecution for 'five whole generations', in 'the hope of winning back their country to our Lord and His Vicar'. Secondly, the Catholic revival of the previous fifty years: 'All ranks of society in England have witnessed a considerable number of men and of women who have given up the errors of the Protestant sects in which they had been educated ... and have embraced the Catholic Faith.' This was a story of conversion, in which neither Irish immigration nor pre-existing Catholic communities, the 'poor remnant' 'beaten to the earth' by long persecution, played much part. Thirdly, the petition invoked 'that original bond between the Apostolic See and our island', which had once 'merited the name of the Isle of Saints, and even of Mary's Dower and Realm'. This short text epitomises Catholic narratives of England. England's Catholic identity was, as the petition put it, 'coeval with its birth' in the Anglo-Saxon centuries. The Reformation robbed England of its true identity, and (almost) eradicated Catholicism through persecution; this was the era both of heroic martyrdom, and of national apostasy. By 1880, the years surrounding Catholic Emancipation had been incorporated into this narrative as the age of conversion and revival, a 'Christian harvest' attributed to 'the blood of our martyrs', whose sacrifice had been patriotic as well as religious – they died to 'win back their country'.

As the iconography of Our Lady and the English Martyrs illustrates, saints constituted a narrative of continuing identity that began with the Romano-British Alban. Canonising the Reformation martyrs emphasised their identity with earlier saints, including those accepted by Anglicans. No Protestant Church, including the Church of England, possessed a process for formally recognising saints, therefore a story of Christian England progressing from 'Saint' Alban to 'Saint' Bede to 'Saint' Thomas More to 'Saint' Edmund Campion expressed an exclusive Catholic claim to continuity.

Devotional texts expressed similar preoccupations. Morris's litany closed with a prayer that 'England may reap the full fruit of the blood her Martyrs have so lovingly shed for her conversion': again, martyrdom and patriotism converge. The prayer continued, 'O God, who hast placed us in this land, hast taught us to love it and all those who dwell therein, grant to all our countrymen the grace of true contrition, faith hope and charity'. Hymnwriters asked the martyrs to 'Pray for the country you once called your own', exhorting them to 'Win our country to Christ again'.[63]

Alongside patriotic and confessional pride, however, the martyrs evoked national guilt. The hymn 'Martyrs of England' makes the prayer for England's conversion into an accusation:

> Jesus, Master, how long, how long
> Shall the nation's rage Thy glory foil?
> The blood of Thy Martyrs – a mighty throng –
> Cries to Thee from our hallowed soil.[64]

Like Christ's, the blood of the martyrs can be salvific. But England is both the land of martyrs and the land that *makes* martyrs. Another hymn contrasts this with pre-Reformation England:

> Remember how our Lady's Dower
> Was England's glorious name,
> Oh, bid her show her former power,
> Her ancient right reclaim.[65]

Both the ancient saints, 'those who prayed at altars now laid low', and the Reformation martyrs, 'those who stood amid the nation's fall' are invoked as barriers against divine wrath – 'For deeds of shame, for faith betrayed / Thy vengeance, Lord, forego'.

As suggested above, this Catholic English 'myth' could also address discourses of liberty and social progress that were central to whiggish narratives. Manning's Tower Hill sermon included

> a brief historical sketch of the growth of our English Constitution and liberties under our Saxon sovereigns, which culminated in King Edward, 'King and confessor', under whom, he said, there could be no hesitation between the duty of their subjects to the Crown and to God, showing also that under the Norman line there arose a constant and ever-growing conflict between these two duties ... The final crash came ... 300 years ago.[66]

Thus the image of Anglo-Saxon liberty threatened by the Norman Conquest could be decoupled from Protestant narratives of a native Church gradually subjugated to papal tyranny.[67] A narrative of political and social regress caused by the Protestant Reformation had been stridently articulated by the Tory radical William Cobbett (1763–1835), in his 1824–27 *History of the Protestant Reformation*, and such ideas were conjoined with the martyrs' sanctity in Catholic texts such as Francis Thompson's poem 'To the English Martyrs' (1906).[68] Thompson (1859–1907) deployed notions of national guilt and national redemption, but England's desolation is imagined as not only spiritual:

> When God was stolen from out man's mouth,
> Stolen was the bread; then hunger and drouth
> Went to and fro; began the wail,
> Struck root the poor-house and the jail.
> Ere cut the dykes, let through that flood,
> Ye writ the protest with your blood;

Thompson equally subverts Protestant constructions of England's destiny when he prays to 'the anointed Kings of Tyburn Tree':

> Your prevalent approaches make
> With unsustainable Grace, and take
> captive the land which captived you
> To Christ enslave ye and subdue
> Her so bragged freedom

This inversion of England's self-image as both imperial nation and home of liberty concludes:

> Hardest servitude has he
> That's gaoled in arrogant liberty;
> And freedom, spacious and unflawed,
> Who is walled about with God.

Thompson alludes to the Church's dogmatic authority, positing its doctrinal prescriptions and proscriptions as guaranteeing freedom of thought within their bounds, safe from the danger of error. It is a defence of papal authority, and probably of papal infallibility in particular – a doctrine defined amid controversy by the First Vatican Council in 1870 – but it depends on triumphally inverting the subjugation and deaths of the English Martyrs.[69]

This links the martyrs to struggles between 'Ultramontanes' and 'Cisalpine' or 'liberal' Catholics. It is difficult to define either of these terms; but, broadly speaking, Ultramontanes took a maximal view of papal jurisdiction and papal authority – sometimes to an extreme which prevented disagreement and discussion even over non-dogmatic questions. Cisalpines or 'English Catholics' emphasised the autonomy of bishops and the local Church, and limited papal jurisdiction – sometimes to an extreme which could render it virtually meaningless. These tensions had a cultural impact: Ultramontanes were inclined to conform religious practice closely to that of Rome (in terms of architecture, devotions, music, etc.), while their opponents tended to reject this modern, 'foreign' Catholicism in favour of indigenous devotional traditions. Ultramontanism was connected with support for the papacy's temporal power (its governance of the 'Papal States'), and agitation for the dogmatic definition of papal infallibility.[70] The later nineteenth century has been seen – largely due to the influence of Henry Manning, Cardinal Archbishop of Westminster – as the era of triumphant Ultramontanism.[71]

The English Martyrs were, in a sense, an Ultramontane cause: they died to maintain communion with Rome and papal authority. Hence it is no surprise to find their cause promoted by Manning and by the Catholic Union (1870) – which cited the restoration of the Papal States among its founding aims.[72] The Union's petition emphasised that 'There is not one among these champions of the Christian faith who did not sacrifice his life for the honour of the Apostle Peter and the rights of the Holy Apostolic See'. The English Martyrs' canonisation would give 'great glory to the Holy See'.[73] Manning's pastoral announcing the 1886 beatifications stated that 'We owe to the head of the Church for this act of love in glorifying our martyrs a faithful imitation of their fidelity'.[74]

Yet the Reformation martyrs were also a national cause. The hymn 'Martyrs of England' emphasised their cultural affinity with the living: 'Our English speech ye can understand / Our cities, and hills, and fields ye know ... Nighest to us of the white-robed Host; / bound to us as our kith and kin.'[75] (Like those who dedicated English

Martyrs Church, Tower Hill, to serve a largely ethnic-Irish population, this hymn-writer was not concerned with contemporary demographics.) The Catholic Union combined affinity to a supra-national Church with national pride in observing that 'among the other nations of Europe scarcely one can be found which has not rejoiced in several additions to the roll of its saints during the last three centuries; while our own country ... has not received a single accession'.[76]

Architecture reflected this dual appeal. Especially during the mid nineteenth century, architectural style was an ecclesiological statement: Ultramontanes had tended to favour Continental Baroque; 'English Catholics', Neo-Gothic – the supposedly 'pure' indigenous style. Perhaps surprisingly, Our Lady and the English Martyrs is a Neo-Gothic extravaganza, from steeple-tip to gargoyles; likewise English Martyrs, Tower Hill. Yet by the later nineteenth century these stylistic choices made sense. The papalist assertiveness of these churches depended on a continuity narrative of Catholic *Englishness*: the Christianity which developed the gothic was the same that rejected the Royal Supremacy for the papacy in the sixteenth century, and which in the nineteenth century rewarded that rejection with honours of sainthood. Perhaps the success of Ultramontanism in shaping English Catholicism during the later nineteenth century was partly due to its ability to incorporate national particularity into a Rome-centred identity; and for that, the Catholic martyrs of the English Reformation had great potential.[77]

'Englishmen', according to *The Times* in 1887, 'are not much concerned with the particular reasons which have moved the Vatican to beatify More and Fisher'.[78] Catholic devotion to, and defence of, More, Fisher, and company was directed towards challenging that definition of Englishness. The fact that, for Catholics, sainthood was connected to papal jurisdiction (because of Rome's exclusive power to confer that status) meant that the beatification of the English Martyrs offered an opportunity not only to re-engage with Protestant narratives of England and its Reformation, but to re-imagine England's relationship with Rome. The significance of the Catholic English Martyrs and the campaign to canonise them needs further research; a short study such as this can perhaps do little more than raise pertinent questions. But it seems clear that the Reformation martyrs and their status as saints proved a focal point in Protestant–Catholic relations, and shaped Catholic contributions to historiography. We have seen how the 'English Martyrs' were also incorporated into a new English Roman Catholic identity, as – in the aftermath of emancipation and restoration – Catholics daringly re-imagined their Church and nation.

## Notes

1  *The Times* (7 January 1887), p. 9.
2  Manning to Morris, 9 December 1886, Archives of the British Province of the Society of Jesus, London (hereafter ABSJ), DZ/M, 10.
3  *Cambridge Chronicle* (1 July 1887), p. 8; (17 October 1890), pp. 4, 8.

4  Standard works such as E. R. Norman, *Anti-Catholicism in Victorian England* (London: Allen and Unwin, 1968), Norman, *The English Catholic Church in the Nineteenth Century* (Oxford: Clarendon Press, 1984), D. J. Holmes, *More Roman than Rome: English Catholicism in the Nineteenth Century* (London: Burns and Oates, 1978), and M. Heimann, *Catholic Devotion in Victorian England* (Oxford: Clarendon Press, 1995) do not address the subject. For twentieth-century canonisations, see A. Atherstone, 'The canonisation of the forty English Martyrs: an ecumenical dilemma', *Recusant History*, 30 (2011), 573–87; J. Davies, 'A cult from above: the cause for canonisation of John Fisher and Thomas More', *Recusant History*, 28 (2007), 458–74; A. Harris, *Faith in the Family: A Lived Religious History of English Catholicism, 1945–1982* (Manchester: Manchester University Press, 2013), pp. 233–50.
5  Norman, *Catholic Church*, pp. 201–43, especially pp. 205–6, 216–20.
6  R. O'Day, *The Debate on the English Reformation* (London: Methuen 1986), pp. 54–83; M. Bentley, *Modernizing England's Past: English Historiography in the Age of Modernism, 1870–1970* (Cambridge: Cambridge University Press, 2005), pp. 45–70; M. Wheeler, *The Old Enemies: Catholic and Protestant in Nineteenth-Century English Culture* (Cambridge: Cambridge University Press, 2006) pp. 77–110; J. E. Drabble, 'Mary's Protestant martyrs and Elizabeth's Catholic traitors in the age of Catholic Emancipation', *Church History*, 51 (1982), 172–85.
7  Norman, *Catholic Church*, pp. 9–11,77–8, 234–43; Holmes, *More Roman*; K. L. Parker and M. J. G. Pahls (eds), *Authority, Dogma, and History: The Role of the Oxford Movement Converts in the Papal Infallibility Debates* (Palo Alto: Academica Press, 2009). See Heimann, *Catholic Devotion*, esp. pp. 1–37, for a reassessment of 'Ultramontanism'.
8  J. H. Pollen (ed.), *Unpublished Documents Relating to the English Martyrs*, Catholic Record Society, 5 (London: Catholic Record Society, 1908), pp. 1–17; Archives of the Archdiocese of Westminster, vols A3, A4, B28; Richard Challoner, *Memoirs of Missionary Priests, ... that have Suffered Death in England, on Religious Accounts* (London: [n.p.], 1741–42).
9  J. H. Pollen, *The Life and Letters of Father John Morris* (London: Burns and Oates, 1896), pp. 212–13. The engravings were based on frescoes painted 1583 for the chapel of the English College, Rome. One of the joint postulators of the cause, Mgr O'Callaghan, submitted the *Ecclesiae Anglicanae Trophaea* to the Congregation of Rites in June 1886, drawing attention to its publication 'cum privilegio' of Pope Gregory XIII.
10  P. Phillips (ed.), *Lingard Remembered* (London: Catholic Record Society, 2004); C. Highley, '"A Pestilent and Seditious Book": Nicholas Sander's *Schismatis Anglicani* and Catholic histories of the Reformation', *Huntington Library Quarterly*, 68 (2005), 151–71.
11  Pollen, *Morris*, pp. 218–34.
12  M. G. Kirkus, 'The relationship between Father John Morris S.J., and the Institute of the Blessed Virgin Mary', *Recusant History*, 26 (2002), 194–209.
13  J. Morris, *The Troubles of Our Catholic Forefathers Related by Themselves*, 3 vols (London: Burns and Oates, 1872–77); *The Life of Father John Gerard of the Society of Jesus* (London: Burns and Oates, 1881); *The Letter-Books of Sir Amias Poulet: Keeper of Mary Queen of Scots* (London: Burns and Oates, 1874); *The Condition of Catholics under James I: Father Gerard's Narrative of the Gunpowder Plot* (London: Longmans, Green, 1871).
14  J. Gillow, *A Literary and Biographical History, or, Bibliographical Dictionary of the English Catholics*, 5 vols (London: Burns and Oates, 1885–1902).

15 H. Foley, *Records of the English Province of the Society of Jesus* (London: Burns and Oates, 1875–83).
16 T. F. Knox, *The First and Second Diaries of the English College, Douay: And an Appendix of the Unpublished Documents* (London: D. Nutt, 1878).
17 R. Mitchell, 'Morris, John (1826–1893)', *Oxford Dictionary of National Biography* (Oxford: Oxford University Press, 2004), online edition.
18 Pollen, *Morris*, pp. 232–3; 'Review of *Troubles of our Catholic Forefathers*', *Athenaeum* (17 January 1887), 111–12; cf. 'Review of *Letter-books of Sir Amyas Poulet*', *Athenaeum* (13 June 1874), 787–8.
19 'Review of Records of the English Province', *Athenaeum* (16 February 1878), 213.
20 Clarke to Morris, 2 March [n.d.], ABSJ, H1/C.
21 B. S. Gregory, *Salvation at Stake: Christian Martyrdom in Early Modern Europe* (Cambridge, MA, and London: Harvard University Press, 1999), pp. 315–41, covers the 'pseudo-martyr' debate.
22 See Drabble, 'Mary's Protestant martyrs'.
23 *The Times* (7 January 1887), p. 9. Sheils's chapter 6 in this volume discusses Protestant appropriations of More.
24 'The Decree of Beatification', *Saturday Review* (22 January 1887), pp. 125–7, at 126.
25 *Ibid.*, pp. 126, 127.
26 'The new martyrs', *Saturday Review* (18 December 1886), pp. 811–12.
27 'Proposed canonization of English Martyrs', *Saturday Review* (10 January 1880), p. 45.
28 *Saturday Review* (22 January 1887), p. 126.
29 *The Times* (9 August 1887), p. 9.
30 J. R. H. Weaver, rev. M. C. Curthoys, 'Jessopp, Augustus (1823–1914)', *Oxford Dictionary of National Biography*.
31 Augustus Jessopp, *One Generation of a Norfolk House: A Contribution to Elizabethan History* (London: Burns and Oates, 1879), p. 263.
32 *Ibid.*, pp. 6–7.
33 *Ibid.*, pp. 282, 309.
34 Pollen, *Morris*, p. 230; Jessopp to Foley, 5 November 1875, 11 November 1875, 4 June 1885, 5 February 1887, ABSJ CH/J.
35 Morris to Fr Stevenson, 24 September 1878, ABSJ, John Morris Letters, 2, f.7r.
36 J. Morris, 'Dr Jessopp's Henry Walpole', *The Month*, 59 (November 1878), 332, 324.
37 T. G. Law, *A Calendar of the English Martyrs of the Sixteenth and Seventeenth Centuries* (London: Burns and Oates, 1876); beatification decrees in Bede Camm, *et al.*, *Lives of the English Martyrs Declared Blessed by Pope Leo XIII in 1886 and 1895*, 2 vols (London and New York: Burns and Oates; Benziger Brothers, 1904–05), I: pp. lix–lxvi.
38 *Ecclesiae Anglicanae Trophaea* (Rome: Bartholomaei Grassi, 1584), plates 27, 30.
39 Cf. J. H. Pollen, *Acts of English Martyrs Hitherto Unpublished* (London: Burns and Oates, 1891), p. xv.
40 Camm, *English Martyrs*, II: pp. 176–7.
41 *Ibid.*, I: pp. 19–20, 23–5.
42 *Ibid.*, II: pp. 1–2, 6–8.
43 *Ibid.*, II: p. xvii.
44 See A. C. Ewald, 'The Gunpowder Plot', *The Gentleman's Magazine*, 251 (August 1881),

193–216 and 'Father Garnet and the seal of confession', *Saturday Review* (2 April 1887), 477–8 for typically hostile assessments.
45 J. Morris, *The English Martyrs: Why They Died, What They Suffered, What Sort of Men they Were* (London: Stonyhurst College, 1887).
46 Pollen, *Morris*, pp. 194–5.
47 Davies, 'Cult from above'.
48 Norman, *Catholic Church*, pp. 216–20.
49 *The Yorkshire Herald and the York Herald* (11 June 1892), p. 2; *Manchester Weekly Times* (15 September 1893), p. 3; *Bristol Mercury and Daily Post* (12 August 1895), p. 6; *The Yorkshire Herald and the York Herald* (14 September 1895), p. 6.
50 J. Morris, *A Shorter and a Fuller Litany of the English Martyrs* (London: Art & Book Company, 1891).
51 *Liverpool Mercury* (23 February 1888), p. 5. See also a 1921 parish history, available at www.englishmartyrspreston.org.uk/history1.htm#The Consecration, accessed 25 July 2014.
52 *British Architect*, 4 (8 October 1875), 93, 205, quotation at 205.
53 *Ibid.*, 4 (10 December 1875), 669.
54 Possibly the churches were not *consecrated* when opened: English Martyrs Preston was formally consecrated in 1921. Further research on Catholic dedications to 'English Martyrs' is needed.
55 *British Architect*, 5 (30 June 1876), 131, 352. In 1866 Cardinal Wiseman proposed the institution of a feast of the 'English Martyrs' for existing canonised saints, but including Reformation martyrs. This was not allowed by Rome: Camm, *English Martyrs*, I: pp. lxi–lxii.
56 See Newman to Canon Scott [n.d.], offering a donation, Archives of Our Lady and the English Martyrs, Cambridge, HA1/3.
57 G. Rupp, 'A Cambridge centenary: the Selwyn Divinity School, 1879–1979', *Historical Journal*, 24 (1981), 426–8.
58 F. Heal, 'What can King Lucius do for you? The Reformation and the early British Church', *English Historical Review*, 120 (2005), 593–614. Lucius appears in *Ecclesiae Anglicanae Trophaea*.
59 For a further statement of this position, see Luke Rivington, *The English Martyrs: Or, Where is Continuity? A Sermon* (London: Kegan Paul, Trench, Trübner, 1892). See Martha Vandrei's chapter 3 in this volume, for Protestant constructions of alternative narratives.
60 See R. Helgerson, *Forms of Nationhood: The Elizabethan Writing of England* (Chicago and London: University of Chicago Press, 1992); L. Colley, *Britons: Forging the Nation, 1707–1837* (New Haven: Yale University Press, 1994); T. Claydon and I. Macbride (eds), *Protestantism and National Identity: Britain and Ireland, c. 1650–c. 1850* (Cambridge: Cambridge University Press, 1998); A. Milton, *Catholic and Reformed: Roman and Protestant Churches in English Protestant Thought, 1600–40* (Cambridge: Cambridge University Press, 1995).
61 C. Highley, *Catholics Writing the Nation in Early Modern Britain and Ireland* (Oxford: Oxford University Press, 2008).
62 *The Times* (6 January 1980), p. 4.
63 Sister Mary Xavier, 'Martyrs of England standing on high', *Westminster Hymnal* (1891; 1903; 5th edn, London: Burns, Oates and Washbourne, 1924), p. 271; N. Jiwon Cho,

'"Martyrs of England! Standing on high!": Roman Catholic women's hymn-writing for the re-invigoration of the faith in England, 1850–1903', in L. Lux-Sterritt and C. Mangion (eds), *Gender, Catholicism and Spirituality: Women and the Roman Catholic Church in Britain and Europe, 1200–1900* (Basingstoke: Palgrave Macmillan, 2010), pp. 131–48.
64 *Westminster Hymnal*, p. 271.
65 T. E. Bridgett, 'O Lord! Behold the suppliant band', *Westminster Hymnal*, p. 193.
66 *British Architect*, 5 (30 June 1876), 352.
67 Bentley, *Modernizing England's Past*, pp. 27–9; F. Heal, 'Appropriating history: Catholic and Protestant polemics and the national past', *Huntington Library Quarterly*, 68 (2005), 109–34; D. B. Hamilton, 'Catholic use of Anglo-Saxon precedents, 1565–1625', *Recusant History*, 26 (2003), 537–55; B. Melman, 'Claiming the nation's past: the invention of an Anglo-Saxon tradition', *Journal of Contemporary History*, 26 (1991), 575–95; B. S. Robinson, 'John Foxe and the Anglo-Saxons', in C. Highley and J. N. King (eds), *John Foxe and his World* (Aldershot: Palgrave Macmillan, 2002), pp. 54–72.
68 B. M. Boardman (ed.), *The Poems of Francis Thompson* (Chestnut Hill: John J. Burns Library, 2001), pp. 288–94.
69 Parker and Pahls, *Authority, Dogma, and History*; Holmes, *More Roman*, pp. 144–8.
70 *Ibid.*, pp. 130–2, 144–8; R. Pezzimenti, *The Political Thought of Lord Acton* (Leominster: Gracewing, 2001).
71 Norman, *Catholic Church*, pp. 244–86.
72 Norman, *Anti-Catholicism*, p. 89; see also *Saturday Review* (10 January 1880), pp. 44–5.
73 *The Times* (6 January 1880), p. 4.
74 *The Times* (17 January 1887), p. 8.
75 *Westminster Hymnal*, p. 271.
76 *The Times* (6 January, 1880), p. 4.
77 Heimann, *Catholic Devotion*, pp. 137–73; J. F. Supple, 'Ultramontanism in Yorkshire 1850–1900', *Recusant History*, 17 (1985), 274–86.
78 *The Times* (7 January 1887), p. 9.

# 9

# Richard Baxter

*Simon Burton*

'IT WAS ENOUGH FOR one age to produce such a man as Richard Baxter.' Such were the words of Dr Wilkins (1614–72), the seventeenth-century Bishop of Chester. Indeed, Wilkins claimed that if Baxter had lived in primitive times he would have been one of the Fathers of the Church.[1] Throughout the century we find similar notes of high esteem pouring forth from the pens of Anglicans and Nonconformists of all stamps. For Baxter's own father, his son was 'sanctified from the womb'. At his funeral sermon his friend, the leading Presbyterian Dr William Bates (1625–99), remembered him as 'this excellent saint', whose preaching was 'animated with the Holy Spirit, and breathed celestial fire' and whose 'prayers were an effusion of the most lively, melting expressions, of his intimate, ardent affections to God'.[2] For the celebrated Nonconformist minister Matthew Sylvester (1636/7–1708) he was another Elisha,[3] and for the latitudinarian Archbishop John Tillotson (1630–94), he was one of God's 'greatest saints', worthy of comparison with Luther, Calvin and even the Apostle Paul.[4]

Clearly, Baxter was revered as a saint even in his own lifetime. While for Puritans the term 'saint' was strictly a biblical one, referring to any elect believer, it is difficult to elude the sense that Baxter was regarded as no ordinary saint. Moreover, such devotion to Baxter was hardly confined to his own century. If anything, as we shall see, it only became more extravagant with time, reaching its zenith in the Victorian age. Indeed, it was in the long nineteenth century especially that Baxter came into his own. By the mid-nineteenth century, widening divides within the Church of England and the increasing opposition between churchmen and Nonconformists left all parties scrambling to construct and defend their own spiritual lineages. Baxter's unique life, ministry and doctrine meant that he could be claimed by everyone. He thus could be portrayed, somewhat bewilderingly, as a staunch Anglican, a Broad Churchman, a founder of the evangelical movement, an inspiration for the Methodists – John Fletcher (bap. 1729, d. 1785) called Wesley the 'Richard Baxter of our age' – and the father of liberal Nonconformity.[5]

This chapter seeks to examine the reasons for Baxter's universal appeal, examining the ways in which different groups took him up and canonised him as a saint. It charts the way in which Baxter came to be regarded not only as a man of exemplary holiness, and thus as a visible link between heaven and earth, but also as a prophetic figure, revered across denominational divides precisely because he was perceived as speaking so directly to the problems and aspirations of the age.

## A Protestant and evangelical saint

Pervading eighteenth- and nineteenth-century accounts of Baxter, just as those of his own contemporaries, is an awareness of the heavenly, even unearthly, quality of his life and writings. To many he appeared as a prophet, an apostle or even an angel amongst ordinary men and women. His own life of devotion and self-sacrifice was thus seen as mirroring that of the Apostle Paul or Christ himself.[6] Indeed, so greatly was he revered by his followers, that the term 'Baxterian' became a commonly accepted designation for those moderates seeking a *via media* between the extremes of Calvinism and Arminianism.[7]

In some cases veneration of Baxter even reached the heights of Catholic devotion. Thus we find evidence of one man who held his name in such reverence that he would always refer to him as 'holy Mr Baxter'.[8] Likewise, Lord Somers's grandfather was buried in the graveyard at Kidderminster due to his belief that its very turf had been hallowed by Baxter's sanctity.[9] Baxter's writings were a subject of special devotion. Many of his admirers revered them next only to the Bible itself, while Henry Venn (1725–97), the famous evangelical, even went so far as to call them holy relics, comparing them to the bones of Elisha in the Old Testament and depicting them as *loci* of extraordinary spiritual power.[10]

Notable here is the way in which traditional, Catholic categories of sanctity of life and sanctity of writings – in other words tradition – were retained or redeployed in order to demonstrate Baxter's credentials as a Protestant saint bringing heaven down to earth. In particular, the eliding of the distinction between Baxter's words and the biblical Word points to ways in which English Protestantism, especially of a more evangelical stamp, was seeking to construct its own notion of tradition, and even its own communion of saints, through recording the historical unfolding and personal instantiation of biblical truth. If this was still an unconscious move on Venn's part, in the more polemical climate of the later nineteenth century securing a lineage became very much a conscious necessity, as Roshan Allpress shows for the Wilberforcean ideal of the 'practical saint' elsewhere in this volume.[11] Baxter's writings, understood as the historical embodiment of the timeless Reformation principle of *sola scriptura*, could thus be interpreted as a vital link in the chain of 'evangelical succession'.

Yet that succession in itself was often highly contested, most notably between evangelical Anglicans and Nonconformists. Due to his unique role in the crisis of 1662, as the most steadfast and heroic, but also most reluctant of Dissenters, Baxter could be, and frequently was, appealed to by both parties. While all drew inspiration from Baxter's heavenly life and his selfless love for Christ, their use of Baxter clearly also registered their own concerns and priorities. In particular, their different ecclesiological loyalties could lead to different interpretations of Baxter's own actions and especially of the spiritual legacy he bequeathed to the troubled nineteenth-century Church. At times this led to open conflict. Indeed, the paper war between Canon John Cale Miller (1814–80) and the Congregationalist R. W. Dale (1829–95), in which Baxter and other Dissenters became pawns in the political and ecclesiological controversies over the bicentenary celebrations of 1662, bears eloquent testimony to this divisive potential.[12] In other, happier times, however, more eirenic and reflective tendencies won out. Then Baxter's role as a tireless promoter of Christian union could be used to bolster a united evangelical front.

One of the most important Nonconformist attempts to appropriate Baxter in the nineteenth century can be seen in the writings of the Scottish Congregationalist William Orme (1787–1830), whose 1830 edition of Baxter's *Practical Works* quickly became the standard work. Here the tension over Baxter's double identity as an establishment evangelical and a Nonconformist becomes fully apparent. A notable populariser of the Puritans – he also produced an edition of the works of John Owen (1616–83) – Orme held Baxter out to his readers as a shining example of practical Christian living. He thus notes his ardour for God and his deep compassion for his fellow men,[13] his willingness to spend himself for Christ and his patient endurance as a 'martyr to disease and pain',[14] and his extraordinary and almost superhuman exertions for the sake of the gospel.[15] Like Bates, whom he drew upon, he also emphasised the unearthly quality of Baxter's life as one who breathed deeply the spirit of heaven, carrying 'its very atmosphere of holy love about him'. For this reason Baxter is singled out by Orme as occupying a 'distinguished place' in the mansions of the blessed'.[16]

Yet Orme was also very concerned to establish Baxter's character as a godly Nonconformist, emphasising his key role in the ecclesiastical struggles of the seventeenth century. Here, very much following in the spiritual tradition of the *Abridgement of Mr Baxter's Narrative of his Life and Times* (1702) and the *Account* of the ejected ministers, both by Edmund Calamy (1671–1732), he depicted Baxter as the champion of Nonconformity. Of Baxter and the fathers of Nonconformity he says that 'the Church and the world were not worthy of them, but they were counted not only worthy to believe, but also to suffer for the sake of Christ; and their names will be held in everlasting remembrance'.[17] Here the theme of martyrdom, which held such fascination for the Victorians, is transposed onto a wider canvas: that of persecution for the sake of the gospel.[18] Speaking directly to his Anglican opponents, Orme says that those who think of Baxter 'only as a sectarian, or a wrangling controversialist, must now regard him with admiration, exercising the faith and patience of the saints; braving danger, enduring pain, despising life, and rejoicing in hope of the glory of God'.[19] This is amplified further in his account of Baxter's later trial before the infamous Judge Jeffreys (1645–89), where we are made to see, in the words of an eyewitness, 'Paul standing before Nero'.[20] Ironically, however, it is Jeffreys himself, the establishment figure, who offers the most fitting verdict on Baxter's character, observing sarcastically to the court 'we have had to do with other sorts of persons but now we have to do with a saint'.[21]

While Orme undoubtedly championed Baxter's Nonconformity he by no means neglected his 'catholic spirit', remarking of his desire for honourable comprehension that he 'hoped for that which is reserved for happier times than his own, or than has yet blessed the Church of God'.[22] Precisely the same tendency can be seen in another nineteenth-century populariser of the Puritans, J. C. Ryle (1816–1900), the influential evangelical Bishop of Liverpool. Writing in *Light from Old Times* (1890), a work which represents a distinctively Anglican *and* evangelical attempt to construct a spiritual genealogy, Ryle remarked of Baxter that 'he could be as zealous as a crusader for the rights of conscience, and yet he was of so catholic a spirit that he loved all who loved Jesus Christ in sincerity'.[23] Like Orme, he also drew attention to the unearthly character of Baxter's 'eminent personal holiness', comparing him to the Apostle Paul as an 'epistle of Christ' written for the benefit of the English people.[24]

Besides his great admiration for his preaching and pastoring – which he says made the 'face of paradise' appear in Kidderminster – Ryle focuses especially on Baxter's conduct in 1662 and its aftermath.[25] Referring to him as 'one of the most patient martyrs for conscience sake that England has ever seen', Ryle says of him that he exemplified that 'dying daily, which, to some natures, is worse even than dying at the stake'.[26] Although an Anglican, Ryle deplored the behaviour of his fellow churchmen who persecuted Baxter, describing the Act of Uniformity as a 'crowning piece of folly' and saying that 'a more impolitic and disgraceful deed never disfigured the annals of a Protestant Church'. Although Ryle did not try to claim the 'saintly old Puritan' for the Anglican Church in the way that some of his Broad Church contemporaries did, he recognised in Baxter and his fellow Puritans the one redeeming feature of the seventeenth-century Church. Many of those ejected he says 'were the best, the ablest, and the holiest ministers of the day'. England, he argues, owes 'an unpaid debt of gratitude' to this 'noble host', the 'saints of the nation'. Chief among them was Baxter, and he thus concludes that 'it is no small thing to be the fellow-countryman of Richard Baxter'.[27] For Ryle, Baxter was clearly a torchbearer of the gospel in a benighted age. If not quite a forerunner of evangelical Anglicanism, he certainly represented the spirit that motivated evangelical Anglicans in their quest for a reformed Church of England and rapprochement with their Nonconformist brethren.

A final evangelical example of quite a different stamp is that of Sir James Stephen (1789–1859), son of the noted abolitionist and father of Leslie Stephen (1832–1904), the well-known Victorian agnostic and first editor of the *Dictionary of National Biography*. Like his son, Stephen senior was fascinated by great lives, but with a very different focus. In his *Essays in Ecclesiastical Biography* (1849) – which, in drawing on Francis of Assisi, Pascal and the Jesuits, represented an ecumenical attempt to construct a spiritual genealogy of activist, evangelical piety – Stephen gave important place to Baxter. Reflecting a more diffuse evangelicalism, Stephen held that Baxter should be assigned an 'elevated rank' amongst those who have taken 'the spiritual improvement of mankind for their province'.[28] As a bookish man of action he was especially drawn to Baxter's practical writings, of which he said that 'among the writings of uninspired men, there are none better fitted to awaken, to invigorate, to enlarge, or to console the mind, which can raise itself to such celestial colloquy'. Reacting snobbishly against Orme's republication of them in octavo format, Stephen remarks 'let not the spirits of the mighty dead be thus evoked from their majestic shrines to animate the dwarfish structures of our bookselling generation'.[29]

Tellingly, such a comment reflects not only his elitism, but also the sense of the sacred and noumenal which pervades his treatment of Baxter.[30] While this reminds us of Venn, his wife's grandfather, it arguably goes beyond this. For Stephen clearly sees Baxter as an ideal type not only of the evangelical Christian – his treatment of Baxter's 'hallowed' marriage draws on the sentimental and familial piety he was steeped in – but also of the spiritual man.[31] It is Baxter's concern for spiritual improvement, his pastoral labours, which he compares to those of apostles and angels, and his 'habitual communion with light' that fired his imagination.[32] In Stephen's hands the evangelicalism that he had inherited from his Clapham forebears was remoulded into a broader, more inclusive spirituality, reflecting allegiance to a general 'radiance from above' rather more than the chapter and verse of Scripture.[33] At the same time, it had by no means yet lost contact with biblical distinctives or a missionary imperative. Describing Baxter's 'revenge' on the authorities who imprisoned him as obtaining the original charter for the Society of the Propagation of the Gospel, he calls this 'a return of good for evil for which his name might well displace those of some of the saints in the calendar'.[34]

## Catholic Christian

While Orme and Ryle both manifested a deep appreciation for Baxter's catholicity, it was Stephen especially who was drawn to his 'mere Christianity'. Baxter epitomised Stephen's own project for a universal Christianity free from the rancour of confessional division. In this he notably demonstrates an important affinity with the great Samuel Taylor Coleridge (1772–1834), the spiritual 'father of the Broad Church movement', and the man who saw deepest into the revolutionary implications of Baxter's thought.[35] For not only was Coleridge almost unique in ascribing value to Baxter's distinctive theological method, he also, more significantly, championed Baxter's charitable ecclesiology.[36] In Baxter he gave his own liberal Anglican followers a prophet of their own latitudinarian ideals.

Coleridge's interest in Baxter can be dated back to at least 1802, when he first expressed his desire to write about the Presbyterians and Baxterians of the reign of Charles II. In the same year his friend Charles Lamb (1775–1834) bought him a copy of Baxter's *Holy Commonwealth*. Coleridge certainly read and admired this work and its constitutional principles, for he used an extended passage as epigraph for an essay in *The Friend*.[37] Coleridge's later *Marginalia* includes extensive annotations on Baxter's

*Reliquiae Baxterianae*, as well as some notes on his *Catholick Theologie*. Indeed, his annotations on Baxter were particularly dear to Coleridge and one copy of his *Aids to Reflection* records his hope to publish further annotations on Bishop Leighton (1611–84) along with those on Baxter and other seventeenth-century divines under the projected title *The Inward Life and Growth of a Christian*.[38] He also planned another book on 'Revolutionary Minds', which would have included discussion of Baxter alongside Aquinas, Scotus, Luther and others.[39] While unfortunately he never completed either of these works, leaving his annotations unpublished and becoming distracted from 'Revolutionary Minds' by his *Opus Maximum*, these proposals do serve to indicate his enduring fascination with Baxter.[40]

While strongly attracted by Baxter's philosophical principles, Coleridge was drawn most of all by his autobiography, the *Reliquiae Baxterianae*, which was to him that 'most inestimable book'. He annotated this book around 1811, seemingly twice over (for we have two differing copies), writing extensive marginal comments, sometimes running to several pages, on passages of particular interest. On the flyleaf to one set of annotations Coleridge declared himself to be a 'bigot to no party', adding: 'highly do I approve of Baxter's conduct, affectionately admire and bless his peace-seeking spirit, and coincide with him as to the necessity of Church discipline in a Christian Church'.[41] For Coleridge one of the great benefits of reading the *Reliquiae* was its 'conquest of party and sectarian prejudices'. Thus although he in fact held Baxter's 'middle way' to be futile and deplored his liturgical views, he still admired the 'mildness of the proposer's temper' and his charitable attempts to heal the breaches of the Church.[42] In this way he found in Baxter a kindred spirit and a true saint of the Anglican Church.

For Coleridge, Baxter was the glorious hero in the tragic drama of the Restoration Church; a period which he described as the 'leprosy' and 'infamy of the Church'. Opposed to Baxter and his Nonconformist brethren he ranged Charles II and the 'Herodian Diocesans' as the villains of the piece.[43] Of these he viewed Archbishop Sheldon (1598–1677), 'the most virulent enemy and poisoner of the English Church', as chief culprit, referring to Bishop Gardiner (c. 1495x8–1555), the anti-hero of Foxe's *Book of Martyrs*, as canonisable in comparison![44] Their persecution of Baxter was not only cruel, but an act of singular ingratitude to the man Coleridge held had done most to bring about the Restoration itself.[45] He admired more than anything the dignity and piety of Baxter and the Nonconformists, referring to them as 'perhaps the largest collective number of learned and zealous, discreet and holy ministers that one age and one Church was ever blest with, and whose authority in every considerable point is in favor [sic] of our Church and against the present Dissenters from it'. He therefore bemoans the attempts of his fellow Anglicans to justify the actions of the episcopate of those days, declaring Baxter and his friends and not the High Church of Laud and Sheldon to be the true representatives of the Church of England of that period.[46]

Concerning Baxter himself he waxes lyrical, saying: 'It is impossible to read Baxter without hesitating which to admire most, the uncommon clearness (perspicuity and perspicacity) of his understanding, or the candour and charity of his spirit. Under such accursed persecutions he feels and reasons more like an angel than a man.'[47] He is to Coleridge not only an angel but also 'an eminent saint of God'.[48] As he put it, in words later oft to be repeated, 'I may not unfrequently doubt Baxter's memory or even his competence, in consequence of his particular modes of thinking; but I could almost as soon doubt the Gospel verity as his veracity'.[49] He also recognised in Baxter a particular innocence, at one point remarking on his 'child-like simplicity'[50] and at another commenting that 'Richard Baxter was too thoroughly good for any experience to make him worldly wise'.[51] Indeed, he regarded Baxter as peculiarly anointed by God, being 'substanziated and successively potenziated by an especial divine grace' which enabled him to endure 'such unremitting and almost unheard of bodily derangements and pains'.[52] Knowing all too well the anguish of bodily pain, he yet felt his own sufferings to be dwarfed in comparison to Baxter's and marvelled that they seem to have impeded him so little, a fact which even made him waver in his customary scepticism towards miracles.[53]

Yet the point to which Coleridge returned again and again, and which certainly impressed itself most on liberally inclined nineteenth-century churchmen, was Baxter's superlative charity towards his fellow Christians. Illustrating this in his *Aids to Reflection* (1825), Coleridge cites the 'following golden passage' from the *Reliquiae* in which Baxter mentions his change in heart about the salvation of Catholics: 'And I can never believe that a man may not be saved by that religion, which doth but bring him to the true love of God and to a heavenly mind and life: nor that God will ever cast a soul into hell, that truly loveth him.' In the paragraph immediately before this Coleridge had famously declared his belief that Unitarians and even Jews could be considered as fellow Christians, and here Baxter's example prompts him to a similar remark about Catholics. Indeed, it is no surprise that Coleridge declared himself to be of exactly the same mind in this issue as that 'man of true catholic spirit and apostolic zeal, Richard Baxter'.[54]

While Coleridge and Baxter would have locked horns over the issues of episcopacy and the liturgy they shared a similar view of the proper constitution of the Church of England. Thus in distinguishing between the *enclesia* of the national Church as an estate of the realm governed by its laws and constitution, and the *ecclesia* of the invisible Church as encompassing all sincere lovers of God whatever their confession, he clearly follows, whether consciously or not, the Baxterian distinction between the charity to be extended to all believers and the Church's need for a definite constitutional structure. Indeed Coleridge's view that Catholics must be excluded from the national Church because of their higher political allegiance to the Pope, which motivated his opposition to the Catholic Emancipation Bill, mirrors closely Baxter's own critique of the Roman Catholics which he had cited favourably earlier in the *Aids to Reflection*.[55]

Coleridge's liberal views on Christian identity, in many respects so redolent of Baxter's own, exercised a deep influence on that loose grouping of mid-century Anglican thinkers variously (and perhaps misleadingly) described as 'Broad

Churchmen' and 'Liberal Anglicans' and whose intellectual and spiritual influences stemmed from a variety of sources, including German idealism, the erastian reformism of Thomas Arnold (1795–1842) and the incarnational Platonism of F. D. Maurice (1805–72).[56] Like Coleridge, a number of them found in Baxter an Anglican very much after their own heart. Thus Archdeacon Julius Hare (1795–1855), who in his younger days had frequented Coleridge's literary salons, declared in his *Victory of Faith* (1840):

> Not to go further back than the Restoration, what a blessed thing would it have been for the Church of England, and for the Church of Christ, if the endeavours of that wise and holy man, Richard Baxter, – one of the wisest and holiest whom the Spirit of God ever purified for the edification of his people, – had been met with hearts desirous, above all things, of preserving the unity of the Spirit in the bond of peace! What a blessing would it have been, if by certain discreet and timely concessions in matters of less moment, at the Savoy Conference, such faithful and gifted servants of God, as Baxter himself, and Owen, and Manton, and Flavel, and Alleine, and Philip Henry, and Howe, had been retained in the bond of Christian communion, as our fellow-servants at the altar of Christ!

He goes on to make a telling comparison between the failure of the seventeenth-century Church to include Baxter and the Nonconformists to the failure of his own Church to comprehend Wesley and the Methodists, thus propelling Baxter into the forefront of nineteenth-century debate about sectarian division, which Hare abhorred.[57]

With both Coleridge and Hare endorsing him so strongly it is unsurprising to find Baxter's name recurring in 'Broad Church' circles throughout the rest of the century. It is found at a critical juncture for Anglican progressives, in the fallout following the 1860 publication of *Essays and Reviews*. Often seen as the 'Broad Church Manifesto', this work promoted a liberal vision of Christianity grounded on the new, German school of biblical hermeneutics.[58] One of the contributors was Rowland Williams (1817–70), Vice-Principal of St David's College, Lampeter. His review of Bunsen's *Biblical Researches*, which was regarded as a frontal attack on the doctrine of biblical inspiration, raised a storm of protest. The situation quickly escalated and Williams was hauled before the Court of Arches to stand trial for heresy.[59] What is significant for us is that in the lengthy defence drawn up for Williams by James Fitzjames Stephen (1829–94), son of the above mentioned Sir James, Baxter was appealed to as the first witness of Williams's fundamental orthodoxy and the continuity of his biblical principles with the historical Church of England.

In particular, Baxter was co-opted by Stephen to argue the point that the Christian religion and not the Bible is the proper 'object of faith'. Here Baxter's distinction between the essentials and circumstantials of the Christian faith is presented as congruent to similar distinctions made by Richard Hooker (1554–1600) and William Chillingworth (1602–44), other spiritual heroes of the liberal Anglican tradition. Stephen was particularly at pains to establish Baxter's Anglican credentials. While he conceded it as 'unhappily true' that Baxter was driven into Nonconformity, he reminded the court that he was also 'an ordained and beneficed member of the Church of England' who was offered the Bishopric of Hereford at the Restoration. Particularly important to him was Baxter's inclusion in an influential manual of theology, the *Christian Institutes* (1837), penned by the impeccably orthodox old-fashioned High Churchman Christopher Wordsworth (1774–1846), which, Stephen told his listeners, was intended by its author to set out the 'fundamental principles of the Church of England'.[60]

Stephen pressed the point that Williams and Baxter were in complete agreement, both affirming the 'characteristic doctrine of the Church of England that Scripture is perfect for the object for which it is intended'. For Stephen, however, the comparison between the two men went beyond doctrinal similarity, for he clearly regarded them as brother sufferers for the cause of truth. Baxter, he cleverly reminded the assembled Lords Spiritual, was also brought to trial on the basis of something he had written – his *Paraphrases of the New Testament* – and charged with subverting the doctrine of the Church of England. However, in this 'shameful prosecution', 'one of the most disgraceful that ever took place in an English court of justice', no mention was ever made of his views on biblical inspiration, even though they were apparent to all. The twofold implication was clear. Not only were Baxter's liberal views of Scripture entirely in line with Anglicanism, but to condemn Williams for holding them would be to commit an injustice to which not even the notorious Judge Jeffreys had stooped. To anyone who still had the temerity to doubt Baxter's Anglican credentials Stephen had the following to say: 'I would say that in the whole list of eminent writers of the English Church a holier or a more learned man than Baxter could not be found. If it is worth while to adduce testimonies to his character in these respects, I could adduce enough, I think, to silence all question upon that matter.'[61]

Williams was a member of the circle of Dean Stanley (1815–81) and of Benjamin Jowett (1817–93), a co-contributor to *Essays and Reviews*. In 1875 Stanley was invited to give an address at the unveiling of Baxter's statute in Kidderminster. In it he depicted Baxter, 'this ever-dying saint', as the prophet who, if alive in his own era, would 'have opened upon us that consuming fire of his love for truth'. Pointing to the new inscription on the statue – 'in a stormy and divided age he advocated unity and comprehension' – Stanley read it as a message for the divided Church of the nineteenth century. Appealing to Baxter's famous programme of 'mere Christianity', Stanley connected it with his own doctrinal minimalism. In particular, Baxter's opposition to religious tests clearly resonated with his own views. He thus saw Baxter as the 'champion of scrupulous consciences' and the standard bearer of a 'Christian liberality ... far beyond his age'. For Stanley, Baxter was a prophet of the coming age of Church unity, and he referred to his prescient last words – 'I would as willingly be a martyr for charity as for faith' – as 'a speech pregnant in far-reaching consequences, the very seed of the Church of the Future'.[62]

In similar vein Stanley also recognised in Baxter a modern and progressive spirit and an ally against the conservative orthodoxy of his own day. In fact he saw an intimate link between Baxter's desire for comprehension and his theological breadth, remarking that 'with this larger view of Christian communion, the whole horizon of Christian thought was enlarged also'. Especially notable for Stanley was the role that Baxter played in Rowland Williams's trial when, as Stanley put it, 'the cause of theological inquiry pleaded for its life before the tribunals of our Church and country'. Like Stephen, Stanley anachronistically saw Baxter's biblical principles as anticipating liberal hermeneutics. Likewise, in attacking what Stanley called the 'scholastic, Lutheran, or Puritan view of "imputed righteousness" and "substitution"', he saw in Baxter a champion of the 'moral and spiritual doctrine of Christian redemption, as set forth in the Gospels and Epistles, or in the most philosophic of German and English divines'. Baxter's confidence in the 'internal evidence of religion' was therefore 'as deeply rooted in his soul as in that of Coleridge, or Arnold, or Carlyle'.[63] In this interpretation Baxter fore-echoes a moral and spiritual, less dogmatic, form of Christianity, something obviously entirely congenial to the aspirations of Stanley and his circle.

In 1891, in one of a series of biographical sermons preached at Westminster Abbey, Jowett offered his own tribute. His admiration for Baxter, whom he called 'one of the greatest Englishmen not only of his own but of any time', was evident throughout the sermon. 'Wonderful stories are told of the effects of his preaching. It might be said of him that as the people of Nineveh repented at the preaching of Jonah, so did the people of Kidderminster at the preaching of Richard Baxter.'[64] In Baxter's willingness to suffer for the sake of the gospel, Jowett found a fit comparison in Saint Paul. Indeed Jowett referred to Baxter's whole life as a 'sermon for posterity', saying of him that:

> When we hear of such men and their labours, who combined the persevering industry of the great scholar with the moral force of a hero and a leader of man kind, we are apt to say, 'There were giants on the earth in those days'. It would be better to say, that they were the sons of God who fought not in their own strength – one man more than a thousand, for they endured as seeing him who is invisible.[65]

Jowett clearly identified Baxter as a hero of the Christian tradition and an 'eminent servant of God'. More than that, however, Jowett also recognised him as true Anglican saint, one who upheld a comprehensive ideal but recognised the need for charity in doing so. The sanctity Jowett found so laudable revolved not so much around Baxter's espousal of unchanging virtues as in his ability to rise above the prejudices of his age; to see beyond forms to the deeper realities that lay behind them. Anyone in the nineteenth century who sought to emulate him 'would not raise questions about the rites of the church, or the canonicity of the books of Scripture: these belong to criticism and ecclesiastical history, not to the spiritual life'.[66] His choice to preach on a leading Nonconformist in the heartland of the Church was no doubt deliberate. For like Stanley before him Jowett saw in Baxter an important bridge between establishment and Dissent, embodying his own desire for union and comprehension. Like Coleridge, he saw in Baxter the saviour of the Church of England, pointing to Baxter's refusal, at a critical juncture in the reign of James II, to join the Catholics in a league against the

Anglicans. 'Certainly', he says, 'no one ever conferred a greater benefit on the Church of England or on the country.'[67]

Two important biographies of Baxter published in the late nineteenth century by clergymen of distinctly Broad Church hues indicate the esteem in which he continued to be held. They also demonstrate Baxter's appeal to more philosophically and sacramentally oriented Maurician Broad Churchmen, as well as to Arnoldians like Stanley and Jowett.[68] The first biography, published in 1883, was by G. D. Boyle (1828–1901), the Dean of Salisbury. Boyle had not only been invited to contribute to *Essays and Reviews*, but was also a friend of Newman and a cautious supporter of the Oxford Movement.[69] For Boyle, himself a former Vicar of Kidderminster, Baxter was both a hero of the faith worthy of comparison with Chrysostom, Anselm and Francis Xavier, and a man who synthesised and anticipated the best aspects of nineteenth-century Christianity: the evangelical zeal of Charles Simeon (1759–1836), the missionary fervour of George Selwyn (1809–78) and the peacemaking spirit of Coleridge and Maurice.[70]

The second biography, published in 1887, was by John Hamilton Davies, a more obscure clergyman. Davies likewise compared Baxter to a host of Catholic saints – Augustine, Francis of Assisi, Xavier and Ignatius Loyola – but his chief emphasis was on Baxter's affinities with German idealism and romanticism.[71] In Schleiermachean manner he held Baxter to have preached that 'absolute dependence upon God, which is the essence of religion', and like Johann Gottlieb Fichte (1762–1814) to have taught that religion is the 'inner spirit which penetrates all our thoughts and actions, and immerses them in itself'.[72] Here we find again the Coleridgean, philosophical appreciation of Baxter, now fused with an important prophetical and even ascetic dimension:

> With all the ardour of his soul, with the tender entreaty of his kindly heart – his face, pale and worn by frequent suffering, kindling as with celestial fire – he exhorted them to look beyond the outline of the present state, and to the serene and compensating future, rejoicing in hope of the glory of God.[73]

Like Boyle, who viewed Baxter as essentially a moderate episcopalian, Davies had no problem in recruiting Baxter to the Anglican cause. Both compared him to Hooker, demonstrating again just how far they differed from Orme.[74] Davies saw Baxter's Anglicanism as embodying practical faith, tolerance and breadth of charity. In its non-dogmatic character it was grounded on the Sermon of the Mount as the 'Magna Charta' of Christianity.[75] Once again we find Davies sounding out the same themes as Coleridge, Stanley and Jowett before him, suggesting that Baxter was by now regarded as a 'Broad Church' patron saint.

Finally, we must remark on the veneration in which Baxter was held among Unitarians, as evidence for the extreme elasticity of the Broad Church ideal. The connection between Baxter's so-called 'rational Dissent' and the Unitarian movement – a development, it is worth noting, that would have horrified Baxter – was remarked on frequently in the nineteenth century. Thus Coleridge, himself once a Unitarian, commented on Baxter's Sabellian tendencies and noted that the English Presbyterians, of whom he had been the leader, formed the core of the later Unitarian movement.[76] Likewise, Alexander Gordon (1814–1931), the Unitarian historian, described him, with John Locke (1632–1704), as 'most potent among the influential sources which tended to the progressive liberalising of the old Dissent'. Elsewhere he went further, calling him the 'founder of liberal Nonconformity'. He held that in representing a 'Catholicism beyond parties' Baxter was able to forge a new route for Nonconformity, away from the rigid orthodoxy of earlier Puritans. In Baxter he therefore discerned the 'germs of enlightened conviction, which time and experience have since fructified to greater issues than were dreamed of in the seventeenth century'.[77]

Gordon was by no means alone in his views. In his Kidderminster address Stanley referred to Baxter as 'the first parent of the extreme school of Nonconformity', describing him as unfurling the 'banner of tolerance and freedom' before the Churches. As evidence for this claim he cited letters from two prominent Unitarians. The first, from J. J. Tayler (1797–1869), spoke of 'Baxter, whom we are proud to claim as our spiritual progenitor'. It described his mind as 'pre-eminently a progressive one, growing in freedom and insight, and expanding in love to the very last'. The second was from the famous Unitarian James Martineau (1805–1900), a close associate of Stanley and other liberal Anglicans, who claimed that 'our spiritual ancestry is undoubtedly found in the Baxterian line'. He clearly recognised in Baxter the point of transition from a dogmatic to a moral and spiritual Christianity. Martineau concluded his letter by deploring the tendency of Unitarians after Joseph Priestley (1733–1804) to form a separate party, saying 'I wish I could say that in departing from the theology of Baxter, we were faithful to the catholicity which has given us the power to change'. In losing this breadth and tolerance he feared that Unitarians were 'fast losing the noblest feature of our historical position, and handing over the future to those who inherit a less [sic] freedom, but appreciate and exercise a greater'.[78]

## Conclusion

In 1914 a small group of Unitarian ministers banded together to form the Society of Free Catholics. Inspired by Martineau, Maurice and the Catholic modernists their desire was to found a Church which combined Catholic sacramental and devotional practice with theological freedom. Their membership included Anglicans, Catholics and Nonconformists. Notably, the Society represented an attempt to move away from the dogmatism of the contemporary institutional Church, including the Unitarian Church itself. One of the founding members of this Society was J. M. Lloyd Thomas (1868–1955), known today for his abridgement of Baxter's *Reliquiae*, who described Baxter as a saint of 'seraphic ardour of devotion'. Like Stanley he also regarded Baxter as a prophet for the twentieth century, standing for a 'Catholicism against all sects'.[79] Indeed, he called Baxter 'a father in the faith' for the Free Catholics and held that the Society's principle of theological freedom derived from Baxter's own desire to 'exclude none that Christ would have received'. While the Society of Free Catholics was short lived, foundering in the early 1920s, its existence is testimony to the deep sway that Baxter's tolerant ideals continued to exercise throughout the long nineteenth century.[80] It thus provides yet more evidence of the Victorian cult of Saint Richard Baxter.

## Notes

1. Cited from Joseph Read, 'To the reader', in Richard Baxter, *Universal Redemption* (London: John Salusbury, 1694), p. 4.
2. William Bates, *A Funeral Sermon for the Reverend, Holy and Excellent Divine, Mr Richard Baxter* (London: Brabazon Aylmer, 1692), pp. 89, 91, 114, 123. Cited from William Orme, 'A life of the author and a critical examination of his writings', in Orme (ed.), *The Practical Works of the Rev. Richard Baxter*, 23 vols (London: James Duncan, 1830), I: pp. 407–8.
3. Matthew Sylvester, *Elisha's Cry after Elijah's God Consider'd and Apply'd with Reference to the Decease of the Late Reverend Mr Richard Baxter* (London: T. Parkhurst, etc., 1696), p. 14. Cited from Orme, 'Life', p. 406.
4. John Tillotson, 'Letter to Matthew Sylvester', in Frederick Powicke, *The Reverend Richard Baxter under the Cross (1662–1691)* (1927; Weston Rhyn: Quinta Press, 2009), pp. 11, 298–9.
5. John Fletcher, *A Vindication of the Rev. Mr Wesley's Last Minutes* (1771; London: R. Hawes, 1775), p. 44. For a discussion of Baxter's influence on early Methodism see Ralph Waller, 'Converging and diverging lines: aspects of the relationship between Methodism and rational Dissent', *Proceedings of the Wesley Historical Society*, 53 (2001), 81–92.
6. See, for example, [Sir James Stephen], 'Review: the life and times of Richard Baxter', *Imperial Magazine*, 12 (1830), 954, 958; [Stephen], 'The practical works of Richard Baxter', *Edinburgh Review*, 70, 141 (1839), 189–90, 196; A. P. Stanley, 'Richard Baxter', *Macmillan's Magazine*, 32 (1875), 389–92; John Tulloch, *English Puritanism and its Leaders: Cromwell, Milton, Baxter and Bunyan* (Edinburgh and London: Blackwood, 1861), p. 387.
7. For discussion of 'Baxterianism' see Geoffrey Nuttall, *Richard Baxter and Philip Doddridge: A Study in Tradition* (Oxford: Oxford University Press, 1951). The inheritance of Baxter's thought in the late seventeenth and eighteenth centuries is discussed in Isabel Rivers, *Reason, Grace and Sentiment: Volume 1, Whichcote to Wesley: A Study of the Language of Religion and Ethics in England 1660–1780* (Cambridge: Cambridge University Press, 1991), pp. 89–163.
8. B. Fawcett, 'Preface', in Richard Baxter, *The Saints' Everlasting Rest*, ed. B. Fawcett (1759; London: T. Nelson & Sons, 1872), p. xvii.
9. Richard Cooksey, *Essay on the Life and Character of John Lord Somers* (Worcester: for the author, 1791), p. 19.
10. Henry Venn, *The Conversion of Sinners the Greatest Charity* (London: S. Crowder, etc., 1779), p. 20.
11. See further Timothy Larsen, 'Victorian nonconformity and the memory of the ejected ministers: the impact of the Bicentennial commemorations of 1862', in R. N. Swanson (ed.), *The Church Retrospective*, Studies in Church History, 33 (Woodbridge: Boydell Press,

1997), pp. 459–73; Gareth Atkins, '"True churchmen"? Anglican evangelicals and history, c. 1770–1850', *Theology*, 115 (2012), 339–49.
12 John Cale Miller, *A Lecture on Churchmen and Dissenters* (Birmingham: Benjamin Hall, 1862), pp. 7–8. Here Miller, citing an earlier work, seeks to drive a wedge between the Old Dissent represented by Baxter and the radical Dissent of the nineteenth century. For further context see Larsen, 'Victorian nonconformity', pp. 465–7.
13 Orme, 'Life', pp. 131–2.
14 *Ibid.*, pp. 739, 786.
15 *Ibid.*, pp. 133, 321.
16 *Ibid.*, p. 391.
17 *Ibid.*, p. 244.
18 *Ibid.*, p. 336.
19 *Ibid.*, p. 349.
20 *Ibid.*, p. 362. Baxter's trial before Jeffreys was a popular theme in Victorian writing and the subject of a famous painting by Edward Matthew Ward (1816–79). See, for instance, Thomas Babington Macaulay, *The History of England from the Accession of James II, Volume I* (1848; Boston, MA: Phillips, Samson 1849), pp. 385–8.
21 Orme, 'Life', p. 359.
22 *Ibid.*, p. 249.
23 J. C. Ryle, *Light from Old Times; or Protestant Facts and Men* (London: William Hunt, 1891), pp. v–xxix.
24 *Ibid.*, pp. 324–5.
25 *Ibid.*, pp. 325–8.
26 *Ibid.*, pp. 331–4.
27 *Ibid.*, pp. 339, 304, 316, 335.
28 Sir James Stephen, *Essays in Ecclesiastical Biography*, 2 vols (London: Longmans, etc., 1849), II: pp. 1–2.
29 *Ibid.*, p. 53.
30 *Ibid.*, pp. 15–16, 25.
31 *Ibid.*, pp. 26–8; see also B. W. Young, *The Victorian Eighteenth Century: An Intellectual History* (Oxford: Oxford University Press, 2007), pp. 110–12.
32 Stephen, *Essays*, II: pp. 15–16, 25.
33 *Ibid.*, p. 5.
34 *Ibid.*, p. 31.
35 Tod Jones, *The Broad Church: The Biography of a Movement* (Lanham: Lexington, 2003), p. 43.
36 In his *Logic* Coleridge made the remarkable claim that Baxter's trichotomous logic anticipated the transcendentalist thought of Kant by more than a century: see Kathleen Coburn and Bart Winer (eds), *The Collected Works of Samuel Taylor Coleridge*, 16 vols to date (London: Routledge, 1969–), XIII: pp. 241–2. The philosophical and theological affinity between Baxter and Coleridge deserves detailed study.
37 Coleridge, *Works*, XII: p. 232; IV: p. 197.
38 *Ibid.*, IX: p. 155n.
39 *Ibid.*, X: p. 134n.
40 Coleridge's editors suggest that his idea to write on 'Revolutionary Minds' formed the seed of his *Opus Maximum*: see *ibid.*, XV: p. xciii.

41 *Ibid.*, XII: p. 242.
42 *Ibid.*, XII: pp. 280–1. For Coleridge's objections to Baxter's liturgical views see pp. 242, 308–11.
43 *Ibid.*, XII: pp. 250, 253.
44 *Ibid.*, XII: p. 255.
45 *Ibid.*, XIV: p. 364.
46 *Ibid.*, XII: pp. 353, 357.
47 *Ibid.*, XII: p. 273.
48 *Ibid.*, XII: p. 259.
49 *Ibid.*, XII: p. 306.
50 *Ibid.*, XII: p. 285
51 *Ibid.*, XII: p. 335.
52 *Ibid.*, XII: p. 344.
53 *Ibid.*, XII: p. 299. For Coleridge's dismissal of Baxter's account of miraculous healing see p. 298.
54 *Ibid.*, IX: pp. 212–13. It should be noted that Coleridge makes this remark of Baxter only in the context of his views about Catholicism and was certainly well aware of Baxter's opposition towards Socinianism.
55 *Ibid.*, XII: pp. 212–13; see also Jones, *Broad Church*, pp. 38–9. Of course such political reasoning was by no means unique to Baxter, but the combination of political opposition and breadth of charity displayed by Coleridge is thoroughly Baxterian.
56 For discussion of Coleridge's theological influence see David Thompson, *Cambridge Theology in the Nineteenth Century: Enquiry, Controversy and Truth* (Aldershot: Ashgate, 2008), pp. 69–95; for the 'Broad Church' see Bernard M. G. Reardon, *Religious Thought in the Victorian Age: A Survey from Coleridge to Gore* (London: Longman, 1995); Jones, *Broad Church*; Jeremy Morris, *F. D. Maurice and the Crisis of Christian Authority* (Oxford: Oxford University Press, 2005).
57 Julius Hare, *Victory of Faith* (London: John W. Parker, 1840), pp. 336–7.
58 See further Victor Shea and William Whitla (eds), *Essays and Reviews: The 1860 Text and its Reading* (Charlottesville: University Press of Virginia, 2000), pp. 1–46.
59 Jones, *Broad Church*, pp. 258–9.
60 James Fitzjames Stephen, *Defence of the Rev. Rowland Williams D.D.* (London: Smith, Elder, 1862), pp. 92–4, 129–31.
61 *Ibid.*, pp. 128–31.
62 Stanley, 'Baxter', pp. 391–6.
63 *Ibid.*, p. 394.
64 Benjamin Jowett, *Scripture and Truth: Dissertations by the Late Benjamin Jowett* (London: H. Frowde, 1907), p. 227.
65 *Ibid.*, p. 229.
66 *Ibid.*, p. 241.
67 *Ibid.*, p. 231.
68 For this distinction see Jeremy Morris, 'The spirit of comprehension: examining the Broad Church synthesis in England', *Anglican and Episcopal History*, 75 (2006), 423–43.
69 A. R. Buckland, rev. H. C. G. Matthew, 'Boyle, George', *Oxford Dictionary of National Biography* (Oxford: Oxford University Press, 2004), online edition.

70 George Boyle, *Richard Baxter* (London: Hodder and Stoughton, 1883), pp. 35–6, 39, 41.
71 John Hamilton Davies, *The Life of Richard Baxter of Kidderminster, Preacher and Prisoner* (London: Church of England Book Society, 1887), pp. 17–18.
72 *Ibid.*, pp. 22, 123, 147. For connections between nineteenth-century Anglicanism and German philosophy see Timothy Gouldstone, *The Rise and Decline of Anglican Idealism in the Nineteenth Century* (New York: Palgrave Macmillan, 2005).
73 Davies, *Life*, p. 35.
74 Boyle, *Baxter*, pp. 100–4; Davies, *Life*, pp. 20–1, 24. Orme, 'Life', pp. 16–17, strongly attacked Hooker and his legacy as well as the 'almost superstitious veneration' in which they were held in his own day.
75 Davies, *Life*, p. 158.
76 Coleridge, *Works*, XII: pp. 249, 346. Elsewhere, Coleridge admitted the absurdity of connecting the Unitarians to Old Dissent: *Works*, XIV: p. 492.
77 Alexander Gordon, *Heads of English Unitarian History* (London: Philip Green, 1895), p. 31 and 'Baxter as a founder of liberal nonconformity', in *Heads*, pp. 97, 101.
78 Cited from Stanley, 'Baxter', p. 394.
79 J. M. Lloyd Thomas, 'Introductory essay', in *The Autobiography of Richard Baxter* (London: Dent & Sons, 1925), pp. xxiii–iv.
80 For discussion of the Society and its connections to Baxter see Elaine Kaye, 'Heirs of Richard Baxter? The Society of Free Catholics, 1914–1928', *Journal of Ecclesiastical History*, 58 (2007), 256–72.

# 10

# The Scottish Covenanters

*James Coleman*

A bloody sword! A bloody sword!
Forged and furbish'd by the Lord!
For thee, O Scotland! 'tis unsheathed –
From thy martyr'd saints bequeathed![1]

THIS VERSE, TAKEN FROM 'Renwick's Visit to the Death-Bed of Peden', by the public lecturer and poet James Dodds (1817–74), is one of a multitude of nineteenth-century texts articulating the debt Scotland owed to the seventeenth-century Covenanters. With a peculiarly Victorian combination of fiery rhetoric and tearful sentimentality, the poem depicts the moment when the dying preacher Alexander Peden (1626?–86) passes on the torch of the Covenant to the young James Renwick (1662–88) while prophesying the downfall of the Stuarts at the Glorious Revolution. Covenanting memory was replete with such moments, depicted time and again in sermons, public speeches, poetry and commemorative monuments.[2] These memories were largely founded upon two complementary ideas: piety and principle. First and foremost the heroes of the Covenant were remembered for their deep and profound Christian piety, humbly giving themselves up to the will of God even in the most trying circumstances. At the same time, the ongoing relevance of the Covenanters to contemporary Scottish faith and nationality was framed by their principles, specifically Christ as the head of a gathered Church on earth and the Bible as the source of ultimate truth. In both of these ways the Covenanters were considered Presbyterian saints: as exemplars of true piety in practice, and an inspiration to those facing correlative challenges in the present.

This chapter will examine the position of the Covenanters as beacons of Christianity within the context of nineteenth-century Scottish Presbyterianism. We will first consider the development of Covenanting memory, from its origins after the Glorious Revolution through to the rise and fall of evangelical Calvinism in the nineteenth century. We will then turn to examine the significance of the term 'saint' in the expression of Covenanting memory, contending that, while it does not signify a deployment of the Covenanters as saints in the Catholic sense, contemporary commentary suggests that there remained a twitchiness about the potential for 'popish error' in ritualised aspects of their commemoration. Finally, we will consider the so-called 'National Commemoration of the Covenanting Struggle' held in 1880. In so doing, we will examine these intertwined threads of piety and principle, arguing that, while the Covenanters' sanctity remained unquestioned, the framing of their piety and principles was subject to considerable change.

## The Covenanting inheritance in the nineteenth century

At its core, the Covenanting struggle was born of Scottish Presbyterianism's resistance to the imposition of prelacy by the Stuart monarchy. The National Covenant, first signed in Greyfriars Kirkyard, Edinburgh, in February 1638, was a statement of intent for everything that followed, rejecting Charles I's attempts to force episcopacy and uniformity of worship on his northern kingdom. In 1643, the Solemn League and Covenant sought to bind all Britons to Presbyterianism, following the Westminster Confession of Faith, the defining standard for Scottish Presbyterianism – other than the Bible – for at least the next two hundred years. When Charles II renewed his father's attempts to force episcopacy on the Scots after the Restoration, over a quarter of Presbyterian ministers refused to conform, choosing instead to preach at illegal 'conventicles', concentrated mainly in south-west Scotland. Declining to accept indulgences from the Crown, as the persecution increased so the Covenanters resisted with force of arms. Their victory at Drumclog and subsequent defeat at Bothwell Bridge (both 1679) ushered in a period of suppression, with summary executions for the most unfortunate – most infamously under the muskets of John Graham of Claverhouse (1648–89) and his dragoons. In 1680, at the height of these 'Killing Times', the followers of the militant Covenanting preacher Richard Cameron published the so-called Sanquhar Declaration, condemning the King and promising his overthrow.[3] By disposing of an unconstitutional, popish monarch, argued later Covenanting memorialists, the Glorious Revolution completed what their heroes began.[4]

For nineteenth-century Scots intent on keeping alive memories of the Covenanters, their struggle and sacrifice provided a wide range of exemplars, whether for the articulation of ecclesiastical grievance or simply for the expression of a broader sense of Scottish nationality.[5] Numerous monuments were raised to events and individuals throughout the century, from the modest pillar to the Covenanting martyr John Brown of Priesthill (c. 1610–79), the 'Christian Carrier', raised in 1825, to the massive obelisk that marks the site of Bothwell Bridge, inaugurated in 1903.[6] These markers were an expression of the fashion for fixing collective memory in stone yet also an established part of Covenanting memory, undertaken with pious enthusiasm long before the cult of commemoration emerged from romantic nationalism in the later eighteenth century.[7] Almost from the moment the martyrs had fallen, grave markers were raised and maintained by the Cameronians, who had remained outside the established Church after 1688. For these few Covenanting diehards, though the Revolution had set the seal on Presbyterianism in Scotland, by not doing the same for all of Great Britain it had failed to follow through on the demands of the Solemn League and Covenant. During the eighteenth century, this Cameronian remnant grew into the Reformed Presbyterian Church who, along with their counterparts in the other Secession denominations, preserved the memorials of their forebears in the face of opposition or neglect from an established Church of Scotland dominated by moderates who preferred to turn their backs on memories of dogmatic rhetoric.[8] Covenanting memory was also sustained by key works preserving tales of the martyrs' heroism and piety: in 1775 *Biographica Presbyteriana* (or 'The Scots Worthies'), by John Howie of Lochgoin (1735–93), the martyrology of *A Cloud of Witnesses for the Royal Prerogatives of Jesus Christ* (1714), and *The History of the Sufferings of the Church of Scotland* (1721–22), by Robert Wodrow (1679–1734). Each was repeatedly reprinted throughout the nineteenth century, taking their place in countless households seeking inspirational tales of Covenanting heroism.[9]

The importance of the Covenanters to Scottish collective memory was highlighted following the publication of Walter Scott's *Old Mortality* in 1816. Scott portrays both the Covenanters and their enemies with characteristic moderation: fanatics suffer appropriately, while the more moderate element endure. For Thomas McCrie (1772–1835), biographer of John Knox (c. 1514–72) and Andrew Melville (1545–1622), Scott's portrayal was one-sided and inaccurate, presenting the Covenanters as narrow-minded zealots bent on imposing their religion and politics on an unwilling nation.[10] In a series of lengthy reviews, McCrie forcefully argued for the Covenanters as 'genuine and enlightened friends of civil liberty', a defence that became hugely influential on subsequent interpretations.[11] In the long term the controversy over *Old Mortality* provided a renewed foundation for the articulation of Covenanting memory.[12] Building on his bestselling biographies, McCrie's defence placed the Covenanters at the centre of an ongoing Scoto-British struggle for civil and religious liberty.[13]

## Champions of civil and religious liberty?

His contentions dovetailed with the Scots' need for a binding thread in their national past that would explain and justify their nation's place as equal partner to England. Alongside national heroes such as Wallace and Knox, the Covenanters could be co-opted into an overarching Unionist definition of Scotland's past and its British present.[14] This model was also adapted to other ends, not least by those intent on political reform. Scottish Chartists, for instance, drank deeply from Covenanting memory, presenting it as a powerful precedent of their stand for the political rights of the commoner.[15] The Chartist press regularly featured inspirational tales of Covenanting heroism and sacrifice, drawing parallels between the suffering of the martyrs and their own persecution in the present day.[16]

Yet growing conflict within Scottish Presbyterianism meant that the Covenanters never lacked for enthusiastic supporters among the religious. In the years leading up to the Disruption in 1843, evangelicals in the Church of Scotland saw in them much that corresponded to their own attempts to free the Kirk from the hand of the state. In 1838, in the midst of this 'Ten Years' Conflict', a large-scale gathering was held in Edinburgh's Assembly Rooms to commemorate the 1638 Glasgow General Assembly, remembering the moment when the Scots clergy had rejected episcopacy and asserted the Church's authority over its own worship and governance, contrary to the demands of the monarchy.[17] Tensions that had been deepening since the Church had adopted the Veto Act (1834), giving parishes the right to reject ministers, were exacerbated by the Court of Session's decision against the Act in May 1838.[18] In response, the General Assembly printed a 'Declaration of Spiritual Independence', asserting the Church's freedom, and appealing to the Westminster Confession and the Covenanting martyrs.[19] The anniversary of 1638 was exploited by leading evangelicals, with almost every speech projecting present political issues back onto the Glasgow Assembly. Seconding a resolution to call upon the Church to 'more fully and faithfully' apply the principles of the Second Reformation, the leading evangelical and social reformer Thomas Guthrie (1803–73) proclaimed that, 'If the patron can get a prison big enough to hold us all, I hold him to be an unworthy minister of the Church that would not rejoice to go there for the cause of Christ'. Such a fate, Guthrie argued, could not daunt 'men in whose veins flows the blood of the Covenanters'.[20] With its renewal of commitment to the doctrinal authority of the Westminster Confession, the Edinburgh commemoration was also a profound expression of evangelical conservatism. Robert Smith Candlish (1806–73), the uncompromising Calvinist who would succeed Thomas Chalmers (1780–1847) as the leader of the Free Church, declared that Scottish Presbyterians, 'were not compelled to suit their system to the times, but [that] they made the times bend to their system'.[21]

After the Disruption, the Free Church became the self-appointed Calvinist conscience of Scottish Presbyterianism.[22] Within months, it was taking a leading role in the celebration of the 200th anniversary of the Westminster Assembly, using the Confession as the rallying point for a show of unity between the various strands of seceding Presbyterianism.[23] Again, Candlish was on hand to connect the present with the past, arguing that the ideal way to commemorate the Assembly was to follow in its progenitors' saintly footsteps:

> For we have served ourselves heirs, as it were, to the memorable men who met on that occasion; and it happens remarkably and ominously enough, that in the course of God's providence, and in the cycle of events, we are brought back again, as it were, to the very same position of affairs in which they conducted their deliberations.[24]

Yet even with 1843's renewal of commitment, the centrality of the Confession was to be gradually eroded as the century progressed. While those such as Candlish were asserting the necessity for sticking close to it, the established Kirk and, from 1847, the United Presbyterian Church, questioned the relevance of historical standards.[25] In 1865, Principal John Tulloch of St Andrews (1823–86), one of the established Church's leading moderates, referred to the Confession as little more than an 'historical monument', portraying all such documents as their authors' 'best thoughts about Christian truth, as they saw it in their time – intrinsically they are nothing more; and any claim to infallibility for them is the worst of all kinds of Popery'.[26] Tulloch saw Westminster as a product of its age, with subscription to it requiring revision in the light of changing times. Contrary to the assertions of evangelicals in 1838 and 1843, and the ever-dwindling number of Calvinist conservatives within the establishment, challenges could not be resolved by 'bending the times' to fit seventeenth-century theology.[27]

As their words lost their bite, so the Covenanting martyrs were repositioned as more generic national heroes, representatives of the Scoto-British tradition of resistance to tyranny. Historians depicting their legacy carried the discourse laid out by McCrie further and further from its seventeenth-century roots.[28] As well as authoring *Lays of the Covenanters*, James Dodds was a popular lecturer, and his *Fifty Years' Struggle of the Scottish Covenanters, 1638–88* (1860) situated them in a British narrative of expanding constitutional liberty, forcefully arguing that what the Covenanters fought for was achieved in 1688.[29] By loosening the ties that bound them to the rigid dogmas of Westminster and Sanquhar, discussions of their memory could be refocused on their martyrdom in a more adaptable and, to nineteenth-century sensibilities, more palatable cause: that of civil and religious liberty.

This is not to suggest that everyone had forgotten about the hard-edged convictions that drove the Covenanters and their opponents. For some, both sides had been as bad as each other. Principal Tulloch argued that the struggle was 'not, as it has been sometimes pictured, that of bleeding patriotism on one side, and relentless domination on the other... [I]t is that of two fierce and intolerant dogmatisms waging a deadly if unequal conflict.'[30] In January 1872, in the second of three controversial lectures on the history of the Scottish Church, another liberal churchman, the Anglican Arthur Penrhyn Stanley (1815–81), Dean of Westminster, declared the Confession an example of 'minute hair-splitting and straw-dividing'. Though the Covenanters' fidelity was to be admired, Stanley patronised them as 'martyrs by mistake' who had stuck unthinkingly to their principles.[31] Others cast the Covenanters as unconstitutional rebels, framing their commemoration as evidence of evangelicalism's continuing threat to the achievements of modernity.[32] Following the 1838 celebration, the *Conservative Journal and Church of England Gazette* referred to the National Covenant as having 'reared the standard of rebellion, bore it through massacre, and through anarchy, till it chased the Sovereign from his throne, waved over the prostrate hierarchy, and consummated its crimes by regicide on the ruins of God's altar'.[33] In the 1860s, in a sustained attack on the martyrology of Covenanting memory, Mark Napier (1798–1879), Sherriff Depute of Dumfriesshire and sympathetic biographer of Graham of Claverhouse, described the cult of the Covenanters as a 'cancerous growth' upon Scotland, even questioning whether some of the executions ever took place.[34] From within the Church of Scotland, James Cooper (1846–1922), Minister at Aberdeen's East Kirk of St Nicholas, preached a sermon on the Glorious Revolution in which he described the 1643 Solemn League and Covenant as bringing about 'the destruction of all that was learned and liberal in the Church'.[35] As one of the Auld Kirk's 'High Church' faction, sympathetic to the aims of the Oxford Movement and a proponent of the observance of Christmas Day and Holy Week, Cooper represented a brand of Presbyterianism that sought to bring together the diverse arms of the 'One Holy Catholic and Apostolic Church' – a mission that had no place for divisive seventeenth-century sentiments.[36]

Being accused of trying to bring down episcopacy or encouraging regicide was unlikely to cause most defenders of the Covenanters to lose much sleep. Whether the focus was on the continued relevance of their doctrine or on their role as Scottish heroes, they were self-evidently champions of civil and religious liberty. For some, however, the commemorative act itself had the capacity to render the expression of Covenanting memory a device for the destruction of reformed religion. Rituals of commemoration contained dangerously popish elements. Indeed, in considering the Covenanters as Presbyterian saints, it may at first appear that one of these popish parallels is apparent in the occasional if by no means consistent identification of the Covenanters as 'saints'. For instance, in 1901 the writings of the Covenanting author Patrick Walker (1666–1745) were collected under the title *Six Saints of the Covenant*, the editor seeing no need to explain the use of this term to describe, amongst others, Peden and Cameron.[37] Such usage was, of course, based upon a Protestant definition of sainthood which denied any intercessory role for those so termed, positioning saints instead as exemplars of God's grace bestowed; as paragons of Christian piety.[38] Following a more strictly Calvinist model, the doctrine of limited atonement further defined saints as the elect, those predestined by God to join him in heavenly communion. Such ideas were set out in the Westminster Confession, which defined 'saint' as referring to the elect and made clear that praying to saints was strictly forbidden.[39] Even as the Confession began to lose its significance this definition remained foundational, and the meaning of saints changed little for Scottish Presbyterians regardless of their attitude towards Calvinism – this was one scriptural truth that was not up for revision.[40] For example, during the 1843 commemorations, a Dr Kettle of the Relief Church argued that the Confession 'advocated Christian communion, not party or sectarian communion, but the communion of the saints – the communion of all who call upon the Lord Jesus Christ in sincerity'.[41] At other times, to refer to a Covenanting martyr as a 'saint' appears to have been little more than malleable shorthand for devout Protestant Christianity, born more of custom than of confessional significance. Its ubiquity is evident in its use by even the most conservative Calvinists. The Ulsterman James Kerr (1847–1905) was one of the most prominent figures in what remained of the Reformed Presbyterian Church after the bulk had joined the Free Church in 1876, and so represented the closest the late nineteenth century got to an ecclesiastical descendant of the Covenanting preachers. At the unveiling of the monument at Bothwell Bridge in 1903, Kerr claimed that: 'The Covenanters never would have been the unflinching opponents of tyranny and the illustrious reformers they were had they not been illustrious saints'.[42] In other words, the Covenanters first had to be supreme examples of Christian piety and principle before they could model Scottish Presbyterianism and British constitutionalism.

To commemorate the Covenanters was to glorify them not as saints in the Catholic sense, but instead as a historic manifestation of God's will working through his elect. From time to time some were at pains to reinforce this distinction: during the 1880 National Covenanting Commemoration discussed later in this chapter, for instance, the Reverend Dr Longmuir of Aberdeen (1803–83) took the bull by the horns when preaching in the Free Church, Stonehaven. '[He] did not represent these martyrs and confessors as saints to whose tombs they made religious processions, but as believers, in whom "they glorified God". He urged all to gratitude for the civil rights and religious liberty for which these men and women so nobly contended until the nation obtained them.'[43] Whether or not these 'believers' were to be defined by strict Calvinist principles, the Covenanters were not Christian superheroes but vessels through which God might work. Such testaments to their humility were a consistent refrain, with many commemorators implicitly or explicitly disavowing any attempt to canonise the dead. In 1834, Andrew Symington (1785–1853) of the Reformed Presbyterian Church, preaching for a collection to raise a monument to two Covenanting martyrs from Paisley, was keen to distance them from such associations. 'We assemble not to consecrate their dust nor to perform masonic ceremonies at the laying of the foundation stone of their tomb. No, we simply tell the story of their martyrdom, in connexion with the noble cause in which they fell.'[44]

During two lectures delivered at Thurso in 1859, a Dr Bannister, a Baptist from Paisley, observed that though the Covenanters 'were but men', anyone reading their lives could not do so 'without feeling their hearts yearn after them, and without embalming their names in their memories as men who struggled for and gained the civil and religious freedom we now possess'.[45] If such lowly Scots were capable of great things, then the present generation must emulate their example. Yet although direct calls for intercession from the Covenanting martyrs would have been instantly denounced as *de facto* popery, commemorative actions spoke louder than words. Notwithstanding Protestant disclaimers, such occasions could still drift close to Catholicism, rendering them potentially the first step down a very dangerous road. Ritual practices had been expressly denounced in the 1638 National Covenant. Lifting a considerable proportion of the Negative Confession of 1581, it had rejected the authority of the Pope as the 'Roman Antichrist', rejecting not only his 'bastard sacraments, with all his rites, ceremonies, and false doctrine', but also 'his canonization of men, calling upon angels or saints departed, worshipping of imagery, relics, and crosses; dedicating of kirks, altars, days, vows to creatures'.[46] Perhaps with this in mind, most commemorations of the Covenanters consisted of sermons preached at sites of significance; yet other celebrations, such as those of Covenanting milestones, either contained unwelcome ritualistic elements or were reminiscent of Catholicism. For instance, a commemoration of the Sanquhar Declaration held there in 1860 involved an ostentatious programme, including the display of sacred 'relics' and readings delivered along a processional route. Sanquhar was decorated with trees, a flag carried at Drumclog and Bothwell Bridge was flown, and two triumphal arches 'composed of evergreens and the beautiful wild flowers of Scotland' were erected along the processional route.[47] The day commenced with a public meeting attended by between 3,000 and 4,000 people, with speeches from the town's Provost and the Reverend Dr Robert Simpson (1792/5–1867), a noted authority on the Covenanters. A procession was then formed, including civic worthies, the local volunteer corps and three brass bands, which proceeded to the first decorative arch, where a local minister read the Declaration and discoursed upon its significance. The procession then moved on to the ruins of Sanquhar Castle where the 'gathered multitude' heard a rousing speech from the classical and Gaelic scholar Professor John Stuart Blackie (1809–95), as well as two Reformed Presbyterian Church ministers.[48]

Critics of commemoration were quick to point out the dangers of all this. In response to a fiery sermon preached in Greyfriars Kirkyard as part of the 1880 Commemoration, a *Scotsman* editorial accused the Reverend James Begg (1808–83) – one of the Free Church's most conservative Calvinists – of engaging in 'an imitation of the practices of that Popery' which he so vigorously denounced. In the same paper's letters column a few days later, 'Original Seceder' directly compared the commemoration with the rituals of the Catholic Church. Even a dogmatic Calvinist, then, could be accused of indulging in 'Romish practices' which had 'more of the modern sentimental enthusiast' about them than of 'the stern principles of Covenanting times'.[49] A second letter appeared the following day, this time from 'A Covenanter', who more openly invoked the Covenant and the practices it rejected:

> The National Covenant condemns, and Scotland in it for ever abjured, the dedication of days to creatures and the veneration of relics, &c., yet professed friends of the Covenants seek to set them forth by the very practices they condemn. Can they hope, in this apeing [sic] of the spirit and devices of the Antichrist, by relics and commemorative services, to attract this country to a due sense of its rights and privileges?[50]

Such comparisons were not lost on those who had the most invested in Covenanting memory. Reverend William Symington (1795–1862) – younger brother of Andrew – was both one of the most vocal defenders of Covenanting commemoration and one of the Reformed Presbyterian Church's leading ministers. An advocate of social reform, Symington was raised to the Reformed Presbyterian Chair of Systematic Theology in 1853 upon the death of his brother and promoted commemoration of the later Covenanting martyrs throughout his public life. In 1831, he preached a sermon entitled 'The Character and Claims of the Scottish Martyrs' in aid of the erection of a monument in Dumfries, in which he mounted a stout defence of the practice. To remember the worthy dead was, Symington argued, 'part of our nature' yet at the same time it was 'no less scriptural than natural'. If the Bible was to be the final arbiter, he insisted, then raising monuments and engaging in public commemorations had all the authority it required. Furthermore, Symington argued that the marking of the graves of the Covenanters was for the benefit not of the dead but of the living. Though fallen in the name of the Covenant, the martyrs' sleep 'is as sweet on the solitary moor where the sighings of the breeze are their only requiem as in the crowded cemetery where art has been tasked to pronounce their panegyric. But instructive and improving to survivors are such touching memorials.'[51]

This was a key consideration. To remember the dead was to bring before the present examples of Christian piety *in extremis*, an example to all of what true faith looked like. This, Symington argued, was why Covenanting martyrs deserved to be remembered:

> What ground of claim for such distinction can be put forth which may not be preferred on their behalf? Is it personal worth? It was theirs. Is it valuable service? Such was theirs. Is it generous sacrifices for public good? There too their claims are unrivalled ... To say that poets, and heroes, and statesmen deserve to be commemorated, while those who loved not their lives unto death in the cause of their country's religion and liberties are to be left to sink into oblivion, is to pay no compliment to either the discernment or the gratitude of the age.[52]

To neglect those who represented the deliverance of Scotland and Britain from tyranny was to turn one's back on the illustrious past. The Covenanters provided, in effect, parables from the past, inspirational memories of the will of God manifest through those most able to hear His voice.

## The 1880 National Commemoration of the Covenanting Struggle

Yet if the martyrs certainly ought to be remembered, how was this memory to be defined, and what was its present-day significance? The taint of Catholicism was easily avoided by referring to the Covenanters' sainthood as thoroughly reformed, being exemplars of piety and devotion to the word of God. How their political principles translated into modern politics was another matter entirely. Should they be placed within a narrative of progressive civil and religious liberty, or should their advocates adhere to the letter of Westminster and even Sanquhar? These different shades of memory were manifest in what was by far the most national Covenanting celebration in nineteenth-century Scotland: the 1880 National Commemoration of the Covenanting Struggle. Whereas in 1838 and 1843 events had been relatively localised, the 1880 Commemoration took place in all corners of the nation. In January, notices appeared in the press indicating that religious services would be held at 'appropriate places across Scotland' in June and July, with the key date being 20 June, the anniversary of the 'publication' of the Sanquhar Declaration. Further gatherings were to take place in Edinburgh, Glasgow, Lanarkshire and Ayrshire.[53] Some were on an impressive scale. On 20 June itself, James Begg of the Free Church and James Kerr of the Reformed Presbyterians preached in Greyfriars Kirkyard to between 5,000 and 6,000 people, while in Dundee an open-air meeting in the Barrack Park in July was attended by around 5,000 people.[54] This was to be the most comprehensive expression of Covenanting memory yet held, organised across all Presbyterian denominations, with even the established Church joining in on occasion.[55]

It is notable that the bicentenary of the Sanquhar Declaration was chosen as the date. The original Declaration was avowedly rebellious, articulating the Cameronians' position as the only true Presbyterians in Scotland and openly declaring war on the King as a 'tyrant and usurper', yet by the 1880s much of its incendiary significance had cooled. Just as the tide of dogmatic Calvinism was ebbing in Scottish Presbyterianism, so key Covenanting texts were losing their authority. Despite conservative harangues, the Westminster Confession was being edged out of its position at the heart of the Kirk. Likewise the Declaration: rather than being remembered as a militant – potentially regicidal – stand against a monarch who had overstepped the bounds of his authority, it was now framed in more moderate terms as a precursor to the much less problematic Glorious Revolution. Other, less adaptable elements of the struggle, such as the projected presbyterianisation of Britain, were glossed over or conveniently ignored in the move to render Covenanting principles usable in the present.

Such pliability was evident in the themes for the 1880 Commemoration circulated by its organising committee. These were to consider 'the history, objects, and results of the Covenanting struggle, with our present duty in connection therewith', specifically:

> The infallibility, inspiration, and supreme authority of the Sacred Scriptures. The agreeableness of the Confession of Faith and Presbyterian Church Government to the Word of God. The mediatorial sovereignty of Christ of His Church and the nations involving submission to His Word and Will. The Scriptural character of national covenanting, with the civil and religious benefits resulting from the great national struggle terminating in the Revolution of 1688.[56]

What stands out is that the only direct historical reference in these themes was to the Glorious Revolution and not to the persecution that prompted the Cameronians to make their Declaration in the first place. In mnemonic terms this was a celebration of the Covenanting principle shorn of its pricklier element. The emphasis was to be on how the Covenanters had ushered in the Revolution.

What Richard Cameron had fought for, then, was realised at the Revolution and had effectively been maintained ever since – his potentially regicidal call-to-arms was quietly edged out of the picture, as was the Cameronian remnant's rejection of the Revolution settlement for failing to stick to the letter of the Solemn League and Covenant. This reframing of past motivations was a recurrent theme, with many of the 1880 speakers keen to qualify the Covenanters' actions. In the Lanarkshire town of Bothwell on 20 June, Dr Thomas Easton of the Reformed Presbyterian Church preached on how it was 'to the Covenanters [that] Scotland owed and Europe owed it that religious liberty had now an actual as well as a constitutional existence. He would not pronounce an unqualified eulogium on all they said and did; it was with the great principles for which these men contended they had specially to do'.[57] Implicit in this was a necessary adaptation of the Covenanters' goals, and that even a member of the Reformed Presbyterian Church should prefer to focus on a modernised reading of their principles, rather than praising their every move, indicates how far their memory was being adopted for broader and less disruptive purposes. Some preachers went even further, rejecting politics entirely and making the commemoration an entirely religious undertaking. At the Dundee Barrack Park meeting in July, the preacher maintained that the commemoration's aim was

> that of promoting a real revival of true religion by becoming acquainted with the principles of our Covenanting ancestors, and by seeking to express, as individuals, families, Churches, and communities that holy living and supreme regard to God's will which distinguished them. This and no political object ought to be our aim.[58]

Thus the purpose of remembering the Covenanters was to inspire the present generation with memories of their piety and principles as Presbyterian saints; to inspire closer adherence to God's will, and not to score political points.

Not everyone was willing to dilute the Covenanters' theology, however. The 1880 Commemoration was replete with doctrinaire Calvinists fully intent on making political points concerning the necessity of counteracting a dangerous increase in the liberality of religious observance in Scotland and in Britain more generally. Deep fears were expressed about the alarming backsliding of Presbyterianism away from Westminster tenets, about the toleration of Catholicism, about biblical criticism as undermining the absolute truth of the Bible, about lack of Sabbath observance, and about the alarming spread of 'prelacy'. Were these not evidence that the evils the Covenanters had faced were once more on the rise? The secretary of the Commemoration's organising committee was the Reverend Dr James Moir Porteous (1822–91), Free Church Minister at Wanlockhead, a parish steeped in Covenanting memory. Across the summer, Porteous preached sermons in Perth, Kinloch Rannoch, Moffat and, perhaps most notably, at North Berwick in commemoration of those Covenanters who had been imprisoned on the Bass Rock. (Revelation 6: 9, on the souls of the slain under the altar crying for vengeance, was his preferred text.) The commemoration, Porteous claimed, 'was not intended merely for the glorification of the martyrs, but to try and stimulate people to revive the history of the Covenant, and preserve the essential spirit of the Covenanters to combat the spirit of Popery and infidelity which was at present threatening to overwhelm our liberties'.[59]

If combating 'popery' was at the heart of much of the Covenanting cult in the nineteenth century, the Commemoration was an ideal opportunity to renew this spirit in Scotland and further afield.[60] To remember the martyrs for their own sake would be counterproductive – the true measure of the Commemoration's success was tangible, practical outcomes in the ongoing war against papal tyranny. By far the loudest Calvinist voice raised in 1880 was Begg, who constantly strove to set forth the establishment principle, the Westminster Confession, and the sanctity of the Sabbath.

Begg's sermons and speeches also contained pragmatic calls for the maintenance of Presbyterian civilisation within Scotland.[61] Along with Porteous, he was one of the moving spirits of the 1880 event, having presented an overture on the 'Cameronian Celebration' to the Free Church General Assembly in May.[62] At each of his several appearances throughout the year, Begg focused on the results of the seventeenth-century struggle and the 'ordinary duties' of Scotsmen in ensuring that those results were maintained. 'The commemoration of the Covenanters had not come a moment too soon', Begg claimed, 'especially if it was to be ruled by God for arresting the shameless backsliding of most of the Presbyterian churches.'[63] Mirroring the commemorations of 1838 and 1843, Begg sought to open his countrymen's eyes to 'the fact that the centuries had brought us back to circumstances similar to those in which Cameron testified and the Covenanting martyrs died'.[64] The solution, he thundered, was 'to go into a new Covenant which would have the effect of arresting the backsliding of the present day and the dragging of them from the high eminences they occupied to lower depths than their father were ever permitted to fall into'.[65] The weapons used in the 1680s to combat the Antichrist were required again in the 1880s to counter new foes. Begg went so far as to draft the text of this new Covenant, presenting it at Newington, Edinburgh, in July 1880 with the hope that it 'might be subscribed by thousands in all parts of Scotland'.[66]

Hurling fire and brimstone from pulpit and platform while clutching his new Covenant, Begg loomed large as a Peden for the nineteenth century, a correspondence not lost on observers. *The Scotsman*'s editorial observed that owing to the bad weather on 20 June and the historical resonances of holding his sermon in Greyfriars Kirkyard, the gathered crowd would have witnessed a Covenanting sermon of decidedly dramatic authenticity. *The Scotsman* likened him to Scott's wrathful Habakkuk Mucklewrath from *Old Mortality*, arguing that 'those who heard Dr Begg, and believed him, could not but think that the present time is not a whit less dangerous than that which Habakkuk thus described and denounced'.[67] Such harangues were, however, an anachronism: 'All the old and obsolete bogeys were to be brought out; the raw head and bloody bones were to be exhibited; and Scotsmen were to be treated as if, instead of living in a time of daily newspapers, electric telegraphs, and railways, they were destitute of all such things, and also of common sense.'[68] Begg was yesterday's man, insisted the *Scotsman*, in his refusal to accept that seventeenth-century texts were no longer usable. The majority of editorial comment surrounding 1880 agreed: if the Covenanters were to endure as symbols of Scottishness, their principles had to be adapted to meet the demands of the present. While the commemoration was, on the whole, successful, then, it elicited acknowledgements about the narrowness of the principles that had pushed the Covenanters into rebellion. An editorial in the *Angus Evening Telegraph*, for example, argued that Scotland 'owed them a debt of everlasting gratitude … By all means let the virtues, the services, and the sufferings of the Covenanters be celebrated with genuine enthusiasm, but do not let it be forgotten that they fell into errors which it is as essential to avoid as it is desirable to imitate their heroic virtues.'[69] A correspondent to the *Dundee Courier* concurred. The spirit of the present age called for toleration of religious differences, not eradication:

> Did our Covenanting forefathers take their stand on toleration? No, they did not. They suffered and died in defence of what they believed to be Divine truth, but they never even hinted at giving liberty of thought to any who differed from them ... We now know the blessings of toleration, and we are gradually discovering that no cause, however sacred, can be promoted by tolerance and persecution. The Covenanters did not see this, neither does Dr Begg.[70]

Covenanting heroism was beyond doubt, but their insistence that a particular brand of Presbyterian Calvinism was the only true path was long past its sell-by date. Few went as far as Tulloch had in declaring a plague on both houses in the struggle, most preferring instead to admit to the Covenanters' flaws while emphasising their fidelity to their principles, and the continuing relevance of their cause. Outwith Scotland, an editorial in *The Standard* of London, echoed this sentiment. The struggles of the 1680s had been

> a struggle between two forms of tyranny, rather than between tyranny on the one hand and intolerance on the other. The Scotch Covenanters had taken a solemn oath that they would not only resist the imposition of Prelacy upon themselves, but that they would utterly overthrow the institution of it in England ... [T]he failure of such an object was both doomed and deserved, though the nobility of the motive and the loftiness of the martyrdom remain.[71]

It was the 'motive' and 'loftiness of the martyrdom' that was the most appropriate subject for commemoration, rather than the strict details of Sanquhar or any other Covenanting text. This focus on the Covenanting martyrs as individual examples of Christian nobility serves to emphasise their position as Presbyterian – indeed, national – saints. Uncoupled from rigid doctrines, they could be reinvented as examples of a broader, more applicable Christian piety. To insist on them as inflexible Calvinists was to risk losing them to memorial irrelevance. Indeed, many argued that if the present generation had failed to take up Begg's new Covenant, the fault lay at the feet of such old-style Covenanting rhetoric. An editorial in Edinburgh's *Evening News* poured scorn on the supposed nationality of the commemoration:

> The results which have followed this deluge of oratory and literature are certainly far from bearing any due proportion to the energy expended. The reasons are obvious to all except those who have endeavoured through these commemoration services to resuscitate the intolerant principles which marked the era of the Covenant, rather than pay homage to its general spirit.[72]

If the Covenanters were to endure as Presbyterian saints, their memory would need to be adapted to the times.

## Notes

1. James Dodds, *Lays of the Covenanters* (Edinburgh: John MacLaren and Son, 1880), p. 208.
2. See James Kerr, *A Third Reformation Necessary ... A Sermon preached in Greyfriars' Churchyard, Edinburgh, on Sabbath, 20th June, 1880, on the Bi-Centenary of the Covenanting Struggle; and Re-Delivered, by Request, on Sabbath, 11th July, in the Dock Park, Dumfries; and on Sabbath, 25th July, at Renwick's Monument, Glencairn* ([n.p.]: James Gemmell, 1880).
3. Ian B. Cowan, *The Covenanters, 1660–1688* (London: Gollancz, 1976).
4. For one of the clearest articulations of this argument, see James Dodds, *The Fifty Years' Struggle of the Covenanters, 1638 to 1688* (London: Houlston, 1868).
5. James Coleman, *Remembering the Past in Nineteenth-Century Scotland: Commemoration, Nationality and Memory* (Edinburgh: Edinburgh University Press, 2014), pp. 143–5.
6. For details on the locations and subjects of the majority of Covenanter memorials, see Thorbjorn Campbell, *Standing Witnesses: A Guide to the Scottish Covenanters and their Memorials* (Edinburgh: Saltire Society, 1996).
7. Coleman, *Remembering*, pp. 9–14.
8. Matthew Hutchison, *The Reformed Presbyterian Church in Scotland: Its Origin and History, 1680–1876* (Paisley: J. & R. Parlane, 1893), pp. 46–7, 55–9, 73–80; Colin Kidd, *Subverting Scotland's Past: Scottish Whig Historians and the Creation of an Anglo-British Identity, 1689–c. 1830* (Cambridge: Cambridge University Press, 1993), pp. 193–5.
9. Edward J. Cowan, 'The Covenanting tradition in Scottish history', in Cowan and R. Finlay (eds), *Scottish History: The Power of the Past* (Edinburgh: Edinburgh University Press, 2002), pp. 124–31.
10. D. M. Murray, 'Martyrs or madmen? The Covenanters, Sir Walter Scott and Dr Thomas McCrie', *The Innes Review*, 43 (1992), 174.
11. Kidd, *Subverting*, p. 203.
12. Andrew R. Holmes, 'The Scottish Reformation and the origin of religious and civil liberty in Britain and Ireland: Presbyterian interpretations, c. 1800–60', in Peter Nockles and Vivienne Westbrook (eds), *Reinventing the Reformation in the Nineteenth Century*, Bulletin of the John Rylands Library, 90 (2014), 138–41; I. B. Cowan, 'The Covenanters: a revision article', *Scottish Historical Review*, 47 (1968), 36; Coleman, *Remembering*, pp. 30–1.
13. Neil Forsyth, 'Presbyterian historians and the Scottish invention of British liberty', *Records of the Scottish Church History Society*, 34 (2004), 92–3.
14. Coleman, *Remembering*, pp. 133–6.
15. W. H. Fraser, *Chartism in Scotland* (Pontypool: Merlin Press, 2010), pp. 212–13.
16. See, for instance, 'John Brown, or the house in the muir', *Chartist Circular* (27 March 1841), p. 331; (3 April 1841), p. 839.
17. Coleman, *Remembering*, pp. 89–92; Holmes, 'Scottish Reformation', 143–4.
18. Andrew L. Drummond and James Bulloch, *The Scottish Church, 1688–1843: The Age of the Moderates* (Edinburgh: St Andrew Press, 1973), pp. 231–4.
19. *Ibid.*, pp. 226, 235–6.
20. *Report of the Great Public Meeting held in the Assembly Rooms, Edinburgh, on Thursday Evening, Dec 20, 1838* (Edinburgh: The Edinburgh Printing and Publishing Company, etc., 1839), p. 66. See also *The Scotsman* (22 December 1838), p. 2.
21. *Report*, p. 39.

22 Forsyth, 'Presbyterian historians', 99–100; A. C. Cheyne, *The Transforming of the Kirk: Victorian Scotland's Religious Revolution* (Edinburgh: St Andrew Press, 1983), pp. 66–7.
23 Coleman, *Remembering*, p. 105; Holmes, 'Scottish Reformation', 145–6.
24 *Bicentenary of the Assembly of Divines at Westminster, held at Edinburgh, July 12th and 13th, 1843* (Edinburgh: W. P. Kennedy, 1843), p. 124.
25 Cheyne, *Transforming*, p. 71.
26 Quoted in *ibid.*, pp. 74–5.
27 Andrew L. Drummond and James Bulloch, *The Church in Victorian Scotland, 1843–1874* (Edinburgh: St Andrew Press, 1975), pp. 298–305; Drummond and Bulloch, *The Church in Late Victorian Scotland, 1874–1900* (Edinburgh: St Andrew Press, 1978), pp. 29–39, 263–71; Cheyne, *Transforming*, pp. 66–71.
28 Forsyth, 'Presbyterian historians', 101.
29 Dodds, *Fifty Years' Struggle*, pp. 1–4.
30 John Tulloch, 'The Wigtown martyrs: a story of the Covenant in 1685', *Macmillan's Magazine*, 7 (1862–63), 145.
31 Stewart J. Brown, 'Dean Stanley and the controversy over his history of the Scottish Church, 1872', *Records of the Scottish Church History Society*, 31 (2001), 157–8.
32 Coleman, *Remembering*, pp. 27–8.
33 Quoted in *Caledonian Mercury* (5 January 1839), p. 2.
34 Quoted in Cowan, 'Covenanting tradition', p. 136; Mark Napier, *The Case for the Crown in re. the Wigtown Martyrs Proved to be Myths versus Wodrow and Lord Macaulay, Patrick the Pedlar and Principal Tulloch* (Edinburgh: Edmonston and Douglas, 1863).
35 'Bicentenary of the Revolution of 1688', *Aberdeen Weekly Journal* (5 November 1888), p. 6; Coleman, *Remembering*, pp. 148–9.
36 Cheyne, *Transforming*, p. 99.
37 Patrick Walker, *Six Saints of the Covenant: Peden, Semple, Welwood, Cameron, Cargill, Smith*, ed. D. Hay Fleming (London: Hodder & Stoughton, 1901).
38 See Franz Courth, 'Sainthood' and R. W. Scribner, 'Cult of Saints', in H. J. Hillerbrand (ed.), *The Oxford Encyclopaedia of the Reformation*, 4 vols (Oxford: Oxford University Press, 1996), III: pp. 472–4, 474–6.
39 *The Confession of Faith, the Larger Catechism, the Shorter Catechism, the Directory for Publick Worship, the Form of Presbyterial Church Government, with Reference to the Proofs from the Scripture* (Edinburgh: Blackwood, 1913), pp. 21, 26, 32.
40 See, for instance, John Thomson, *The Idolatry of the Church of Rome, in the Worship of Saints and Images* (Paisley: Alex. Gardner, 1851), pp. 4–7, 15–18.
41 *Bicentenary of Westminster*, pp. 51–2.
42 'Battle of Bothwell Bridge: unveiling of national memorial', *Glasgow Herald* (21 June 1903), p. 6.
43 'Bi-centenary commemoration of the Covenanting struggle', *Aberdeen Journal* (6 July 1880), p. 4.
44 A. Symington, *The Blood of the Faithful Martyrs Precious in the Sight of Christ: a Discourse Delivered in the Church of Paisley, on the 24th October, 1834* (Paisley: Alex. Gardner, 1834), p. 47.
45 'Lectures at Thurso on the Covenanters', *John O' Groats Journal* (2 June 1859), p. 2.
46 Gordon Donaldson (ed.), *Scottish Historical Documents* (Edinburgh: Scottish Academic Press, 1974), pp. 151–2, 194.

47 'The Sanquhar Declaration: great public demonstration at Sanquhar', *Dumfries and Galloway Standard* (27 June 1860), p. 3.
48 *Ibid.*
49 'The Covenanting Commemoration,' *The Scotsman* (24 June 1880), p. 3.
50 *Ibid.*
51 William Symington, 'The character and claims of the Scottish Martyrs', in Symington, *Discourses on Public Occasions* (Glasgow: Bryce, 1851), p. 93.
52 *Ibid.*, p. 94.
53 *Daily News* (5 January 1880), p. 6.
54 'Covenanting Commemoration', *The Scotsman* (21 June 1880), p. 6. See also 'The Covenanters' Commemoration: meeting in Dundee', *Dundee Courier* (23 June 1880), p. 3.
55 Coleman, *Remembering*, pp. 136–8.
56 Quoted in *Dundee Courier* (7 January 1880), p. 2.
57 *The Scotsman* (21 June 1880), p. 6.
58 'The Covenanters' Commemoration: great open-air meeting in the Barrack Park', *The Northern Warder and Bi-Weekly Courier and Argus* (20 July 1880), p. 2.
59 'Moffat, Covenanting Commemoration', *Glasgow Herald* (24 August 1880), p. 3.
60 Coleman, *Remembering*, p. 147.
61 Thomas Smith, *Memoirs of James Begg, D.D.*, 2 vols (Edinburgh: James Gemmell, 1885–88), II: pp. 148–50; see also H. J. Hanham, *Scottish Nationalism* (London: Faber, 1969), pp. 74–6.
62 *Proceedings of the General Assembly of the Free Church of Scotland* (Edinburgh: Ballantyne, Hanson, 1880), p. 121.
63 'Dr Begg on "Backsliding Presbyterianism"', *Edinburgh Evening News* (13 July 1880), p. 2.
64 *The Scotsman* (21 June 1880), p. 6.
65 *Dundee Courier* (23 June 1880), p. 3.
66 *Edinburgh Evening News* (13 July 1880), p. 2.
67 *The Scotsman* (21 June 1880), p. 6.
68 *Ibid.*
69 *Angus Evening Telegraph* (23 June 1880), p. 2.
70 'The Covenanter Commemoration', *Dundee Courier* (23 July 1880), p. 7.
71 *The Standard* (14 September 1880), p. 4.
72 *Edinburgh Evening News* (18 September 1880), p. 2.

11

# John and Mary Fletcher

*David R. Wilson*

IN THE DECADES FOLLOWING the deaths of John (1703–91) and Charles Wesley (1707–88), succeeding generations of Methodists began to construct histories of the movement, seeking to define it as a denomination in its own right, and to explain and justify their departure from the Church of England. Central to these histories was the recounting of the lives of those considered to be representatives of early Methodist piety, exemplars worthy of imitation. Collecting, editing, and printing served the dual purpose of propagating devotion while constructing a tradition after the model of Wesley's 'experimental religion', with its own line of holy lives and devoted ministers as evidence of the providential hand of God in establishing the denomination.[1] Yet the project, often driven more by evolving Methodist culture than by a single co-ordinated effort, served a *de facto* tertiary purpose. Methodism was birthed within the Church of England and used the Book of Common Prayer for its Liturgy, Calendar, and Articles.[2] However, after 1786, Methodists (especially those who had stopped attending their parish churches) increasingly used Wesley's abridgement of the Prayer Book, *The Sunday Service of the Methodists*,[3] which had excised 'the sanctoral calendar along with certain liturgical seasons and holy days'.[4] The formal means for remembering the saints of Christian history as part of Methodist practice were thus limited. However, the exercise of reprinting lives and 'accounts of happy deaths' once printed by Wesley,[5] and writing and collecting new lives for both personal and public reading, gave rise in the nineteenth century to a functional if informal Methodist hagiography. Amongst early models of Methodist sanctity put into print, few were called upon by Methodist historians and hagiographers more than John and Mary Fletcher.

John William Fletcher (1729–85) was a francophone Protestant Swiss émigré who settled in England (c. 1749), experienced evangelical conversion under the ministries of John and Charles Wesley (c. 1754), and was subsequently ordained in the Church of England (1757). In 1760 he was inducted as Vicar of Madeley, an industrialising parish in East Shropshire, where he served until his untimely death in 1785.[6] He maintained a friendship with the Wesley brothers (especially Charles) throughout his life.[7] In the 1770s, Fletcher came to John's aid in defending the Arminian theology of the Wesleyan Methodists against the attacks of the attacks of opponents who aligned themselves with the Calvinistic Methodism of George Whitefield (1714–70), the Countess of

Huntingdon (1707–91), and Sir Richard Hill (1703–1808), amongst others. Through these and his other writings he achieved some notoriety amongst the Methodists.[8] Indeed, Wesley was so pleased with his performance that he repeatedly urged Fletcher to leave his parish in order to assist him with the Methodists as his 'designated successor'.[9] By the mid-1770s, despite the fact that Fletcher declined Wesley's inducements, there were yet some who thought of Fletcher as Wesley's presumptive successor as the leader of the Connexion. By the end of his life, he was well known and highly regarded amongst evangelicals – including some of his theological opponents – as one of the most assiduous clergymen and pious churchmen of the eighteenth century.

Mary Fletcher, née Bosanquet (1739–1815), was born in Essex to a wealthy family.[10] She was raised in the Church of England amongst the Huguenot congregations of London, catechised by her father when she was five years old, and confirmed at St Paul's Cathedral when she was thirteen. Some years before her confirmation, she had heard of the Methodists from a maid, and eventually she was drawn into Methodist circles in London. Having left her parents' home, she established a small community of Christian women and an orphanage in Leytonstone, Essex.[11] When this outgrew its premises, and her income, she and it moved to Morley, Yorkshire in 1768, where her influence as a society and class leader increased. Believing that she was called to relate what God had done for her soul, she became one of the first female preachers of Methodism.[12] In addition, she published several religious works. Concerned that marriage would restrict her ministerial activity, she resisted various proposals, although she had, since her early contact with the Methodists, considered John Fletcher the one possible exception – and he had held the same sentiment. In 1781 they renewed their acquaintance and were married. Mary removed with John to Madeley to serve as a partner in ministry. Following his death less than four years later, she continued to reside in the vicarage, and was (astonishingly for the times) allowed by her husband's non-resident successor to appoint the curates. Over the next thirty years she continued to meet the local Methodist societies, lead classes, and act as a spiritual guide, preaching and effectively overseeing the parish until her death in 1815.

This essay first examines Wesley's ideas about saints and sanctity, going on to explore, through the Fletchers' self-understanding and through their posthumous construction, the evolution of a distinctively Methodist tradition of 'sainthood' and its often striking expression in texts, rituals, relics, and commemorations.

### Early Methodist views of sainthood

The most obvious source apart from Scripture for early Methodist understandings of the 'communion of saints', and of saints as individuals, was the Thirty-Nine Articles of the Church of England, the twenty-second of which stated that 'The Romish Doctrine concerning ... Worshipping and Adoration as well of Images, as of Reliques, and also Invocation of Saints, is a fond thing, vainly invented, and grounded upon no warranty of Scripture'. John Wesley asserted, throughout his life, that Methodism was a movement within the established Church, and his views on the subject were concordant with this, as has been shown elsewhere.[13] Yet a summary is useful for understanding not only how later Methodists followed Wesley, but also where they diverged or even dissented from his teaching. The Protestant iconoclasm which was intrinsic to early Methodism created a lasting tension as later Methodists sought to remember and reclaim their saints.

Wesley had a genuine appreciation for the Calendar and Liturgy. Journal entries reveal that he regarded one day with particular affection – All Saints' Day, 1 November – referring to it as 'a festival I dearly love'.[14] He thought that the Liturgy for the day, including the collect ('Grant us the grace so to follow the blessed Saints in all virtuous and godly living') was constructed with 'admirable piety'.[15] Even so, his appreciation for it was not enough to compel him to keep either the festival, or indeed the sanctoral calendar, in his revision for Methodist worship.[16] Wesley's view of the saints was guarded by a Protestant wariness of the temptation to move from expressing gratefulness to God for the saints, and seeking to emulate them, to adoration of them, when only God was worthy of such worship.[17] To do so, however, was a problem not only of idolatry, but of soteriology and ecclesiology; it was, he thought, a misunderstanding of the 'communion of saints', which had implications for the self-understanding of the Church as 'those in paradise as well as those upon earth as ... one body united under one Head'.[18] Wesley believed that there were indeed those within that communion whose lives were especially worthy of imitation, but that this did not confer a status beyond that of others. He deplored the Catholic doctrine of supererogation, or in his words, the 'overplus of the satisfactions of Christ and the saints'.[19] Although recent work has shown the depth of Wesley's engagement with the 'primitive Church', he nevertheless appears either to misunderstand or disregard the distinction between worship (*latreia*) of God, and adoration (*douleia*) of the saints made at the Second Council of Nicaea (787).[20]

Yet Wesley clearly believed that some communication between saints departed and saints living was possible, although imperceptible except by those who had been given a special blessing. In the other direction, he was willing to state unambiguously that the 'saints in paradise' had full access to happenings on earth. 'They no doubt clearly discern all our words and actions, if not all our thoughts too ... but we have in general only a faint and indistinct perception of their presence, unless ... where it may answer some gracious ends of Divine Providence.'[21] As Wainwright has observed, Wesley's *Collection of Forms of Prayer for Every Day of the Week* (1733) included prayers, in accordance with the Book of Common Prayer, for the 'faithful departed', demonstrating a belief in an intermediate state between death and final judgement.[22] Even so, he was unwilling to pray for or to departed saints by name.[23] 'Wesley valued the saints as honoured exemplars,' Maddox argues, 'not intercessors.'[24] Following Wainwright, however, Colón-Emeric attributes Wesley's reticence to invoke saints as shaped more by 'anti-Catholic tendencies than [by] his eschatological reserve'.[25] Wesley was aware that Scripture was not prescriptive on the issue, and that the only descriptive instance was the story of Dives and Lazarus (Luke 16: 19–31). 'I do not remember in all the Bible any prayer made to a saint but this,' he wrote. 'And if we observe who made it, a man in hell, and with what success, we shall hardly wish to follow the precedent.'[26]

Perhaps Wesley's most important contribution to Methodist understandings of sainthood was his emphasis on a model of discipleship shared across 'divers spectrums of churchmanship' based on the imitation of Christ.[27] To be a Christian was to be a saint. 'We are all indeed "called to be saints"', he wrote, 'and the name of Christians means no less.'[28] Yet the Methodist pursuit of holy living and holy dying was dependent upon examples of Christian holiness against which one could test one's own experience.[29] This emphasis is clear throughout Wesley's printed corpus, most clearly in the series of edited lives included in his fifty-volume *Christian Library*,[30] as well as others printed in an early edition of his *Works* recommended to every Methodist society.[31] The surest way to participate in the communion of saints was to live as one by accepting God's gift of salvation by faith, and applying the means of grace.[32] By stressing this point repeatedly, Wesley was simultaneously making holiness of life (and thus sainthood) understandable and available to all who desired 'to flee the wrath to come', and by making this the only prerequisite for society membership.[33] A testimony by the American Methodist minister Freeborn Garrettson (1752–1827) exemplifies this. At the beginning of his path to conversion,

> [T]here seemed to be a question asked me, 'do you know what a saint is?' I paused awhile and then answered to myself, 'There are no saints on earth in this our day.' The same voice seemed to reply, 'A saint is one that is wholly given up to God.' ... I was much affected and wished to be a saint, and it was pressed upon my mind that I should be one.[34]

Wesley solicited such experiences from Methodists generally, and wrote to his preachers requesting accounts of their own conversions, which he began to publish in his *Arminian Magazine* (*AM*) in 1778. In addition to these and the lives in the *Christian Library*, Wesley printed several of his favourites independently, among which were the missionary David Brainerd (1718–47), the Scottish Presbyterian Thomas Halyburton (1674–1712), Gaston de Renty (1611–49), and Gregory Lopez (1616–91), the last two being Catholics.[35] There were several layers to imitation as well, for it was not uncommon for Methodists in their mention of Lopez and others to notice that both of these found inspiration in reading the *Lives of the Saints*.[36] Eamon Duffy suggests that Wesley had 'waited for much of his life for an exemplar to match them', which he found in John Fletcher, who had all the devotion without the faults of 'some touches of superstition, and some of idolatry, as the worship of images, angels and saints', which he saw in his Catholic heroes of holiness.[37]

## The Fletchers' views of sainthood

The Fletchers' own views were influenced by Wesley's, although they allowed for a greater degree of mystery and mysticism regarding the communion of saints. The

Fletchers used the term 'saint' sometimes to refer to one who had experienced salvation,[38] at other times to refer to one who lived as a model Christian to be emulated,[39] or again, to refer to since-departed holy ones.[40]

Both of the Fletchers were from strongly Protestant backgrounds and had Huguenot connections which moulded their negative conceptions of Catholicism. As a parish priest, John Fletcher found himself in what was the Catholic centre of the coalfield and clashed with his Catholic parishioners.[41] On several occasions he preached against their doctrines, circulating handwritten tracts including statements against the idea that saints are in any way mediators, and, over and against the Catholic belief (as he stated it) in 'the worship of the host, and of angels, saints, images, and relics', that Christians yet living have no recourse to 'the virgin Mary, St. Peter, and departed saints in general'.[42] 'As to prayer', he continued, 'it is perverted by them, being ridiculously addressed to saints and angels'.[43] In another sermon he explained, 'If saints could save us, it would be rather living saints than dead ones. It is well for the Virgin Mary and the saints, that they know nothing of the prayers which poor superstitious Christians address to them ... the very thought of such a piece of idolatry ... would damp all the joy in heaven.'[44]

Mary Fletcher's sentiments concerning Catholicism were more mild-tempered, perhaps because the constituency which had been so strong in the 1760s had waned by the time of her arrival in the parish in 1782. Her kindly correspondence with the Catholic priest in Madeley between 1806 and 1808 reveals moderation in her relationships with Catholics she knew personally, acknowledgement of their shared faith despite divergences in doctrine. The correspondence also reveals a sense of remorse for the loss at the Reformation of some means of promoting pious devotion amongst true believers, and, following Wesley, she expressed her appreciation for the holiness she saw in the lives of de Renty, Ignatius of Loyola, and Xavier. Furthermore, she lamented the dissolution of the monasteries.[45] Her biographer, the preacher Henry Moore (1751–1844), appended an edited version of this letter to his 1817 *Life of Mrs Mary Fletcher*, leaving in the comment regarding de Renty, but excising the references to Ignatius and Xavier. Nor did he share her comments on religious houses. In reference to the community at Leytonstone, he warned the reader that: 'Those ... who form and govern such a house, should beware of any approach to the confinement of the *Cloister*.'[46]

These posthumous attempts to tweak Mary Fletcher's opinions were at odds with her own position, for, although avowedly Anglican, she saw little problem in making some small attempt at moving beyond 'standard' Protestant rhetoric. She articulated her views systematically in a treatise on *Communion with Happy Spirits*.[47] Her purpose for writing was to explain her hope for continued communion with the spirit of her late husband.[48] But she also wanted also to exhort those to whom she continued to minister in an aspect of spirituality which she felt lacked proper treatment. The work was a piece of speculative theology, based on deductive reasoning, and borrowed in several parts from John Wesley's own thoughts on the subject.[49] The two key elements of Fletcher's argument were: (1) belief not only that saints departed have access to the thoughts of saints still living, but that they are indeed 'concerned for the dear fellow-pilgrims whom they have left behind'; and that they 'may still see and serve the souls committed to [their] care ... to act as ministering spirits'; and (2) belief that, after the pattern exemplified by Elisha's request for a double portion of Elijah's spirit, some believers may be granted a special perception of 'the spirits of just men made perfect', and that this blessing may be more normative for the sanctified Christian life than exceptional.[50]

Like many Protestants, Mary Fletcher returned repeatedly to the idea that the early Church had espoused beliefs that were later lost and that ought to be reclaimed. 'It is probable', she wrote,

> [that] the primitive church knew [of communion between saints on earth and saints in heaven] perfectly; but ... When *they left their first love*, they ... ran into the false humility of the worship of angels, instead of worshipping God only, and adoring Him for the angelic ministry. Perhaps some communion with departed spirits caused the first step into the egregious errors of the Papists; and man ever prone to extremes, knew not now to throw away the abuse, without throwing away the use of this heavenly secret.[51]

In a similar statement, drawing upon Swedenborg, John Fletcher had written that: 'It is certain, that if Believers were more detached from earthly things & more concentred [sic] in $X^t$ by Faith, they wou'd converse $w^h$ angels & $w^h$ the spirits of departed [sai]nts, as the Patriarchs & first Xtians were accustom'd to do.'[52]

## Nineteenth-century continuity and revision

In 1870 the novelist Wilkie Collins (1824–89), wrote of a character who 'went down to the little room ... which had once been her brother's study. There she ... took some books from a shelf ... The books were the Bible, a volume of Methodist sermons, and a set of collected Memoirs of Methodist saints.'[53] Although a fictional reference, this suggests that at least an informal collection of Methodist saints was conceivable. However, the lack of formal mechanisms meant that Methodist hagiography developed haphazardly as they sought to tell their story by pointing to eclectic collections of others who epitomised their ideals.[54] This had been initiated by Wesley, but was sustained in the succeeding generation in the *AM*, and in the biographical anthologies compiled by Charles Atmore (1759–1826), Thomas Jackson (1783–1873), and others.[55] Yet these early hagiographical writings were only the first indication of popular acceptance of a Methodist hagiology. Because there was neither an official canon nor the structures to create one, the question of who was to be included was always under negotiation. It is because of their longstanding and frequently acknowledged status as 'Methodist saints' that John and Mary Fletcher might offer the best view into that process.

Running through Wesley's edited *Lives* was a sense that sanctity is possible and desirable in every age, and that the Church's identity should be shaped by the practice of piety and experience of sanctification in every generation. Perhaps this was why he removed the sanctoral calendar from the Sunday service, and encouraged the reading of the lives in the societies: that is, to prioritise present sanctification over the celebration of those departed with whom we have no communication. But a by-product of that perspective was a functional disconnect between the hundreds of accounts gathered by Wesley and the fact that there was no clear form of expression similar to the calendar with its feasts and festivals.[56] It is paradoxical, given the way early Methodism has been pointed to by some as developing a heightened individualism, that rather than highlighting individuals, with their different callings, such practices dissolved lives into a generalised formula for the experience of (1) conversion (2), sanctification, and (3) a happy death.[57]

In the face of claims by Anglo- and Roman Catholics there were always those who wanted to repossess those saints who were believed to belong to the Universal Church. One Methodist, writing on Francis of Assisi in 1895, reflected that 'There are treasures of great price hidden away in the kalendar [sic] of the Church of Rome. Herein is a great loss, and also a great wrong; for saintly lives, which are the common possession of all Christendom, have ... been appropriated by an ecclesiastical monopoly.' Like many other Protestants, the same author was simultaneously critical of the hagiographical glosses that had entered over the centuries into the *Acta Sanctorum*.[58] What was required was a new edition, written by someone with 'an intimate knowledge of contemporary history, an expert familiarity with the ways of hagiography, and an exact discriminating skill in dealing with evidence', in order to 'make real to us the times and circumstances in which these children of God lived, and help us to see and hear them as they were seen and heard by those among whom their lives were passed'.[59] T. Alexander Seed (d. 1926), summarised both the dilemma and what he hoped was the means to reclaim sainthood as genuinely universal:

> Cardinal Newman was neither well informed nor happily inspired when ... he declared that 'Catholics have the idea before them which a Protestant nation has not; they have the idea of a Saint; they believe they realize the existence of those rare servants of God who rise up from time to time in the Catholic Church like angels in disguise, and shed around them a light as they walk on their heavenward way.' It would, of course, be as ignorant as it would be illiberal to deny to a church that is still illustrious with a galaxy of names as bright as those of St. Teresa, Madame Guyon, and the two Saints Francis the advantage of their shining piety. But, in presence of the saintly pair whose lives we are about to sketch [i.e. John and Mary Fletcher], it is impossible to concede to the Romish Communion a monopoly in the production and possession of saints.[60]

Seed's premise was that Methodists *had* in fact been developing 'the idea of a Saint' (with a capital 'S'). They had been developing it in ways that looked very much like what Christians in all ages had done. The first step was the use of biographies which were disseminated not only in print, but through Methodist connexionalism. Methodist saints, argued Seed, developed organically, manifesting as they did so the ancient traditions of gathering relics, going on pilgrimages, erecting monuments, dedicating memorials, and creating likenesses, all of which mutually reinforced hagiographical biographies. As Clyde Binfield has simply but keenly stated, the 'nineteenth century was hagiography's high noon. All sorts of men and women were candidates for treatment.'[61] Methodists were no exception.

## The Fletchers in hagiography

The earliest biography of John Fletcher was a compilation of two letters written by his widow immediately after his death, which she described as 'some Account of a Life the most Angelic I have ever known'.[62] Fletcher's second biographer was John Wesley, who wrote a eulogistic sermon two months later.[63] Subsequently Wesley wrote a fuller biography, the only one he authored himself, in 1786.[64] This was supplemented by a series of biographical *Notes* which Joshua Gilpin (c. 1755–1828), a clergyman from a neighbouring parish, appended to a work in which Fletcher listed the pious traits of Saint Paul.[65] Gilpin's *Notes* became a dual hagiography, recommending both Saint Paul and 'St' Fletcher. In 1804 a fourth *Life* was printed by a leading preacher and editor of the *Methodist Magazine* (*MM*), Joseph Benson (1749–1821).[66] An indicator of the way in which Fletcher was being used to shape a distinct Methodist identity was the publication of yet another *Life* by the Anglican Robert Cox (fl. c. 1810–35), an evangelical who attempted to highlight Fletcher's churchmanship as a corrective.[67] Benson's *Life* was the most popular and was reprinted throughout the nineteenth century.[68] Wesley and Gilpin were reprinted, although with less frequency, while Cox's *Life* was translated into German and French soon after its initial publication.[69]

Mary Fletcher's *Life* appeared in 1817 in a heavily edited version by Moore, composed largely of extracts from her journals, correspondence, and autobiographical notes.[70] Moore's preface stated that this was to be seen 'not as a common religious Biography, but as the record of an uncommon work of God ... not ... expected to fall short of any account which has come forth in the great revival of Scriptural Christianity in our day'.[71] Those who had read and appreciated the lives of Madame Guyon, Chantel, and Bourignon, 'will be glad to see a life in the Protestant Church superior to any of them'.[72] Moore's edition was frequently reprinted throughout the nineteenth century, and was the basis of treatments of Mary Fletcher in numerous anthologies.[73]

Numerous hagiographical anecdotes are to be found amongst the 'lives' of the Fletchers. Many are the accounts by Mary of God's providence in supplying the needs of her household and orphanage. One tells of how she had set aside insufficient money in order to give to the poor out of her income. She found herself weakening, not having sustenance enough. Yet, unwilling to take from what she had 'set apart', she prayed, laying her 'case before the Lord for divine direction', and a few days after, funds which she needed arrived unsolicited.[74] Perhaps even more frequently recounted in Methodist circles, especially in the earlier nineteenth century, were stories of Mrs Fletcher's dreams. As Phyllis Mack has so lucidly shown, dreams 'were recorded and analysed because they validated an individual's vocation or helped move him from one stage to another' in the spiritual life cycle.[75] Like Saint Anthony in the desert, Mrs Fletcher fought evil spirits in her dreams, and thus prayed before sleep that her mind would be stayed on God, and thus strengthened against the devil.[76] More frequently cited, though considered similarly as a sign of God's providence, were visits to Mary Fletcher by her late husband. Thomas Cooper (1760–1832) wrote about how Mrs Fletcher had told him during his time Madeley of how John had 'promised ... [that] he would always attend her as her guardian angel; and after his decease, she informed me of the certainty she had of his being near her'. 'Knowing that she possessed strong intellectual powers, and was no enthusiast,' Cooper added, slightly apologetically, 'I could not disbelieve.'[77]

Another 'miraculous' anecdote explains how John Fletcher had entered the pulpit, but could not recall the text or the sermon he had prepared. So, he preached extempore upon the first lesson for the day, which happened to be the third chapter of Daniel. 'I found in doing it', he wrote, 'such an extraordinary assistance from God ... that I supposed there must be some special [i.e. providential] cause for it.' He asked his congregants to report to him any effect the sermon had, and a few days following, one parishioner related that both text and sermon had been efficacious. Her irreligious husband had threatened her with death if she continued attendance at the parish church, saying that if she went once more, he would slit her throat and throw her into the furnace when she returned home. Screwing up her courage, she went anyway, and was emboldened by the sermon on the three faithful servants who were themselves thrown into the furnace of Nebuchadnezzar. She returned home to see her husband on his knees in the house, praying for forgiveness, and he had 'continued diligently seeking the Lord ever since'.[78]

## Pilgrimage and relics

Madeley is at the heart of the East Shropshire coalfield, a centre of early industrialisation which drew visitors from far and wide, especially after the construction of the first iron bridge there in 1779–81. Tourists from America, Europe, and even New Zealand visited what the writer and local businessman Charles Hulbert (1778–1857) thought 'the most extraordinary district in the world', and they included a number of religious visitors, even during the Fletchers' lifetimes, precedents for what in the nineteenth century would be described by Methodists and evangelicals themselves as 'pilgrimages'.[79] Between John's death in 1785 and Mary's in 1815, Madeley became known as the sacred place not only of his former labours, but of her ministry in its own right. Wesleyan preachers considered appointment to the circuit that included Madeley a special blessing. 'I was honoured', wrote one, 'with a particular intimacy with that blessed woman, Mrs. Fletcher; and I felt it a great privilege to go to Madeley in my turn to preach.'[80] Thomas Blanshard (c. 1765–1824), appointed in 1796, compared peaceable Madeley under Mrs Fletcher to the biblical land of Goshen where the Israelites were protected from the storms.[81] When Sarah Hawkes (1759–1832) stopped at Madeley on a visit to her family elsewhere, she had originally been drawn by John Fletcher's legacy, but it was Mrs Fletcher's hospitality and ministry over the course of the three-hour visit which became one of Mrs Hawkes's 'choicest favours'.[82] By the end of the nineteenth century, Madeley was known to some by the ironic eponym the 'Mecca of Methodism'.[83] The locally born preacher William Tranter (1778–1879) wrote more seriously that Madeley had become 'the rendezvous for religious persons and purposes … a privileged and honoured place; a sort of Christian Jerusalem'.[84] George Mather (d. 1888) described it as 'a place hallowed by the saintly lives and labours of John and Mary Fletcher'.[85] All of this served to reinforce belief in Madeley as a place of sanctity, as accounts of pilgrimages were shared in correspondence, and written for publication amongst Methodists in England and abroad.

Some pilgrims even made their way to Nyon, Switzerland, to pay homage to Fletcher's birthplace. 'It is endeared to Englishmen as having given birth to Fletcher of Madeley – a name connected with all that is pure and exalted in piety, and amiable and disinterested in benevolence.'[86] In the same letter, the visitor related a conversation he had with one of his travelling companions, a French-speaking Catholic woman, who had asked him if he was a Catholic himself, whereupon he launched into a diatribe on the corruptions of Rome. Ironically, amongst its offences against true religion, he listed pilgrimages, and idolatrous worship of the saints. There is no indication that he saw any incongruity between his own visit and his criticisms. Others made their ways to Mrs Fletcher's homes at Leytonstone and Leeds. These accounts exhibit the tension that persisted between the Methodist impulse to collect and cherish the relics of their saints and their negative views of similar practices in Catholicism. There was not necessarily a single Methodist view of this. While some wrote articles for the *MM* detailing the absurdities of Roman 'relic-mongers', others wrote unselfconsciously of their experiences in visiting the home of the Fletchers.[87] Still others appreciated Methodist relics as mnemonic aids, such as in the article concerning 'curios' at the Mission House in 1897, which advertised the collection and explained its rationale.[88]

Mary Tooth (1777–1843), who lived with Mary Fletcher from the mid-1790s, was until her death guardian of the reliquary that comprised the Madeley vicarage, church, and churchyard. Benjamin Gregory recorded that on his visit she 'seemed proud to show me all the Fletcheriana: the lanthorn which he used in his night-visits to the sick, a curious piece of Continental mechanism, etc'.[89] It was the holiness of the Fletchers that drew the revivalist preacher and founder of the American Holiness Movement Phoebe Palmer (1807–74) to Madeley in 1862, where she received several relics, including 'an original letter of Mrs. Mary Fletcher … the Testament of Mr. and Mrs. Fletcher, one used by her in her closet devotions, doubtless as it is marked with her own hand in many places … Also, a manuscript-copy of one of Mr. Fletcher's sermons, never published'.[90] Although various relics of other eminent Methodists were collected and valued – as for example those listed in the catalogue of the Museum of Methodist Antiquities in 1889, including numerous items once owned by the Wesleys, Adam Clarke (1762–1832), and other early Methodist leaders – the Fletchers seem to have given rise to particularly substantial collections.[91] When the various extant accounts are tallied, they include books, locks of hair belonging to both, Mary Fletcher's purple cloak, John Fletcher's pulpit, a needle case and materials for sewing, manuscripts, the parish registers, John Fletcher's razor, a handkerchief, and several other items.[92]

## Monuments, memorials and likenesses

The most significant monument to the Fletchers is their above-ground cast-iron tomb, the single grave in which they were buried along with two other members of their household. John's epitaph was penned by Mary, and was cast into the original lid, her own being engraved beneath it thirty years later. Cast-iron tombs or iron graveside accoutrements were by no means uncommon in Coalbrookdale, although the size of the tomb, the elaborate inscription, and its location near the front of the churchyard are relatively unique. Like most Protestants, Methodists were censorious of Catholic, Buddhist, Hindu, and Muslim worship at shrines, and thus avoided the word in reference to graves or monuments. Yet descriptions by visitors to the Fletchers' grave and excitement over seeing their relics betrays the shrine-like way in which they were viewed. Benjamin Gregory wrote of the significance of his visit in 1843:

> In the evening, with 'clear shining after rain,' [I] made my longed for pilgrimage to Fletcher's tomb – with emotions differing widely from those which I had gazed upon the grave of Shakespeare. In Madeley churchyard I felt conscience-stricken and humbled to the dust. There is no character which so realizes my ideal of *sainthood* as that of Fletcher, or for which I cultivate a reverence so profound ... I felt guilty in approaching Fletcher's tomb without having prepared for the solemnity by meditation and prayer.[93]

For Methodists reading his account he made clear that 'A pilgrimage to the grave of a genuine *Scriptural* saint, as a means of grace, is not without countenance ... but to ordain it as a *penance*, or to make the sepulchre a *shrine*, is most preposterous.'[94]

Wesleyan chapels were not commonly named after saints. But there were exceptions. The one built in 1841 at Madeley eventually became 'John Fletcher Methodist Church', and another constructed in 1877 was dedicated as 'Mary Fletcher Memorial Chapel'.[95] Both, however, appear to have been seen as memorials and not shrines, being mentioned only rarely in accounts of visits there. If more space were available, much could be said regarding the various paintings of the Fletchers – there is not one of them together, for instance – but what is noteworthy for our purposes is how portraits were copied, sold, bought, collected, revered.[96] That art also includes pictures of the old tithe barn where Mrs Fletcher used to preach, pictures of Fletcher's chapels, and even an engraving of the couple's bedroom, albeit without the saintly pair, whose portraits are displayed on the wall.

## Conclusion

'There were saints in John Fletcher's day and he was one of them.'[97] This bald statement by a commentator in 1937 reflects the legacy of the previous century. Even if the informal doctrine drawn from the so-called 'Wesleyan Standards' suggested that all true Christians were saints, whether living or departed, as the stories of those who were considered eminently pious amongst the early Methodists were fashioned, edited, told, and retold, some became perceived as saints in a more particular sense. Narratives of their lives became unapologetically – and often intentionally – hagiographical. Anecdotes demonstrating the working of God's providence, including 'miracles', answers to prayers, and spiritual combat, served two purposes. In the first instance, following Wesley's intention of publishing biographies of 'some persons, eminent for understanding and piety', they served to bolster 'experimental religion' by providing examples against which one could test one's own religious experience, also emulating how they charted their experience in diaries, journals, and other autobiographical materials, and sharing them in societies and classes.[98] Yet, a secondary result of publishing the lives of such exemplars was the cultural (although not doctrinal) adoption of certain persons as pre-eminent holy ones in the communion of saints. This was not just a top-down endeavour: Methodist publishing houses were so prolific because there was such a strong demand for such lives by eager purchasers and readers. While nineteenth-century Catholics and Anglo-Catholics were happy to claim hagiology for their respective traditions, Methodists were already constructing it at a popular level. Seed called the Fletchers 'typical Methodist saints'.[99] To list just a few other titles from the later nineteenth and early twentieth centuries is to underline the extent to which they had been successfully established amongst the saints of Methodism.[100]

## Notes

Note on abbreviations: JF and MF refer to John Fletcher and Mary Fletcher. *AM*, *MM*, and *WMM* refer to the *Arminian Magazine* (1778), retitled the *Methodist Magazine* (1798), and the *Wesleyan Methodist Magazine* (1823). Two editions of John Wesley's *Works* are cited: Frank Baker, *et al.* (eds), *The Bicentennial Edition of the Works of John Wesley*, 20 vols to date (Nashville: Abingdon, 1984–), hereafter *Works* (BE); and Thomas Jackson (ed.), *The Works of the Rev. John Wesley*, 14 vols (3rd edn, London: Wesleyan Conference Office, 1872), hereafter *Works* (J). John Telford (ed.), *The Letters of the Rev. John Wesley*, 8 vols (London: Epworth, 1931), is hereafter *JWL*. The Fletcher-Tooth Collection at the Methodist Archives and Research Centre, John Rylands University Library of Manchester, is hereafter MARC.

1 See Isabel Rivers, *Reason, Grace, and Sentiment: A Study of the Language of Religion and Ethics in England, 1660–1780*, Volume 1, *Whichcote to Wesley* (Cambridge: Cambridge University Press, 1991), pp. 214–21.
2 Kenneth A. Wilson, 'The Devotional Relationships and Interaction Between the Spirituality of John Wesley, the Methodist Societies and the Book of Common Prayer' (PhD thesis, Queen's University, Belfast, 1984); cf. Randy L. Maddox, *Responsible Grace: John Wesley's Practical Theology* (Nashville: Kingswood Books, 1994), pp. 205–9.
3 William Myles, *A Chronological History of the People Called Methodists* (4th edn, London: Thomas Cordeux, 1813), pp. 171–7.

4 Karen B. Westerfield Tucker, 'Mainstream liturgical developments', in William J. Abraham and James E. Kirby (eds), *The Oxford Handbook of Methodist Studies* (Oxford: Oxford University Press, 2009), p. 299.
5 See Isabel Rivers, 'John Wesley and religious biography', *Bulletin of the John Rylands Library*, 85 (2003), 209–21.
6 David Robert Wilson, 'Church and Chapel: Pastoral Ministry in Madeley, c. 1760–1785, with Special Reference to John Fletcher' (PhD thesis, University of Manchester, 2010).
7 See Peter S. Forsaith (ed.), *Unexampled Labours: Letters of the Revd John Fletcher to Leaders in the Evangelical Revival* (Peterborough: Epworth, 2008).
8 Fletcher's *Works* were first published as bound sets between 1788 and 1796. The first collected *Works* with an index were edited by Joseph Benson and published in nine volumes in 1809–13. Subsequent editions were reprinted throughout the nineteenth century, the latest edition appearing in America in 1891.
9 Peter S. Forsaith, 'Wesley's designated successor', *Proceedings of the Wesley Historical Society*, 42 (1979), 69–74; Wilson, 'Church and Chapel', pp. 163–82.
10 See Grace Lawless Lee, *The Story of the Bosanquets* (Canterbury: Phillimore, 1966), p. 20.
11 Henry Moore, *The Life of Mrs. Mary Fletcher, Consort and Relict of the Rev. John Fletcher*, 2 vols (Birmingham: J. Peart and Son, 1817), I: pp. 1–14.
12 Paul Wesley Chilcote, *John Wesley and the Women Preachers of Early Methodism* (Metuchen: Scarecrow Press, 1991); David R. Wilson, '"Thou shal[t] walk with me in white": afterlife and vocation in the ministry of Mary Bosanquet Fletcher', *Wesley and Methodist Studies*, 1 (2009), 71–85; Wilson and Phyllis Mack, 'Mary Fletcher's Bible', in Scott Mandelbrote and Michael Ledger-Lomas (eds), *Dissent and the Bible in Britain, 1650–1950* (Oxford: Oxford University Press, 2013), pp. 57–84.
13 Laurence Hull Stookey, 'The Wesleys and the saints', *Liturgy*, 5 (1985), 77–81; Eamon Duffy, 'Wesley and the Counter-Reformation', in Jane Garnett and Colin Matthew (eds), *Revival and Religion Since 1700: Essays for John Walsh* (London: Hambledon Press, 1993), pp. 1–19; Geoffrey Wainwright, *Methodists in Dialogue* (Nashville: Kingswood, 1995), pp. 237–49.
14 Maddox, *Responsible Grace*, p. 206; Wainwright, *Methodists*, p. 238.
15 Quoted in Wainwright, *Methodists*, p. 238.
16 Maddox, *Responsible Grace*, p. 208, n. 92.
17 John Wesley, *A Word to a Protestant* (8th edn, London: W. Strahan, 1745), p. 3; *Works* (BE), III: pp. 103–14.
18 *JWL*, VI: pp. 26–7.
19 *Works* (J), X: p. 97.
20 See Geordan Hammond, *John Wesley in America: Restoring Primitive Christianity* (Oxford: Oxford University Press, 2014).
21 *JWL*, VI: pp. 26–7; cf. *Works* (BE), IV: p. 195.
22 Hammond, *Wesley in America*, pp. 54–64.
23 Wainwright, *Methodists*, 244–5.
24 Maddox, *Responsible Grace*, 208.
25 Edgardo Antonio Colón-Emeric, 'Perfection in Dialogue: An Ecumenical Encounter Between Wesley and Aquinas' (PhD thesis, Duke University, 2007), p. 126.
26 *Works* (BE), IV: p. 14.

27 Geordan Hammond, 'John Wesley and "Imitating" Christ', *Wesleyan Theological Journal* 45 (2010), 198.
28 *Works* (BE), IV: pp. 399–400; see Romans 1: 7.
29 See Phyllis Mack, *Heart Religion in the British Enlightenment: Gender and Emotion in Early Methodism* (Cambridge: Cambridge University Press, 2008).
30 John Wesley (ed.), *A Christian Library: Consisting of Extracts from, and Abridgements of, the Choicest Pieces of Practical Divinity*, 50 vols (Bristol: Farley, 1749–55). The Fletchers owned a complete set which is still extant at MARC: MAW Fl. 61–110: see D. R. Wilson, *An Annotated Catalogue of the John and Mary Fletcher Library* (forthcoming).
31 For titles, see Rivers, 'John Wesley'.
32 *Works* (BE), I: pp. 376–97.
33 *Ibid.*, IX: pp. 68–75.
34 'The experience and travels of Mr. Freeborn Garretson, minister of the gospel, in North America', *AM* (1794), 3.
35 Rivers, *Reason, Grace, and Sentiment*, p. 221.
36 See *AM* (1780), 22, 533.
37 John Wesley, *A Sermon Preached on Occasion of the Death of the Rev. Mr. John Fletcher* (London: J. Paramore, 1785), p. 31.
38 John William Fletcher, *The Works of the Rev. John Fletcher*, 10 vols (London: John Mason, 1859–60), IX: pp. 54, 130.
39 *Ibid.*, IX: p. 151.
40 *Ibid.*, VIII: p. 493.
41 See Wilson, 'Church and Chapel', pp. 250–65.
42 Fletcher, *Works*, VIII: p. 493; see also John Fletcher, 'An Answer to Popish Quibbles', MARC: MAM Fl. 18/11/1,
43 Fletcher, *Works*, VIII: p. 494.
44 *Ibid.*, VIII: pp. 418–19.
45 MF to John Austin Reeve [1808], MARC: MAM Fl. 37/4/17.
46 Moore, *Mary Fletcher*, I: pp. 24–5n.
47 Mary Fletcher, *Thoughts on Communion with Happy Spirits* (Birmingham: William Rickman King [n.d.]). Moore incorporated it into *Mary Fletcher*, II: pp. 3–25.
48 Mary Bosanquet Fletcher, 'Some Thoughts on the Comunion [sic] of Spirits', 15 December 1785. MARC: MAM Fl. 12/2/10.
49 Primarily 'Sermon 71: On Good Angels', in *Works* (BE), III: pp. 3–15, dated January 1783, and originally published in *AM* (1783), 6–13, 61–6. See also 'Sermon 115: Dives and Lazarus', in *Works* (BE), IV: pp. 4–18, and 'Sermon 132: On Faith', in *Works* (BE), IV: pp. 187–200.
50 Moore, *Mary Fletcher*, II: pp. 24–5.
51 *Ibid.*, p. 25.
52 JF to Rev. Mr Bouverot, [c. 1783], MARC: MAM Fl. 36/5.
53 Wilkie Collins, *Man and Wife*, 3 vols (London: F. S. Ellis, 1870), III: p. 224.
54 Clifton F. Guthrie, 'Why a sanctoral cycle? Or, are we ready for Methodist hagiography?', in particular Guthrie's examination of relics, memorials, and calendars, is a starting place for what follows. See www.materialreligion.org/journal/saints.html, accessed 1 January 2015.

55 See Rivers, 'John Wesley'.
56 Although see Robert Cubitt Nightingale, 'The Methodist saints and martyrs', *Contemporary Review*, 72 (1897), 378–9.
57 See D. Bruce Hindmarsh, *The Evangelical Conversion Narrative: Spiritual Autobiography in Early Modern England* (Oxford: Oxford University Press, 2005).
58 See especially 'Introduction', pp. 1–3, 14–16, in this volume.
59 G. Stringer Rowe, 'St. Francis of Assisi', *WMM* (1895), 103.
60 Thomas Alexander Seed, *John and Mary Fletcher: Typical Methodist Saints* (London: Charles H. Kelly, 1906), pp. 9–10.
61 Clyde Binfield (ed.), *Sainthood Revisioned: Studies in Hagiography and Biography* (Sheffield: Sheffield Academic Press, 1995), p. 13.
62 Mary Fletcher, *A Letter to Mons. H. L. De la Flechere* (London: G. Clark, 1786).
63 Wesley, *Sermon on the Death of John Fletcher*.
64 John Wesley, *A Short Account of the Life and Death of the Rev. John Fletcher* (London: J. Paramore, 1786).
65 'Letter DXXXVII: From Mrs. Fletcher, to the Rev. J. Wesley [7 July 1782]', *AM* (1790), 390–1. Gilpin's *Notes* were appended to later editions of Wesley's *Short Account*.
66 Joseph Benson, *The Life of the Rev. John W. de la Flechere* (London: Conference Office, 1804).
67 R. Cox, *The Life of the Rev. John William Fletcher* (London: J. Butterworth, 1822).
68 French translations were published at Lausanne in 1826 and on Jersey in 1845, and in German in 1833.
69 Robert Cox, *Vie Du Rd. J. G. De La Fléchère, Curé de Madeley, en Shropshire* (2nd edn, Paris: Servier, 1827); Robert Cox, *Das Leben des Ehrwürdigen Joh. Wilh. Fletscher* (Frankfurt: H. C. Brönner, 1833).
70 See David R. Wilson, 'A Sermon by Mary Fletcher (Née Bosanquet), on Exodus 20, preached at Madeley in the parish vicarage on the evening of Whitsunday, 8 June 1794', *Wesley and Methodist Studies*, 2 (2010), 115–22.
71 Moore, *Mary Fletcher*, I: p.vi.
72 Ibid., I: p. xxiii.
73 John Hodson, *A Widow Indeed: A Sermon Occasioned by the Lamented Death of Mrs. Fletcher* (Wednesbury: J. Booth, 1816); Samuel Burder, *Memoirs of Eminently Pious Women of the British Empire* (1823; Philadelphia: J. J. Woodward, 1827), pp. 704–30; Zechariah Taft, *Biographical Sketches of the Lives and Public Ministry of Various Holy Women*, 2 vols (London: Kershaw, 1825), I: pp. 19–40; D. L. Child, *Good Wives* (Boston, MA: Carter, Hendee, 1833), pp. 43–74; Thomas E. Gill, *The Life of Mrs. Fletcher* (London: Easingwold, 1845); Stephen Cox, *'Holiness Unto the Lord.' Illustrated in the Character and Live of Miss Bosanquet, of Leytonstone* (London: Wesleyan Conference Office, 1876); W. H. Withrow, *Makers of Methodism* (London: Charles H. Kelly, 1903), pp. 124–45.
74 W. Woodall, 'The providence of God asserted', *MM* (1817), 526–8.
75 Mack, *Heart Religion*, p. 229.
76 Ibid., pp. 240–1.
77 'Memoir of the late Rev. Thomas Cooper', *WMM* (1835), 83.
78 John William Fletcher, *The Furious Butcher Humbled: A True and Remarkable Story as Related*

by the Late Rev. Mr. Fletcher, Vicar of Madely [sic], in Shropshire (London: A. Paris, [1795?]), p. 8.
79  See e.g. Benjamin Gregory, 'Methodism in the middle of the century: chapter viii. Methodism in the midlands fifty years ago (continued)', WMM (1893), 698.
80  'Thomas Cooper', 83.
81  Cited in Henry W. Shrewsbury, 'A Methodist shrine', WMM (1896), 573.
82  'Biographical sketch: Mrs. Hawkes. By the Editor', The Scottish Christian Herald, third series, 1 (1839), 20–1.
83  Luke Tyerman, Wesley's Designated Successor: The Life, Letters and Literary Labours of the Rev. John William Fletcher (London: Hodder and Stoughton, 1882), p. 505. See also Edward J. Sturdee, 'A visit to the "Mecca of Methodism"', Annals of Church Pastoral-Aid Work Series, 5 (London: Church Pastoral-Aid Society [n.d.]); James John Hissey, A Leisurely Tour in England (London: Macmillan, 1913), pp. 221–9.
84  William Tranter, 'Methodism in Madeley', WMM (1837), 900–3.
85  George Mather, 'To the Editor of the Wesleyan-Methodist Magazine', WMM (1862), 457–9.
86  Daniel Wilson, 'Travels on the continent of Europe … in the summer of 1823', in Jonathan Going, et al. (eds), The Christian Library, 8 vols (New York: Thomas George, Jr, 1836), VII: pp. 87–123.
87  'Popery', WMM (1840), 33.
88  William G. Beardmore, 'Curios and pictures at the Mission House', WMM (1897), 756–63.
89  Gregory, 'Methodism in the midlands', 699.
90  Phoebe Palmer, 'Letter from Mrs. Palmer [14 May 1861]', Mansfield and Austa M. French (eds), Beauty of Holiness in Heart and Life, 13 vols (New York: M. French, 1861), XII: p. 229.
91  Edward G. Harmer, 'The Museum of Methodist Antiquities', WMM (1889), 933–7.
92  See e.g. MARC: MAM Fl. 1/4/8; Tyerman, Wesley's Designated Successor, p. 505.
93  Gregory, 'Methodism in the midlands', 699.
94  Ibid., 698.
95  Caroline Churchill, 'Birthplace of Mary Fletcher' The Christian Miscellany, and Family Visiter [sic], second series, 21 (1875), 99. The building has since been torn down.
96  For an excellent treatment of this subject, see Peter S. Forsaith, 'Portraits of John Fletcher of Madeley and their artists', Proceedings of the Wesley Historical Society, 47 (1990), 187–201.
97  [Paul S. Rees], The Valiant Vicar of Madeley (University Park: John Fletcher College, 1937), p. 1.
98  John Wesley, 'To the Reader', AM (1779), unpaginated front matter.
99  Seed, John and Mary Fletcher.
100  Eldon Ralph Fuhrman, 'John Fletcher: Saint of the Eighteenth Century' (unpublished paper); Georges Gallienne, 'Jean-Guillaume de la Fléchère. Un saint du Pays de Vaud. 1729–1785', Le Chrétien Évangélique: Revue Religieuse de la Suisse Romande, 32 (1889), 108–18; Jabez Marrat, John Fletcher: Saint and Scholar (London: Charles H. Kelly, 1901).

## 12

# William Wilberforce and 'the Saints'

*Roshan Allpress*

IN HIS 1837 FUNERAL sermon for Thomas Babington (1758–1836), one of the inner circle of the 'Clapham Sect', William Acworth (1803–99), Vicar of Rothley, numbered his late friend among

> those, whose characters are so resplendent in holiness, who in their tempers and lives so visibly reflect the image of Christ, who enjoy such decisive proofs of the Divine favour, … they are denominated by St. Paul, 'saints in light,' because even in this world they grope not in thick darkness, as the rest of mankind, but have the light of life.[1]

Venerated in death, Babington was also among those parliamentarians derided and admired in life as 'the Saints', and held in high regard by successive generations of evangelicals.[2] During their lifetimes these reputations served the political and ecclesiastical ends of the Saints, and after their deaths came under the management of their heirs and protégés.[3] While speaking of evangelical 'saints' may seem a misnomer, the persistence of the language of sainthood in the veneration or derision of these particular evangelical personalities is noticeable, but has rarely been analysed. The central argument of this chapter is that the history of the reputation of this cohort of Saints and their associates during the first half of the nineteenth century illuminates the emergence of a new kind of distinctive, evangelical hagiography – that of the 'practical' or 'useful' saint. This new figure of sainthood, epitomised by William Wilberforce (1759–1833), was construed as a mediator between Britons and the world, and, equally importantly, between evangelical communities and processes of historical change. With particular reference to funeral sermons and other post-mortem memorials, and by juxtaposing these with the historiographical sense represented by the *Essays in Ecclesiastical Biography* of Sir James Stephen (1789–1859), this chapter seeks to go beyond the frames of politics and filial piety that have characterised recent treatments of the Clapham Sect to trace the development of the ideal of the 'practical saint' from its eighteenth-century precursors to its fruition in the 1830s and 1840s. In doing so, it represents an attempt to historicise the hagiographies with which accounts of the historiography of the Saints usually begin.[4]

## History and eulogy

In his landmark article on Joseph Milner's *History of the Church of Christ* (1794–1809), John Walsh underscored the importance of Milner's historiographical vision to evangelical identity.[5] According to Walsh, Milner (1745–97) aimed to trace the shining thread of real or practical Christianity as it was manifested in the lives of pious individuals, and occasionally, 'by periodic effusions of the Spirit',[6] in pious communities, and so to demonstrate that the vital religion that many feared as innovation was in reality 'ancient orthodoxy'.[7] With such an emphasis on continuity, Milner 'had no real concept of change or adaptation', but rather presented a harmonious sequence of biographical portraits, interacting with wider society insofar as they faithfully represented the unchanging truths of the gospel.[8] This assessment of Milner's historiography can comfortably be extended to other contemporary evangelical writers on history, until at least the 1820s. In his *Review of Ecclesiastical History* (1770), for example, John Newton (1725–1807) traced the genealogy of 'a spiritual people, who ... retained so much of the primitive truth'.[9] Though Erasmus Middleton (bap. 1739, d. 1805) was less regular in his churchmanship, his *Biographia Evangelica* (1779–86) invoked the presence or absence of that evangelical favourite, 'the One Thing Needful', as indicating the health of the Church in any age.[10] Middleton's concluding narrative was of variations in adherence to the 'Doctrines of Grace', which inspired the Reformation, were preserved in the lives of a faithful remnant during the controversies and crises of the sixteenth and seventeenth centuries, and re-emerged in a 'lively promulgation' from the 1740s.[11] Similarly, in his 1829 *Christian Student*, Edward Bickersteth (1786–1850) traced what he called the 'rich vein of gold' that was 'the doctrine ... of justification by grace through faith'.[12] The emphasis was on the perseverance of the faithful despite periods of adversity, confusion or controversy.

To evangelical writers of the mid nineteenth century, such as Stephen, the relationship between historical societies and past lives was subtly but importantly different. Their portrayal of continuity was overlaid by the Victorian sense that their society was a qualitative improvement on that of their eighteenth-century antecedents.[13] Stephen's attribution of this improvement in large part to the activities of the members of the 'Evangelical Succession', and the 'Clapham Sect', exemplifies the historiographical positioning of the new evangelical hagiography. Evangelical saints were those whose characters were such that they modelled good living, 'even in this world', motivated by the inner life of the gospel. As Bruce Hindmarsh has argued, eighteenth-century evangelical writing reflected 'a high level of individuation', and was therefore not merely a reworking of the medieval hagiographical trope of the 'unity of sanctity'.[14] However, a further shift occurred during the early nineteenth century: pious individuals came to be re-imagined as historical agents. Emblematic of the transition to the hagiography of practical sainthood was Stephen's emphasis on a particular relationship between history and biography, which brought to the fore the transformative, or conversionary, nature of the relationship between the individual life and its wider social milieu.[15]

Unlike in Milner's account, and in the myriad of biographical and autobiographical conversion narratives, the beneficiaries of the pious life expanded beyond those edified by knowing or hearing of the saint, to include those on whose behalf the saint laboured in the past, and the community of historical heirs to this improving work. That is, the 'saint' was no longer only a synecdoche for the belief patterns and pious practice of the true Church, but also now for the historical change wrought by the gospel. This development explains in part the ambivalence that Stephen felt towards Robert Isaac (1802–57) and Samuel Wilberforce (1805–73) writing their father's *Life*. The duty as he saw it was not merely that of filial piety to curate memory, but the fuller historical task of explaining the causal link between religion and reform. As Stephen wrote in an 1833 letter to Babington,

> I can scarcely forego the Conviction that great Changes in human Society are impending, and that the greatest of all, will consist in a growing Conformity between the Laws of God and the Policy of man. I have often thought what noble a topic W. Wilberforce's Biographer would have, in tracing the Extent to which his Life and Labours had conduced to that result.[16]

At the conclusion of his essay on William Wilberforce, Stephen wrote that the task of 'ecclesiastical biography' was that of '*mémoires pour servir*, in the composition of an historical picture of English society, political and religious, as it existed in the most eventful epoch of the history of England, and as it clustered round one of its most admirable members'.[17] The evangelical hagiographical form was therefore by the late 1840s a site for the interaction between evangelical personal mythologies and British national narratives.

An illustration of the characteristics of this posited trope of evangelical hagiography can be seen by comparing two funeral sermons preached fifty years apart. In 1808, Thomas Scott (1747–1821), an evangelical clergyman and associate of the Saints, preached *The Duty and Advantage of Remembering Deceased Ministers*, on the death of his friend and co-religionist Thomas Pentycross (1748–1808).[18] In 1858, his grandson, John Scott (1809–65), also a beneficiary of Claphamite patronage, preached a sermon under the same title, on the death of his friend John King (1761–1858).[19] Because the younger Scott intentionally wrote his sermon with reference to that of his grandfather, it provides useful evidence of the change that had taken place. Thomas's emphasis, like Joseph Milner's, was on the unchanging gospel, quoting Jude 3 on 'the faith once delivered unto the saints'.[20] To be worthy of remembrance, the 'deceased minister', 'must speak the word of God ... [H]e must shew the tendency and effect of it in his own example'.[21] Congregations could most honour their departed pastor by recalling to mind his preaching and exhortation in the gospel, and 'imitate' him primarily in his acceptance of salvation.[22] By contrast, the focus of John's sermon was on the manner in which his subject had 'lived and laboured', the 'services rendered to this town by our departed friend ... [and the] many excellencies which adorned his character'.[23] In the earlier sermon, the personality of its subject was almost entirely denuded – replaced by a formalised delineation of the virtues of Christ and the excellencies of the gospel. In the latter, the personality of John King is expressed by listing his habits of life, and his various involvements in activism within the community. The reader learns that King read 'solid history, sterling biography, sound theology and poetry, and above all whatever tended more directly to elucidate or throw light on the meaning of God's Word'.[24] His activism was also to the fore, as worthy of emulation:

> Deep was the interest which he took in all our great Christian and Evangelical Societies. Ardently did he long, and fervently did he pray, for the diffusion of true religion throughout the world. When health permitted it, he was rarely absent from his post, at any of our public meetings. The Bible, Church Missionary, and Religious Tract Societies, with the Protestant Associations of various kinds, found in him a ready, able, and earnest advocate.[25]

The gospel was visibly present, but as the motivation behind lived habits and contextualised activism, not solely as unchanging doctrine. It is telling that John omitted the second part of Thomas Scott's biblical source text, 'Jesus Christ the same yesterday, and today, and for ever'.

A further comparison can be drawn between the manner in which the two sermons depict the process of death, and the state of the saint in paradise. Thomas Scott portrayed Pentycross's death as a kind of martyrdom to his message. Having faced earlier persecution as one of the six students expelled from Oxford in 1768 for attending Methodist meetings, in dying with his hope in Christ intact, Pentycross's witness was of final faithfulness to his conversion.[26] John Scott maintained this connection, but extended the metaphor of martyrdom into his subject's trials, opposition and sicknesses during life.[27] His saint was one whose forbearance and continued faithful action in this life was worthy of remembrance.[28] Similarly, the differences in portrayal of the saint in paradise expose the contours of the new hagiography. Thomas Scott's friend was now, concisely, 'delivered from sin and temptation, and admitted into the presence of his beloved Redeemer',[29] whereas John Scott's useful saint had entered into

> A rest from sin, from care, from temptation, from conflict, and from death! Not a rest from employment, – that would be wretchedness to a mind of immortal strength and unbounded activity, – but the delightful occupation of a free, unfettered, perfected, and ennobled spirit in that which will yield continually increasing satisfaction to everlasting ages. 'Blessed are the dead which die in the Lord; for they find rest from their labours; and their works do follow them.'[30]

This remarkable language of activity, employment, occupation and work, applied to the saint in glory, is consistent with evangelical self-identity, but also with the wider mid-nineteenth-century vocabulary of practicality, vocation and morality.[31]

## From pious philanthropy to moral celebrity

The origins of the use of this vocabulary within evangelical hagiography lie in the late eighteenth century, and can be seen in an embryonic form in a relatively unknown short biography of Sir John Barnard (c. 1685–1764), a prominent London MP, merchant and magistrate, published in 1776 and authored by the leading pious clergyman Henry Venn (1725–97).[32] Venn's intent was to demonstrate that Barnard's faith underpinned his reputation as a prominent public figure of character: 'that the world should know on what he built his hope of everlasting life'.[33] His approach was to show that Barnard held to 'the principles of truth, which the Church universal has embraced in all ages', and that these explained Barnard's uniqueness among his peers.[34] This was continuing a tradition of hagiography that stretched back to the Puritans, in which unusual public probity was appropriated for the purposes of recommending religion to 'great men'.[35] That Venn did not publish the *Memoir* until twelve years after Barnard's death suggests that this was not merely an act of gratitude for patronage, but an early attempt to lodge evangelicalism in the public mind. Venn, however, went further, explaining to his audience that Barnard's 'various plans of public utility' owed their inception to his 'great piety', his 'spirit of benevolence, watching for the public good', and that 'his ruling intention was to prove a permanent benefactor to society'.[36] By connecting Barnard's faith to an idea of public engagement, Venn laid the rhetorical groundwork for the ideal of the practical saint, with the central thesis that evangelical faith was a necessary precondition of 'real greatness'. However, there were limitations on the application of this language. Important among these was contemporary upper-class and middling antipathy to evangelical piety itself. Venn felt the need to defend even the writing of his account from the charge of irrelevance and insult to his subject, lest he be perceived to 'reproach, by the particular mention of his great piety, the excellent person [whom he] ... designed to honour'.[37]

A second thread in the development of an evangelical hagiographical vocabulary was the concept of a 'sphere' of usefulness and influence, an idea that found widespread use as evangelical laymen tried to articulate non-ecclesiastical forms of vocation without raising challenges to the Church establishment.[38] From at least 1773, John Thornton (1720–90), a friend of Henry Venn and a London-based merchant with strong connections to Yorkshire, was using the language of a 'sphere' of influence to describe new business ventures, and the opportunity they presented for the gospel.[39] This became the lens through which his immediate evangelical successors understood his life:

> from the most enlarged and expanded philanthropy, he adopted, supported and patronized every undertaking, which was suited to supply the wants, to relieve the distresses, or to increase the comforts of any of the human species, in whatever climate, or of whatever description, provided they properly fell within his sphere of action.[40]

Published memorials to Thornton represent a halfway point in the emergence of the practical saint, stressing the subservience of his philanthropy to his faith. Tied to commercial metaphors of opportunity, investment and efficacy, the key value judgement for evangelicals was not profit, but philanthropy: whether the resources available had been used well for the spread of the gospel and on behalf of mankind.[41] What was being expressed was a new ideal of lay evangelical professionalism, which extended and built on many of the ideals of the clerical profession, but applied them to new areas.[42] Those shaped by this late eighteenth-century idea of a 'sphere of influence' approved of saints, then, insofar as they had used their station and talents on behalf of others. Thomas Babington, who made a pilgrimage to visit places associated with William Cowper (1731–1800) after his death, reflected on the effect of Cowper's physical and social contexts on his poetry, writing about how the poet had been distinguished by 'influencing in no small degree the fate of others of his species during endless ages by the use he made of his time & faculties'.[43] What mattered further about the 'sphere of influence' was the way in which it contextualised the effects of the gospel. In common with Barnard in Venn's *Memoir*, philanthropic exemplars like Thornton and Cowper were not essentialised by their contexts – no explicit connection was made between their piety or philanthropy and national identity – but rather by their vocational faithfulness in context. They were central to the move to considering how the gospel inspired not merely individual conversions, but also the redemptive transformation of a particular domain of human life.

A further crucial intermediate stage to the development of practical hagiography came with the formation of the pious community at Clapham from the 1790s. Collective action by the group created a collective reputation and an enlarged sphere of influence, but also increasingly specialised reputations, based on each member's functional contributions. Henry Thornton (1760–1815), for example, felt that he could be most 'useful' to his friends and country by coupling his banking experience and thinking in political economy with leadership in parliamentary select committees on economic matters, most notably the bullion issue. Even before the publication of his educational treatises, Babington developed a reputation as an authority on the raising of children, and his letters to his wife during the 1800s and 1810s contain frequent examples of solicitations for advice, including accounts of invitations to 'consult' with parents about how best to educate their children.[44] Publications and parliamentary speeches by members of the Clapham community drew on the expertise of other members of the group. By appropriating and rejuvenating the late seventeenth- and early eighteenth-century language of the 'reformation of manners', they effectively expanded their collective 'sphere of influence', to include fashionable and political society.[45] The result was that many of the individuals who would later be collectively labelled the 'Clapham Sect' became what can best be described as 'moral celebrities'. Though the term may seem a strange category of analysis, especially as some studies have seen a nadir in Britain's national celebrity culture from the 1790s through until the 1810s in the context of wartime uncertainty and social unrest, a better account of these decades is that of a shift in the kinds of celebrities that captured the imagination of the public and polity.[46]

Moral celebrity, or at least renown, was the key precursor to the later, usually posthumous, invocation of practical sainthood. It tied the public reputation of their faith to the perceived successes and public personae of the group. Wilberforce in particular, who had remained something of a celebrity since his 1784 election in

Yorkshire, took this association furthest in the publication of his *Practical View* in 1797, a book that achieved its success largely as a result of its author's fame, but which did so at the risk of tying perceptions of evangelical religion to those of its author. By 1807, Wilberforce's moral celebrity had become widely acknowledged, and linked to national character, most famously in Samuel Romilly's 'living eulogy' during the Abolition Bill debate, which positioned Wilberforce as Britain's moral answer to Napoleon. In Romilly's rhetoric, Wilberforce was the juncture between imperial Britain's stained past and her benevolent future, the mediator between black and white races, between whom the latter had hitherto 'acknowledged no community of law, nor of justice, nor of species'. He was the dispenser of 'benign effects' upon 'the whole property of the colonies, and upon the prosperity of the empire at large', and was even figuratively beatified by the 'innumerable voices that would be raised in every quarter of the world to bless him'.[47] Outside Parliament, stories describing Wilberforce's encounters with rulers and labourers alike fostered a sense that the universality of his moral character allowed him to mediate between social ranks.[48] His national reputation added impetus to his claim, expressed in the *Practical View*, that just as living well required inner transformation, so the spiritual health of the nation was 'intimately connected' with its temporal greatness.[49] While this process helped evangelical leaders mobilise larger numbers of people at greater distance, it also ensured that they, especially Wilberforce, were inundated with requests for advice, support and patronage for philanthropic projects. It also attracted criticism. The primary insinuation of the derogative 'Saints' was of hypocrisy – a critical charge to a faith-system in which inner transformation was supposed to diffuse itself in good character and action. Each of the Saints was also conscious of the implications of their public and semi-public behaviour and patterns of consumption. Conspicuous piety, such as Sabbath observance, avoidance of theatre and other improper amusements, and appropriate management of their households, was fostered in order that their public image might reflect their ideals.[50] During the 1800s and beyond, various reputational strategies such as anonymous and pseudonymous authorship, even the titular rhetoric of practicality itself, were deployed to preserve public reputations, and the Saints were quick to defend the reputations of their associates in Parliament and the press.

As the generation of evangelicals who had come of age during the last decades of the eighteenth century passed away during the nineteenth century, funeral sermons, obituaries and the historical accounts of their lives drew on these earlier threads in presenting many of them as 'saints'. As with John Scott's account of John King, inner piety was reflected in the transformative effects of the deceased's character and labours on the surrounding community. The earliest glimmers of this trend can be seen in the obituaries, especially of non-clergy, in the *Christian Observer*, founded in 1802. To the common narrative patterns of conversion and the good death were added an account both of the deceased's accomplishments, and of the gratitude of the community.[51] A very early example is the obituary of Katherine Venn (1760–1803), wife of John, the Rector of Clapham. Such was 'the unwearied assiduity of her attentions' on behalf of the poor in the parish that 'when the summons of death reached her, she may be said to have had nothing to do but to die', and to join 'the society of saints'.[52] The death of Thomas Robinson (1749–1813) in Leicester was said to have so affected the community that 'the whole town seemed to have moved from its foundations'.[53] Sophia Cunningham (1780–1821), wife to a former curate of John Venn, was mourned at a funeral packed by 'the poor and the young ... the special objects of her anxious and unwearied care ... unite[d] in lamenting the loss of their benefactress'.[54] By the 1820s, evangelical funeral sermons were directly linking the faith of their subject to their activism. For the future Bishop of Calcutta Daniel Wilson (1778–1858), speaking of the East India Company grandee Charles Grant (1746–1823), it was the 'sincere and honest dedication of every talent and acquirement to the service and glory of God, which constituted him, in the proper sense of the term, a Christian'.[55] Similarly, the leading evangelical clergyman William Dealtry (1775–1847) devoted a large part of his sermon on the death of Charles Simeon (1759–1836) to encouraging his audience to 'go abroad into the world, and observe how he exercised his increasing influence'.[56]

## A second Reformation

At a national level, this was understood in terms of a second Reformation – one in which the manners, laws and practices of the British people were being shaped towards Stephen's perceived 'conformity between the Laws of God and the Policy of man'.[57] As John Coffey has argued, evangelical abolitionists thought in terms of providence and used biblically resonant imagery in presenting their case, though this was about more than the identification of British, or Protestant, interests with divine favour.[58] After their deaths, these activists were imagined in transposed biblical metaphors, in a reflection of the process by which it was understood that biblical Israel had become a righteous nation with a role in history. The commemorative plaque in Holy Trinity, Clapham, to the Sect records that they 'laboured ... abundantly for national righteousness', and concludes with the Psalmist's cry, 'O God we have heard with our ears and our fathers have declared unto us, the noble works that Thou didst in their days and in the old time before them'.[59] Evangelical reformers were thus compared to the great men of ancient Israel.[60] Lord Teignmouth, for example, 'lived a patriarch's life, and ... died a patriarch's death', exemplified by the manner in which he blessed his children, and his nation.[61] God had raised Wilberforce to be 'a witness to Himself worthy of the patriarchs of old',[62] and upon Babington's death, his relationship with his mother was placed in a lineage of holy maternal educators from Hagar to the present.[63] As had been the case with Israel's patriarchs, their faithfulness underwrote Britain's place in the redemptive narrative of history, and they became, in the imagination of writers such as Stephen, a central pillar to Britain's claim to being a Christian nation, and a witness to posterity. Ford K. Brown's 'Fathers of the Victorians' were therefore mediators of divine blessing but, more importantly, metaphorically laden bearers of the seed of faith: their actions and achievements were signs and fruit of the covenantal promise of the nation.

The imagery of the patriarch served further as a counter to competing claims upon Church tradition. The Saints were directly compared with 'the Fathers of the four first centuries [and] ... the Reformers and Martyrs of the sixteenth',[64] and claimed as 'Evangelical Fathers'.[65] In an advance upon Milner, mid-nineteenth-century evangelicals claimed that saints represented a tradition not merely of faith, but of faithful cultural presence and reform, as contrasted with what they held to be the unworldly and wilfully impractical eccentricity held out, for instance, by supporters of the Oxford Tract writers.[66] Two contrasts in Stephen's connection of biblical imagery to sainthood illustrate this. First, 'Practical' saints differed in the *Ecclesiastical Biography* from those of the first Reformation, for whom prophetic images and linkages drawn from biblical Exilic period were more commonly used to express their alienation from culture.[67] Secondly, biblical allusions in his article on the eighteenth-century 'Evangelical Succession' primarily link to an extended metaphor of the four evangelists.[68] Both of these tropes serve to underline for the the reader the importance of doctrinal purity. When contrasted with what Stephen had to say about the Clapham Saints, it becomes clear that a shift had occurred in the meaning of 'reformation', away from the renovation of Christianity towards an appreciation of how the renewal of embedded institutions and persons would affect wider society.[69] That Stephen's essay constituted a historiographical shift can be further illustrated by comparison with John White Middleton's 1822 *Ecclesiastical Memoir*, in which the author's 'examination of the existing condition of the outworks of the national Zion' framed the failings of leaders as their lack of 'purity of sentiment, or attachment to the distinguishing tenets of the Reformation', rather than their failure to bring about redemptive change.[70]

Like that of the patriarch, the imagery of royalty was also pervasive within evangelical funeral sermons. At Wilberforce's funeral in Westminster Abbey, the 'star of royalty' shone most brilliantly when 'it let its rays fall into his hallowed tomb'.[71] Just as the lawyer and MP Samuel Romilly (1757–1818) had compared Wilberforce to Napoleon, in their deaths the Saints were compared favourably with the conquerors, emperors and 'mere earthly king[s]' after whose death men anticipated 'the excitement of a funeral discourse'.[72] In becoming 'kings' and 'judges' in heaven, the Saints were held up as a new model of national leadership. They were those who had during life fulfilled 'the important duty of serving, it may be of saving, their country ... by that sure and radical benefit of restoring the influence of religion'.[73] There is also a strong thread of vicarious action and suffering – especially from the 1830s. While eighteenth-century evangelical eulogists noted the patient perseverance of their subjects in faith and suffering for their witness, their nineteenth-century counterparts were more likely to speak of overcoming opposition through action, even suffering for the sake of others.[74] Their subjects were aligned with biblical Israel's restoring monarchs, and, as agents of restoration after a period of public faithlessness, deserved their memorials, 'in the venerable mausoleum of our kings'.[75] The trope reflected a confidence in the success of the national reformation that had occurred and the transformation that was occurring – not merely were they the patriarchal founders of a new moral nation, but its epitomes; its truest leaders.

'As goes the leader, so goes the nation.' So the character of the Saints was claimed as the wellspring of national character. Evangelical thought posited a metaphorical relationship between inner life or character and the exterior world, which provided what the leading Scottish evangelical and social reformer Thomas Chalmers (1780–1847) called a 'moral investment' on the face of reality.[76] As in Venn's biography of Barnard, the inner renewal of evangelical religion provided the foundation for true greatness, but it also added a 'moral investment' to its aesthetic qualities. For Stephen, this was a restoration of the old 'alliance' between English theology and 'philosophy and eloquence, wit and poetry'.[77] The emphasis in evangelical funeral sermons and other writing on the attractive playfulness and cheerfulness of their subjects reflects this, and is a perceptible change in style from that of the earlier generation. Chalmers further described the relationship between the beautiful personality and moral character: 'Sublimity in the one is the counterpart to moral greatness in the other; and beauty in the one is the counterpart to moral delicacy in the other.'[78] The gaiety and aesthetic appreciativeness of evangelicals as they were remembered and venerated was not just a counterpoint to their perceived seriousness, but an exterior reflection of their inner moral state. Babington's mourners heard of 'the religion of this pre-eminent saint, which was associated with great natural cheerfulness and equanimity of temper, was incorporated with the whole frame and habits of his life'.[79] The practical saint was one who 'adorned' his or her belief with good habits and demeanour.

## A second empire

The way in which the outworking of this new moral state was conceived, however, was strikingly non-national, and connected different localities with national and global identities. As the Saints' 'sphere of influence' had expanded to encompass the British nation, so now it also connected Britain to the world: 'Wilberforce was not the man of one parish, or of one country, but of the whole world of that God whose doctrine he adorned.'[80] Unlike missionaries, who were arguably defined by foreign residence, the context for the 'practical' saint's work was in the British side of the ubiquitous dichotomy of 'British and Foreign', and as such the benefit conveyed beyond the nation was not a mere export of civilisation, but a mediated relationship. A saint was one who 'augmented the sum of human happiness',[81] and made 'unwearied efforts to benefit his fellow-man'.[82] This was not a reductionist universalism, but a differentiated and expansive understanding of humanity, in which the gospel was understood to have different benefits in different contexts. An aspect of this can be seen in the Saints' memorials. John Oldfield has detailed how various localities sought to use monuments to incorporate abolitionist achievement into local identity – a phenomenon that extended to other areas of evangelical activism.[83] Wilberforce had hoped to be buried in Stoke Newington, not Westminster Abbey, but was commemorated the year following his death by a column in his hometown of Hull, the foundation of which was laid on the day that the Abolition Act came into effect.[84] Charles Grant's memorial in St George's, Bloomsbury celebrated his role in improving the 'ancient and famous nations' entrusted to his governance, and in the transformation of the Scottish Highlands. In this way, the memory of the local saint was framed in terms of a global connection, mediating and reinforcing the relationship between British parishes and the wider world. Stephen described Wilberforce as 'forming the interior of many circles', the outermost of which was a, 'remoter multitude ... from Gades to Ganges'.[85] This outer sphere too was subdivided, and within the pious community of Clapham, 'Every human interest had its guardian, every region of the globe its representative. If the African continent and the Caribbean Archipelago were assigned to an indefatigable protectorate, New Holland was not forgotten, nor was British India without a patron.'[86] The various regions of the globe were each assigned their own patron saints, who also mediated Britain's growing second empire to a domestic audience.

## A second revolution

The Saints were also constructed in the context of the growth in mass media, and the changing patterns of production and consumption in the early nineteenth century. Their reputations became part of the mass promotion of piety, a process which started well before their deaths, with appearances at society meetings, publications and other functions of their moral celebrity helping to develop the machinery of evangelical activism, a machinery that continued to grow after their deaths. Within their funeral sermons are anecdotal narratives of universal approbation – of the King wishing that all MPs were as diligent and good as Wilberforce, or of wagon-drivers giving way from deference to character.[87] Evangelical societies published tributes emphasising the role leading Saints had played in their work.[88] Avid audience interest led to the rapid publication by Wilberforce's sons of their father's 1838 *Life*, and a quick succession of abridged and foreign-language versions, as well as to the various eulogies and sermons published by evangelical magazines.

A consequence of the ubiquity of such accounts, the speed with which they were produced, and the emphasis on their subjects' this-worldly habits and projects was a stress on the immanence of their piety. Thomas Acworth wrote of Babington,

> I am not reading to you the history of some eminent servant of God, who lived in a remote age, or in a distant country; the person of whom we say these things lived and died among ourselves. You have all seen, the greater part of you have seen from your infancy, how 'holy and unblameably' he behaved himself in the elevated station which he occupied in this parish for more than half a century.[89]

Evangelical saints were involved in parish churches, in raising their families and improving local communities. They were accessible, and to be emulated, regardless of social station. Narratives of improving habits and daily devotions underlined the claim that all were called and capable of similar religious discipline and activism. This immanent practicality was in contrast to those 'nice self-observers' of religion – usually High Churchmen – whose discipline extended to minor acts of self-denial, but who lacked a broader vision. Instead, the practical saint's habits were directed towards control over the 'various springs of human action', so as to foster self-control, but on behalf of 'the great brotherhood' of humanity.[90]

The frame of this spreading practical piety is best illustrated through the most common metaphor used in the funeral sermons of the Saints – that of spreading light as an image of the improvement of society. To Victorian evangelicals, a denouement had been reached – such that Stephen could write of living after 'the most eventful epoch of the history of England' – in which the gospel had been revealed through the lives and works of their forebears as the pre-eminent force in human progress.[91] In his funeral sermon for Wilberforce, the Minister of Camden Town Chapel, Alexander D'Arblay (1794–1837), equated those who walked in the 'path of light' with those who 'augmented the sum of human happiness'.[92] Further, he argued that 'not only are the just children of light, but children of a constantly *increasing* light … Here, then, we have the necessity of unceasing *improvement*'.[93] In this narrative, present in other written memorials, the saints, 'who have appeared as lights in the world',[94] were pitched against the forces unleashed by the rupture of 'mechanical industry', 'vice, ignorance, poverty, and discontent' among the lower classes, and 'selfishness, sensuality, hardness of heart, and corruption' among the higher classes.[95] The 'miracles' of 'mechanical art … by the aid of commercial capital' of Watt and Arkwright were directly comparable to the advancements in education and religious knowledge fostered by the Saints. To Stephen, churches, Sunday Schools and evangelical societies of all forms were factories of piety and departments in the 'eleemosynary government' of the 'disjointed state', of which Wilberforce was 'prime minister', in a concerted project to 'diffuse the light of the gospel, and to increase the sum of temporal comforts'.[96] It was this vision that gave him the confidence to assert that humanity itself was undergoing a fundamental, even eschatological, transformation.

### 'Mémoires pour servir'

The hagiography of the practical saint was intrinsically tied to a way of understanding the role of 'practical Christianity' in the world, and particularly in history. The inwardly redeemed saint served the historical process of the salvation of humanity, by a constant process of self- and national improvement. As such, the practical saint functioned as mediator between God and nation, between national and global, between the happy and the helpless. By participation in improvement while alive, and as an ongoing symbol of the reformation of the nation, and its place in the globalising world, the practical saint became a kind of agent for providential improvement of his or her fellow human beings. The early hagiographies of the Saints suggest that their reputations were not merely being managed by their families, contested by ecclesiastical parties, or rolled into early liberal–imperial historiographies, as Catherine Hall has recently argued.[97] Rather, the shift in hagiography from the late eighteenth to the mid nineteenth centuries may suggest another angle in addressing Stuart Piggin's rhetorical question about evangelicalism's persistent interest to historians, 'is it just that it has become adept at writing its own history?'[98] It may be, as Stephen suggested, that its historiographical fascination is due to its creation of a distinctive form of 'ecclesiastical biography', which uniquely connected national history and global consciousness with the piety of 'its most admirable members'.[99]

## Notes

I owe a debt of gratitude to Jane Garnett and to the anonymous reader for their helpful comments and suggestions on drafts of this chapter.

1 William Acworth, *A Sermon, Occasioned by the Death of Thomas Babington, Esq.* (Leicester: [n.p.], 1837), pp. 5–9. See Col. 1: 12.
2 Thomas Babington to Jean Babington, 9 April 1805, Trinity College Cambridge, Wren Library (hereafter Wren), Babington Papers, 14/50.
3 See Christopher Tolley, *Domestic Biography: The Legacy of Evangelicalism in Four Nineteenth-Century Families* (Oxford: Clarendon, 1997); Anne Stott, *Wilberforce: Family and Friends* (Oxford: Oxford University Press, 2012).
4 See, for example, Ian Bradley, *The Call to Seriousness* (London: Cape, 1976); Stott, *Wilberforce*; Stephen Tomkins, *The Clapham Sect: How Wilberforce's Circle Transformed Britain* (Oxford: Lion, 2010).
5 John Walsh, 'Joseph Milner's Evangelical Church History', *Journal of Ecclesiastical History*, 10 (1959), 174–87. See also Gareth Atkins, '"True churchmen": Anglican Evangelicals and history, c.1770–1850', *Theology*, 115 (2012), 339–49.
6 Walsh, 'Evangelical Church History', 187.
7 *Ibid.*, 186.
8 *Ibid.*, 185.
9 John Newton, *A Review of Ecclesiastical History* (London: Edward and Charles Dilly, 1770), p. xiv.
10 Erasmus Middleton, *Evangelical Biography*, 4 vols (1779–86; London: W. Baynes, 1816), I: p. ii.
11 *Ibid.*, IV: pp. 497–512.
12 Edward Bickersteth, *The Works of Rev. E. Bickersteth* (New York: Daniel Appleton, 1832), p. 632.
13 Brian W. Young, *The Victorian Eighteenth Century* (Oxford: Oxford University Press, 2007), pp. 3–5, 118, 122.
14 Bruce Hindmarsh, *The Evangelical Conversion Narrative* (Oxford: Oxford University Press, 2005), p. 347.
15 For further discussion of the importance of biography to the Stephen family, see Young, *Victorian Eighteenth Century*, pp. 114–18.
16 Sir James Stephen to Thomas Babington, 14 October 1833, Wren, Babington Papers, 20/87.

17 Sir James Stephen, *Essays in Ecclesiastical Biography* (1849; 5th edn, London: Longmans, etc., 1867), p. 522.
18 For Pentycross's evangelicalism, see Charles H. E. Smyth, *Simeon & Church Order* (Cambridge: Cambridge University Press, 1940), pp. 237–8.
19 John Scott succeeded his father to the living of St Mary's, Hull, in 1834, under the patronage of the merchant and banker Samuel Thornton (1754–1838). John King was incumbent of Christ Church, Hull, and a fellow evangelical.
20 Thomas Scott, *The Duty and Advantage of Remembering Deceased Ministers* (Buckingham: J. Seeley, 1808), p. 17.
21 *Ibid.*, p. 9.
22 *Ibid.*, p. 17.
23 John Scott, *The Duty and Advantage of Remembering Deceased Ministers* (London: Seeley, Jackson, and Halliday, 1858), pp. 5, 23, 27.
24 *Ibid.*, p. 15.
25 *Ibid.*, p. 17.
26 Thomas Scott, *Duty*, p. 23.
27 Bob Tennant identifies early examples of this trope of living martyrdom in Church Missionary Society anniversary sermons in *Corporate Holiness: Pulpit Preaching and the Church of England Missionary Societies, 1760–1870* (Oxford: Oxford University Press, 2013), pp. 132–4. *Contra* Tennant, however, this rhetoric was not merely about psychological impact, but about turning the metaphorical equivalence between missionary self-sacrifice and Christ's self-sacrifice into the basis by which to claim the missionary as saint: the foundation of the Society's claim to historical significance.
28 John Scott, *Duty*, p. 18.
29 Thomas Scott, *Duty*, p. 25.
30 John Scott, *Duty*, pp. 25–6.
31 There is a substantial literature that addresses this vocabulary, and the relationship between evangelical belief and action. See, for example, John Wolffe (ed.), *Evangelical Faith and Public Zeal* (London: SPCK, 1995); Mark Noll, 'Revolution and the rise of evangelical social influence in North Atlantic societies', in Noll, David Bebbington and George Rawlyk (eds), *Evangelicalism: Comparative Studies of Popular Protestantism in North America, the British Isles, and Beyond, 1700–1990* (New York: Oxford University Press, 1994), pp. 113–36.
32 Henry Venn, *Memoirs of the Late Sir John Barnard, Knight, and Alderman of the City of London* (London: W. Oliver, 1776).
33 *Ibid.*, p. 20.
34 *Ibid.*, p. 21.
35 See discussion in Michael Walzer, *The Revolution of the Saints: A Study in the Origins of Radical Politics* (Cambridge, MA: Harvard University Press, 1965), esp. p. 264; and in Jeremy Gregory, '*Homo religiosus*: masculinity and religion in the long eighteenth century', in Tim Hitchcock and Michèle Cohen (eds), *English Masculinities, 1660–1800* (London: Longman, 1999), pp. 85–110. See also Geordan Hammond, 'The revival of practical Christianity: the Society for Promoting Christian Knowledge, Samuel Wesley, and the clerical society movement', in Kate Cooper and Jeremy Gregory (eds), *Revival and Resurgence in Christian History*, Studies in Church History, 44 (Woodbridge: Boydell, 2008), pp. 116–27, esp. p. 119.

36  Venn, *Memoirs*, pp. 9, 12, 15.
37  *Ibid.*, p. 15.
38  See Wesley D. Balda, 'Spheres of Influence: Simeon's Trust and its Implications for Evangelical Patronage' (PhD thesis, University of Cambridge, 1981).
39  John Thornton to John Newton, February 1772, 7 July 1774, Cambridge University Library, Thornton Papers, MS Add. 7674/1/A, fos. 2, 14.
40  *The Love of Christ the Source of Genuine Philanthropy* (London: J. Johnson, 1791), p. 6.
41  *Ibid.*, pp. 6–9.
42  See, for example, Thomas Gisborne, *An Enquiry into the Duties of Men* (London: B. and J. White, 1794), p. 3; William Wilberforce, *A Practical View of the Prevailing Religious System … Contrasted with Real Christianity* (London: T. Cadell, etc., 1797), pp. 268–9. See also Deryck Lovegrove, *The Rise of the Laity in Evangelical Protestantism* (London: Routledge, 2002).
43  Thomas Babington to Jean Babington, 8 November 1813, Wren, Babington Papers, 14/191.
44  E.g. Thomas Babington to Jean Babington, 29 January 1806; 30 January 1806, Wren, Babington Papers, 14/67, 68.
45  Joanna Innes, 'Politics and morals: the reformation of manners movement in later eighteenth-century England', in Eckhart Hellmuth (ed.), *The Transformation of Political Culture: England and Germany in the Late Eighteenth Century* (Oxford: Oxford University Press, 1990), pp. 57–118.
46  Simon Morgan, 'Celebrity: academic "pseudo-event" or a useful concept for historians?', *Cultural and Social History*, 8 (2011), 95–114, esp. 110.
47  *Cobbett's Parliamentary Debates*, 8 (1807), cols 977–9.
48  Joseph Brown, *A Sermon Occasioned by the Death of W. Wilberforce* (London: J. Hatchard & Son, 1833), p. 18.
49  Wilberforce, *Practical View*, p. 3. See also John Coffey, '"Tremble, Britannia!": fear, providence and the abolition of the slave trade, 1758–1807', *English Historical Review*, 127 (2012), 844–81.
50  See discussion in Stott, *Wilberforce*, p. 81.
51  For broader context, see Hindmarsh, *Conversion*, and Patricia Jalland, *Death in the Victorian Family* (Oxford: Oxford University Press, 1996).
52  *Christian Observer*, 2 (1803), 255.
53  *Ibid.*, 12 (1813), 271.
54  *Ibid.* 20 (1821), 68.
55  Daniel Wilson, *A Sermon Occasioned by the Death of Charles Grant, Esq.* (London: George Wilson, 1824), pp. 16–17.
56  William Dealtry, *Honour from God the Sure Portion of them that Honour Him* (Cambridge: J. & J. J. Deighton, etc., 1836), p. 13.
57  Sir James Stephen to Thomas Babington, 14 October 1833, Wren, Babington Papers, 20/87.
58  Coffey, 'Tremble', 844–5. See also Coffey, *Exodus and Liberation: Deliverance Politics from John Calvin to Martin Luther King Jr* (Oxford: Oxford University Press, 2014), pp. 7–9.
59  The translation of Ps. 44: 1 is that of the Litany from the Book of Common Prayer. See 'Holy Trinity Clapham: The Clapham Sect', www.londonremembers.com/memorials/

holy-trinity-clapham-clapham-sect, accessed 2 May 2014. Wilberforce's monument in Westminster Abbey uses a similar language of 'public labour', talking of 'exertions' to remove God's curse on the nation and to bring blessing to its people. See 'William Wilberforce & Family', www.westminster-abbey.org/our-history/people/william-wilberforce, accessed 2 May 2014.

60  See also Coffey, *Exodus*, pp. 114–15.
61  Robert Anderson, *To look on the Things of Others: A Sermon … on the Sunday after the Funeral of John, Lord Teignmouth* (London: J. Hatchard and Son, 1834), p. 21.
62  Alexander C. L. D'Arblay, *The Path of the Just, or, Christian Improvement, Consisting of Two Discourses Occasioned by the Death of W. Wilberforce* (London: Hatchard, 1833), p. 26.
63  Acworth, *Babington*, pp. 23–4.
64  Wilson, *Grant*, p. 43.
65  Stephen, *Essays*, p. 445.
66  See Macfarlane's chapter 14, pp. 245–61, in this volume.
67  Stephen, *Essays*, p. 230.
68  Ibid., p. 401.
69  For the earlier conception, see Brian W. Young, *Religion and Enlightenment in Eighteenth-Century England* (Oxford: Clarendon, 1998), pp. 19–20.
70  John White Middleton, *Ecclesiastical Memoir of … the Reign of George the Third* (London: L. B. Seeley, 1822), pp. vi, 10.
71  Brown, *Wilberforce*, p. 18.
72  D'Arblay, *Wilberforce*, p. 25.
73  Ibid., p. 42.
74  See, for example, Newton, *History*, pp. x–xi.
75  D'Arblay, *Wilberforce*, pp. 29–30.
76  Thomas Chalmers, *On the Power, Wisdom, and Goodness of God*, 2 vols (1833; 5th edn, Glasgow: William Collins, 1839), I: p. 81.
77  Stephen, *Essays*, p. 379.
78  Chalmers, *Power*, p. 131.
79  Acworth, *Babington*, p. 16.
80  D'Arblay, *Wilberforce*, p. 27.
81  Ibid., p. 25.
82  Brown, *Wilberforce*, p. 25.
83  John R. Oldfield, *Chords of Freedom: Commemoration, Ritual and British Transatlantic Slavery* (Manchester: Manchester University Press, 2007), pp. 56–87.
84  'The Wilberforce Monument', *Hull Museum Collections*, www.hullcc.gov.uk/museumcollections/collections/storydetail.php?irn=227&master=443, accessed 2 December 2015.
85  Stephen, *Essays*, p. 512.
86  Ibid., p. 553.
87  Brown, *Wilberforce*, pp. 16–18.
88  Anderson, *Teignmouth*, pp. 25–9.
89  Acworth, *Babington*, p. 17.
90  Stephen, *Essays*, p. 481.
91  Ibid., p. 522.
92  D'Arblay, *Wilberforce*, p. 25.

93 *Ibid.*, p. 15.
94 'Obituary: Henry Thornton', *Christian Observer*, 14 (1815), 129.
95 Stephen, *Essays*, pp. 497–8.
96 *Ibid.*, pp. 498–9.
97 Catherine Hall, *Macaulay and Son: Architects of Imperial Britain* (New Haven and London: Yale University Press, 2012).
98 Stuart Piggin, 'Preaching the new birth and the power of godliness and not insisting so much on the form: recent studies of (mainly English) evangelicalism', *Journal of Religious History*, 33 (2009), 366.
99 Stephen, *Essays*, p. 522.

# 13

# Elizabeth Fry and Sarah Martin

*Helen Rogers*

IN HER INFLUENTIAL LECTURE 'Sisters of Charity' (1855) championing women's involvement in public service, the art historian and social commentator Anna Jameson (1794–1860) called her countrywomen to emulate Catholic women, past and present, by forming 'active charitable Orders'. By 'Sisters of Charity' she spoke not merely 'of a particular order of religious women, belonging to a particular church, but also in a far more comprehensive sense, as indicating the vocation of a large number of women in every country, class, and creed.' Jameson was careful, however, to reassure Protestants she was not advocating nunneries or any superstitious and idolatrous practice they might associate with Papacy and the Roman Church: 'We may smile at the childish and melancholy legend of St. Ursula and her eleven thousand virgins', she acknowledged, 'but of the Ursulines, as a community', with a 'vocation' to care and instruct poor children, 'we may be allowed to think seriously and even reverently'.[1] Jameson's mock-serious aside on Saint Ursula makes an interesting starting point for investigating Victorian attitudes towards female sainthood and saintliness at a time when women's rights and duties were conceived overwhelmingly within a broadly religious discourse of 'woman's mission'. Her reference to the myth of Saint Ursula, a Romano-British Christian princess supposedly slaughtered with her handmaidens in Cologne following a pilgrimage, is all but lost on the modern secular reader.[2] Perhaps the anecdote was comic and knowing, for it is not the saintly British Ursula she commended but the Ursuline Order, a continental community of women devoted to good work which, founded in 1537, represented for Jameson a historical precedent for contemporary women's philanthropic action.

The figure of the woman saint offered activists part-historical, part-mythical examples of female vision, ministry and vocation to legitimise their own desire for purposive action. Yet saintliness was also a quality associated with that stifling, saccharine image of idealised womanhood, 'the angel in the house'. Concerned with women's efforts to challenge representations of the devoted, self-sacrificing priestess of the hearth, feminist historians have paid almost no attention to the meanings or attractions of sanctity for Victorian women.[3] Susan Mumm, for instance, examines the establishment of Anglican sisterhoods, many named after saints, but does not consider the significance of sanctity for those communities or the women who joined them.[4] As

Alison Twells observes, the focus of women's history has been 'on the role of religion in providing motivation, sustenance and justification for women's involvement in feminism and other public campaigns. Questions of faith and devotion, spirituality and Christian selfhood ... remain largely unaddressed.'[5]

In an exceptional and pioneering investigation of the uses of sanctity for Protestant women, Eileen Janes Yeo argues that Catholic saints, houses and sisterhoods helped mid-Victorian reformers imagine femininised and androgynous models of divinity that validated female forms of authority and public service.[6] As an art historian, for example, Jameson took inspiration from the ultimate embodiment of female sainthood, 'the divine image of the Madonna', for a radical reworking of gender identity. In *Legends of the Madonna* (1852) she claimed the Virgin Mary was just one incarnation of 'a divine maternity' that, 'as the voice of a mighty prophecy, sounded through all the generations of men, even from the beginning of time, of the coming moral regeneration, and complete and harmonious development of the whole human race, by the establishment, on a higher base, of what has been called the "feminine element" in society'.[7] In *Sisters of Charity* and *The Communion of Labour* (1856), Jameson proposed that this 'feminine element' should complement the 'masculine element' in the social sphere, in order to regenerate public institutions, such as prisons and workhouses, and foster sympathy between the classes.

Saintliness, then, could be a way of legitimating the courageous and visionary leadership of women activists when their public action was deeply controversial. Cannily, in *Sisters of Charity*, Jameson cited the historian Thomas Babington Macaulay (1800–59), pointing out that the Roman Church made space 'for female agency', assigning to 'devout women ... spiritual functions, dignities, and magistracies', while 'in our country':

> If a pious and benevolent woman enters the cells of a prison, to pray with the most unhappy and degraded of her own sex, she does so without any authority from the Church; no line of action is traced out for her, and it is well if the Ordinary does not complain of her intrusion, or if the Bishop does not shake his head at such irregular benevolence. At Rome, the Countess of Huntingdon would have a place in the calendar as Saint Selina, and Mrs. Fry would be foundress and first Superior of the blessed Order of the Sisters of the Gaols.[8]

The reference to Elizabeth Fry (1780–1845) is unsurprising, for few women were made to embody the ideal of sisterhood in charity as much as the prisoner reformer, or would be more associated with lay constructions of saintliness. In popular representations of Fry's work at Newgate Gaol we can detect the quasi-secularisation of female sanctity to validate women's public service. Indeed, Victorian ideals of female saintliness were heavily influenced by these imaginative reconstructions of Newgate's dungeons. As I shall show, Mrs Fry became the saintly model other women were urged to follow, while subsequent portraits of laudable women would be drawn in similarly hallowed hues. By way of example, I explore Fry's contemporary, Sarah Martin (1791–1843), prison visitor at Great Yarmouth Gaol, also effectively canonised by the

Victorians. By depicting women reformers in saintly terms, their advocates mythologised and sentimentalised their accomplishments, I argue, and certainly obscured less conventionally 'feminine' aspects of their dogged commitment. I begin, however, by outlining the posthumous 'canonisation' of the two prison visitors and their place in hagiographic accounts of 'worthy women'.

## Hagiography and 'prison heroines'

Elizabeth Fry started to acquire celebrity status when reports began to circulate in the press in 1818 of her work at Newgate. While Fry garnered most attention, her Ladies' Association for prison visiting provided a model of practical Christian vocation, networking and campaigning that was adapted by women in the growing campaign to abolish slavery and by later reform movements.[9] While the Ladies' Association showed what women could do collectively under the direction of a charismatic, well-connected leader, Sarah Martin was praised for demonstrating what could be achieved by a 'humble' individual acting alone. Most posthumous memoirs cited the eulogium given by Prison Inspector Williams:

> She was no titular sister of charity, but was silently felt and acknowledged to be one by the many outcast and destitute persons who received encouragement from her lips, and relief from her hands, and by the few who were witnesses of her good works.[10]

After their deaths, Martin and Fry were lauded as exemplary, saintly women. Pledging his contribution to a stained-glass window commemorating Martin at St Nicholas's Church, Yarmouth, the Bishop of Norwich declared, 'Could I canonize Sarah Martin, I would do so.'[11] In 1852, a French memoir reckoned Fry would have been canonised had she belonged to the Catholic faith while Baron von Bunsen (1791–1860), the Prussian Ambassador to London, described her as 'my favourite saint'.[12] According to her biographer in the *Eminent Women* series (1884), to the prisoners whom she served, 'the memory of Mrs Fry was something almost too holy for earth. No orthodoxly canonized saint of the Catholic Church ever received truer reverence, or performed such miracles of moral healing.'[13]

Canonisation, as Tricia Lootens suggests, is largely textual and is highly mediated.[14] The saintly reputations of the two 'female Howards' were secured by posthumous memoirs – Martin's in 1844 and Fry's in 1847 – and by eulogistic treatment in magazines and collections of 'eminent' or 'worthy' women.[15] Hagiographic studies were enormously popular through the second half of the century, and a major force in establishing the pantheon of 'great women' in which Fry and Martin featured prominently. Fry, depicted in thirty-six of the volumes examined in Alison Booth's survey of Victorian women's prosopography, was second only to Joan of Arc in popularity (the subject of thirty-eight portraits). Of the social reformers, Martin (with twenty entries) was superseded only by Fry, Florence Nightingale (1820–1910) and Hannah More (1745–1833).[16]

Victorian portraits of exemplary women were shaped by Christian hagiography. Many offered not so much a secular version of the earlier 'Lives of the Female Saints', nor even a specifically Protestant one, but rather a universal and surprisingly inclusive model of Christian womanhood, characterised by faith and service to others. In an influential example of the genre, *Women of Christianity, Exemplary for Acts of Piety and Charity* (1852), the Irish writer and devout Catholic Julia Kavanagh (1824–77) assembled an eclectic bunch of Christian martyrs, holy women, mystics, nuns, saints, queens and benevolent women 'of every land; every race; every rank', who were united by the same spirit of devotion and charity. She ended this illustrious history with two contemporary examples to illustrate precisely that point: Elizabeth Fry, the well-connected and famous Quaker minister, and Sarah Martin, the Anglican dressmaker: 'With ... an humble working-girl of our own times, we close this series of generous women, who for eighteen hundred years and more, steadily followed in the path opened by Dorcas, a lowly Christian of the first Christian age.'[17] It is notable that for Kavanagh and other hagiographers, saints renowned for benevolence to the poor and outcast, rather than for mysticism or vision, provided inspiration for the modern-day philanthropist. As Emma Raymond Pitman (fl. 1870s–c. 1900) declared of Fry:

> Such saints were Elizabeth of Hungary, around whose name legend and story have gathered, crowning her memory with beauty; Catherine of Sienna, who was honored by the whole Christian Church of the fourteenth century, and canonized for her goodness; and Sarah Martin, the humble dressmaker of Yarmouth, who, in later times, has proved how possible it is to render distinguished service in the cause of humanity by small and lowly beginnings ... [A]nd towering above all her contemporaries in the grandeur of her deeds and words, Mrs. Fry still lives in song and story.[18]

Potentially, these ideals of female saintliness and female service could be achieved by any woman, regardless of class, creed or colour. Closer examination of the memorialisation of Fry and Martin reveals, however, the ideological workings of mythology in these hagiographies.

## The Newgate heroine: Elizabeth Fry

Sainthood is generally conferred posthumously but in the case of Fry it followed soon after she established schools for women and children at Newgate Gaol, when Thomas Fowell Buxton (1786–1845) included an account of the Proceedings of the Ladies' Committee at Newgate in his 1818 *Inquiry* on prison discipline.[19] Much of his report was reproduced verbatim in the periodical press and in later memoirs and sketches of Fry.[20] Buxton's survey drew on accounts by the eleven Quaker women on the Ladies' Committee but it was Fry, the only woman he named, who acquired the reputation as Newgate heroine. Her entry into the gaol and influence over its inmates provided the thrilling centrepiece to all the exemplary biographies, for it gave the story narrative drive while symbolising a new female power, born in the prison cells. This dramatic episode set the scene for future portrayals of women's philanthropy in and beyond the prison.

Fry's visualisation of the Newgate scene, related to Buxton, coloured later portraits: 'all I tell thee is a faint picture of the reality; the filth, the closeness of the rooms, the ferocious manners and expressions of the women towards each other, and the abandoned wickedness, which everything bespoke, are quite indescribable'. She found the women begging, playing cards and fighting over winnings, reading 'improper books', and in thrall to an imprisoned fortune-teller for, 'believing nothing else', they 'were eager and implicit believers in the truth of her divinations'. Added drama was lent by the more affective account of Mary Sanderson, the Quaker (unnamed in most accounts and illustrations) who accompanied Fry to the female wards: 'She felt as if she were going into a den of wild beasts, and she well recollects quite shuddering when the door closed upon her, and she was locked in with such a herd of novel and desperate companions.'[21] Repeated in most versions of the Newgate story, Sanderson's recollection fixed in the popular imagination the ladies' 'descent' into the inferno and their 'miraculous' influence over its demonic inhabitants. In gothic re-workings of the Newgate scene, the terror of the unnamed Quaker woman enhances Fry's courage and stature.[22] The myth is distilled in the iconic painting *Mrs Fry Visiting Newgate* (1875), by Henrietta Ward (1832–1924). It depicts Sanderson peering timidly at the imprisoned fiends from behind Fry's protective body (figure 6). The virtue of the two benevolent women illuminates the gaol's netherworld. As Alison Booth notes, the Newgate myth relied on the heroic convention 'of the rescuing woman bearing light into darkness, like a virgin confronting a dragon, a Demeter/Persephone figure'. The same convention was applied to Florence Nightingale, whose name was frequently yoked with Fry's, and to other intrepid reformers lauded as 'Ladies with the Lamp'.[23]

While the gothic sensationalism of the Newgate accounts gripped readers and galvanised some into action, for many recent historians it betrays the disciplinary rhetoric underpinning contemporary philanthropy and humanitarianism. Soon after she organised women inmates into classes, Fry proclaimed, 'Already, from being like wild beasts, they appear harmless and kind'.[24] Her programme of kindness mixed with strictness, devised in her first few weeks at Newgate, constituted a 'powerful sympathy', claims Randall McGowen, defined by class ideology as much as Christian piety.[25] In this view, philanthropic recognition of the outcasts' humanity – that they were 'poor' rather than 'beasts' – depended upon their adoption of gendered roles as Christian men or women, appropriate to their class. From the perspective of the Foucauldian critique of the will to discipline, it is telling Buxton found that under 'the rule of kindness' the female wards 'exhibited the appearance of an industrious manufactory, or a well regulated family'.[26]

Though the model of Christian sisterhood, Yeo contends, proved empowering for many middle- and upper-class women, too often it was secured by infantilising less privileged women.[27] In *The Communion of Labour* (1856), for instance, Anna Jameson invoked Fry's venture into the 'den of wild beasts' to illustrate the role that women

6  *Mrs Fry Visiting Newgate, 1818*, exhibited 1876; engraving by T. D. Atkins.

should play in rescuing the 'perishing and dangerous classes'. In her version of the famous scene, two gaolers stand 'jeering' at the cell door.[28] In popular representations, too, the Newgate women were shown to be brutalised as well as brutish, while Fry's courage and benevolence indicted the gaol authorities. The intransigence and complacency of Newgate's authorities is stressed by *Women of Worth: A Book for Girls* (1859), which echoes Jameson's call for the extension of sisterhood across the classes: under the 'peace, cleanliness, and order' instilled by the Ladies' Association, the prisoners were no longer 'a herd of irreclaimable creatures'; 'their reciprocal sentiments' awakened by 'those fine sisters of charity'.[29]

While historians have rightly scrutinised the unequal power relationships that structured philanthropic encounters, their emphasis on discipline has obscured a crucial element in what Buxton saw as the Quaker Ladies' 'experiment … as important as any … attempted by ingenious humanity'.[30] Committed to the Christian imperative of personal communication and reciprocal kindness, Fry and her associates appear to have responded to inmates' demands and understanding of their own needs, rather than simply imposing upon them their authority. Fry's 'calling' came not just from God; the 'Newgate heroine' was called into being by the women themselves, as suggested by an extract from her diary, cited by many memoirs. It was only on her third visit to the gaol that Fry was moved to speak, despite trepidation, after her Quaker friend Anna Buxton had addressed 'the poor female felons'. Fry had not intended to speak but was inspired to do so by the prisoners: 'I heard weeping, and I thought they appeared much tendered; a very solemn quiet was observed: it was a striking scene; the poor people on their knees around us, in their deplorable condition.'[31] As Annemieke van Drenth and Francisca de Haan indicate, phrases like 'our women', 'poor prisoners' and 'poor creatures' appear to have been more typical of Fry's intercourse with inmates than her reference to 'wild beasts'.[32] It was a point stressed by many memoirists. Her 'simpleness and gentleness', claimed Kavanagh, was more effective than 'admonition or reproach'.[33]

Though Fry's biographers focused on how she communicated with her flock, they suggested, more obliquely, how her congregation responded to female pastorship. From the start, Fry believed reclamation depended on gaining the consent of inmates, and her programme developed in response to their demands: 'Want of employment, was the subject of *their continual lamentation. They complained* that they were compelled to be idle' (my emphasis). Fry planned initially to open a school for their children. The extension of schooling to the women was requested by prisoners: 'Their zeal for improvement, and their assurances of good behaviour, were powerful motives and *they tempted* these ladies to project a school for the employment of the tried women, for teaching them to read, and to work' (my emphasis).[34] With a show of hands, prisoners consented to rules devised by the Ladies, unanimously renouncing reading novels, gaming, singing popular songs, dancing and 'dressing up in men's clothes' in return for Bible reading, education and needlework.[35] They had powerful incentives – the acquisition of new skills and learning – but they also seem to have responded to mutual responsibility. Forming prisoners into groups, Fry required them to elect their own monitors and left them alone to select 'the most proper person' from their ranks as schoolmistress.[36]

The prisoners' commitment to the 'rule of kindness' – and their susceptibility to religious impression – are suggested by an anecdote mentioned by Buxton and frequently repeated. Fearing that the women continued gaming, one of the ladies urged them to give up their cards, if not for their own sakes then out of kindness to their teachers. Five women handed over their cards and were remunerated with a new muslin handkerchief each. One girl 'looked disappointed', confessing she had hoped for a Bible with her own name written inside it, 'which she should value beyond anything else, and always keep and read'.[37] We might be tempted to read the episode more sceptically than Fry's biographers, and it appears to have inspired the most iconic and complex image of her work at Newgate – Jerry Barrett's *Mrs Fry Reading to the Prisoners in Newgate, 1816* (c. 1860; figure 7) – a version of which has illustrated the Bank of England's five-pound note since 2002. As Booth suggests, the seated Mrs Fry in the 'well-lit focal point of the painting', with her plain dress, open palm, and hand resting on the Bible, 'all do much to refer the viewer to the saints in art'.[38] The two Magdalene figures on whom her gaze seems fixed embody the ambiguous appearance of female reclamation, one apparently bowing in repentance, the other concealing a pack of cards behind her friend's back.[39]

Bible reading was at the heart of Fry's ministry and the core activity of female

7 Jerry Barrett, *Mrs Fry Reading to the Prisoners in Newgate, 1816*, engraving.

visiting societies established across Britain on the lines established by the Ladies' Committee.[40] Watching and listening to a lady reading, prisoners would not only absorb scriptural lessons but model themselves on her open and gentle demeanour, a process further reinforced by the monitorial system. According to Booth, exemplary studies of Fry and other women philanthropists 'mimic the pedagogical methods of the ministering women themselves', focusing on the 'scene' where the woman reads the Bible aloud to 'subordinated ranks of other women or conscripted groups of men'.[41] Readers, likewise, would learn to model themselves on these exemplary women. Sarah Martin, too, would be pictured as this kind of philanthropic heroine, though as we shall see, she did not view her reclamation work at Great Yarmouth in the terms of 'female mission' set out by Fry.

## 'The jail missionary': Sarah Martin

It is likely that Martin was influenced by the Newgate experiment, for she began visiting Yarmouth Gaol in 1818 to read the Bible with inmates. She met Fry just once, in 1832, showing her around the prison on one of the reformer's many unofficial 'inspections' of British and foreign gaols. Fry commended 'the regular order of the prisoners' and the women's needlework, produced under the eye of the professional dressmaker, Martin; she purchased baby linen to show the Ladies' Committee, 'as they were much better both in Quality of Materials and in that of sewing work'.[42] Following their meeting, Martin received £5 annually from the Ladies' Committee to support her prison work.[43] Fry, however, made no mention of Martin in public, and neither did Martin refer to Fry or other prison philanthropists in her short memoir. Both women, however, were frequently linked in memoirs and sketches.

Unlike Fry, Martin made no effort to publicise her work. Some years before her death, she was urged 'to write an outline of my life with the view of encouraging others in instructing prisoners' but laid aside the manuscript owing to 'the strange impropriety' of a public account. On her deathbed Martin resumed the narrative, resolving to excise all 'egotistical appearance'. Paradoxically for a woman later hailed as an exemplary figure, she read the lives of philanthropic and 'enlightened people' only 'sparingly', preferring to search Scripture as her guide to God's work. Nevertheless, she presented her 'simple account' to demonstrate what could be achieved by the lone Christian acting under divine agency: 'in the absence of all human sufficiency on my part, whether of money, or influence, or experience, it is plain that God alone inclined my heart ... Hence arises the boundless encouragement which it presents to others; for the most humble individual, in any department of the providence of God.'[44] The message would be reiterated in her memorialisations.

Martin revealed little personal detail, other than that she was the orphaned daughter of a village tradesman, raised by her grandmother, a glovemaker and 'meek and lowly Christian'. She barely mentioned her work as a dressmaker or the personal sacrifices she must have made by devoting all her spare time and resources to the poor. Her narrative avoided sentimentality and sensation, though these were used by her biographers to lend character and drama to her tale. The only 'personal' element in the memoir was the story of Martin's youthful fall from grace and subsequent spiritual conversion, which defined her life and work and served to warn and inspire others: rejection of the Bible, seduction by novels and atheistic literature, intellectual pride, the mercy of salvation, and the divine grace that girded her lifelong struggle against doubt. The anonymous editor – and later biographers – framed Martin's memoir in the conventions of the evangelical 'good life', concluding with an account of her pious, brave and joyous death. For Victorian readers, these parts of the memoir probably established Martin, not as the sinner she saw herself, but as a self-sacrificing saint along the 'practical' lines discussed by Roshan Allpress in chapter 12 of this volume. 'It made me shed many tears, from the sense of her superior virtue, and my own inferiority', wrote the writer Amelia Opie (1769–1853), collaborator with Fry in establishing female nursing societies. 'What an example she was, and how illustrative her life of what that of a humble, but real, and confiding Christian should be! and her end was one of intense bodily suffering!'[45]

Martin planned to include 'a few short accounts of some prisoners, to whom God brought the truth with power to their conversion'; for her, their testimony of divine benevolence was as significant as her own.[46] Their inclusion would have been appropriate for a woman whose life was defined by those she served, but illness prevented its realisation. Instead, the editor supplemented Martin's 'brief sketch' of prison visiting (thirty-three pages) with extracts (twenty-five pages) from her 'Every Day Book' and 'Liberated Prisoners Book' in which she traced her students' conduct while under instruction and after release: 'It astonishes me to observe how strictly and constantly the prisoners labour to learn their verses from the Holy Scriptures, every day. Poor old S. takes uncommon pains to remember one.'[47] No previous study had drawn in such detail the day-to-day interaction between prisoners and their teacher. Unlike the dramatised portrayals of the Newgate women, the extracts hint at the diverse and complex responses of inmates to Christian reclamation.

Journal entries were selected to show Martin's approval of contemporary approaches to prison discipline; her desire that the gaol might have a treadmill and separate prisoners more effectively: 'in the absence of fixed occupation of a deterring kind, these boys may well be always full of spirits, just like school-boys on a playground'. The excerpts demonstrated the effectiveness of useful employment: 'The boy B is making patch-work for a quilt to cover a poor child ... W. told me the more work I gave them to do the quieter they are, and then there was plenty of time to learn their lessons: the other men joined in the observation.'[48] Combined with details of Martin's careful accounting – how subscriptions and sale of prisoners' work enabled her to supply them with more employment and help destitute families – the extracts showed how to undertake practical Christian charity. Including several of Martin's gaol sermons, the volume illustrated how Christian women – not only Quakers like Fry – might conduct religious services. Other excerpts recording snatches of conversations between Martin and inmates suggested how philanthropists should communicate with the poor. They also revealed Martin's intimate and inquisitorial intervention in the lives of former prisoners who sought her approval and assistance:

> T.B. came this morning to tell me, he had obtained work as a bricklayer's labourer ... 'I have earned 4s ... it is all for victuals and clothes. I went to the Sunday school and took my sister's little boy with me: I told Mr F. you sent me, and he was very kind ... I met B., and he asked me to go with him in a boat on Sunday, but I told him I would not, for I should go to school, and said "You had better go too".'
> T.B. has no work to-day but ... I found him ... playing at marbles. I advised him, if he had time and wished for a little play, to drive a hoop or throw a ball, but strongly deprecated marbles as children's gaming, which was not likely to end there.[49]

Particularly striking in these excerpts – and the journals from which they were extracted – is the absence of the class condescension found in other philanthropic discourse. Renting a small apartment near the prison in the working-class district where most inmates lived and worked, Martin was their neighbour rather than a distant visitor. She never referred to prisoners as savages, beasts or heathens but addressed them as fellow sinners like herself. Neither did she invoke the ideal of 'woman's mission' to sanction her work, nor to appeal to prisoners, though this was a pervasive feature of contemporary female activism.

It is notable that the delineation of Martin's personality in her biographies owed more to the Prison Inspector's reports that closed the memoir than the journal jottings of the stern, exacting teacher. His eulogium firmly aligned her with the feminine ideals of contemporary gender ideology: 'Her simple, unostentatious, yet energetic devotion to the interests of the outcast and the destitute, her gentle disposition, her temper never irritated by disappointment nor her charity straitened by ingratitude ... are rarely embodied in humanity.'[50] The Inspector had watched Martin work with prisoners – they listened to her sermon with 'the profoundest attention and most remarked respect, and ... appeared to take a devout interest' – but the character that emerges from her journals is formidable rather than 'gentle'.[51]

The Inspector's commendations provided material for Martin's hagiographic transformation, which took shape in an 1847 *Edinburgh Review* notice of her biography, which later accounts quoted heavily. Martin was 'a poor dressmaker; a little woman of gentle, quiet manners, possessing no beauty of person, nor, as it seemed, any peculiar endowment of mind'.[52] Her saintliness was implied by comparison with Fry – 'a woman of education' who moved 'in the higher walks of life', was trained for public speaking by a religious community, and was 'supported by influential and well-tutored assistants'. The contrast validated the distinctiveness of a working woman's charity: 'we think there was something far more simple, and far more nearly heroical, in the conduct of [Mrs Fry's] humbler sister'. 'Humble' became the term most frequently associated with Martin. The dressmaker was a 'noble' example of labouring-class philanthropy in works aimed at the artisan and mechanic classes.[53] The example of what a poor woman could achieve, working alone, emphasised what her more privileged sisters might do. Martin was, claimed *Women of Worth*, an example to her sex: 'moral loveliness enshrined in female form'. Its illustration of the 'Jail Missionary' depicted her not as the middle-aged author of the journals but as a young woman (figure 8). All Victorian portraits presented Martin in the same youthful, chaste, demure and humble guise.[54] These provided young readers with appealing and unthreatening images of a Christian activist whom they could identify with and emulate.

Sentimentalism deflected potential criticism regarding two conceivably controversial areas of Martin's activity: her unsupervised work with male prisoners and her daring intrusion into the masculine preserve of preaching.[55] While the *Edinburgh Review* noted that she was guided at all times by the Bible, her actions were depicted as springing from a feeling heart. Rather than enforcing 'religious terror', her teachings, urged with 'a kindly, warm-hearted sincerity', won 'the respect and attention' of her hearers because they 'flowed naturally out of a knowledge of their feelings'. Martin's 'lowly' and 'natural' ministry was more suited to the current time than outdated religious authority, asserted the *Edinburgh Review*, using her gaol services to vindicate wider claims for female ministry. In a much-quoted passage, it censured men who 'stiffly' condemned lay, and especially female, preachers only to 'inflict upon us ... the theology (as it is called) of the Fathers, or of the middle ages'; 'the cold, laboured eloquence' of the 'boy-bachelors ... sink[s] into utter worthlessness by the side of the jail addresses of this poor uneducated seamstress'.[56] Here, as we see in other studies

8  W. Dickes, *The Jail Missionary*, reproduced from *Women of Worth: A Book for Girls* (1859: New York, 1863), p. 85.

in this volume, sanctity was closely linked with this-worldly practicality and a repudiation of the priestly and ascetic exemplars set forth by Anglo-Catholics and others.[57] By stressing how Martin gave voluntarily the spiritual and moral guidance that should have been provided officially, the hagiographical sketches implicitly criticised institutional neglect and urged a more intimate and involved response to the outcast (figure 9).

### Sisters in charity

Saintliness was a quality assigned to Elizabeth Fry and Sarah Martin rather than claimed by them. Unsurprisingly, the Quaker Fry was much disturbed by saintly iconography. Though in 1839 she was impressed, for instance, by the Brethren and Sisters of St Joseph at Avignon, who lived with inmates and worked as turnkeys, she told a meeting of Protestants and Catholics in the town of her concerns:

9 [Joseph] Swain, *Sarah Martin Conducting Service in Yarmouth Gaol*, wood engraving. Reproduced from Edwin Hodder, *Heroes of Britain in War and Peace* (London, [1879–80]), p. 186.

But the mixture of gross superstition is curious, the image of the Virgin dressed up in the finest manner, in their different wards. I feared, that their religion lay so much in form and ceremonies, that it led from *heart work*, and from the great change which would probably be produced, did these Sisters simply teach them Christianity. Their books appeared to be mostly about the Virgin; not a sign of Scripture to be found in either prison or refuge [my emphasis].[58]

Fry's reference to 'heart work' epitomises not only how she understood Christian philanthropy, but how female vocation and ministry would be represented in hagiographic treatments of charitable women. Such portrayals have been overshadowed by recent histories which claim that the language of Christian pastorship masked the class and gender authoritarianism of Victorian philanthropy. The work of prison reformers — however benignly intended — has been presented as leading inexorably to the rise of the modern penitentiary.[59] Returning to the popularisations of Fry's and Martin's work, however, suggests that philanthropy, while implicated in disciplinary society, retained a powerful critique of dehumanising public institutions that found its way even into exemplary stories aimed at Sunday-school readers and young Christian women.

While early responses to Fry lauded her as the 'guardian angel of the *prison house*' who had domesticated Newgate and civilised its female inmates by turning it 'from a *den* of thieves into a *house* of prayer [my emphasis]', by the 1830s her insistence on the superiority of moral reclamation over more punitive forms of discipline faced sustained critique.[60] Under intense interrogation before parliamentary select committees in 1832 and 1835 Fry defended the employment of prisoners in productive labour and challenged the use of the treadmill, silence and solitary confinement: 'I think there is more cruelty in the gaols than I have ever seen before.'[61] In 1836, while acknowledging the moral improvement brought about by female visitors at Newgate, the Prison Inspectors effectively proscribed their work, listing numerous complaints including the impropriety of their recent visits to male prisoners and the 'injudicious' attendance of outside spectators at Fry's Friday services. By the 1840s, the Inspectorate was dominated by supporters of separate confinement. The call for Societies for Discharged Prisoners along the lines set out by Martin, made by the Inspector to Yarmouth in 1840, was ignored.

With prison philanthropy on the back foot, Fry's memoirs provided an extended exposition and defence of the necessity of women's involvement in moral reclamation while reports of Martin's work sought to provide a practical outline of how reclamation could be extended to include discharged prisoners and their families. Hagiographic portrayals of the two philanthropists therefore helped popularise a forceful critique of punitive discipline and institutionalisation. Asking why Protestant women could not become sisters of mercy like their Catholic counterparts in Europe, Fry's daughters concluded:

The best regulated and well-planned institution is but a body without a soul, whilst rules and regulations are enforced, unaccompanied by *personal influence or individual communication*. The prisoner, the lunatic, the hospital patient require these to touch the heart, to reach the malady, or give confidence under suffering and painful treatment [my emphasis].[62]

This passage was quoted by Louisa Twining (1820–1912) in the *Journal of the Workhouse Visiting Society* in 1859.[63] Twining was also inspired by Sarah Martin's account of her gaol services. After reading the prison visitor's memoir she began delivering sermons to inmates too ill to attend chapel, much to their delight, she found. Anna Jameson urged Twining to read *Sisters of Charity* and accompanied her around the Strand Workhouse while she was working on the *Communion of Labour*.[64] As Booth notes, women reformers' emphasis on practical action is found in the popular biographies of eminent women, from the mid-century onwards, which 'move beyond the common legend of the angel of mercy' to show that 'women's service was systematic rather than miraculous, public as well as personal'.[65]

Fry's and Martin's emphasis on personal intercourse and connection with the sinner and outcast has tended to be viewed as one-way communication but their memoirs remind us that fellowship was supposed to be, and in practice could be, reciprocal. Occasionally, if we are attentive, we can just catch in their memoirs and retellings, snatches of the voices of those touched by these ministering women. When Henrietta Ward was preparing her painting of *Mrs Fry Visiting Newgate*, Katharine Fry (1801–86) gave the artist some roses from the plant from which her mother picked flowers to give the women prisoners, for, she said, 'they proved a means of softening their hearts and giving them a vision of beauty'.[66] In Ward's painting Fry has a red rose pinned to her breast, to which she holds her red-covered Bible, each symbolising her 'heart work' (figure 6). Following Fry's death, her family received a letter from a former Newgate prisoner, Hester Clark (born c. 1791), sentenced to seven years' transportation for shop-lifting. Elected by fellow inmates as schoolmistress, Clark effectively became one of Fry's sisters of charity. Departing Newgate, Fry gave the convict 'a pound lump of sugar, and half a pound of tea'. Married for twenty years, Clark now wished 'her former benefactress' to know that in New South Wales she had 'plenty of pigs and fowls; buys her tea by the chest; and that the patchwork quilt which now covers her bed, was made of the pieces given to her by the ladies when she embarked.' To the ministering woman who brought red roses to the women at Newgate Gaol, the former prisoner sent a calabash from her very own garden.[67]

## Notes

1 Mrs [Anna] Jameson, *Sisters of Charity; and, The Communion of Labour, Two Lectures on the Social Employments of Women* (London: Longman, etc., 1859) pp. 34, 11, 25.

2 'Ursula, St', in Hugh Chisholm (ed.), *Encyclopaedia Britannica*, 29 vols (11th edn, Cambridge: Cambridge University Press, 1911), XXVII: pp. 803–4.

3 With the exception of occasional references to women's critiques of Saint Paul's injunction

against female preaching, saints are conspicuously absent from the following seminal histories of women and religion: Gail Malmgreen (ed.), *Religion in the Lives of English Women, 1760–1930* (Bloomington: Indiana University Press, 1986); Susan Morgan (ed.), *Women, Religion and Feminism in Britain, 1750–1900* (Basingstoke: Palgrave, 2002); Sue Morgan and Jacqueline deVries (eds), *Women, Gender and Religious Cultures in Britain, 1800–1940* (London: Routledge, 2010).

4   Susan Mumm, *Stolen Daughters, Virgin Mothers: Anglican Sisterhoods in Victorian Britain* (London: Leicester University Press, 1999).
5   Alison Twells, '"The innate yearnings of our souls": subjectivity, religiosity and outward testimony in Mary Howitt's *Autobiography* (1889)', *Journal of Victorian Culture*, 17 (2012), 310.
6   Eileen Janes Yeo, 'Protestant feminists and Catholic saints in Victorian Britain', in Yeo (ed.), *Radical Femininity: Women's Self-representation in the Public Sphere* (Manchester: Manchester University Press, 1998), pp. 126–48. See also Kimberley van Esveld Adams, *Our Lady of Victorian Feminism: The Madonna in the Work of Anna Jameson, Margaret Fuller, and George Eliot* (Athens: Ohio University Press, 2001).
7   Mrs Jameson, *Legends of the Madonna, as Represented in the Fine Arts* (1852; London: Longman, etc., 1857), p. xvii.
8   Jameson, *Sisters of Charity*, p. 26. See [Thomas Babington Macaulay], 'Ranke's *History of the Popes*', *Edinburgh Review*, 72, 144 (1840), 227–58, and Gareth Atkins, 'Ignatius Loyola', pp. 127–43, in this volume.
9   For which, see Alex Tyrell, '"Woman's Mission" and pressure-group politics in Britain (1825–60)', *Bulletin of the John Rylands Library*, 63 (1980), 194–230; Clare Midgley, *Women Against Slavery: The British Campaigns, 1780–1870* (London: Routledge, 1992); Helen Rogers, *Women and the People: Authority, Authorship and the Radical Tradition in Nineteenth-Century England* (Aldershot: Ashgate, 2000); Michael J. D. Roberts, *Making English Morals: Voluntary Association and Moral Reform in England, 1787–1886* (Cambridge: Cambridge University Press, 2004); Alison Twells, *The Civilising Mission and the English Middle Class, 1792–1850: The 'Heathen' at Home and Overseas* (Basingstoke: Palgrave, 2009).
10  [John Bruce], 'Life of Sarah Martin – prison-visiting', *Edinburgh Review*, 85, 122 (1847), 320–40; *Sarah Martin, the Prison Visitor of Great Yarmouth, with Extracts from her Writings and Prison Journals* (1844; London: Religious Tract Society [1847]), p. 143.
11  Cited in [George Mogridge], *Sarah Martin, The Prison Visitor of Yarmouth: A Story of a Useful Life* (London: Religious Tract Society [1872]), pp. 167–8.
12  Cited by Annemieke van Drenth and Francisca de Haan, *The Rise of Caring Power: Elizabeth Fry and Josephine Butler in Britain and the Netherlands* (Amsterdam: Amsterdam University Press, 1999), p. 195, n. 6; and Janet Whitney, *Elizabeth Fry, Quaker Heroine* (London: George G. Harrap, 1937), p. 277.
13  Emma R. Pitman, *Elizabeth Fry* (London: W. H. Allen, 1884), p. 186.
14  Tricia Lootens, *Lost Saints: Silence, Gender, and Victorian Literary Canonization* (Charlottesville: University Press of Virginia, 1996), p. 9.
15  *Sarah Martin, the Prison Visitor* [1844]; Katherine Fry and Rachel Elizabeth Cresswell (eds), *Memoir of the Life of Elizabeth Fry, with Extracts from her Journals and Letters*, 2 vols (London: Gilpin, 1847).
16  Alison Booth, *How to Make It as a Woman: Collective Biographical History from Victoria to the Present* (Chicago: University of Chicago Press, 2004), pp. 394–5.

17  Julia Kavanagh, *Women of Christianity: Exemplars for Acts of Piety and Charity* (London: Smith, Elder, 1852), p. 466.
18  Pitman, *Fry*, pp. 164–5. Kavanagh wrote at length on the charity of Saint Elizabeth and Catherine of Siena. While she commended Teresa of Avila's learning, she conceded that many readers would be mystified by her mystical writings. See Kavanagh, *Women*, pp. 140–1. Frances Power Cobbe (1822–1904) compared Fry with Saint Monica and Saint Elizabeth alongside holy and illustrious women since the classical age in 'The final cause of woman', in Josephine E. Butler, *Woman's Work and Woman's Culture: A Series of Essays* (London: Macmillan, 1869), pp. 2–3.
19  Thomas Fowell Buxton, *An Inquiry, Whether Crime and Misery are Produced or Prevented, by Our Present System of Prison Discipline* (London: John and Arthur Arch, 1818).
20  Long extracts appeared in 1818 in, for example, 'Prison discipline', *Edinburgh Review*, 30, 60 (1818), 479–86; 'Mrs. Elizabeth Fry', *Lady's Monthly Museum*, 7 (1818), 301–12; *Edinburgh Magazine*, 82 (1818), 356–8; *Christian Observer*, 17 (1818), 446–56; 'Moral reformation at Newgate' and 'Proceedings of the Ladies Committee at Newgate, London', *Christian Herald and Seaman's Magazine*, 5 (1818), 513–22, 545–52.
21  Buxton, *Inquiry*, pp. 114–15, 118.
22  In her examination of early Victorian depictions of Lady Jane Grey in the Tower, Billie Melman argues that her 'transformation into a saint involves various inroads on Victorian gender ideology' and that the popular, gothic 'image of the dungeon ... was feminized and domesticated in the early 1840s'. That process had already begun with Fry, however, and might be traced back further to representations of female captivity in gothic novels by Ann Radcliffe (1764–1823) and Mary Wollstonecraft (1759–97). See Melman, *The Culture of History: English Uses of the Past, 1800–1953* (Oxford: Oxford University Press, 2006), p. 157.
23  Booth, *How to Make It*, pp. 148, 125–7, 160–5.
24  Fry's journal, 14 April 1817, cited in Fry, *Memoir*, I: p. 261.
25  Randall McGowen, 'A powerful sympathy: terror, the prison, and humanitarian reform in early nineteenth-century Britain', *Journal of British Studies*, 25 (1986), 312–34.
26  Michel Foucault, *Discipline and Punish: The Birth of the Prison*, trans. Alan Sheridan (1975; Harmondsworth: Penguin, 1991); Buxton, *Inquiry*, pp. 134, 127.
27  Yeo, 'Protestant feminists'.
28  Jameson, *Sisters of Charity*, p. 200.
29  *Women of Worth: A Book for Girls*, ill. W. Dickes (London: James Hogg, 1859), p. 42.
30  Buxton, *Inquiry*, p. 133.
31  Fry's journal, cited in Pitman, *Fry*, p. 29.
32  Van Drenth and de Haan, *Caring Power*, p. 70. See, for example, Fry's address delivered to prisoners at Berne in 1839: Thomas Timpson, *Memoirs of Mrs Elizabeth Fry* (New York: Stanford and Swords, 1847), pp. 324–30.
33  Kavanagh, *Women*, p. 443.
34  Buxton, *Inquiry*, pp. 114, 117, 118–19.
35  *Ibid.*, pp. 123–6.
36  Fry, *Memoir*, I: pp. 260, 277.
37  Buxton, *Inquiry*, p. 130.
38  Booth, *How to Make It*, p. 151.

39  Helen Rogers, 'The Bank of England's £5 note, Elizabeth Fry and the women of Newgate', *Crime in the Community*, www.crimeinthecommunity.wordpress.com/2013/04/29/the-bank-of-englands-5-note-elizabeth-fry-and-the-women-of-newgate, accessed 29 July 2014.
40  Matilda Wrench, *Visits to Female Prisoners at Home and Abroad* (London: Wertheim, 1852).
41  Booth, *How to Make It*, p. 137.
42  22 November 1832, Gaol Keeper's Journal, 1825–35, Norfolk Record Office, Y/L2/46.
43  *Sarah Martin*, pp. 21, 23; Wrench, *Female Prisoners*, p. 56.
44  *Sarah Martin*, pp. 5, 13, 36, 11, 37.
45  Extract from journal, c. 1847–48, Cecilia Lucy Brightwell (ed.), *Memorials of the Life of Amelia Opie* (London: Longman, Brown, 1854), p. 376.
46  *Sarah Martin*, p. 24.
47  *Ibid.*, p. 112.
48  *Ibid.*, pp. 126–7.
49  *Ibid.*, pp. 130–1. Helen Rogers, 'Thick as thieves', *History of the Emotions Blog*, 28 March 2014: https://emotionsblog.history.qmul.ac.uk/2014/03/thick-as-thieves, accessed 2 December 2015.
50  *Sarah Martin*, p. 137, citing *First Report of the Prison Inspectors* (1836), and p. 142, citing a letter from Captain William John Williams, 11 November 1843.
51  *Ibid.*, pp. 137–8.
52  [Bruce], 'Life of Sarah Martin', 323.
53  *Eliza Cook's Journal* (17 April 1852), 385; Samuel Smiles, *Brief Biographies* (Boston, MA: Ticknor and Fields, 1856), pp. 489–90.
54  *Women of Worth*, pp. 51–69, 68.
55  I have found no commentary that questioned either of these extraordinary aspects of her work.
56  'Sarah Martin', *Edinburgh Review*, 323–5, 330, 328–9.
57  See 'Introduction', pp. 14–17, and 'John Henry Newman's *Lives of the English Saints*', pp. 245–61, in this volume.
58  Fry, *Memoir*, II: p. 28.
59  Helen Rogers, 'Kindness and reciprocity: liberated prisoners and Christian charity in early nineteenth-century England', *Journal of Social History*, 47 (2014), 721–45.
60  'Eminent philanthropists', *Christian Examiner*, 2 (1825), 24.
61  Evidence of Mrs Elizabeth Fry, Mrs Elizabeth Pryer, Mrs Jane Pirie and Miss Catherine Fraser, *Second Report of the Select Committee of the House of Lords Appointed to Inquire into the Present State of the Several Gaols and Houses of Correction in England and Wales* (London: The House of Commons, 1835), pp. 327–43, quotation at p. 339: *House of Commons Parliamentary Papers Online*, https://.parlipapers.proquest.com/parlipapers, accessed 4 December 2015 .
62  Mrs Francis Cresswell, *A Memoir of Elizabeth Fry: By Her Daughter* (London: Piper, Stephenson & Spence, 1856), pp. 262–3.
63  *Journal of the Workhouse Visiting Society*, [1] (London: Longman, etc., 1859), p. 28.
64  Louisa Twining, 'Extracts from my diary', 12 February 1858, *Recollections of Workhouse Visiting and Management During Twenty-Five Years* (London: C. Kegan Paul, 1880) pp. 111–12, 95–6.

65 Booth, *How to Make It*, p. 127. For the practical nature of women's activism and writing in the mid nineteenth century, see Rogers, *Women and the People* and Kathryn Gleadle, *Borderline Citizens: Women, Gender, and Political Culture in Britain, 1815–1867* (Oxford: Oxford University Press, 2009).
66 Van Drenth and de Haan, *Caring Power*, p. 195, n. 7.
67 Fry, *Memoir*, I: pp. 445–6; Trial of ESTHER CLARK, April 1823, t18230409-103, *Old Bailey Proceedings Online*, www.oldbaileyonline.org, version 7.0, accessed 9 May 2012.

# 14

# John Henry Newman's *Lives of the English Saints*

## Elizabeth Macfarlane

'WHAT'S A SAINT?' HOWL the high-kicking demon chorus in *The Dream of Gerontius*, answering themselves: 'a bundle of bones / which fools adore'.[1] John Henry Newman's poem of 1865 picks up a major theme in the previous year's *Apologia Pro Vita Sua*, where he took considerable pains to defend an earlier endeavour, his *Lives of the English Saints* project of the mid-1840s. The recurrence in *Gerontius* is poignant, and suggestive of how the failure of the project continued to rankle with Newman two decades later. Events surrounding the *Lives* marked a climacteric within the Tractarian movement. The series was initiated by Newman as he contemplated resigning as Vicar of Oxford's University Church. It involved many from his circle, and its prospectus appeared in the final edition of the *British Critic* before its closure by Francis Rivington (1805–85). Newman's disappointment at what he termed the inability of the Church of England to tolerate the lives of her saints has rightly been assigned as a milepost on the path to his reception into the Catholic Church in October 1845, and the injudicious assault on Newman's integrity by Charles Kingsley (1819–75), almost twenty years later, found fuel in the project.

Yet the *Lives* have received scant attention in studies of Newman. Ian Ker's biography barely mentions them; nor does Sheridan Gilley. Martin Svaglic's *Apologia* edition attributes the Bollandist project to a mysterious contemporary, 'John van Bolland, who in 1843, began the work' of the eponymous productions of the Belgian Jesuits; Derek Holmes seeks to minimise Newman's involvement in the project, and to demolish any suggestion that his few contributions might be seen as inconsistent with a commitment to recognisable standards of objective accuracy.[2] It fell to the late Frank Turner to tease out a narrative of the production, demonstrating as he did so the vacillations in Newman's approaches to the project.[3] Recent work by H. S. Jones and Ciaran Brady, too, has given greater prominence to the *Lives*, demonstrating their place in the intellectual development of Mark Pattison (1813–84) and James Anthony Froude (1818–94), both contributors who recalled the project in later writings.[4] In fact, Newman's initial plans projected work by an array of rising scholars including R. W. Church (1815–90), John Sherren Brewer (1809–79) and A. W. Haddan (1816–73), 'towards a complete hagiography for England', through which a more sympathetic apprehension of Catholic history might be inculcated.

The *Lives of the English Saints* have been a subject of intrigue, misinformation, and little scholarship. This essay examines the *Lives* and their reception, arguing that Newman's relatively slight authorial contribution and his relinquishing the editorship of the series have caused the depth of his personal involvement to be overlooked. It suggests that though the short-lived project failed to provide the consolation Newman advertised and sought, it had an enduring effect upon his coterie and how others perceived it. The uneasy compromises between hagiography and history that the project engendered serve to underline broader contemporary discussions about history, truth-telling, what saints were for, and, above all, how one ought to write about them.

## Newman's saints

Aside from local and antiquarian productions, there had been no significant publication on English saints' lives from within the Church of England since Henry Wharton's *Anglia Sacra* (1691) had printed a number of episcopal lives as part of a history of English dioceses depicting pre-Reformation ecclesiastical history. Wharton (1664–95) had published the accounts he transcribed from monastic historians such as Eadmer and William of Malmesbury, rather than synthesising and commenting as the Catholic Alban Butler did in his *Lives of the Fathers, Martyrs and Other Saints* (1759). Butler (1709–73) worked with the encouragement of Richard Challoner (1691–1781), who had himself produced *Britannia Sancta* (1745) and *A Memorial of Ancient British Piety* (1760), both of which offered brief accounts of British saints as a prompt to domestic piety and remembrance. Beyond a spate of publication following the excavation of Cuthbert's tomb in Durham in 1827, comment on the saints from within the Church of England was extremely limited, prompting the then President of Oscott College, Nicholas Wiseman (1802–65), to indict the English in 1843 for ignorance of their saints.[5] Contemporary publications bear out his accusation: *Hierologus: Or, the Church Tourists* (1843), by the ecclesiologist John Mason Neale (1818–66), took in sites such as Guthlac's Crowland, but depicted the saints as evanescent shadows among the venerable ruins, while a *Christian Remembrancer* article on pilgrimage to St Albans made only passing mention to Alban.[6] Perhaps the most representative productions of the saints were the faux-medieval *Ingoldsby Legends* which Richard Barham (1788–1845), Minor Canon of St Paul's, published in *Bentley's Miscellany*, where figures such as Dunstan and Becket appear as humorous vehicles for commentary on contemporary veniality, with comic illustrations by George Cruikshank (1792–1878) and others. With the Bollandists' scheme wrongly perceived to have fallen into abeyance, but offering an intriguing model, the saints offered a *tabula rasa* for inscription by Newman and his circle.

In a sermon on Hebrews 12: 1, preached in September 1834, Newman made bold assertions on the benefits of a Christian believer's contact with the past in the persons of the saints through a process of learned sympathy and elective affinity: 'He by degrees learns to have [the saints] as familiar images before his mind, to unite his cause with theirs, and since their history comforts him, to defend them in his own day ... He had rather the present day should be proved captious, than a former day mistaken'.[7] The devotee of the saints was a liminal figure, mediating and defending the past, and locating his consolation within it: the sermon depicted seeking the company of the saints not as self-indulgent escapism, but a source of solace and, tellingly, conflict. The sermon echoes remarks made in the combative preface to the second part of Hurrell Froude's *Remains*, where readers were exhorted to follow divine dictates especially when they seemed to conflict with present-day *mores*.[8]

The development of Newman's ideas is evident in *Lyra Apostolica*, published in the *British Magazine* in 1833–36, where his section 'Hidden Saints' offered contrasting views of them as necessarily recessed from the common view of history and reason ('The hidden ones'), but also perceptible through personal revelation ('Transfiguration').[9] Newman's understanding of the role of the saints continued to reflect this uneasy opposition: on the one hand there was the austere cultivation of figures distant in time as a conscious act of educative piety and, on the other, the almost romantically charged moment of recognition.

Newman dated the inception of the project to correspondence with his earliest friend, John William Bowden (1798–1844). On 4 April 1841, Newman sought to discover whether Bowden had a new intellectual object in mind following his work on Gregory VII, and suggested to him that he might take up where Hurrell Froude (1803–36) had left off, in writing about Anselm: the brilliant but unstable Froude was to be an absent presence throughout the project. Newman's later annotation marked this letter as his immediate response to reading Wiseman's essay on the Donatists: 'It led me to publish "Lives of the English Saints."'[10] Newman's idea was that the life of Anselm he proposed to Bowden might be part of the renewed effort to persuade people towards a reawakened English catholicity: 'In order to kindle love for the national Church *and yet* to inculcate a Catholic tone, nothing else is necessary but to take our Church in the middle ages.'[11]

The programmatic development of the scheme began in the spring of 1843, with Newman asking Pattison to copy catalogues of saints in the Bodleian, and seeking suggestions of contributors from R. W. Church: by 1 April, Rivington had agreed to publish the *Lives*, pleased by the 'highly respectable' list of writers.[12] Writing to Bowden almost exactly two years after his initial approach, Newman had refined his objectives: 'I mean the work to be historical and devotional, but not controversial. Doctrinal questions need not enter.'[13] This view is somewhat contradicted by a letter to John Keble on 18 May, in which Newman set the project out as both a 'practical carrying out of Tract 90' and a means of occupying 'the minds of men in danger of running wild', giving them 'an interest in the English soil and the English Church' and bring them 'from doctrine to history, from speculation to fact'.[14] It was at least in part aimed at countering the Romeward drift of his unruly coterie.[15]

Newman's definition of a saint was fluid, including even the founders of Oxford colleges: he offered Keble Walter de Merton, and Froude Walter Stapleton; filial piety towards Oriel College accounts for his initial inclusion of its nominal founder, Edward II; and his admission of Anselm and Lanfranc illustrates the elasticity of the designation 'English'.[16] The initial allocation of all the Celtic saints to David Lewis (1814–95) of Jesus College proved excessive, and the prospectus published in October 1843 demarcated the Cornish saints as being too numerous to be attempted. Later in July, Brewer, future editor of the Rolls papers from the reign of Henry VIII but for now lecturer at King's College, London, set out the necessity of a plan for the *Lives*, lest the sheer volume of materials prove unmanageable.[17]

## Prospectus and reaction

The prospectus for the series, which had altered from 'History of the British Saints' to 'Lives of the English Saints', revisited Newman's theme of the consolation of the past in the traces and echoes of blessings received by early Christians from their apostolic forebears. Newman insisted that there were 'special reasons at this time' for looking to the saints of 'our own dear and glorious, most favoured, yet most erring and most unfortunate England'. His use of intensifiers emphasised the difficulty of the current position, while his studied ambiguity in referring to the duties owed to the Church 'which was in former times the Mother of St Boniface and St Ethel[d]reda' created an unsettling effect, suggestive not only of restiveness and dissatisfaction, but of questions about the validity of the English Church in his own day.[18] The *Lives* were to be the work of diverse hands, and would be published anonymously.

The prospectus was welcomed in some High Church circles: here was a project emulating the Benedictines' patristic library and completing the Bollandists' work.[19] Some correspondents offered contributions, though none was accepted. Others were more equivocal: Sir Francis Palgrave (1824–97), Deputy Keeper of the Rolls, was concerned that the series could do great good or great harm, and later commended the inclusion of an instance of Abbot Ceolfrid of Jarrow directing his monks to scriptural study to allay suspicions that the medieval Church held the Bible in low regard.[20] As proof sheets of the first life for publication, an account of Stephen Harding, Abbot of Citeaux, by J. B. Dalgairns (1818–76) began to circulate in November, further disquiet was expressed. In correspondence with the lawyer James Robert Hope (1812–73), Newman became aware of Gladstone's misgivings, the ostensible cause of his eventual withdrawal from editing the series. Whilst Gladstone expressed revulsion at the apparent approval of doctrines to which the Church of England was opposed, and the implication that there could be no communion with the saints of the Middle Ages without acquiescence to Rome, his greatest unease was with the tone adopted towards the English Church, which thought likely 'to cherish and aggravate estrangement'.[21] He portrayed his reservations in terms of caveats and modifications, criticising not 'the writer's mind, but the sound of his language': for the time being, these were criticisms not of design, but of execution.

Newman's response to these expressions of concern was far from sanguine. To

Hope he refused to concede that others might find the series 'repugnant and prejudicial' and would not admit to being aware of any 'tone' that his correspondent might have identified as problematic, following this with a tirade ironically echoing the closing remarks of Saint Paul's great paean to charity: 'Now Church History is made up of these three elements – miracles, monkery, popery.'[22] Unlike Gladstone, from whose comments he distanced himself, Hope was anxious to reassure Newman that he had read the proofs 'greedily', but he suggested that some passages were 'needlessly direct and pointed' and might be given 'obliqueness'.[23] Seeking to alleviate Newman's sense of obligation regarding the financial expectations of contributors, and predicting of Rivington's withdrawal as publisher, Hope offered up to two hundred pounds to cover the expense of cancellation.

In the event, Rivington indeed declined to publish material inconsistent with his firm's role as a Church of England publisher. Having read the first three *Lives* – Dalgairns's *Harding*; *The Family of Richard the Saxon*, by Thomas Meyrick (1817–1903); and *St Augustine of Canterbury*, by Frederick Oakeley (1802–80) – he felt their tendency to be 'essentially Roman Catholic' and stated his (ultimately correct) impression that 'their writers will in course of time join the Roman communion'. He framed his rejection within his support for the views propounded in the Tracts, for which he was publisher, seeing the new enterprise as a deviation from those views.[24] Newman initially regarded it as beneath his dignity to approach a publisher, but early in January 1844, and with interest also expressed by John Murray, James Toovey was engaged. At around the same time Newman's brother-in-law, the printer John Mozley (1805–72), expressed significant misgivings: 'One cannot read the prospectus without feeling that such a work would be sure to contain much to do violence to the feelings of many who yet are very far from thinking themselves ordinary Low Churchmen': he, too, declined to undertake publishing the *Lives*.[25]

Turner's observation that Newman recoiled from exercising editorial discretion for fear of losing friendship must therefore be seen in the context of growing trepidation on the part of those who initially supported the idea. Their mild suggestions for revision were met with vehement rejection, and treated as tests of personal loyalty: Bowden recommended that the series be styled 'Acts' rather than *Lives*, on the basis that lives were hidden in God, to which Newman responded that Acts 'looks rather affected', especially given the paucity of activity.[26] Newman's decision in December 1843 to abandon schematic publication under his editorship, even before the publication of the first instalment, was, he told Hope, a highly personal sacrifice not to Gladstone's opinions, but to his own respectful feelings towards Gladstone, a comment illustrative of how far he had internalised his sense of the project.[27] At the close of 1843, Newman wrote to one of the most prolific authors, Frederick Faber (1814–63), that Rivington 'has got frightened at our Lives'. His tone bespoke his mounting frustration at the stalling of the series: 'Please, let yours, though not yet written, be published also.'[28]

## The Littlemore *Lives*

Over a period of eighteen months from March 1844, thirty-three lives appeared, ranging from a few pages long to the two-part life of Augustine.[29] The first to appear, Dalgairns's *Stephen Harding*, was anomalous in that it seemed to institute a series of 'The Cistercian Saints of England'; subsequent titles were to carry the uniform heading 'Lives of the English Saints', though they continued to use the same blackletter Gothic for the title. Most had Pugin frontispieces depicting the saints stylised in later medieval dress and settings, and all bore the series epigraph: 'Mansueti haereditabunt terram, et delectabuntur in multitudine pacis' (The meek shall inherit the land and delight in abundance of peace: Ps. 37: 11). Little survives in correspondence or later recollections to explain their authors' choice of subject, methods of research or composition. Both Froude and Pattison recalled the project as part of their intellectual development, Froude adducing it as part of his disillusion with dogmatic claims, Pattison as an awakening of academic vocation.[30] The treatment was uneven, with some, such as Church's *Wulstan*, presenting a thorough synthesis of sources, whilst others, especially those written by Faber, veered between sentiment and polemic. The 'series' created confusion: its numbers were inconsistent, being neither critical editions of texts nor Church history, but a hybrid which detailed the extreme ascetic piety of bishops and hermits in devotional language, intermingling this with accounts of the medieval English political scene. They did not offer academic apparatus or bibliographies; they were not commentaries on the vagaries of the source texts, but narratives. Some commentators drew unfavourable comparisons with T. E. Tomlins's translation of the Camden Society's text of Jocelin of Brakelond's *Chronicles of Bury St Edmunds*, also published in 1844.[31]

Newman's contributions were limited to two short lives and half of a third in *Hermit Saints*, as well as the advertisement for the second volume published, the *Family of St Richard*. There he stated that there was no 'prima facie' reason for the rejection of miracles, and suggested a dual epistemology, distinguishing the 'kinds of facts' proper to ecclesiastical history from those proper to secular history, and the distorting elements particular to each: in the former, credulity and superstition, and in the latter, 'party spirit, private interests, personal attachments, malevolence'.[32] A 'properly taught religious mind' would be able to discern the difference, he asserted, a feline if opaque distinction that perhaps revealed more about Newman's sense of *ethos* – how an individual's life and beliefs constantly shaped one another – than it did any practical advice for the reader.[33]

In his introductory comments for the 'Legend of St Bettelin', Newman used metaphors of unresolved distinction – homecoming travellers being given 'direction and confidence' by optical illusions of proximity, and medicinal herbs necessarily being impure compounds – to express why the truths saints represented were still compelling, although not always possible to analyse critically. The verification of particulars was unnecessary for devotion: 'There is no room for the exercise of reason – we are in the region of faith. We must believe and act, where we cannot discriminate.'[34] His conclusion, frequently misattributed to Froude's 'Legend of St Neot', is probably the only sentence from the entire project that has achieved some level of repetition and recognition, albeit as the apotheosis of the authors' collective abandonment of reason: 'And this is all that is known, and more than all, – yet nothing to what the angels know, – of the life of a servant of God, who sinned and repented, and did penance and washed out his sins, and became a Saint, and reigns with Christ in heaven.'[35] After the justificatory tenor of the prefatory comments, the deliberate choice of a simplistic, even childish register, emphasised the acceptance that the writers sought for their work.

Newman's other significant contribution to the volume, his 'History of St Edelwald' being almost entirely in quotation from Bede, was the account of a Welsh saint, Gundleus. Six and a half of the eight pages comprise introductory comments, in which Newman argued for the duty 'to make the unknown known' through a process of meditation, which 'does for the Christian what Investigation does for the children of men'.[36] The subjective work of the imagination was depicted in sacramental terms: hagiography was a means of building the Church, its 'holy' authors putting dialogues 'into the mouths' of saints to inculcate ideas which 'live within us by being broken into detail'. Newman's conclusion reverts to the unknowability of the subject, an appeal to the personal authority of the anonymous writer, and a creedal formula:

> Whether St Gundleus led this very life, and wrought these very miracles, I do not know; but I do know that they are Saints whom the Church so accounts, and I believe that, though this account of him cannot be proved, it is a symbol of what he did and what he was, a picture of his saintliness and a specimen of his power.[37]

## The tenor of the series

Writing to Bowden in February 1844, Newman admitted that it would have been better to have begun the series with well-known names. The *Lives* were, he maintained, 'an Anglican form', and the idea of their being a practical carrying-out of Tract 90 resurfaced in the preface to Dalgairns's 'Legend of St Helier'. Stating that there was 'no proof that the writers intended these stories to be believed at all', Dalgairns cited the Church of England's Sixth Article, suggesting that they might instead be 'read for example of life and instruction of manners', the same status afforded to the Apocrypha.[38] The precise ways in which the *Lives* were truly Anglican was to be expressed in a variety of ways by different contributors.

In the first part of his *Life of St Augustine*, the third number in the series, appearing in mid-1844, Frederick Oakeley went on the offensive against imagined complaints regarding the dearth of evidence. If the existence of a Saint George might be exploded by a skilful advocate as 'the unwritten record of empty pageants and bauble decorations', this was to demand the wrong sort of proof. 'What Catholic is there but would count it a profaneness to question the existence of St George?'[39] Oakeley's robustly patriotic invocation of England's patron saint, and references to how the supposed substance of unwritten folk belief supplemented the slender documentary evidence surrounding George, show that he failed (or maybe refused) to grasp what might make a medievalising and credulous account of Augustine so indigestible, not least the fact that, as several other chapters in this volume show, British Protestants continued to expend so much energy constructing narratives of early Christianity that bypassed the papal mission.[40] As ritualising incumbent of the Margaret Street chapel, Oakeley gradually took over the editorship of the series from Newman, converting to Catholicism only three weeks after him in October 1845.

Faber's opening salvo in *St Wilfrid*, also published in 1844, fuelled the impression that the series was to be understood in autobiographical terms:

> To be striving to do good and to follow conscience, to be secretly sure that, with many miserable failures, we are doing God's work, and yet the while to be misunderstood, cruelly misinterpreted by persons whom we not only acknowledge to be good but indeed far better than ourselves – this is a cross which Saints have sometimes had to bear.[41]

Faber's *Wilfrid*, consistent in this tenor, drew the majority of adverse comment, partly due, as Church observed of his career in general, to 'a want a severity of taste and self-restraint'.[42] One review suggested erroneously that Newman's editing might have moderated *Wilfrid*'s 'self-defeating tone': in reality, Newman not only urged Faber to write, but consoled him in the face of criticism, deriding parents who feared their children might turn hermit, and imagining 'many a pater-familias ... saying "Such trash shalln't come into my house"'.[43]

It is especially curious that Newman's words at the conclusion to 'St Bettelin' have been misattributed to Froude, whose prefatory remarks to his 'Legend of St Neot' brought nuanced psychological insights into the respective roles of readers and writers of hagiography. Newman had advised Froude on the desirability of maintaining 'the *religious* effect, and without pledging oneself to the truth of this or that fact, to imply that one does not know *how much* truth there might be in it, and that it reminds of truth and is edifying, even where it is fictitious' and the preface shows him carrying out the instruction.[44] Froude argued that the *Lives* were not 'strict biographies' but works to 'produce a religious impression in the mind of the hearer', a means of teaching character in which the facts are 'but ... frail, weary weeds': provided character-forming instruction may be adduced, it is of no matter whether they are 'true or not as facts'.[45] In excess of his brief, he reflected upon the basis of the whole undertaking: all historical writing must be shaped by its writers' subjectivity, and individuals might observe their own perceptions altering over the course of time, illustrating the human capacity to remould and revisit personal history, demonstrating that 'we all write Legends'.[46] Such reflections did not please everyone: the High Church *Christian Remembrancer* took exception, contrasting it unfavourably with Newman's 'Advertisement' in the *Family of St Richard*: Froude's 'ingenious' and 'consoling' analogies of the quotidian fictions of representation were irreverent and over-familiar. Would it be acceptable to produce a mythic life of the recently deceased Dr Arnold?[47] Nor did psychological speculation please Newman, whose aims in propagating tradition as a source of Catholic authority were not served by it: correspondence between the two suggests a coolness over 'Neot' that became icy when Froude eventually withdrew his proposed volume on Patrick.[48] His later repositioning was fundamentally a reiterative exercise, indicating his gradually expansive sense of the varieties of truth available to the writer and historian, and along with it his repudiation of the Oxford Movement as a whole.[49]

Newman's stated aim in the April 1841 letter to Bowden was to dissuade people of their 'prejudices against Catholicity as anti-national' and yet throughout the series there was recurrent criticism of the insular national Church. Faber diagnosed 'the true disease of England' as being its narrow temper of self-praise, 'leading the great mass of common minds to overlook with a bigoted superciliousness almost the very existence of the Universal Church'.[50] Few statements in the extensively reviled *Life* were as revealing as Faber's defence of Wilfrid's action in appealing to Rome over the head of the Archbishop of Canterbury: what was 'in modern language' the betrayal of the national Church was 'translated into catholic phraseology' the rescuing of England from nationalism. This was a red rag to critical bulls. It was only too easy to read Wilfrid as a portrait of Newman and his teaching.[51]

## Critical responses

Contrary to Newman's much-rehearsed prediction – 'What then, cannot the Anglican Church bear the Lives of her Saints?' – and their subsequent excoriation as 'an oglio of unwholesome trash', early responses were far from discouraging.[52] The *Christian Remembrancer* was swift to discern, in Dalgairns's *Stephen Harding*, Newman 'writing with his whole heart' and 'perhaps unconsciously, picturing his own trials in those of his subject', not to mention reading significant lessons for the nineteenth-century Church in the corruption of the twelfth.[53] The reviewer objected to the asceticism of the *Lives*, mocking Pugin's frontispiece depicting 'the stern abbot of Citeaux', surrounded by beautiful objects in a Salisburyesque cloister, as incongruous: like Gregorian chant performed by young ladies in a drawing room.[54] Asceticism was especially problematic for commentators versed in the models of modern 'practical' sainthood analysed by Roshan Allpress in his chapter on Wilberforce and 'the Saints'.[55] There was no personal virtue in imitation, and no social good would have ensued from Howard or Wilberforce retiring to caves, or Lord Ashley enclosed in La Trappe.[56] Besides, the affected self-denial of present-day 'man-milliners' could hardly match the severe mortifications of a medieval saint. The *Edinburgh* could not resist wheeling out the much-mocked passages from Froude's *Remains* about the subject's temptation by 'roast goose and buttered toast'.[57]

In July, the *Remembrancer* expressed cautious approval, while warning against a 'dreaming church idealism' which might affect 'the young and ardent of either sex'.[58] It suggested a preface addressed to the 'Good English reader', who would be reminded that miracles no longer occurred, but reassured that this did not mean that the English

Church was especially diseased. The Good English reader stood in contrast to the 'unreal reader', who, imperilled by the hybrid form's elision of fact and fable, might then fail to distinguish the respect due to monkish legend from that due to Scripture: 'if thinkers are once led to the impression that the written Word is rather subjective than objective, we own that we could not answer Strauss'.[59]

Elsewhere, the need was identified to make the *Lives* more accessible. A correspondence grew up in the *English Churchman* following a complaint that they were expensive and that their price, between 3s. and 4s. for 120–30 pages, put them beyond the reach of the poor, who might benefit from them, the Derby Reprints of major Roman texts being cited as a model for affordable publishing.[60] Toovey replied that these works were longer, the Pugin plates adding a further £20 to the costs.[61] The publication in 1844 of a cheap edition of Conyers Middleton's 1749 *Free Inquiry into the Miraculous Powers Which are Supposed to have Subsisted in the Christian Church*, a vitriolic attack on the credibility of the Fathers, was widely regarded as an evangelical prophylactic against the *Lives*.[62]

The *Lives*' chief critic was John Clark Crosthwaite (1800/1–74), Rector of St Mary at Hill in London, an old-fashioned High Churchman who, through the pages of the *British Magazine*, undertook a prolix commentary on the volumes, later compiled into book form. His critique ranged from the personal, in which he wrongly associated Pusey with the project, to more wide-ranging accusations of undermining and 'explaining away' the Scriptures through allegorical reading, and on to rebellion and revolution. Like other critics he saw the danger as principally to the malleable young, 'who but lately would have traded on moustaches or a Byron tie', and decried the precocious sexualisation of children implicit in the 'fanatical panegyrics of virginity'.[63]

Although more belated, Kingsley's reaction was similar. While he was later famously to dredge up Newman's conduct of the project, his initial response was *The Saint's Tragedy*, a sub-Shakespearean account of Elizabeth of Hungary, begun as a wedding gift for his future wife at a time when he was composing refutations of the Tracts.[64] In it he contended that saints could only be recognised 'as they are felt to have been real men and women', and indeed, real Protestants.[65] Kingsley's vehement reaction against marital celibacy led him to caricature Elizabeth as the victim of monastic sadism, but at its publication five years later, F. D. Maurice's preface identified *The Saint's Tragedy* as an intervention against clergy who had betrayed their vocation 'in perverting history to their own ends'.[66] The target was clear. Interestingly, in his inaugural lecture as Regius Professor of Modern History at Cambridge in 1860, Kingsley referred to the necessity of understanding medieval lives, particularly those of the saints, by befriending the dead, bringing them back to life and trying 'to see with his eyes, and feel with his heart'. Gone was Newman's apprehensive liminality; in its place was sympathy and physical connection.[67]

## Afterlives

Just as Newman returned to the *Lives* in the *Apologia* and *Gerontius*, the project continued to resonate for other participants long after publication ceased. Faber's essays introducing volumes in his series of Oratorian *Lives* presented hagiography as a form of mystical theology, necessarily separate from literary biography, whose interest lay in the sympathy between reader, subject and form. Devotional reading allowed the reader and the *Life* to form 'a world of their own', far removed from the 'English activity' of intellectual argument.[68] Protestant biography, he averred, was a mere pastime, rather than a serious religious undertaking, and its readers were wilful children who would not take their medicine: 'To you the life of the Saint is the pill which you can only swallow when it is disguised as the life of the great man.'[69] In an extension of Newman's ideas about the Littlemore *Lives*, Faber argued for the essentially national character of lives shaping their writing 'for the taste of that country, directed against its prejudices, or moulded to them'.[70]

Froude repudiated the Littlemore enterprise in a paper given in 1850, while reserving saints' lives as a potential means of moral education through the example of the perfection of character and 'personal purity'.[71] He had resigned his Exeter fellowship the previous year following the scandal caused by his agnostic semi-autobiographical novel, *The Nemesis of Faith*, which, among other things, vividly portrayed its hero's struggle to subscribe to the ossified dogmas of the past. Not surprisingly, he rejected anachronistic approaches to medieval belief to enliven contemporary spiritual practice: there was no threshold for mediation, and no bridge by which saints might communicate.[72] The Littlemore enterprise was 'as foolish as, if the attempt had succeeded, it would have been mischievous'; an attempt to make devotion out of an unreality, rather than seeing saints for what they were: a reflex of the need to project ideal attributes onto scarcely known figures. Thirty years later, Froude revisited the project in his reminiscences about 'a series of biographies of distinguished English saints', in which he delineated himself as a somewhat naive participant.[73] He depicted it in dramatically personal terms, using metaphors of earthquake and shipwreck to describe the effect of discovering cracks in the historical foundations of Christianity. More revealing, perhaps, were his reflections on the creation of the Oxford Movement itself as a legend. If Keble had become 'a Saint of the Church of England', it was because: 'Now, and always, remarkable persons become mythical. Anecdotes are told of them, almost always inaccurate; words are assigned to them which they never spoke. Smaller luminaries are robbed to swell the greatness of the central orb.'[74] Making 'saints' was inextricably linked to the romances of impressionable youth and the idealising vagaries of memory.

On All Saints' Day 1863, Mark Pattison preached in Lincoln College Chapel on the rectitude of the English Church's approach to the saints, an approach characterised by 'moderation', 'wariness', and 'wisdom' in commemorating them but tempered with an awareness that invocation or prayer *to* them was not permitted. If they 'lived' it was through the continuing life of the Church. His *Stephen Langton* had attempted to demarcate its subject as 'public history', arguing for Langton's importance rather than presuming acquiescence on the part of readers.[75] Now, his sermon drew on many elements familiar from the Littlemore period, including reference to the violence of Protestant rejection of the saints; the hidden nature of the inner life; and the Church as a society of higher and invisible values, quoting from both Saint Bernard and Newman. For a generation too concerned with 'commercial' virtues and self-admiration, Pattison argued, saints' lives provided a moral corrective. Yet far from being due veneration for their eccentricities and prodigies of penance, they were and had always been examples of good living that all could and should follow. True saintliness was 'unobtrusive, retiring', consisting in simple sincerity, uprightness and wisdom. Pattison's hearers were pointed not just towards the early Church but to 'the biographies of Donne, Hooker, Sanderson, Hammond, Bull, Nelson', as well as modern lives and those beyond the Church of England, including (but not especially) holy men in the medieval Catholic Church.[76] It is indicative of this more liberal Protestant approach that Pattison could conclude his monumental 1875 account of Isaac Casaubon regretting the failure of his subject's intellectual objectivity 'in the service of a religious interest'.[77]

Yet the series had other, less self-exculpatory after-echoes. In 1877 an anonymous *Life of St Willibrord* appeared, dedicated to Newman. The preface indicated that it was originally intended to have been part of the *Lives* series: the text had lain 'dead and buried thirty three years' and now the 'resuscitated innocent' saw public life under Newman's auspices.[78] The following year, another Life appeared 'by the author of *St Willibrord*', its subject Saint Winfrid or Boniface. The *Lives*' themes were entirely of a piece with the original series: Willibrord imagined Victorian England's being under the spiritual darkness of an interdiction, as had *Stephen Harding*, whilst *Winfrid* stated that 'Alfred and Charlemagne ... were great because they were Catholics'.[79] They were the work of Meyrick, whose father had paid for the suppression of the original print run, and who had spent the intervening years alternating between the English and Roman Churches.

## 'England of Saints! Thy hour is nigh'

Neale's optimistic announcement of a time when English saints would be acknowledged was not realised through the Littlemore *Lives*.[80] Whilst Faber opined that the world lived in dread of Dunstans, Anselms, and Beckets, Anglicans considered them in very different terms.[81] Crosthwaite attributed to the English a vague sense of traditional veneration of saints as 'good and holy men', but this impression, he argued, was imperilled by the *Lives*' production of 'theatrical personages' working for effect.[82] Many of the *Lives* sought, as Gladstone had feared, to reserve the saints to the Roman Church, the project ultimately becoming a narrative of personal estrangement from Oxford and the Church of England, especially for its most prolific authors. 'Fairy tales of monasticism' were read by many as an extended autobiography of the Newman set:

a pastiche life was published of Saint Oldooman, an Anglican clergyman whose ludicrous medievalism and asceticism created social disorder and derision of the Church, but whose oblivious 'triumphant sect' established a monastic community with a rule of irrationality at Littlebitmore.[83]

Just as seriously for an age that prized truth-telling almost above all else, the series sat uneasily between scholarship and hagiology. While in the 1860s Newman's *Apologia* trumped Kingsley because of its account of its subject's strenuous quest for the truth, whatever the price, the events of the 1840s left a lingering sense of falsity and distortion. Kingsley later recalled the failures of differentiation, whereby some writers demanded that the 'common laws of evidence' be waived, and produced legendary material, whilst other *Lives* were 'told in earnest'.[84] In this most negative sense, the project was portrayed as a practical carrying out of Tract 90: a disingenuous reading of past statements (in this case exaggerated medieval eccentricity) for present purposes. Unlike James Stothert's *Justorum Semita* (1843), and a rash of other publications exploring the details of the Book of Common Prayer – including the saints in its Calendar – the Lives had no liturgical purpose, nor did they argue for Calendar revision. While at the time this was decades in the future, it is possible to discern threads linking Newman's half-formed ideas of the 1840s with a much more enduring intellectual achievement, his *Essay in Aid of a Grammar of Assent* (1870), but that lies beyond the bounds of this chapter.

In some ways, of course, Neale was right: change was at hand. When Charles Merivale (1808–93), the Dean of Ely, initiated the events of the Etheldreda commemoration in October 1873, it was with some hesitancy concerning her distinctly un-Victorian disobedience to her husband and vow of perpetual virginity, not to mention the fact that this was the first post-Reformation English celebration of its kind. Yet perhaps he should not have worried. Kingsley was the seemingly unlikely choice as preacher, and within twenty-five years ideas and images of saints were increasingly present in English churches.[85] Cathedral restorations and diocesan renewal, both placing emphasis on local identity, were the primary agents of change. As Newman was engaging with Kingsley in 1864, another Ely and Cambridge clergyman, William Selwyn (1806–75) published *Winfrid*, a poem dedicated to his brother, George Augustus Selwyn (1809–78), Bishop of New Zealand. It drew on accounts of medieval missionary heroism in depicting an idealised missionary bishop leading a band of faithful disciples. The saints were no longer languishing in ascetic reserve, but being deployed afresh in a variety of contexts, most strikingly, perhaps, in building the imperial Church.

## Notes

1 John Henry Newman, *The Dream of Gerontius and Other Poems* (London and New York: Oxford University Press, 1914), p. 19.
2 Ian Ker, *John Henry Newman: A Biography* (1990; Oxford and New York: Oxford University

Press, 2009), pp. 281–2; Sheridan Gilley, *Newman and His Age* (1990; London: Darton, Longman and Todd, 2003), pp. 220–1; John Henry Newman, *Apologia Pro Vita Sua*, ed. Martin J. Svaglic (Oxford: Clarendon Press, 1967), p. 585; J. Derek Holmes, 'Newman's reputation and *The Lives of the English Saints*', *Catholic Historical Review*, 51 (1966), 528–38.

3   Frank M. Turner, *John Henry Newman: The Challenge to Evangelical Religion* (New Haven and London: Yale University Press, 2002), pp. 474–526. For a recent if patchy treatment, see also Devon Fisher, *Roman Catholic Saints and Early Victorian Literature* (Farnham: Ashgate, 2012), pp. 53–86.

4   H. Stuart Jones, *Intellect and Character in Victorian England: Mark Pattison and the Invention of the Don* (Cambridge: Cambridge University Press, 2007), pp. 31, 146–7; Ciaran Brady, *James Anthony Froude: An Intellectual Biography of a Victorian Prophet* (Oxford: Oxford University Press, 2013), pp. 86–111.

5   [Nicholas Wiseman], 'National holydays', *Dublin Review*, 28 (1843), 481–505.

6   John Mason Neale, *Hierologus: Or, the Church Tourists* (London: James Burns, 1843); 'A summer's day pilgrimage', *Christian Remembrancer*, 6 (1843), 218.

7   John Henry Newman, 'The visible church an encouragement to faith', in Newman, *Parochial Sermons*, 6 vols (London: Rivingtons, 1834–42), III: p. 267.

8   John Henry Newman and John Keble (eds), *Remains of the late Reverend Richard Hurrell Froude, M.A., Fellow of Oriel College, Oxford, Part II*, 2 vols (London: J. G. and F. Rivington, 1839), I: p. xxxiii.

9   Newman, *Poems*, pp. 63–4, 110.

10  Anne Mozley (ed.), *Letters and Correspondence of John Henry Newman during His Life in the English Church*, 2 vols (London and New York: Longmans, Green, 1891), II: p. 345.

11  C. S. Dessain, *et al.* (eds), *The Letters and Diaries of John Henry Newman* (hereafter Newman, *Letters and Diaries*), 32 vols (London: Thomas Nelson and Sons; Oxford: Clarendon, 1961–2008), VIII: p. 155.

12  *Ibid.*, IX: pp. 277, 279.

13  *Ibid.*, IX: pp. 298–9.

14  *Ibid.*, IX: pp. 346–50.

15  Turner, *Newman*, p. 481.

16  Newman, *Letters and Diaries*, IX: pp. 324, 393. Oriel College continued prayers for Edward II, and repaired his tomb three times in the eighteenth century: Seymour Phillips, *Edward II* (New Haven and London: Yale University Press, 2010), pp. 62, 556.

17  Newman, *Letters and Diaries*, IX: pp. 442–3.

18  Newman, *Apologia*, ed. Svaglic, pp. 280–1.

19  *English Churchman* (19 October 1843), p. 667.

20  Palgrave to Newman, 18 October, 7 November 1843, Newman, *Letters and Diaries*, IX: p. 576, X: p. 16.

21  William Ewart Gladstone to James Robert Hope, 3 December 1843, *ibid.*, X: p. 43.

22  Newman to Hope, 2, 6 November 1843, *ibid.*, X: pp. 5, 12.

23  Hope to Newman, 5 December 1843, *ibid.*, X: p. 45.

24  Francis Rivington to Newman, 10 November 1843, *ibid.*, X: pp. 22–3.

25  John Mozley to Newman, 2 December 1843, 8 January 1844, *ibid.*, X: pp. 41, 81.

26  Bowden to Newman, 23, 31 October 1843, *ibid.*, IX: pp. 594, 596.
27  Newman to Hope, 16 December 1843, *ibid.*, X: p. 60.
28  Newman to Faber, 30 December 1843, *ibid.*, X: p. 74.
29  J. B. Dalgairns, *Stephen Harding*; Thomas Meyrick, *Family of St Richard*; Frederick Oakeley, *Augustine*, in two parts; John Henry Newman, Dalgairns, John Barrow and J. A. Froude, *Hermit Saints*; R. A. Coffin and R. W. Church, *William and Wulstan*; Frederick Faber, *Northumbrian Saints*; William Lockhart and J. B. Dalgairns, *Gilbert*; Faber, *Wilfrid*; John Walker, *German*, in two parts; Mark Pattison, *Stephen Langton* (all published London: James Toovey, 1844); Dalgairns and Barrow, *Aelred and Ninian*; Pattison and Dalgairns, *Edmund and Richard, Waltheof and Robert* (all published London: James Toovey, 1845). See S. L. Ollard, 'The Littlemore Lives of the English Saints', *St Edmund Hall Magazine* (1933), 82–3.
30  James Anthony Froude, 'The Oxford Counter-Reformation' in Froude, *Short Studies on Great Subjects*, 4 vols (new edn, London: Longmans, Green, 1895), IV: pp. 316–17, 323–32; Francis Charles Montague, 'Some early letters of Mark Pattison', *Bulletin of the John Rylands Library*, 18 (1934), 166–7; Mark Pattison, *Memoirs* (London: Macmillan, 1885), p. 186.
31  *Edinburgh Review*, 80, 162 (1844), 367; *Christian Observer*, 43 (1844), 764.
32  [John Henry Newman], 'Introduction', in *Family of St Richard, the Saxon* (2nd edn, London: James Toovey, 1844), pp. iii–iv.
33  See James Pereiro, *'Ethos' and the Oxford Movement* (Oxford: Oxford University Press, 2007).
34  [John Henry Newman], 'Legend of St Bettelin', in *Hermit Saints* (London: James Toovey, 1844), pp. 57–9.
35  *Ibid.*, p. 72.
36  [John Henry Newman], 'A Legend of St Gundleus', in *Hermit Saints*, p. 1.
37  *Ibid.*, p. 8.
38  [J. B. Dalgairns], 'A Legend of St Helier', in *Hermit Saints*, p. 11.
39  [Frederick Oakeley], *The Life of St Augustine, Archbishop of Canterbury, Apostle of the English* (London: James Toovey, 1845), p. 10.
40  See especially Martha Vandrei, 'Claudia Rufina' (chapter 3) and Andrew R. Holmes, 'Patrick' (chapter 4), in this volume.
41  [F. W. Faber], *St Wilfrid, Bishop of York* (London: James Toovey, 1844), p. 1.
42  Richard W. Church, *The Oxford Movement: Twelve Years 1833–1845* (London and New York: Macmillan, 1891), p. 205.
43  *Christian Remembrancer*, 9 (1845), 311; Newman to Faber, 31 January 1845, Newman, *Letters and Diaries*, X: pp. 517–18.
44  Newman to Froude, 28 November 1843, Newman, *Letters and Diaries*, X: p. 36.
45  [J. A. Froude], 'A Legend of St Neot', in *Hermit Saints*, pp. 74, 80–1.
46  [Froude], 'St Neot', pp. 75–9.
47  *Christian Remembrancer*, 8 (1844), 55.
48  Brady, *Froude*, pp. 105–6.
49  Elinor S. Shaffer, 'Shaping Victorian biography', in Peter France and William St Clair (eds), *Mapping Lives: The Uses of Biography* (Oxford and New York: Oxford University Press, 2002), p. 129; Froude, 'Oxford Counter-Reformation', pp. 323–4, 330–4.

50 [Faber], *Wilfrid*, p. 36.
51 John C. Crosthwaite, *Modern Hagiology: An Examination of the Nature and Tendency of some Legendary and Devotional Works*, 2 vols (London: John W. Parker, 1846), I: p. 81.
52 Newman to Hope, 6 November 1843, Newman, *Letters and Diaries*, X: p. 14; *Christian Observer*, 43 (1844), 765.
53 *Christian Remembrancer*, 7 (1844), 491–2.
54 *Ibid.*, 492.
55 See pp. 209–25 of this volume.
56 *Christian Observer*, 43 (1844), 754.
57 *Edinburgh Review*, 80, 162 (1844), 368.
58 *Christian Remembrancer*, 8 (1844), 42–3.
59 *Ibid.*, 54–6.
60 *English Churchman* (3 October 1844), pp. 633–4.
61 *Ibid.* (10 October 1844), p. 649.
62 *Christian Remembrancer*, 9 (1845), 309; *Edinburgh Review*, 80, 162 (1844), 365; *Christian Observer*, 43 (1844), 746.
63 Crosthwaite, *Modern Hagiology*, I: pp. 125, 26.
64 F. E. Kingsley (ed.), *Charles Kingsley: His Letters and Memories of His Life*, 2 vols (London: Henry S. King, 1877), I: p. 97.
65 Charles Kingsley, *The Saint's Tragedy* (London: John W. Parker, 1848), pp. 262, xxiii.
66 *Ibid.*, p. xiv.
67 Charles Kingsley, *The Limits of Exact Science as Applied to History* (Cambridge and London: Macmillan, 1860), pp. 4–6.
68 Frederick W. Faber, *The Life of S. Francis of Assisi, with an Essay on the Characteristics of the Lives of the Saints*, 2 volumes (London: Richardson and Son, 1853), I: pp. 122–3.
69 *Ibid.*, pp. 1, 17, 19.
70 *Ibid.*, p. 17.
71 James Anthony Froude, 'Lives of the Saints', in Froude, *Short Studies*, I: p. 567.
72 Froude, 'Saints', p. 562.
73 Froude, 'Oxford Counter-Reformation', p. 316.
74 *Ibid.*, pp. 332–3, 319.
75 [Mark Pattison], *Stephen Langton, Archbishop of Canterbury* (London: James Toovey, 1845), p. 1.
76 Mark Pattison, *Sermons* (London: Macmillan, 1885), pp. 279, 285, 287, 292–3, 296–7.
77 Mark Pattison, *Isaac Casaubon 1559–1614* (London: Longmans, Green, 1875), pp. 524–5.
78 [Thomas Meyrick], *Life of St Willibrord* (London: Burns and Oates, 1877), unpaginated prefatory note.
79 [Meyrick], *Willibrord*, pp. 1–2; [Dalgairns], *Stephen Harding*, p. 187; [Thomas Meyrick], *Life of St Winfrid* (London: Burns and Oates, 1878), p. 15.
80 Neale, *Hierologus*, p. 102.
81 [Faber], *Wilfrid*, p. 149.
82 Crosthwaite, *Modern Hagiology*, I: pp. 140–1, 105.
83 *Christian Observer*, 43 (1844), 762; [Caroline Clive], *Saint Oldooman: A Myth of the Nineteenth Century* (London: Simpkin, Marshall, 1845).

84 Charles Kingsley, *What, Then, Does Dr Newman Mean?* (London and Cambridge: Macmillan, 1864), p. 22.
85 See Elizabeth Clare Macfarlane, 'Cultures of Anglican Hagiography c.1840–1940, with Special Reference to the Diocese of Truro' (DPhil thesis, University of Oxford, 2012).

# 15

# Thérèse of Lisieux

*Alana Harris*

IN 1912, TWO YEARS before the process for her canonisation was opened, a priest teaching in a seminary in the Diocese of Glasgow wrote a short hagiography comparing a relatively obscure and recently deceased French Carmelite nun to 'a Campion or an Ignatius, a Teresa of Avila, or a John of the Cross'.[1] Saint Thérèse of Lisisux was canonised in 1925 and declared by Pope Pius X (1835–1914) to be 'the greatest saint of modern times'. This chapter examines the little-known part played by British Catholics in the development of her worldwide devotion after her death in 1897 and through the globalisation of her cult in the first three decades of the twentieth century.[2]

Focusing on the pivotal part played by Father Thomas Nimmo Taylor (1873–1963) in the beatification process, and the part played by other bishops and clergy throughout Britain, including both Lancashire and London, this chapter also explores the role of ordinary Catholic women and men in the 'making' of devotion to this now ubiquitous saint. British Catholics were foundational to the evolution of the *fin de siècle* cult of the 'Little Flower' – from providing one of the first miracles considered by the Vatican (a Glaswegian woman cured of a tumour in 1909) through to the consolidation of Thérèsian devotion when commemorated in stone or invoked through image, holy cloth and bone. Through examining the processes surrounding the construction of her sanctity, and understandings of her intercessional and therapeutic efficacy, it is possible to identify the persistence of the sort of late nineteenth-century Ultramontane commitments that Lucy Underwood's chapter on the English Catholic martyrs discusses.[3] Simultaneously, in the consolidation of her cult and the deployment of a self-consciously 'modern' and 'mass-market' Catholicism using different devotional rhetorics and communicative mechanisms, it is also possible to see the adaptation of conceptions of sanctity into the new century and particularly after the First World War. One key context for this chapter is the spread of eclectic international spiritual healing movements, both Protestant and Catholic, across the globe.[4]

Utilising a cachet of ex-votos from British Catholics preserved in the archives of the Carmelite convent in Lisieux, as well as material housed in Monsignor Taylor's reliquary centre at Carfin, Motherwell, this chapter analyses the growing appeal of Thérèse in the early years of the twentieth century. The Little Flower, recognised within a decade of her death as 'very sweet [yet] very powerful', was invoked by her

English and Scottish clients to address their fears and anxieties about their health, families, and the fulfilment of domestic responsibilities.[5] Through her metaphorical and sometimes material 'embodiment', and her 'envisioning' as a heavenly advocate, British Catholics reworked ideas about Christian virtue (and its democratisation), shifting gender roles, and the distinctiveness of a British (while simultaneously continental) Catholic identity for this growing and increasingly confident minority within a Protestant nation.

### 'Apostle of the cause': Monsignor Canon Thomas Nimmo Taylor

In a requiem sermon delivered on 5 December 1963 by Monsignor John Conroy DD – given the absence of the entire Scottish Hierarchy at the second session of the Second Vatican Council – the Vicar General eulogised the recently deceased 89-year-old Thomas Taylor to the vast congregation which packed Motherwell Cathedral:

> His mind was attuned to sanctity: he was after holiness, wherever he could find it. ... This attraction to sanctity manifested itself in various ways – his love for modern saints, for example ... Holy places, too, filled him with delight ... . Relics too he cherished – a chapel full of them. Some of them may be of doubtful authenticity but, in his childlike faith he reverenced them for what they purported to be ... [I]t is not for us to judge him. But may we not say that his very faults were the result of his exuberant enthusiasm.[6]

As Monsignor Conroy had earlier surmised, his role as 'promoter of the spirituality of St. Teresa' was 'surely ... the crowning point of [his] life' and 'well may we be proud to acclaim one of our own Scottish priests as the apostle of such a cause'.[7]

Born in Greenock in 1873 to an English teacher father and Irish mother, Thomas Nimmo Taylor was the eldest of four boys, three of whom trained for the priesthood. Tellingly, his own priestly formation was at the seminary of Saint-Sulpice in Paris and then the Catholic University, which immersed him in a distinctive nineteenth-century French devotional piety and theological landscape.[8] Long before worldwide fame prompted the institution of national pilgrimages to the Marian pilgrimage site of Lourdes, in the Pyrenees, from 1893 Father Taylor repeatedly visited the shrine[9] and sought to publicise it and its seer Bernadette Soubirous (1844–79) to an anglophone audience, chiefly through his 1911 handbook *Lourdes and its Miracles*.[10]

In a similar vein, Taylor's francophone religious networks alerted him to the distinctive spirituality and believed sanctity of an enclosed and recently deceased Carmelite nun, Marie-Françoise-Thérèse Martin (1873–97). In 1897, after an austere and seemingly uneventful life in a convent, and now dying of tuberculosis, Soeur Thérèse was requested by her Prioress (and elder sister) to write an account of her childhood and fervent prayer life.[11] The resulting three documents, published posthumously as a spiritual autobiography *L'Histoire d'une âme* (The Story of a Soul), were circulated to 2,000 Carmelite convents in lieu of an obituary and obtained an almost immediate wider appeal in their programmatic description of 'the little way' – a 'way of spiritual childhood' as Thérèse described it, or 'trust and absolute self-surrender', offering to God 'the flowers of little sacrifices'.[12] Father Taylor was ordained the year that Soeur Thérèse died and he read *The Story of a Soul* shortly after its publication in 1898. From 1901 he became a frequent pilgrim to the Carmelite convent in Lisieux (in which her two sisters still resided) and thereafter assumed an important role in the promotion of knowledge of Thérèse's life and the 'Roses' (or favours) which the Little Flower was already bestowing on those asking for intercessions or assistance in living a Christ-like 'little way'.

There is a well-established tradition that Father Taylor was the first person to suggest that the cause for Thérèse's canonisation be introduced.[13] Irrespective of the truth of this claim, it is certainly the case that his writings – undertaken around his post-ordination duties as Chair of Sacred Scripture and Church History at St Peter's Seminary, Glasgow – played an essential part in the dissemination of information about the Little Flower, and in laying the foundations of devotion to her. Beginning with *As Little Children*, which very quickly sold over 100,000 copies, his 1912 translation of *The Story of a Soul* was the first full autobiography of Thérèse Martin and was immensely popular throughout the English-speaking world.[14] The volume's successor, *A Little White Flower*, similarly went through reprint after reprint.[15] Detailed correspondence between Father Taylor and the Convent in Lisieux survives, with a first letter in fluent French praising *L'Histoire d'une âme* as an incomparable book and asking for a relic.[16] Intimate, detailed and directive correspondence with Sister Anne is preserved from around the time of the first publication of *The Story of a Soul*, discussing sales (9,000 copies for the first edition, 3,000 more in reprint, and 8,000 copies of the second edition – 'breaking every publishing record'),[17] the reproduction of photographs and illustrations of Thérèse,[18] and the perils of literal translations.[19] Father Taylor took great pleasure in these letters to notify Carmel of striking (English and Scottish) 'Roses' that should publicised,[20] but he also seized the opportunity to dispense advice on the management of the momentum behind the beatification, such as avoiding:

> references to 1/8 for masses ... I have heard it criticised. You are not 'touting' for Masses, *I know*, but I'd avoid all shadow of seeking for them, espec[ially] as they do not benefit the cause in any way.[21]

Alongside the exchange of familial news and greetings, and pleas for the continued prayers of Thérèse's sisters for his ministry, these letters also make clear Father Taylor's intense involvement, micro-management and emotional investment in the canonisation cause.[22]

The role of Father Taylor in personally forging and fostering networks of promotion and devotional patronage within British lay and clerical circles is also beyond doubt. His energy and enthusiasm for furthering devotion to the saint knew few bounds, especially upon leaving his teaching post in 1915 for parish duties at St Francis Xavier in Carfin. An important enlistment in the task of mainstreaming devotion to Saint Thérèse was Taylor's fellow Sulpician seminary graduate and friend Francis Bourne

(1861–1935). The youthful Bishop of Southwark, who was then translated to the Archdiocese of Westminster (and promoted to the red hat of Cardinal) was introduced to the spirituality and writings of the Little Flower of Jesus by Taylor, who asked for Bourne's input on his translation of *L'Histoire d'une âme* and enclosed a relic with the manuscript.[23] Devotion to Saint Thérèse was to be an enduring and fundamental component of Archbishop Bourne's prayer life,[24] evidenced not only through the preface he wrote for the 1912 autobiography,[25] but also through his frequent pilgrimages to Lisieux[26] and the Thérèsian shrine Taylor later created at Carfin.[27] Another important convert to the saint's cult, following his conversion to Catholicism when reading *The Story of a Soul*,[28] was the charismatic preacher Father Vernon Johnson (1886–1969). Confessing in correspondence to Mother Agnes in 1920 that Thérèse 'took me out of Anglicanism only just in time [as] I can see now how perilous my presence was in the midst of so much popularity and success',[29] Father Johnson worked with Archbishop Bourne in Westminster fostering late vocations[30] before his appointment to the University of Oxford chaplaincy and foundation of the Association of Priests of St Teresa.[31] These clerical promoters were joined by laity of all classes – 'busy mothers and toiling men', as Father Taylor put it[32] – as well as numerous women religious – including those within the raft of newly established Carmelite convents in Great Britain – which were themselves unequivocally attributed by Taylor to the intercession of Thérèse.[33] Interviewed about his part in the saint-making process towards the end of his life, Taylor's self-effacing summation of his efforts was as follows:

> I have tried to make the Servant of God known, both by distributing little pictures of her, and by helping her autobiography to reach a wide circle of readers, especially in Great Britain, the Colonies, and the United States.[34]

As we will see, his efforts extended well beyond the mere production of pictures and publications, important as these were, to include active participation in the furtherance of Thérèse's cause as the second person to speak, after her sister (and Mother Superior), at the Vatican beatification tribunal.[35] To this end, as early as 1909 Taylor persuaded *The Glasgow Observer* (a Scottish Catholic weekly) to publish acknowledgements of 'favours received' through the believed intervention of the Little Flower. By 1910, there were already eighty-seven such notices in print, and Taylor ensured that dramatic miracles attributed to the future saint were carefully documented and forwarded to Lisieux for publication in *Pluie de Roses*.[36] From 1907 until Thérèse's canonisation in 1925, these Carmel-produced volumes detailing healings and favours obtained from all parts of the globe were published annually, amounting to over 3,000 pages.[37] Father Taylor's role in stimulating and stoking devotion to Soeur Thérèse cannot be overestimated – indeed in this vein Pope Benedict XV (1854–1922) is reported to have said:

> I am not surprised at the enthusiasm of the French over their country-woman, but the extraordinary devotion of the English-speaking nations is to me the Finger of God. HIC MIHI EST DIGNUS DEI. I shall canonise her as speedily as possible.[38]

She was beatified by Pope Pius XI (1857–1939) on 29 April 1923, and canonised by the same pope two years later on 17 May 1925. In explaining how this came about, the unappreciated role of ordinary British men and women in endorsing and substantiating this making of a modern saint will now be discussed.

### Thérèse's roses in an English (and Scottish) garden

In his 1927 publication *St Thérèse of Lisieux*, Father Taylor outlined the intricacies of the canonisation process to an interested public and described the six supporting miracles considered by the Vatican,[39] including the two French cases which were examined in detail to substantiate Thérèse's designation as Blessed.[40] The publication also included a section entitled 'The British Isles and St Thérèse', which outlined the first recorded 'Rose' across the channel on 8 November 1908. This healing of the badly injured foot of a Good Shepherd postulant in a London convent was much publicised, especially in her hometown of Glasgow,[41] and within the space of a year over 450 favours had been reported in the British Catholic press.[42] Within this same publication, Father Taylor sought to create a transnational holy genealogy between the French Carmelite and the medieval British Isles, asserting that

> the Little Flower is deeply loved in the land where once lived St Simon Stock, to whom Our Lady revealed the scapular of Mount Carmel. Of the Roses forwarded to the convent in Lisieux from St Thérèse's English garden, two are chosen for publication here.[43]

Tellingly, the two favours reproduced were both from Anglicans who had read *A Little White Flower* and, under quite different circumstances, converted to Catholicism. The first from 'a grateful client' centred on receipt of a relic from the Carmel of Lisieux and the reactions of her vicar who was 'scorn[ful] of my "superstition"', leading to the realisation that 'since the religion of my birth rejected her, I too, would be a Catholic'.[44] The second 'Rose' came from an anonymous writer who, in florid terms, dwelt upon Thérèse's intercession in 'draw[ing] me back from the brink of hell', and overcoming 'innumerable defilements with which I sullied my soul'. Contrasting 'the spotless purity of her soul and the utter vileness of mine!', the writer styled themselves 'the Little Flower of Thérèse' and recounted 'feeling the sensible presence and continual assistance of the sweet Saint' over a period of nine months until 'the devil took flight'.[45] These two exemplars present a triumphalist Catholicism which is pure, powerful and self-consciously distinctive in the face of Protestant prejudice. Yet these case-studies were hardly representative and served a clear authorial purpose, defensively claiming Thérèse for an Ultramontane (and indigenous) Catholicism in the face of buoyant Edwardian Anglo-Catholicism and particularly pronounced Scottish sectarianism. These 'conversion narratives' continued to feature as the decades went on, prompting increasing interest in the saint and her intercessory reputation from those outside the flock. The most famous example of this cross-denominational affection and admiration, from one clearly on the fringes of organised religion, was Vita Sackville-

West's double biography of Teresa of Avila and Thérèse of Lisieux, *The Eagle and the Dove* (1946).[46]

Perhaps the most publicised favour, and certainly the 'cure' that served as a stimulus to early British interest in the Carmelite wonder-worker was the miraculous healing of a Glaswegian widow, Mrs Helen Dorans, from inoperable cancer.[47] This was the intercession advanced by Father Taylor to the beatification tribunal (witness 28), though excluded because 'it makes no reference to either Thérèse's virtues or her renown for holiness'.[48] Nevertheless, its inclusion in the tribunal process ensured that the specifics of the case are recorded in some detail within the archive at Lisieux. These include firsthand accounts from the *miraculée* and her children (Agnes and Joseph), verbatim statements attributable to the patient's doctor, and the testimony of a longstanding personal friend and spiritual adviser, Sister M. Teresa RSM. The bare facts of Mrs Dorans's condition are uncontrovertibly described within these documents: suffering from a tumour that had grown for at least eight years, she had been in constant pain and, since 1907, had hardly been able to move out of bed or to sleep for sustained periods of time. She had visited the Western Infirmary in Glasgow on two or three occasions and had been told that her cancer was proliferative and inoperable. In July 1909, Dr Carmichael told the family that there was nothing now to be done, save pain alleviation, and that the patient would gradually become weaker and weaker before slipping into unconsciousness. Mrs Dorans was described by Sister Teresa as 'a most religious good woman and possessed of a warm Faith',[49] and Novena after Novena had been made by her friends and relatives for her recovery; Lourdes water was brought by Sister Teresa on one of her visits. On 22 August 1909, when the patient had not taken solid food for ten weeks and was on the point of dying, Sister Teresa recounted to Father Taylor the enlistment of Thérèse's help:

> I said to [Mrs Dorans] then 'Now that we have tried nearly all the known Saints in the Court of Heaven suppose we try a little one who has not yet been Canonized?' I talked to her a little about Sr Thérèse, then proposed a Novena in her honour. That she should go to Our Lady, St Joseph and St Teresa [of Avila] and ask them to take *her*, Thérèse, to Our Divine Lord; but that *she* was to obtain from the S[acred] Heart Mrs D's recovery.[50]

At a time when the life and legacy of Soeur Thérèse Martin were little known, expediency and an insurance of orthodoxy were served by the addition of these well-known saints and devotions to the new intercessor.

Helen Dorans herself provided an account of the effect of the Novena and her miraculous cure on 27 August 1909 – though transcribed by Sister Teresa, and written as an official testimony in the third person:

> About 11 P.M. having taken a small piece of ice, the poor patient had a severe vomiting attack, after which quite exhausted she fell asleep – this would be about 11.30... For the last two days previously the poor invalid's sight had become much impaired. She could only see very indistinctly, just distinguish figures. She slept on quietly (her first restful, natural sleep for many years) until about half past five next morning (Friday 27th) when

she was aroused by a gentle pressure on each shoulder, as if someone lent over her. At the same time she felt a sweet, warm breath in her face, and she knew an unseen presence about her bed. On opening her eyes she saw distinctly everything in the room even to the pattern on the wallpaper – all distress and pain were gone and she felt perfectly well, being able to move her arms and limbs freely. The dear 'Little Thérèse' had come down to pass on some of her 'Heaven' in bringing health and happiness to that sorrowing family.[51]

The testimonies written and signed by Mrs Dorans's children dwelt on the terminal medical prognosis given by those at the Western Infirmary and the treating physician, which they juxtaposed with verbatim quotations from Dr Carmichael when he examined the patient next day:

Mrs Doran can you give me any reason for this great change [?] … everything is normal, no trace of anything here, save a tiny lump about the size of a marble. I have never had a case like this and I say if this is going to be permanent it is nothing short of a miracle.[52]

This external affirmation of the occurrence was summarised by Mrs Doran in her official statement:

The Doctor was perfectly puzzled and though a Protestant he declared that if any other doctor were brought in to the patient and told what had been her state a few hours before, he would not have believed it. He said that she had been beyond any medical skill to help and that a Higher Hand had wrought the cure, which could not have been brought about by any human means.[53]

Dr Carmichael subsequently provided a medical certificate attesting to this profound and permanent change in the patient's health, which was forwarded to Lisieux.[54]

This 'Rose' has been given extended treatment here not only because of its early date and formative role in the establishment of the cult of Thérèse in Britain (and elsewhere), but also because it exhibits many of the features which became hallmarks of the Thérèsian miracles over the years.[55] The intervention of the Little Flower at the point of death and a sudden miraculous transformation in medical condition were reoccurring tropes, alongside the intellectual incredulity and 'conversion' of medical professionals (particularly if Protestant). As I, and others such as Mary Heimann, have discussed in more detail elsewhere, the complex interaction of the 'supernatural' and the 'scientific', and a critique of modernist epistemologies were explanatory glosses often placed upon these favours by their interpreters and promoters.[56] Also of note here and throughout many of the reported favours was an assertion of the fervent, childlike faith of the recipient – in mimesis of Thérèse herself – and reports of an experiential, bodily and sensory encounter with the soon-to-be saint. While this material, incarnational encounter is a well-established element of many saints' cults, it was given particular encouragement in the case of Thérèse through modern means of communication and technology. Inevitably Taylor also played a prominent role in this envisioning and embodiment of the Little Flower of Lisieux, through his creation of spaces of encounter and sites of commemoration.

## Carfin and Ribbleton: materialising British Catholic devotion to Saint Thérèse of Lisieux

Shortly after her death, Soeur Thérèse Martin became an instantly recognisable celebrity not only through her bestselling writings but also through the reproduction of her photographs and illustrations and the circulation of her relics, including clippings of hair, pieces of clothing, bone splinters, fragments of letters, earth from her coffin and threads from her pillow.[57] As Sophia Deboick has extensively charted, modern Weberian notions of charisma were combined with technologically facilitated mechanisms of reproduction and distribution to create a readily reproducible, commercially packed ideal of sanctity.[58] Within the formative years of 1897 and 1925, around 17,500,000 relics and 30,500,000 pictures of Thérèse were distributed: 'most early accounts of her miracles show that supplicants possessed or were given a portrait or relic of her'.[59]

The familiarity of British Catholics with the image of Thérèse was equally facilitated by these mechanisms but also by the little-known activities of Father Taylor in creating the first shrine to the Little Flower in the British Isles. Harnessing what he called the 'enforced leisure' of around 300 parishioner-colliers during the 1921–26 mining strikes, Taylor sought 'to make a long cherished dream a reality, the building in Scotland of an open-air Basilica to the Mother of God'.[60] The result was a 'Scottish Lourdes' and the replication of the grotto and its rituals,[61] complete with its own 'miraculous spring' which facilitated a raft of healings and cures well into the 1960s.[62] Father Taylor also saw an opportunity here to augment growing devotion to Soeur Thérèse, and wrote to Lisieux for consent to establish a Little Flower shrine. In an account written by Taylor in the 1950s about the history of Carfin, he outlined the response of Mother Agnes to the incorporation of a statue of Thérèse alongside the copy of the rock of Massabielle:

> the child who had loved Mary so passionately would certainly not rob Our Lady of her glory. Keep her statue in the Grotto! We will ask our Thérèse to draw souls to Carfin and so prove how she loves Our Lady.[63]

The fame of the shrine (co-opting both Marian and Thérèsian devotion) grew in anticipation of the beatification, drawing 250,000 pilgrims in the first three months of 1923,[64] and prompting a newspaper to quip jocularly that 'every char-a-banc in Scotland can find its way to Carfin unattended'.[65] A statue of Carrara marble, made to specifications provided by her sisters at Lisieux, was installed beside the grotto, and the shrine was improved several times until it eventually became a mound-shaped, raised rockery surrounded by roses.[66] Thérèse's canonisation three months earlier was publically celebrated at Carfin on 30 September 1925, when over 30,000 people came to this little mining village outside Glasgow see her statue and relics carried around the rose-decorated shrine and to participate in a torchlight procession.[67] In effusive, self-congratulatory terms Father Taylor exulted:

> [This] was doubtless the most striking torchlight procession in the history of Scottish devotion ... The enthusiasm was unbounded, and the widespread joy was a clear sign that the rainfall of spiritual roses had grown into a torrent. May it be a prelude to the homecoming of the children of St Margaret to the Faith of their fathers! And may these words, laid like a wreath of simple flowers at the feet of Mary and Thérèse, draw a multitude of hearts unto them, wherever the English tongue is spoken.[68]

From these beginnings, the creative invocation and celebration of Saint Thérèse would take many different forms, including the staging of a Thérèsian Rosary pageant centred around the procession of a parishioner dressed as the Carmelite nun, and the attribution of many healing cures to Father Taylor's prized relic of Saint Thérèse.[69] Again we see the recurring Thérèsian theme: the contact of a saintly body with a broken, infirm or fragile pilgrim body. Accounts in the archive describe its effectiveness against more prosaic ailments such as a large goitre,[70] blood poisoning[71] or disfiguring warts,[72] through to the spectacular healing in 1934 of Miss Mary Traynor from debilitating rheumatoid arthritis and a wasting illness that had brought her near to death. Writing later about the application of the relic to her joints and legs, alongside a blessing from Father Taylor, Miss Traynor described a warming sensation, 'like a thread of fire', and before the eyes of those assembled she left her wheelchair and walked to her car.[73] Generating a huge correspondence within the mainstream and religious press, and an entire file of testimony and medical reports,[74] Miss Traynor's sudden recovery from her various illnesses was not reversed, nor was there a relapse of symptoms until her death of old age in 1970.[75]

The fame and appeal of Carfin soon extended throughout Scotland and beyond, and with the development of a small train station, the 'Grotto Halt', pilgrimages of the laity from 'across the border' commenced from Manchester, Bolton, Tyneside and Liverpool in 1925.[76] Some English dioceses developed a particularly strong affection for Saint Thérèse and her shrine at Carfin – for example, there were four separate pilgrimages from Preston in 1930.[77] Yet Carfin also provided a stimulus for the development of Thérèsian shrines elsewhere, particularly throughout the newly created Diocese of Lancashire.[78] Father James Fleming was ordained in the Liverpool Archdiocese on 17 May 1913 and was serving as a parish priest at St Joseph's Preston when the decision was taken in 1928 to open a new church in Ribbleton (Preston).[79] He was inducted as first rector of the Parish of the Blessed Sacrament in early November 1928 and immediately conceived of the idea of creating a shrine to Saint Thérèse – officially enlisting 'Fr T. N. Taylor, of Carfin' to open 'the Shrine of the Little Flower' on 18 November 1928.[80] A statue of the 'Rose Queen' was commissioned and a framed image of the saint – based on the 1899 charcoal portrait executed by her sister Céline (Soeur Geneviève of the Holy Face) – was enshrined within the church (figure 10). Almost immediately people came from miles around on pilgrimage, and the shrine became a site of fervent devotion and countless 'favours'.

From the outset Father Fleming sought the spiritual support of the Carmel in Lisieux for this endeavour and remained keen to demonstrate, through letters of

10 Unknown photographer, *Postcard of the Shrine of the Little Flower*, Ribbleton, c. 1928.

thanksgiving and details of 'Roses' received, the success of the shrine and support for this French saint across the channel.[81] In 1931 he sent to Lisieux a bound, typed folio entitled 'Letters of Gratitude to "The Little Flower"', which outlined in detail the favours received by ten of Thérèse's clients in the north of England.[82] In subsequent years, he also forwarded individual letters of thanksgiving and this correspondence, present without comment in the archive, provides an intimate portrait of the anxieties and struggles of ordinary Catholic men and women in the context of interwar Britain. These favours are also illuminating, especially when compared to the more spectacular, health-related 'Roses' attributed to Carfin,[83] or Thérèse's palpable assistance with the trauma of the trenches and the distribution of over a million devotional medals to French soldiers in 1915.[84] In contrast, the favours at Ribbleton catalogue a cross-section of the laity's relational difficulties, material worries and everyday lives given a providential interpretation through the believed intercession of Thérèse. A great many of these letters relate to economic and chiefly working-class preoccupations, including the fulfilment of gendered responsibilities relating to 'work' and 'breadwinning' at a time of severe economic downturn. As the Catholic weekly *The Universe* termed it in 1931, while reporting on the institution of a third Novena service on a Thursday evening to accommodate crowds of over 2,300 people each week, these devotions to Saint Thérèse were an 'Out-of-Work Service'.[85] Father Fleming explained:

> Quite a large proportion of the people who come here have been out of work for a long time. Many of them are on the 'dole'. Up to date, more than 200 people have given me detailed proof that after long periods of unemployment they have come to one of our services, placed their petitions in the box, and very soon afterwards obtained positions. I could give you literally columns of instances of other authenticated 'favours' received here through the intercession of St Theresa of Lisieux.[86]

In his letters to Lisieux, Father Fleming gave further details of some of these instances, including 'one of the first big favours granted by her at the Shrine of Ribbleton, Preston' and dated Easter Sunday 1930, when the petition of a non-Catholic nurse for her brother was believed to have secured his employment after three years out of work.[87] Given the severity of the Depression in the north of England, as well as parts of Scotland, there was clearly a localised need being served by the shrine and a mass appeal, through the creation of hope and a sense of agency.[88] Yet Thérèse's clients were not all out-of-work husbands and fathers – petitioning on their own behalf, or as the subjects of their wives' prayers. Devotees also included a 16-year-old girl dying of pneumonia[89] and frustrated lovers who, after four years of obstacles and misunderstanding, 'have the pleasure of [each others'] company' and regard this saintly matchmaking 'not as a rose, or a bouquet, but as a vast rose garden'.[90] A letter of thanksgiving headed 'A Shower of Roses' from a woman in Preston demonstrated Thérèse's efficacy across a wide field of activity. Itemising the 'graces and blessings [which] have been showered down upon me and my family', her interventions included assistance with one daughter's nuptial mass and subsequent pregnancy, redress of another daughter's ill-health, attention to the intercessor's own 'financial straits' and, for her husband, 'the grace of [re]conversion' after ten years of bitter separation from the Church.[91] As Sheila Kaye-Smith observed some years later in her confessional study of early twentieth-century sanctity:

> [Thérèse] comes with a special message for an age that badly needs inspiration. It is an age that has lost its aristocracy, its kings, its geniuses, its great men. It is an age of mass production, of mediocrity, of democracy, the rank and file, the common man. ... Thérèse's call is to the average man, who in our day exists for the first time as a real person instead of a statistical calculation. She calls even him to be a saint.[92]

In the case of many of the ex-votos that have been preserved from the Novena services in Ribbleton, the use of the male pronoun in respect of the Saint's devotees seems largely justified.[93] Despite nineteenth-century, cross-denominational fears of the 'feminisation of religion', Thérèse seems to have generated fervent affection from soldiers, factory workers and miners, as well as the high-profile priests committed to her promotion.[94] In this, she echoes the appeal generated by the Scottish nun and former factory worker Venerable Margaret Sinclair, who was commonly known as 'Scotland's Little Flower'.[95] In contrast to the near contemporaneous cause for the beatification of the Bootle mystic, Teresa Higginson, and the divergent reactions which her extraordinary life and mystical experiences elicited from English Catholics,[96] Thérèse's 'littleness' and the self-conscious promotion of her 'domesticity' and 'ordinariness', as well as her 'sweetness', seemingly made her a more accessible and palatable patron to British men and women.[97]

## Conclusion

At a meeting on 11 October 1938, the Scottish Hierarchy made a remarkably generous decision to sponsor one of the memorial chapels to be created in the newly erected International Basilica of St Thérèse in Lisieux. The decision to raise the £3,000 from Advent collections was taken 'because our country was a pioneer in the devotion to the Little Flower' [and] 'to create a new bond between herself and the land of St Margaret'.[98] In what would become a pantheon of international Catholicism following the Second World War, the altar bore the inscription:

> Built in honour of the Child Jesus and as an example of gratitude to the Little Flower of Jesus to hasten the conversion of Great Britain and to implore for it and 'Sweet France', mother of saints, the shower of roses of blessed Thérèse of the Child Jesus.
> Revd. Thomas N Taylor, of the Diocese of Glasgow.

This chapter has charted the pioneering and strenuous efforts of Monsignor Canon Thomas Taylor, beginning more than twenty years before her canonisation, to publicise the life of Soeur Thérèse and to promote her veneration and emulation. It has also explored the evolving bond between Saint Thérèse and the land of Saint Margaret, as well as that of Saint George. While Glaswegian Catholics were at the forefront of devotion to the Little Flower, particularly with the establishment of her first British shrine at Carfin, the faithful across the country – religious and clergy from Lancashire to London – were readily convinced of her sanctity and her powerful, intercessional efficacy. As the inscription on the Scottish Memorial Chapel attested, Thérèse was mobilised to channel the devotion and to hasten the conversion of Great Britain. As this understanding of British Catholic identity encompassed regional and national variations, it could also incorporate and correspond with continental sensibilities and affectations.

This chapter has also explored the role of ordinary Catholic men and women, through their prayers, offerings, veneration of statues and relics, and through their testimonies at Ribbleton or to Lisieux, in the 'making' of this modern saint. Whether as the saint of those 'out-of-work', particularly working-class men in the late 1920s, or as a miracle worker renowned for healing cancer and mending familial relationships, Saint Thérèse was perceived to be a 'saint of the people' and her clientele – as explored within this chapter – encompassed the great and the good, as well as the more ordinary within cities and villages across the British Isles.

## Notes

1 Thomas N. Taylor (ed.), *Soeur Thérèse of Lisieux, the Little Flower of Jesus* (London: Burns and Oates, 1912), p. 12.
2 See B. Ulanov, *The Making of a Modern Saint* (London: Jonathan Cape, 1967).
3 See pp. 155–6, this volume.
4 For healing, see J. Shaw, *Octavia, Daughter of God: The Story of a Female Messiah and her Followers* (New Haven: Yale University Press, 2011); Joel Cabrita, 'The people of Adam: divine healing and racial cosmopolitanism in the early twentiety-century Transvaal, South Africa', *Comparative Studies in Society and History*, 57 (2015), 557–92.
5 Francis Colchester SJ to Lisieux, 11 September 1911, Archives du Carmel de Lisieux [hereafter ACL], Angleterre A–Z.
6 Typed note headed 'Right Rev. Mgr. Thomas N. Canon Taylor', p. 3, ACL, Taylor, Thomas Nimmo Mgr. 1873–1963 [hereafter TNT].
7 *Ibid.*, p. 2. See also R. P. Stéphane-Joseph Piat, OFM, 'Un promoter du culte Thérèsien dans les pays de langue Anglaise', *Annales* (November 1964), pp. 10–13, ACL TNT.
8 See Richard D. E. Burton, *Holy Tears, Holy Blood: Women, Catholicism and the Culture of Suffering in France, 1840–1970* (Ithaca: Cornell University Press, 2004).
9 Thomas Taylor to his brother, James Bede, autumn 1906, Scottish Catholic Archives [hereafter SCA], HC9/2 TNT, 9.
10 It was reprinted by the Catholic weekly *The Universe* in 1919. See Susan McGhee, *Monsignor Taylor of Carfin* (Glasgow: J. Burns, 1972), p. 176.
11 For an extended discussion of the hagiography of Saint Thérèse, see Alana Harris, *Faith in the Family: A Lived Religious History of Catholicism, 1945–1982* (Manchester: Manchester University Press, 2013), pp. 208–24.
12 Thérèse Martin, *The Story of a Soul: A New Translation* (Brewster: Paraclete Press, 2006), pp. 210–25.

13 See 'Witness 2: Thomas Nimmo Taylor', www.archives-carmel-lisieux.fr/english/carmel/index.php/2-thomas-nimmo-taylor, accessed 7 August 2014.
14 McGhee, *Monsignor Taylor*, p. 278.
15 E.g. Thomas N. Taylor, *'A Little White Flower': The Story of Saint Thérèse of Lisieux* (London: Burns, Oates and Washbourne, 1926).
16 Taylor to Lisieux, 24 February 1902, ACL Taylor, TNT.
17 Taylor to Anne of Jesus, [n.d.], 1, ACL TNT.
18 For a gallery of photographs of Thérèse, mostly taken by her sister Céline, see www.archives-carmel-lisieux.fr/english/carmel/index.php/47-photos-english/gallery/27-47-photos-english#fwgallerytop, accessed 7 August 2014.
19 Taylor to Anne of Jesus, [n.d.], 2, ACL TNT.
20 Taylor to Anne of Jesus, [n.d.], 3, ACL TNT.
21 Taylor to Anne of Jesus, [n.d.], 2 ACL TNT.
22 Taylor to Anne of Jesus, [n.d.], 3, ACL TNT.
23 McGhee, *Monsignor Taylor*, p. 278.
24 Mark Vicars, *By the Thames Divided: Cardinal Bourne in Southwark and Westminster* (Leominster: Gracewing, 2013), pp. 583–4.
25 Taylor, *Soeur Thérèse*, p. xii. See also the preface to Taylor, *Little White Flower*, p. x.
26 Archbishop Bourne was one of the first Englishmen to visit the saint's grave, and returned to Lisieux in 1919. See Vernon Johnson, *Our Guiding Star: A Short Life of St Teresa of Lisieux* (London: Burns and Oates, 1951), p. 89.
27 'Memorable day at Carfin, Cardinal Bourne greeted at grotto by 50,000' *Glasgow Evening News* (21 June 1926), filed in Carfin Shrine Archives [hereafter CSA], Note Book 7 [hereafter NB], p. 116.
28 Vernon Johnson, *One Lord, One Faith: An Explanation* (London: Sheed and Ward, 1929).
29 Vernon Johnson to Mother Agnes, 2 November 1920, ACL Ther-13 Vernon Johnson.
30 Vicars, *Thames Divided*, pp. 474–5. See also 'St Teresa and her mission', in Vernon Johnson (ed.), *The Mission of a Saint: Essays on the Significance of St Thérèse of Lisieux* (London: Burns, Oates and Washbourne, 1947), pp. 14–21, and *Spiritual Childhood: A Study of St Teresa's Teaching* (London: Sheed and Ward, 1953).
31 On the complex relationship of Thérèse herself with priestly vocation, see Steffen Lösel, 'Prayer, pain and priestly privilege: Claude Langlois' new perspective on Thérèse of Lisieux', *Journal of Religion*, 88 (2008), 273–306.
32 Taylor, *Little White Flower*, p. xii.
33 *Ibid.*
34 Christopher O'Mahony, *St Thérèse of Lisieux by Those who Knew Her: Testimonies from the Process of Beatification* (Dublin: Veritas Publications, 1975), p. 75.
35 See 'Note of Thanksgiving from Thomas Nimmo Taylor', ACL TNT.
36 O'Mahony, *St Thérèse*, p. 76.
37 F. Lang, *Smiles of God: The Flowers of St Thérèse of Lisieux* (London: Burns and Oates, 2003), p. 144.
38 McGhee, *Monsignor Taylor*, p. 286.
39 Thomas N. Taylor, *Saint Thérèse of Lisieux, the Little Flower of Jesus* (London: Burns, Oates and Washbourne, 1927), pp. 250–1.

40 For full details, see 'Les miracles', www.archives-carmel-lisieux.fr/english/carmel/index.php/les-miracles, accessed 7 August 2014.
41 Taylor, *Saint Thérèse* (1927), p. 392.
42 *Ibid.*
43 *Ibid.*, p. 393.
44 *Ibid.*, p. 394.
45 *Ibid.*, pp. 394–5.
46 Vita Sackville-West, *The Eagle and the Dove: A Study in Contrasts, St Teresa of Avila, St Thérèse of Lisieux* (London: Michael Joseph, 1943).
47 Lang, *Smiles*, p. 149.
48 See 'Witness 28: Hélène Knight', www.archives-carmel-lisieux.fr/english/carmel/index.php/28-helene-knight, accessed 7 August 2014.
49 Sister Teresa to Father Taylor, 7 September 1909, ACL Dorans (Mmn), Glasgow Ecosse (Dorans).
50 *Ibid.*
51 Testimony of Mrs Helen Dorans, transcribed by Sr Teresa, ACL Dorans, 6–7.
52 'For Father Taylor', signed testaments of Helen, Agnes and Joseph Dorans, ACL Dorans, 1–2.
53 Testimony of Mrs Helen Doran, transcribed by Sr Teresa, ACL Dorans, 10–11.
54 'Pluie 1, 56. –X., Angleterre, 15 October 1909', ACL Pluie de Roses, I.
55 Antoinette Guise, 'Thérèse de Lisieux et ses miracles: recompositions du surnaturel 1898–1928' (PhD thesis, Sorbonne, Paris, 2006).
56 Alana Harris, 'Bone idol? British Catholics and devotion to St Thérèse of Lisieux', in Nancy Christie, Michael Gauveau and Stephen Heathorn (eds), *The Sixties and Beyond: Dechristianization as History in North America and Western Europe, 1945–2000* (Toronto: University of Toronto Press, 2013), pp. 429–52, and Mary Heimann, 'Mysticism in Bootle: Victorian supernaturalism as an historical problem', *Journal of Ecclesiastical History*, 64 (2013), 335–56.
57 Thérèse Taylor, 'Photos of St Bernadette and St Thérèse', *Nineteenth Century Contexts*, 27 (2005), 269–92.
58 Sophia Deboick, 'Image, Authenticity and the Cult of Thérèse of Lisieux, 1897–1959' (PhD thesis, University of Liverpool, 2011); Deboick, 'The creation of a modern saint', in Peter Clarke and Tony Claydon (eds), *Saints and Sanctity*, Studies in Church History, 47 (Woodbridge: Boydell & Brewer, 2011), pp. 376–89.
59 Lang, *Smiles*, p. 144.
60 Thomas N. Taylor, *The Carfin Grotto* (Glasgow: Burns, 1952), p. 9.
61 For a brief history of the Carfin Grotto and its expansion into a vast complex of various saints' shrines, see www.carfingrotto.org, accessed 2 December 2015.
62 Alana Harris, 'Astonishing scenes at the Scottish Lourdes: masculinity, the miraculous, and sectarian strife at Carfin, 1922–1945', *The Innes Review*, 66 (2015), 102–29.
63 Taylor, *Carfin*, p. 10.
64 'Carfin honours Our Lady', *Novena*, 8 (1958), 45–52.
65 'Scottish Lourdes: striking rise in fame of tiny village: Protestant interest', unlabelled clipping filed in CSA NB 7, p. 78.
66 McGhee, *Monsignor Taylor*, p. 294.

67  Taylor, *Little White Flower*, p. xxiii.
68  *Ibid.*
69  'Carfin Grotto's fifteenth anniversary: Rosary can save Christian civilization', *Scottish Observer* (8 October 1937), filed in CSA NB 8, p. 47.
70  Letter from M. Gilmore (Harrington) to Thomas N. Taylor, 'Rose – Goitre' [n.d.], CSA Box No. 12.
71  'Carfin Grotto: – cure of volunteer worker John Roche – 29 January 1937', CSA NB 8, p. 10.
72  'Carfin Grotto: a little Rose Flower', *Catholic Times* (8 April 1938), filed in CSA NB 8, p. 65.
73  File: 'Claims of cures mostly Grotto and L. F. "Roses"', CSA Box No. 5.
74  File: 'Grotto and L. F. Cures and Favours', CSA Box No. 12.
75  McGhee, *Monsignor Taylor*, pp. 264–5.
76  *Ibid.*, p. 225.
77  *Ibid.*
78  'Spread of devotion in Lancashire', handwritten note from Father Fleming [c. 1930], listing the establishment of shrines at St Mary's and the Sacred Heart (Preston), St Patrick's (Walton-le-Dale), St Michael's (Alton Lane), St William's (Longridge), St Ann's (Westby near Blackpool), St Patrick's (Barrow-in-Furness) and at the Church of Christ the King (Broadgreen, Liverpool) and St Mary's (Ambleside), ACL A–Z, Father Fleming.
79  'Lanpriests' file, Preston, The Talbot Library. With thanks to the Rev'd Michael Dolan.
80  Lancaster Diocesan Directory (1928), 17.
81  Fr Fleming PP to Mother Agnes, 7 February 1934, ACL A–Z Fleming.
82  'Letters of Gratitude to "The Little Flower"', ACL A–Z Fleming.
83  See Harris, 'Astonishing scenes'.
84  Lang, *Smiles*, p. 157. For a selection of correspondence, publications and ex-votos from soldiers, see 'Thérèse and the First World War', www.archives-carmel-lisieux.fr/english/carmel/index.php/apres-1897/la-1ere-guerre, accessed 7 August 2014.
85  'Crowd at "Little Flower services" still increasing: long queues gather in spite of heavy rain', *The Universe* [c. 1931], ACL A–Z Fleming.
86  *Ibid.*
87  'Letters of Gratitude', 1, ACL A–Z Fleming.
88  Concerns about employment during the Depression were also present in Carfin petitions: see Harris, 'Bone idol?', p. 436.
89  Fr Fleming to Mother Agnes, 7 February 1934, ACL A–Z Fleming.
90  F. S. Kitchen to Fr Fleming, January 1931, ACL A–Z Fleming.
91  Unnamed female client, January 1931, 'Letters of Gratitude', 5, ACL A–Z Fleming.
92  Sheila Kaye-Smith, *Quartet in Heaven* (London: Cassell, 1952), p. 217.
93  The large majority of petitions archived were from Catholic men, in contrast to other devotional cults: see Robert Orsi, *Thank You, St Jude: Women's Devotion to the Saint of Hopeless Causes* (New Haven: Yale University Press, 1999).
94  See Tine Van Osselaer and Thomas Buerman (2008) 'Feminization thesis: a survey of international historiography and a probing of the Belgian grounds', *Revue d'Histoire Ecclésiastique*, 103 (2008), 1–31, and Lucy Delap and Sue Morgan, 'Introduction', in Delap and Morgan

(eds), *Men, Masculinity and Religious Change in Twentieth-Century Britain* (London: Palgrave, 2013), pp. 1–29.
95 Karly Kehoe, 'The Venerable Margaret Sinclair: an examination of the cause of Edinburgh's twentieth-century factory girl', *Feminist Theology*, 16 (2008), 169–83.
96 See Heimann, *Mysticism*, and John Davies, 'Traditional religion, popular piety or base superstition? The cause for the beatification of Teresa Higginson, *Recusant History*, 23 (1996–97), 123–44.
97 For more on the cult of Saint Thérèse and her slightly different appeal to men and women, see Harris, *Faith in the Family*, pp. 217–24.
98 'The Scottish Memorial Chapel', Declaration of the Scottish Hierarchy, filed in ACL TNT.

# Index

'n.' after a page reference indicates the number of a note on that page. Page numbers in italic refer to illustrations. Page numbers in bold refer to main references.

Abbott, Edwin 106
*Acta Sanctorum* 9–10, 15, 130, 199, 245
Adrian IV, Pope 80, 86
Alban 8, 17, 152–3, 246
Alexander III, Pope 100
Amos, Prophet 3
Anglo-Catholicism 6, 14, 46–8, 49, 50–1, 55, 67–8, 100, 103–5, 199, 204, 226–7, 237, 266
anthropology 19–20
  Frazer, J. G. 20
  Tylor, Edward Burnett 19–20
anti-Catholicism 7, 8, 9–10, 14, 16, 20, 46, 51, 65–6, 93–4, 102–3, 114–16, 119, 127–9, 146, 183, 187–8, 194–7
Arnold, Matthew 37, 39
Arnold, Thomas 5, 97, 138, 168, 170, 202
Arnold-Forster, Frances 12, 110nn.75, 77
asceticism 13, 16, 33, 128, 130, 134, 137, 236–7, 253
Athanasius 3
Augustine of Canterbury 8, 16–17, 62–5, 69, 152, 249–52
Augustine of Hippo 3, 8, 21, 50, 104, 138, 171

Baxter, Richard 3, 9, 15, **161–76**,
  Christlike 162–4
  Jeffreys, George 163–4, 169
  Kidderminster 162, 164
  statue (1875) 169–70
  'martyr for charity' 15, 169
Becket, Thomas (Saint Thomas of Canterbury) 7, **92–111**, 152, 246, 256
  medieval scholarship 102–6

  *see also* Gladstone, William Ewart; pilgrimages; Stanley, A. P.; Tennyson, Alfred
Bede, Venerable 8, 62–4, 153, 251
Begg, James 185–9
Benedict XV, Pope 265
Benson, Edward White 12–13, 106
Bible
  biblical criticism 15, 18, 29, 31, 34–7, 39, 88, 106, 134, 170, 187, 254
  *Essays and Reviews* (1860) 168–71
  biblical definitions of sanctity 7, 19, 29–39, 161–2, 165, 169-70, 178, 184, 187, 195–6, 198–201, 216–17
  British and Foreign Bible Society 1, 135
  English Bible 4, 116, 195–6
*Book of Common Prayer* 4, 7–8, 103, 147, 193, 194–5, 257
Borrow, George 132
Bowles, William Lisle 66–7
Broad Church 5, 13, 15, 161, 165, 167–71
  *see also* Kingsley, Charles; Stanley, A. P.; Tulloch, John
Brompton Oratory 44, 52–3
Buckland, William 95, 98
Buddha 5, 21
Butler, Alban
  *Lives of the Fathers, Martyrs, and Other Principal Saints* (1756–59) 10, 13, 246

calendars 7–8, 12, 19, 78, 83, 96, 127, 165, 193–9, 257
  *Calendrier Positiviste* (1849) 5, 137
  *see also Book of Common Prayer*
Calvin, John 3, 131, 161

canonisation 9–10, 62, 123, 134, 144–56,
    262–6
  *de facto* 4, 5, 16, 82, 161, 166, 183, 227–9
Caractacus 60–73, *61*
Carlyle, Thomas 5, 15, 19, 100, 136, 170
Catherine of Siena 15, 48, 229
Catholic Emancipation 65, 112–23, 153, 167
celibacy 14, 16, 82, 101, 226, 254
Challoner, Richard 46, 48, 145, 150, 246
Champneys, Basil 1
Charles Borromeo 13
Chaucer, Geoffrey 96
children's books 5, 16, 33, 93–4, 137, 147
Church, R. W. 245, 247, 250
Clapham Sect ('the Saints') 16, 135, 164–5,
    **209–25**
  biblical imagery and memorials to 216–18
  practical piety 211–16, 219–20
Claudia Rufina (Saint Gwladys) 12, **60-76**,
    *61*, 78
  early modern antiquarianism 62–5
  Pudens 60–1, *61*, 65, 66, 71
  Welshness 68–70, 72
Clough, Arthur Hugh 132–3
Cobbett, William 112
  *History of the Protestant Reformation* (1824–27)
    95, 113, 118, 120–3, 154
Coleridge, Samuel Taylor 5, 15, 19, 114, 119,
    165–8, 170–1
Columba/Colum Cille 17, 82–4, 87
Comte, Auguste 5, 19, 137
  *see also* calendars
Confucius 5
Cornish saints 13, 248
Counter-Reformation 9–10, 129–33
Cromwell, Oliver 3, 15, 53, 86, 152
Crosthwaite, John Clark 254, 256

Dale, R. W. 1, 3, 163
Darby, John Nelson 137
Darling, Grace 17
Darwin, Charles 18
Dickens, Charles 94, 97, 98
Dissent *see* Nonconformity
Dodds, James 177, 181
Donne, John 14, 256

early modern scholarship, persistence of, in the
    nineteenth century 4, 7–8, 14, 31–3,
    60–73, 78–80, 112–14, 129–31,
    145–52, 162–5
Eliot, George, 5, 10, 17–18

Elisha, Prophet 96, 161, 162, 198
Elizabeth, Queen 7–8, 45, 53, 115–16, 145,
    147–9
Elizabeth of Hungary 229, 254
  *see also* Kingsley, Charles
English Catholic martyrs 8, **144–60**
  canonisation process 145, 147–50
  and national identity 152–6
  *see also* Fisher, John; More, Thomas;
    Thompson, Francis
Enlightenment 8–9, 30, 31–2
evangelicalism 11, 17, 29, 30, 31, 33, 37,
    77–88, 130, 133, 135, 161–3,
    177–89, 193–204, 234
  Chalmers, Thomas 3, 12, 180, 218
  Gorham Judgment (1850) 104–5
  More, Hannah 30, 228
  Simeon, Charles 14, 171, 226
  *see also* Stephen, (Sir) James; Venn,
    Henry (1725–97); Venn, Henry
    (1796–1873); Wilberforce, William

Faber, Frederick William 13–14, 15, 44, 47,
    71, 100, 102, 130, 135, 249, 250,
    252–3, 255, 256
Farrar, F. W. 15, 35, 71, 101, 104, 142n.67
  *Darkness and Dawn* (1891) 71–2
  *The Life and Work of St Paul* (1874) 35
Feuerbach, Ludwig 5
Fisher, John 113, 120–3, 144, 146–8, 150–2,
    156
Fletcher, John 9, 10, 161, **193–208**
  early hagiography 200–1
  miraculous anecdotes 201
  relics and tomb 202–3
  Wesley's ideal Protestant saint 196
Fletcher, Mary, née Bosanquet, 9, 10, **193–208**
  communion with 'happy spirits' 197–8
    primitive Church 198
    Swedenborgian influences 198
  eirenicism towards Catholics 197
  Leytonstone female community 194, 197,
    200, 202
  mysticism 197–201
  relics and tomb 202–3
Foxe, John, *Actes and Monuments* 8, 113–16,
    119, 147, 166
Francis of Assisi 3, 5, 14, 132, 135, 137, 164,
    171, 199
  Protestant positivity towards 14–15, 136–7,
    164–5, 199
Francis Xavier 16, 135, 136–7, 171, 197, 264

Freeman, Edward Augustus 92, 97, 100
freethought 4–5, 17–19, 34
Froude, James Anthony 19, 97, 122, 132, 138–9, 245, 250–3, 255
Fry, Elizabeth 3, 16, 127, **226–44**, *231*, *233*
   female activism 226–8
     obscured by hagiography 238–40
   Newgate heroine 229–33

George 12, 13, 17, 251–2, 273
Giles, John Allen 105
Gladstone, William Ewart 95, 99, 103, 136, 248–9, 256
Gregory I, Pope ('the Great') 8, 62–3
Gregory XIII, Pope 145

Hales, William 67–9
Henry VIII, King 44, 94, 145, 147, 149, 151–2, 248
Herbert, George 14, 17
Heron, Henry 81–3
holy days 4–5, 7–8, 49–50, 62, 103, 137, 144–5, 184, 195, 255–6, 266
   *see also* calendars
Hooker, Richard 3, 14, 168, 176 n. 74, 256
Hume, David 94, 97, 105, 131
   'Of Miracles' (1748) 9

Ignatius Loyola 18, **127–43**, 171, 197, 262
   charisma 133–5, 137–8
     pedagogy 133–4, 135–6, 138
   Spanishness 131–3, 138–9
   *Spiritual Exercises* 135–6
Ireland 67–8, 77–88, 100–1, 137
   immigration from 120–2, 151–3, 156

Jameson, Anna 19, 51, 226, 230–1
Jesus Christ 6, 15, 29, 49, 51, 52, 96, 134, 154, 162, 173, 182, 186, 196, 209, 212, 264, 273
   quest for the historical Jesus 18, 19, 104
   *see also* Farrar, F. W.; Renan, Ernest; Seeley, J. R.
Joan of Arc 17, 228
Jowett, Benjamin 35–9, 169–71

Keble, John 13, 46, 49, 100, 104, 247, 255
Killen, W. D. 81, 85, 87
Kingsley, Charles 14, 15, 136, 137, 245, 257
   *The Saint's Tragedy* (1848) 14, 254

Leo XIII, Pope 1, 147
Lingard, John 94, 113–14, 121–2, 145
Locke, John 31–2, 172
Luther, Martin 9, 15, 17, 36, 63, 121, 131, 133–4, 138, 139, 161, 166, 170

Macaulay, Thomas Babington 120, 127–8, 227
Manning, Henry 94, 99, 103, 144, 152–5
Mansfield College, Oxford 1–3, *3*
Martial 65, 68, 71, 721
Martin, Sarah 15, **226–44**, *237*, *238*
   humble origins 234–7
   preaching 236–7
martyrdom 1, 6, 8–10, 14, 16–17, 71–2, 94–7, 100, 112–20, 144–60, 163–4, 177–89
Mary, Queen 8–9, 119, 121, 147–8
Mary, Queen of Scots 148
Maurice, F. D. 13, 15, 96, 168, 172, 254
Mill, John Stuart, 'saint of rationalism' 27n.105
miracles 1, 4, 9, 14–16, 19, 29–30, 85, 95, 106, 123, 128, 167, 201, 204, 228, 253–4, 267–8
   scepticism regarding 18–20, 35–6, 38, 98, 106, 134–5, 148, 167, 250
missions 16–17, 84–8, 135, 136–7, 212, 226–40, 257
   Livingstone, David 3, 16, 137
   Martyn, Henry 13, 16, 137
Mohammed 5, 15, 34
More, Thomas **112–26**, 144, 146–8, 150–6
   ghost of 10, 117–21
     mistaken for a tourist 120
   paintings 122
muscular Christianity 97, 101–2, 128, 137
   *see also* Kingsley, Charles; soldier-saints

Neale, John Mason 246, 257
Newman, Francis William, 17–18, 137
Newman, John Henry 12, 13, 15, 17, 46–7, 97–8, 102, 104, 122, 136, 152, 199
   *Dream of Gerontius* (1865) 1, 21, 245
   *Lives of the English Saints* (1844-45) 14, 19, 70, 102, **245–61**
Nightingale, Florence 17, 136, 228, 230
Nonconformity 1–3, 4, 16, 32–3, 51, 66, 70, 102–3, 115, 118–19, 127, 133, 135, 161–73
novels 4, 10, 16, 18, 19, 52, 71–2, 99, 104, 112, 128, 179, 188, 198, 232, 234, 255

Origen 3
Oxford Movement 10–11, 46–7, 95, 96, 102–4, 128, 182, 217, 245–57
  *British Critic* 96, 245
  Marian devotion 46–7
  Wales 67–8
  *see also* Anglo-Catholicism

Paley, William 33–6
Patrick 12, **77–91**,
  missionary to Ireland 84–8
  Presbyterian historical scholarship 80–4
  primitive Christianity 81–4, 85–6
Pattison, Mark 245, 247, 250, 255–6
Paul 7, **29-43**, 61, 63, 66, 72, 83, 137, 138, 162–4, 200, 249
  conversion 30, 33, 34, 35–7
  cross-confessional appeal 4, 161
  Enlightened apologetics 31–4
  liberal Protestant fascination 31–9, 170
  mission to Britain 64, 65, 67
  writings 30, 39, 137, 209
Paul III, Pope 130
Peter 7, 61, 63, 72, 83, 134, 155, 197
phrenology 137–8
pilgrimage 9, 44, 51, 95–7, 130, 151–2, 183–4, 199, 202, 226, 262–74
  Canterbury 95–7, 99
  Carfin ('the Scottish Lourdes') 269–72
  Croagh Patrick 19
  Lourdes 263, 267
  Madeley ('the Mecca of Methodism') 201–3
  Montserrat 129–30, 136
  Walsingham 44, 51, 55
Pius V, Pope 13, 147
Pius IX, Pope 50, 100, 135
Pius X, Pope 262
Pius XI, Pope 266
Plato 3
Positivism 18, 34
  *see also* Comte, Auguste
Prayer Book *see* Book of Common Prayer
pre-Reformation Christianity 8, 10, 14, 95, 112-23 , 152–3, 236, 246
Presbyterians 21, 135, 161, 165, 171–2, 196
  Scottish 8, 9, 20, 79, 80, 83–4, 85, 87–8, 177–89
    Free Church of Scotland 180–4, 185, 187, 188
    Reformed Presbyterians 179, 182–9
  Ulster 12, 77–91

psychology 31, 34–9, 128, 133–4 , 137–8
  James, William 20–1, 38–9, 136
Pugin, A. W. N. 17, 48, 50, 250, 253–4
Puritans 3, 81, 92, 112, 161–73, 212
Pusey, Edward Bouverie 46–7, 50, 95, 254

Reformation 6, 7–9, 29, 44–5, 62, 79, 83–4, 94, 113–23, 131, 144–56, 162, 210, 216–17
Reid, James Seaton 79–81, 84
relics 3, 6, 8–10, 16, 17, 95, 96, 98–9, 103, 113, 162, 183–4, 199, 262, 263, 270, 274
  Museum of Methodist Antiquities 10, 202
Renan, Ernest 19, 36–7, 38, 104, 131, 138
Robertson, James Craigie 105–6
Rossetti, Christina 49

Sackville-West, Vita 266–7
Saint Jude's Church, Hampstead Garden Suburb 17
Schleiermacher, Friedrich 3, 171
Scott, (Sir) Walter 10, 68, 100
  *Ivanhoe* (1820) 100
  *Old Mortality* (1816) 179, 188
Scottish Covenanters 8, **177–92**
  bicentenaries 180, 182
    Glasgow General Assembly (1838) 180
    Sanquhar Declaration (1860) 183–4, 185–9
    Westminster Assembly (1843) 180–2
  monuments 177, 178–9, 182–4
Seeley, J. R. 19
  *Ecce Homo* (1865) 19, 104
shrines 3, 4, 7, 16, 17, 44, 50, 51, 55, 94–5, 98, 105, 165, 177, 178–9, 199, 203, 263, 265, 269–74
sisterhoods 12, 47–51, 103, 127, 194, 197, 200, 202, 226–8, 230–1, 237–9, 262–74
Smiles, Samuel 16, 95, 243n.53
Socrates 5
soldier-saints 17, 128, 133, 137
Southey, Robert 10, 66, 112–23, 133
Spinoza, Baruch 19
spiritualism 29, 37–8
stained glass 3, 5, 17, 50, 60–1, *61*, 72, 152, 228
Stanley, A. P. 5, 15, 36, 96–7, 99, 101, 104–5, 136, 137, 169–71, 181

Stephen, (Sir) James 15, 135, 164–5, 209, 211, 216–17
Stephen, James Fitzjames 168–9
Stillingfleet, Edward 64–5, 69, 78
Stubbs, William 92, 100, 105

Tacitus 64, 71–2
Taylor, Isaac 34, 133
Tennyson, Alfred 96
   *Becket* (1884) 95, 99, 100
Teresa of Avila 5, 127, 129, 138–9, 199, 242 n. 18, 262, 266–7
Thérèse of Lisieux (Marie-Françoise-Thérèse Martin) **262-78**, 271
   healings 13, 265–6, 270–3
   working-class appeal 272–4
Thompson, Francis 1
   'To the English Martyrs' (1906) 154–5
Tractarians *see* Oxford Movement
Tulloch, John 15, 130–1, 136, 180–1

Unitarians 5, 21, 32–4, 167, 172–3
   Belsham, Thomas 31–2, 36
   Martineau, James 15, 36, 172
   Society of Free Catholics 172–3
Ussher, James 63–4, 72, 77–80, 84, 87

Venn, Henry, of Huddersfield (1725–97) 162, 165, 213–14, 218
Venn, Henry, of the Church Missionary Society (1796–1873) 136–7
Victoria, Queen 17, 52–4, 95, 100
Virgin Mary 7, 12, 13, **44–59**, *45*, 153–4, 269–70
   cross-confessional appeal 4, 51, 46–51, 52, 55
   devotion to 47, 52
      Immaculate Conception, doctrine of 59
   in contemporary art 50–1
   Pre-Raphaelite Brotherhood 50–1
   Protestant attitudes 82, 197, 227, 239
   statues 44–6, 49–50, 52–3, 55
Voltaire 134

Wesley, John 3, 13, 127, 133, 136, 138, 161, 193–204
   as saint 3, 10, *11*
   on sanctity 194–6, 198–9
      prayers for the faithful departed 195–6
Wilberforce, William 16, 162, **209–25**, 253
   imperial 'saint' 215, 218–19, 220–1
Wiseman, Nicholas 47, 61–2, 98, 101, 103–4, 140n.14, 246, 247

EU authorised representative for GPSR:
Easy Access System Europe, Mustamäe tee 50,
10621 Tallinn, Estonia
gpsr.requests@easproject.com

www.ingramcontent.com/pod-product-compliance
Lightning Source LLC
Chambersburg PA
CBHW021348300426
44114CB00012B/1134